The Challenge and Burden
of Historical Time

The Challenge and Burden of Historical Time
Socialism in the Twenty-First Century

ISTVÁN MÉSZÁROS

foreword by JOHN BELLAMY FOSTER

MONTHLY REVIEW PRESS
New York

Library of Congress Cataloging-in-Publication Data

Mészáros, István, 1930–

The challenge and burden of historical time: socialism in the twenty-first

century / Mészáros, István ; foreword by John Bellamy Foster.

p. cm.

Includes bibliographical references and index.

ISBN 978-1-58367-169-6 (alk. paper) — ISBN 978-1-58367-170-2 (alk. paper)

1. Capitalism. 2. Imperialism. 3. Socialism. I. Title.

HB501.M6223 2008

335–dc22

2008028197

Monthly Review Press

146 West 29th Street, Suite 6W

New York, NY 10001

5 4 3 2 1

Contents

to the memory of

ANTONIO GRAMSCI (1891–1937)

ATTILA JÓZSEF (1905–1937)

CHE GUEVARA (1928–1967)

el carbón, el hierro y el petróleo,
la materia real nos ha creado
echhándonos hirvientes y violentos
en los moldes de esta
sociedad horrible,
para afincarnos, por la humanidad,
en el eterno suelo.

Tras los sacerdotes, los soldatos y los burgueses,
al fin nos hemos vuelto fieles
oidores de las leyes:
por eso el sentido de toda obra humana
zumba en nosotros
como el violón profundo.

~

real matter created us,
coal, iron and petrol,
threw us into the mould
of this horrible society,
ardently and untrammelled,
to make our stand for humanity,
on the eternal soil.

After priests, soldiers and burghers,
thus we became at last
the faithful listeners to the laws:
this is why the sense of all
human work throngs in us
like the deep viola.

—Attila József

Foreword

by John Bellamy Foster

Karl Marx once wrote that "theory . . . becomes a material force as soon as it has gripped the masses."[1] For this to happen, István Mészáros explains in his new book, theory must take on *The Challenge and Burden of Historical Time*, grasping the human requirements of a particular moment while holding on to the "radical openness of history."

Today Mészáros's theoretical insights are becoming a material force, gripping the masses through various world-historical actors in the context of Latin America's Bolivarian Revolution. Thus a *New York Times* article on January 24, 2007, referred to Venezuelan President Hugo Chávez's well-known "admiration of István Mészáros, a relatively obscure Hungarian-Marxist scholar, who argues that there is an alternative to capitalism in his 1,000 page book, *Beyond Capital.*"

Mészáros, though, is far from being a "relatively obscure" thinker. Born in 1930, he entered the University of Budapest in 1949 where he soon became a young assistant to the towering twentieth-century Marxist philosopher Georg Lukács. He left Hungary following the Soviet invasion in 1956, and eventually took a position as professor of philosophy at the University of Sussex. He has written a host of philosophical, political-economic, and cultural works including books on Marx, Lukács, and Sartre. His 1970 *Marx's Theory of Alienation* won the prestigious Issac Deutscher Memorial Prize.

It was in his Issac Deutscher Memorial Lecture "The Necessity of Social Control" and in his 1971 preface to the third edition of *Marx's Theory of Alienation* that Meszáros first raised the issue of the "global structural crisis of capital."[2] Recognizing the enormity of the changes occurring both within capitalism and in the post-capitalist Soviet system, he was to set aside the major philosophical works that he had

been writing for many years (in the form of two unfinished book manuscripts, *The Social Determination of Method* and *The Dialectic of
Structure and History*) to concentrate on these more urgent issues. The
result was a set of three key works: *The Power of Ideology* (1989), *Beyond
Capital* (1995), and *The Challenge and Burden of Historical Time*.

Mészáros's monumental *Beyond Capital* represented a turning
point in the development of Marxist thought—a radical change in
perspective and a recapturing of the revolutionary potential of classical Marxism. A work of enormous philosophical, political, and economic range, its title reflected its threefold goal: to develop a vision
that went beyond the system of capital, beyond Marx's *Capital*, and
beyond the Marxist project as it was understood in the historical conditions of the nineteenth and twentieth centuries.

A number of key theoretical innovations stood out in this work:

1. an emphasis on the "capital system," i.e., the regime of capital
   rooted in the exploitation of labor power, as distinct from the historically specific institutional order of capitalism associated with
   private ownership of the means of production;[3]
2. the treatment of the capital system as a particular order of "social
   metabolic control" permeating all aspects of society;
3. an analysis of the "activation of capital's absolute limits";
4. a critique of post-capitalist society, particularly the Soviet system,
   as failing to eradicate the capital system in its totality; and
5. an account of the historical conditions for capital's complete eradication, involving an alternative order of social metabolic control
   rooted in "substantive equality."

As Daniel Singer summed up the revolutionary implications of
Mészáros's argument, "What must be abolished is not only classical
capitalist society but the reign of capital as such. Indeed, the Soviet
example proves it is not enough to 'expropriate the expropriators' if
you do not uproot the domination of labor on which the rule of capital rests."[4] Using a metaphor drawn from the life of Goethe, Mészáros
argued in *Beyond Capital* that each story of the building that constitutes the home of humanity must be replaced from the bottom floor
up—so that in the end there is an entirely new structure—even while
we as human beings are living within it.[5]

Beyond Capital helped extend the range of the Marxian critique
by including powerful gender-based and ecological conceptions of

human emancipation as integral components in the transcendence of the regime of capital, without which the needed conditions of substantive equality and genuine sustainable development could not be attained. More than any other work, it highlighted the uncontrollability and wastefulness of capital. The entire reign of capital, Mészáros argued, was approaching its absolute limits as a result of its increasing inability to displace its internal contradictions, creating a global structural crisis of capital.

Rather than accepting Margaret Thatcher's proclamation "there is no alternative," *Beyond Capital* insisted that the only viable alternative required a complete shift in control over society from capital to the associated producers. The social democratic dream of a "hybrid" system (a reconciliation of capitalism with social welfare) had to be discarded as illusory. Failing to touch the capital system's inner metabolism through its reforms, social democracy was everywhere devolving into neoliberalism or crude capitalism.

The penetrating nature of the analysis exhibited in *Beyond Capital* can be seen in Mészáro's recognition as early as 1995 that Hugo Chávez in Venezuela was charting the necessary alternative path when he stated: "The sovereign people must transform itself into the object and the subject of power. This option is not negotiable for revolutionaries."[6] Subsequently, Chávez as Venezuelan president was to draw directly on *Beyond Capital*'s analysis, incorporating within his own perspective its insistence on the need for communal exchange of activities in opposition to capitalist commodity exchange. Chávez thus followed Mészáros in designating communal exchange as the "Archimedean point" of revolutionary social transformation.[7] Through the direct exchange of activities between nations in the Bolivarian Alternative for the Americas (ALBA), the rise of Venezuela's communal councils, new Constituent Assemblies in Venezuela and Bolivia aimed at dissolving the political hegemony of transnational capital, and the spread of workplace cooperatives in the current Latin American revolt—the near-absolute dominance of capitalist commodity exchange is being loosened.

The Challenge and Burden of Historical Time is not meant to displace *Beyond Capital* as the indispensable key to Mészáros's critique of the capital system. Rather the two volumes overlap and complement each other in numerous ways. *The Challenge and Burden of Historical Time* has the advantage of being shorter and more accessible. In this respect, Mészáros's new book might be read as either a lengthy introduction to or as an extensive afterword to *Beyond Capital*. But it is much more than simply that. If the emphasis of *Beyond Capital* is on the global structural crisis of capital and the necessary path of socialist transition, *The Challenge and Burden of Historical Time* focuses on historical time itself. It addresses the necessary forms of socialist temporality and the radical openness of history. The latter has been a central theme of Mészáros's thought since *Marx's Theory of Alienation*, in which he singled it out as the defining feature of Marx's revolutionary world-view.

What Mészáros calls the "decapitation of time" operates at every level within the capital system. The greatest bourgeois thinkers—such as Locke, Smith, Kant, and Hegel—all pointed in various ways to the "end of history" identified with the rise of capitalism. The same ideological closure to history is visible today in dominant conceptions of globalization, in ideas of modernism/post-modernism, in the incessant neoliberal mantra that "there is no alternative," and in Francis Fukuyama's claim that the fall of the Soviet Union confirmed the earlier Hegelian view of the end of history.

This illusory closing off of the future is intended to rationalize as inescapable what Albert Einstein in his 1949 article "Why Socialism?" criticized as the "crippling of individuals," which he saw as "the worst evil of capitalism" and the reason why the historical pursuit of socialism was essential.[8] Free human control over disposable time is minimized under the capital's system of time accountancy, which seeks to reduce life to endless minute decisions directed at the enhancement of productivity and profits for the benefit of the vested interests. Under these conditions, as Marx observed, "time is everything, man is nothing; he is, at the most, time's carcase."[9] The lived-existence of the individual human being is given over to an abstract entity—the promotion of abstract value.

Capital's "truncated time accountancy" thus has its roots in its promotion to the nth degree of the detailed division of labor, excluding all other considerations. The capital system regards the terrible human, social, and ecological losses that its myopic pursuit of speed and quantity imposes as mere "collateral damage." In contrast, as Simón Rodríguez, the great utopian-socialist teacher of Latin America's Liberator, Simón Bolívar, wrote in 1847: "The division of labour in the production of goods only serves to brutalize the workforce. If to produce cheap and excellent nail scissors, we have to reduce the workers to machines, we would do better to cut our fingernails with our teeth."[10] For Mészáros a genuine emphasis on the self-development of human beings would allow the normal working day to be cut to twenty hours a week or less, while creating the preconditions for egalitarian social relations.

The capital system, *The Challenge and Burden of Historical Time* insists, is unable to rise above "short-termism" in its outlook. This is linked to the threefold contradictions of:

1. its innate "uncontrollability," which derives from the antagonistic nature of its mode of social metabolic control;
2. its unceasing dialectic of competition and monopoly; and
3. its inability to integrate politically on the global plane despite its globalizing economic tendencies. It therefore displays a deep aversion to planning.

The result is a maximum of waste and destruction, marked by the incessant degradation of human labor, a decreasing rate of utilization, ballooning financial parasitism, a rising threat of nuclear annihilation, expanding barbarism[11] and accelerating planetary ecological catastrophe. On October 19, 1999, Mészáros delivered a public lecture in Athens entitled "Socialism or Barbarism," which was later expanded into a small book under the same title that was published in Greek and Italian in 2000 and in English in 2001 (and is included as chapter 4 of the present book). There he argued, well before the events of September 11, 2001, that the world had entered "the potentially deadliest phase of imperialism." The United States is now effectively at war with the entire planet in a futile attempt to become the state of the capitalist system, even at the risk of the annihilation of humanity itself.[12]

The alternative mode of social metabolic control provided by socialism in its most revolutionary egalitarian form, Mészáros explains in *The Challenge and Burden of Historical Time*, demands an entirely different time accountancy. Sustainable development based on "rational husbandry" is impossible outside of a society of substantive equality. What is required is a system in which the associated producers become the subject and object of society in line with the principle, stressed most eloquently by Bolívar, that equality is "the law of laws."[13] This can only be accomplished by means of comprehensive social planning—not through commandism from above, but arising from collective needs and the most widespread democratic participation.[14] The goal would be a radically altered time accountancy aimed at qualitative human development transcending the current disjuncture between needs and productivity. A revolution that moved decisively in this direction would become "historically irreversible."

It is not surprising that Mészáros, who drew inspiration from a very young age from the revolutionary poetry of his Hungarian compatriot Attila Jószef, should quote him frequently in his work, dedicating his new book in part to him. It was Jószef, he notes, who wrote:

> After priests, soldiers and burghers,
> thus we became at last
> the faithful listeners to the laws . . .[15]

This represents the challenge and burden of historical time—the emergence of a new material force as theory grips the masses, who thus become "the faithful listeners to the laws."

Introduction

1.

This book is dedicated to the memory of three great human beings of the twentieth century—Antonio Gramsci, Attila József, and Che Guevara—seventy years after the tragic death of the first two, and forty years after that of the third. For, against all odds, in unyielding defiance of the tragic consequences that had to be suffered, they faced up to the enduring challenges of an age torn by the succession of extreme crises, and they carried to its ultimate limits the burden of their historical time. The time to which they were confined by the most unfavorable circumstances which they were nevertheless able to transcend, thanks to their exemplary commitment and far-sighted vision, towards the consciously adopted perspective of humanity's only viable—socialist—future passionately advocated by them.

Gramsci, József and Che Guevara were great witnesses to the deepening crisis of capital's social order in the course of the twentieth century. They were fully conscious of the unprecedented intensity of that crisis which was beginning to threaten the very survival of humanity. First through the violent Fascist and Nazi Fascist attempt to redefine the international political and military power relations, and later, in Che Guevara's final years, through the new aggressive design to dominate the world order on a permanent basis by the global hegemonic imperialism of the United States.

All three of them clearly realized that only the most radical societal transformation, instituting a veritable *epochal change*, could offer a way out from the perilous succession of crises that characterized the whole of the twentieth century. Such epochal change became necessary because the established order carried on producing destruction all over the world, with no end in sight to the devastating clash of interests. Not even the dreadful bloodletting of two world wars seemed to be able to make the slightest difference to the underlying antagonisms.

It was totally ironical, if not much worse, that the defenders of the ruling order were promising, in the midst of the First World War, that the sacrifices endured in it were destined "to end all wars." Yet in no time at all the most sinister preparations for an even more ruinous confrontation were well on the way, gathering strength in the aftermath of the great world economic crisis of 1929–1933. The rival parties embarked upon these preparations as a self-delusory guarantee against the possibility of sinking into yet another all-embracing economic crisis. The perverse logic of capital made it impossible for them to understand the far-reaching and disastrous implications of their blindly pursued course of action.

To be sure, the preparations for the new war had brought their fruit soon enough, exploding in 1939 in a global armed conflict lasting six years. Just before the outbreak of the Second World War, the United States was in fact heading for another severe recession, notwithstanding the remedial attempts pursued by Roosevelt's New Deal. But their active industrial and military involvement in the war quickly reversed that trend, bringing with it, in the country, previously unimaginable economic expansion. However, the emergence of the United States from the war as by far the most powerful economic power did not resolve any of the capital system's fateful contradictions. It only provided the United States with the overwhelming advantage to take over in due course, in one way or another, the role of imperialist domination formerly exercised by the British and the French colonial empires, consigning to oblivion at the same time also the minor colonial powers, the Portuguese and the Dutch. Thus, under the utterly false promise of the end of imperialism and the alleged onset of the new era of universally beneficial as well as fully equitable democracy and liberty, the country with the mightiest arsenal of military destruction, capable of easily exterminating humanity in a matter of hours, laid its claim to dominating the world at first in the so called "American Century," the twentieth, and then announced even its firm determination to rule over the entire self-decreed "American Millennium" ahead of us.

Gramsci and József died long before the United States had assumed the role of the global imperialist hegemon. But Che Guevara already passionately and clear-sightedly followed the unfolding of the Vietnam War, which pointed in that direction. For in the Vietnam War the United States tried to impose its overwhelming military might over the area once dominated by the French, hoping to establish thereby an unassailable bridgehead for their future adventures in the service of global domination. This was part of the same imperial design in which the United States is now engaged in the Middle East, menacing to extend its military aggression in the "indefinite" future, as they say, also against the countries of the arbitrarily denounced "Axis of Evil," whenever that kind of action might suit its "pre-emptive" convenience, threatening in the service of that end also the self-proclaimed "morally justified" use of nuclear weapons even against non-nuclear powers.

2.

Che Guevara well understood that the literally vital question was not simply which particular country was trying to impose on humanity the most horrendous suffering and sacrifices under the prevailing historical circumstances. For in that respect the role of the aggressor could be transferred from Hitler's defeated Nazi Germany to the victorious capitalist antagonist, the United States. What really decided the issue was not some changeable, and at times even reversible, *historical contingencies* but the underlying *structural necessities*. In other words, the all-important decider was the incorrigible nature of capital's social reproductive control, which could not find any solution to its own insuperable *systemic antagonisms*. Consequently, under the conditions of monopolistic imperialist development, the overwhelmingly dominant power—if not a particular one then another—had to attempt to impose its might (if needed in the most violent form, irrespective of the consequences) over its real or potential adversaries.

This is why in Che Guevara's vision the struggle against American imperialism—in which he heroically sacrificed his life—was inseparable from an uncompromising dedication to the establishment of a positively sustainable and historically viable new social order on a global scale. That was the only feasible way to face up to the challenge of our historical time, accepting the burden of responsibility arising from it. Only the positive foundation of the envisaged new social order could provide the necessary guarantee against the renewal of ever more destructive antagonisms in the future. Thus, there could be absolutely no time to lose. The dedicated work for laying the positive foundations for such a genuinely cooperative social order, combating the ubiquitously promoted diffusion of *anti-value* by the established one, had to start right in the present, in plain awareness of the fact that nothing less than the survival of humanity was at stake in this dangerous time of history.

In this spirit, appealing to our consciousness of humanity, Che Guevara addressed the people in his years in Cuba:

> It is necessary to have a great devotion to humanity, a great sense of justice and truth, so as not to fall into extreme dogmatisms, into cold scholasticisms, in isolation from the masses. *It is necessary to fight every day in order to transform this active love for humanity into concrete facts, into actions which serve as mobilizing examples.*[1]

Che Guevara fully shared with Gramsci and József this line of approach that asserted the vital need for maintaining an intense commitment to the enduring values of humanity, under the circumstances of ever more openly threatening barbarism. In Gramsci's time the promoters of the rising fascist menace not only repeatedly denounced in public the outstanding Italian political leader, who passionately raised his voice in the name of humanity against Fascism, but cruelly imprisoned him for the best years of his life, until he became a dying man.

At the time of his incarceration, the Italian Fascist Procurator, inspired by Mussolini—the turn-coat former editor of the socialist newspaper—wrote with brutal cynicism: "We must prevent this brain from functioning for twenty years."[2] They were hoping to destroy Gramsci's spirit and thereby render impossible the diffusion of his ideas. Instead, under the circumstances of unbelievable hardship, deprivation, and even great illness suffered in Mussolini's jail, Gramsci produced his *Prison Notebooks*, a magnificent work whose influence will last for a very long time. Indeed, for long enough to be able to say that the power of capital has been irretrievably relegated to the past, in the spirit in which Gramsci envisaged it.

In the same period when Gramsci had to confront and endure the inhumanities of fascism, also the Hungarian socialist poet, Attila József—who perceived with his profound and far-sighted vision the devastating prospects of the coming Nazi-fascist global military adventure—had put at the center of several of his great poems his impassioned concern for the fate of humanity, trying to raise the alarm against the unfolding barbarism by underlining that:

> new infamy rises up to set
> against one another the races.
> Oppression croaks in squadrons,
> it lands on living heart, as on carrion—
> and misery dribbles all over the world,
> as saliva on the face of the idiots.[3]

And in a poem addressed to Thomas Mann, who was at the time reading from his work at a public meeting in Hungary, József wrote:

> *Al pobre Kosztolányi* [4] *enterramos ayer*
> *y, como abrio en su cuerpo el cáncer un abismo,*
> *Estados-Monstuo roen sin tregua al humanismo.*
> *?Qué más vendra, inquirimos—las almas de horror plenas—*
> *de dónde nos azuzan nuevas ideas-hienas?*
> *?Hierven nuevos venenos que quieren infiltrarnos?*
> *?Y hasta cuándo habrá un sitio en que puedas hablarnos?* [5]

> Just now we buried poor Kosztolányi,
> and the way in which cancer engulfed him,
> monster-states are devouring humanity;
> we ask, in horror, what else could overwhelm us?
> From where could new ferocious creeds assault us?
> Is there new poison being prepared for us?
> For how long will there be a place for you to address us?

The apologists of capital did—and continue to do—everything they could in order to obliterate people's awareness of historical time, in the interest of eternalizing their system. Only those who have a vital interest in the institution of a positively sustainable social order, and thus in securing the survival of humanity, can really appreciate the importance of historical time at this critical juncture of social development. Gramsci, at the time when he was already gravely ill in prison, kept on repeating: "Time is the most important thing; it is a simple pseudonym of life."[6] The defenders of the ruling order could never understand the meaning of his words. For them time can have only one dimension: that of the *eternal present*. The past for them is nothing more than the backward projection and blind justification of the established present, and the future is only the self-contradictorily timeless extension of the—no matter how destructive, and thereby also self-destructive—"natural order" of the here and now, encapsulated in the constantly repeated mindless reactionary dictum according to which "there is no alternative." Perversely, that is supposed to sum up the future.

3.

If people in general really accepted this capital-apologetic conception of time, they would inevitably sink into the abyss of bottomless pessimism. Gramsci, even when personally suffering the greatest of hardship, and at the same time perceiving the Nazi-fascist catastrophe for humanity around the corner, absolutely refused to yield to utter pessimism. Notwithstanding the darkest clouds everywhere on the horizon, he forcefully rejected the idea that human will should be allowed to be subdued by pessimism, no matter how unfavorable might be the visible trends and circumstances, as they undoubtedly were at the time. He adopted as one of his maxims the words of Romain Rolland who spoke of "the pessimism of the intellect and the optimism of the will."[7]

Gramsci's conviction, predicated on the "optimism of the will," stood and stands for the irrepressible determination of a radical social force to overcome the destructive trends of development, inspired by a sustainable vision of the future and defying the established relation of forces. The "personifications of capital" are more than happy to glorify the "no alternative," eternal present, deluding themselves that— just because with all means at their disposal they are dominating society—the historical process itself has already ended. They even pontificate about the happy neoliberal "end of history" in vastly promoted pseudo-scholarly propaganda concoctions, à la Fukuyama, wishfully preaching to themselves—the converted—the forever conflict-free consummation of history while pursuing genocidal wars.

However, the time of the oppressed and the exploited, with its vital dimension of the future, cannot be obliterated. It has its own logic of unfolding, as the irrepressible historical time of our age of make or break. Only the total destruction of humanity could put an end to it. This potentially emancipatory time is inseparable from the social subject capable of asserting through struggle Gramsci's "optimism of the will," despite all adversity. This is the real historical time of the present and the future that appears in one of József's poems:

> Time is lifting the fog, so that we can better see our summit.
> Time is lifting the fog, we have brought time with us,
> we brought it with our struggle, with our reserves of misery.[8]

Nothing and no one can destroy or subdue this time that helps to make the exploited and the oppressed become aware of the outlines of a radically different future society. There can be no illusions as to the arduous climb that must be undertaken in order to reach the summit in question. For the inhuman, alienating, one-dimensional present time of capital's social reproductive order is still in control of the situation. Attila József depicts it with great evocative power in another of his poems:

> *Este tiempo presente*
> *es el de los generales y banqueros.*
> *Frio forjado, relumbrante*
> *cuchillo-tiempo.*
>
> *El cielo chorreante está blindado.*
> *La helada perfora, hiende el pulmón*
> *y el pecho desnudo detrás de los harapos.*
> *En piedra de amolar chirria el tiempo.*
>
> *Detrás del tiempo !cuanto pan silencioso*
> *y frio!, y cajas de hojalata,*
> *y un montón de cosas heladas.*
> *Escaparate-vidrio-tiempo.*
>
> *Y los hombres gritan: ?Dónde está la piedra?*
> *?Dónde el escarchado pedazo de hierro?*
> *!Arrojaselo! !Hazlo trizas! !Penetra!*
> *!Qué tiempo! !Qué tiempo! !Qué tiempo!* [9]

This is the time of bankers
and generals: the present time.
Forged iron, freezing time,
this lightning knife-time.

Thundering sky in armour,
frost piercing lung
and naked breast beneath rags,
time shrieking like whetstone.

How much silent cold bread
and tin boxes piled-up in
frost-bitten heaps behind
this frozen shop-window time.

And people shout: where is the stone?
Where are the icy pieces of iron?
Throw them at it! Break it! Tread on it!
—What a time!—Oh, what a time!

But be it as it may be, capital's "eternal present," with its "frozen shop-window time," cannot possibly wipe out humanity's aspiration for establishing a historically sustainable social order for as long as there is oppression and exploitation in the world. By the time when they shall be irretrievably consigned to the past from our world, as they must be if humanity is to survive, the capital system itself shall be only a bad memory.

4.

Capital cannot tolerate any limitations to its own mode of social metabolic reproduction. Accordingly, considerations of time are totally inadmissible to it if they call for restraining its uncontrollable imperative for capital-expansion. There can be no exemption from that imperative. Not even when the devastating consequences are already glaringly obvious both in the field of production and on the terrain of the ecology. The only modality of time in which capital can be interested is *exploitable labor time*. This remains the case even when the ruthless exploitation of labor time becomes a *historical anachronism* through the potential development of science and technology in the service of human need. Since, however, capital cannot contemplate such an alternative, for pursuing it would require transcending the fetishistic structural limitations of its own mode of operation, capital becomes the *enemy of history*. That is the only way in which capital can presume extricating itself from its objective predicament of historical anachronism.

Thus, capital must negate history in its vision of the world, so that the question of any historical alternative to its own rule should not even conceivably arise, no matter how anachronistic and dangerous its—despite all self-mythology very far from economically efficient—labor-exploitative control of social reproduction. But the trouble is that capital's negation of history is not a leisurely mental exercise. It is a potentially lethal practical process of enlarged capital-accumulation and concomitant destruction in every domain, and not only on the military plane.

As we know, in the ascending phase of its development the capital system was immensely dynamic and in many ways also positive. Only with the passing of time—objectively bringing with it the intensification of the capital system's structural antagonisms—had it become a dangerous regressive force. If, however, the ruling reproductive order has no sense of historical time, as happens to be the case today, it cannot even perceive the difference, let alone make the necessary adjustments in accord with the changed conditions.

Nihilation of history is the only feasible course of action, inseparable from capital's blindness to the painfully tangible future that must be faced. This is why capital has no alternative to abusing historical time. Its callous maxim, according to which "there is no alternative," is only a propagandistic variant of the general negation of history corresponding to capital's innermost nature at the present stage of our historical development. This determination of capital was not always the case, but it has become inalterably so. Thus, capital's only way to relate to history in our time is to violently *abuse it.*

Here we have an obvious combination of historical contingency and structural necessity. If humankind had an "infinity of time" at its disposal, then one could not talk about "capital's abuse of time." The infinity of time could not be abused by any historically given force. Under such circumstances ongoing "capital-expansion" would be a harmless quantitative concept, with no end in sight. But humanity has no infinity of anything at its disposal, as it is absurdly presumed by capital's willing personifications, and certainly not of time. Besides, talking about an infinity of human historical time would be a grotesque contradiction in terms.

Only the most insensitive force, devoid of all human consideration, could ignore the limitations of time. This is what we witness today in a characteristic way. It happens to be our given historical contingency that activates the insuperable—absolute—structural limits of capital. These are absolute structural limits of the capital system that become destructive determinations bent on blocking off humanity's future. At this juncture in history, capital cannot be different in any way from what it actually is. This is how capital's structural necessity becomes devastatingly fused with its brutally—but totally in vain— ignored historical contingency. This is so precisely because capital does not have, and cannot have, the consciousness of historical time. Only structurally open-ended social reproductive systems can have it. Consequently, there can be no way out from this destructive entrapment of humanity without eradicating the capital system itself from its long entrenched control of the social metabolic process.

In the same poem from which the epigraph of this book is taken Attila József calls our attention to the burden of historical time and to the tremendous responsibility inseparable from it. He speaks of the human beings who must meet the great social and historical challenge of our age as "faithful listeners to the laws," underlining that only in that way can we qualify for being worthy inheritors of the mandate bequeathed to us in the course of humanity's historical development. He is fully conscious, as one absolutely should be, both of the historical continuity on which we can build our future, and of the vital differences, which must be instituted and duly consolidated in the ongoing process of qualitative transformation. These are József's words:

> *la materia real nos ha creado*
> *echhándonos hirvientes y violentos*
> *en los moldes de esta*
> *sociedad terrible,*
> *para afincarnos, por la humanidad,*
> *en el eterno suelo.*
>
> *Tras los sacerdotes, los soldatos*
> *y los burgueses*

al fin nos hemos vuelto fieles
oidores de las leyes:
por eso el sentido de toda obra humana
zumba en nosotros
como el violón profundo.[10]

Real matter created us,
coal, iron and petrol,
threw us into the mould
of this horrible society,
ardently and untrammeled,
to make our stand for humanity
on the eternal soil.

After priests, soldiers and burghers,
thus we became at last the faithful
listeners to the laws:
this is why the sense of all
human work throngs in us
like the deep viola.

The vital requirement to be "faithful listeners to the laws" stressed by József does not refer simply to manmade laws. It stands above all for the absolutely fundamental law of humanity's relationship to nature itself: the objective *substratum of our very existence.* This must be the ultimate foundation of the whole system of human laws. Yet, this is the relationship that is being violated by capital in our time in every possible way, irresponsibly ignoring the consequences. One requires no prophetic insight to understand that the ruthless violation of the natural basis of human existence cannot continue indefinitely.

5.

To be sure, manmade laws are very much involved in the overall destructive process. József's appeal to our sense of unavoidable necessity and conscious responsibility—which call for *faithfully listening to the laws*—covers also them. It is all a question of *priority*, concerning the relationship between the *absolute* and the *relative.* It should be perfectly obvious to us which of the two should take precedence. We can reverse their relationship—by irresponsibly *absolutizing the relative* and recklessly *relativizing the absolute*—only at our peril.

However, capital *always* operated on the basis of such reversal. One might say that capital is "color blind" in that respect. It could not operate in any other way than by overturning that vital relationship because of its innermost nature. For capital always defined itself as *the absolute* and everything else in relation to its primary self-determination as the dependent and dispensable *relative*. Indeed, in a positive sense—for as long as it could be done without destructive consequences—this mode of operation was always the secret of its incomparable dynamism and success, sweeping aside everything that stood in the way.

Moreover, on the face of it there seems to be no reason at all why this should not be so. There is nothing in principle absolutely reprehensible about the *destruction of determinate parts or forms of nature* through their transformation into something else, even if only into combustion and waste products. It is happening in nature itself, in one way or another, all the time. The point is, however, that at the time when capital, with its irrepressible and all-encroaching dynamism, appeared on the historical stage the *margin of safety* for its objective impact on nature—irrespective of the magnitude of destruction generated by its direct prodigal intervention in the metabolic process—was so *immense* that the negative implications seemed to make no difference whatsoever. This happened to be the case simply because the "moment of truth"—necessarily arising from the interchange between the *finiteness* of our natural world and a *certain type* of (inalterably *wasteful*) reproductive control—was still very far from knocking at the door. This is what gave to the self-complacent liberal economists even in the twentieth century the astonishing illusion that their system would forever qualify for the grand characterization of "productive destruction" (Schumpeter) when in reality it was already becoming ever more dangerously plagued by its irreversible tendency toward *destructive production.*

Like all values, productivity and destruction acquire their meaning only in the human context, in the closest possible relationship with the relevant historical conditions. What makes the *destruction of nature* we now witness an irredeemably—and in the longer run catastrophically—negative process is its ultimate impact on human life as such. This is why under the circumstances of our time capital's absolutization of the historically created relative—its own self—and the reckless relativization of the absolute (the natural basis of human life itself) is much worse than playing Russian roulette. For it carries with it the *absolute certainty* of human self-destruction in the case that capital's ongoing social metabolic process of reproduction is not brought to a definite end in the near future, while there is still time to do so. Capital's overturning of the objective relationship between the absolute and the relative is driving humanity in the opposite direction, without even giving the odd chance of pulling the trigger of the Russian roulette gun a few times before the statistically probable fatal shot.

Here again we can see the perilous combination of historical contingency and structural necessity. The original *vast margin of safety has disappeared forever.* Our given historical contingency irreversibly activated the structural limits of capital with a vengeance, turning them into overwhelmingly destructive determinations bent on blocking off the future. The established system's structural necessity and voracious destructiveness is now inextricably fused with its anachronistic—but to capital inadmissible—historical contingency. For capital continues to deny the possibility of being historically transcendable from the height of its fictitious self-absolutization.

The imperative of instituting an open-ended social reproductive system in the foreseeable future arises from these conditions. It goes without saying, there can be no future without *faithfully listening to the laws.* But to be able to do so the proper priority must be established in our overall system of laws. Capital's laws were *always* based on the false priority of reversing the relationship between the *absolute* and the *relative,* in the interest of making absolute its own rule even at the cost of the destruction of nature; in the same way as capital had to—and must always—deny its historical determinateness in order to eternalize its own domination of the social metabolic process. Humanity never needed a more faithful listening to and observance of the laws than at this crucial juncture of history. But the laws in question must be *radically remade:* by bringing into fully sustainable harmony the absolute and the relative determinations of our conditions of existence, in accord with the unavoidable challenge and burden of our historical time.

6.

The twentieth century witnessed not only the first major attempt to establish a post-capitalist society, but also the implosion of that type of society both in the Soviet Union and all over Eastern Europe. Not surprisingly, the uncritical defenders of capital's social order celebrate that implosion as the healthy return to their "natural" order after an erratic deviation. They have the nerve to postulate now the absolute permanence of the established conditions, notwithstanding all disturbing signs of dangerous instability, ignorant of the deepening economic and ecological crises and of the more or less permanent war endemic to their system.

It would be extremely naive to imagine that the move from capital's social metabolic order of reproduction to a historically viable alternative could take place without painful contradictions and even relapses. For no social transformation in the entire course of human history required an even remotely comparable qualitative change. This is so not only because of the almost prohibitive scale and magnitude of the task, involving a great variety of interrelated national groups—with their long history and deeply rooted traditions as well as diverse interests—in a truly *global setting*. What is radically different on top of that from all of the historically witnessed changes from one social formation to another—i.e., the "non-negotiable" constituent of the required socialist transformation—is the absolute necessity to permanently overcome all forms of *structural domination and subordination*, and not only that of the capitalist variety. In our time no "change of personnel," however well intentioned at first, could even begin to match up to the task. In other words, the *adversarial and conflicting* relationship between human beings—which has been far too obvious in all known history—is what must be *positively superseded* through the creation and firmly secured consolidation of the new social order. Otherwise, uncontrollable contradictions and antagonisms will begin to mushroom on the newly established foundations sooner or later, as they actually did in Soviet-type societies, undermining and destroying them in the end.

Only a genuine critical—and *self-critical*—engagement in the course of socialist historical transformation can produce the sustainable result, by providing the *necessary correctives* as the conditions change and call for meeting their challenge. Marx made this amply clear from the very beginning, when he insisted that socialist revolutions should not shirk from criticizing themselves "with unmerciful thoroughness"[11] in order to be able to accomplish their vital emancipatory objectives.

The twentieth century made a significant difference with regard to Marx's admonition. For in the light of seven decades of extremely costly *practical experience* the original Marxian warning about the necessary practical critique of one's own actions—a warning which could not be in the mid-nineteenth century more than a very general exhortation—had acquired an unavoidable urgency in the socialist movement. For, on the one hand, given the deepening structural crisis of our established social metabolic order, the well grounded institution of the socialist alternative is more urgent today than ever before, despite the self-complacent propaganda assault by the ruling ideology visible everywhere. But at the same time, on the other hand, due to the weighty historical evidence of the Soviet type of development, and the immense sacrifices that had to be endured in its long decades, no one can deny today the necessity for confronting "with unmerciful thoroughness" the problems that are bound to arise. For only through the fully conscious and self-critically committed socialist re-examination of the intended emancipatory steps taken—both in the past and in the present—can it become feasible to make the foundations of socialism in the twenty-first century more secure than they turned out to be in the twentieth.

All three great human beings to whom this book is dedicated had approached the historic task of socialist transformation in this vital critical spirit. Gramsci and József firmly asserted their belief in the uncompromising socialist integrality of the radical epochal change not only against the class adversary but even when they had to suffer the sectarian incomprehension of their own side. And Che Guevara did not hesitate to proclaim with great clarity his principled disagreement with the course of action pursued in the Soviet Union—prophetically indicating that it pointed in the direction of the capitalist restoration—although that outspoken disagreement carried with it his dismissal as a heretic and even as an adventurer. As Fidel Castro underlined in one of his interviews:

> My admiration and fellow feeling for Che have grown as I have seen what has happened in the socialist camp, because he was categorically opposed to the

use of capitalist methods for the construction of socialism. . . . [Che's writings] are of enormous value and should be studied, because I think that the use of those capitalist methods and concepts had an alienating influence in those countries. I think that Che had a prophetic vision when, as early as the first few years of the 1960s, he foresaw all of the drawbacks and consequences of the method that was being used to construct socialism in Eastern Europe.[12]

In this way, even after his death Che Guevara's prescient insights could exercise an essential influence in Cuba's period of rectification. To quote Fidel Castro's impassioned words again:

> We had fallen into the bog of bureaucracy, of overstaffing, of work norms that were out of date, the bog of deceit, of untruth. We had fallen into a whole host of bad habits that Che would have been really appalled at. If Che had ever been told that one day, under the Cuban Revolution there would be enterprises prepared to steal to pretend they were profitable, Che would have been appalled . . . Che would have been appalled if he had been told that money, money was becoming people's concern, their fundamental motivation. He who warned us so much against that would have been appalled.[13]

Gramsci's fascist enemies wanted not only to "prevent his brain from functioning for twenty years" but also to prevent him from exercising any influence in history. As we all know, they failed in every way. Likewise in the case of Che Guevara, his executioners—at the time the Bolivian client regime of U.S. imperialism—intended for him the fate of oblivion, attempting to make disappear forever even his earthly remains. They miserably failed even in that. Che Guevara's influence is alive today not only in Cuba but everywhere in Latin America—as we have seen it testified by one of the most important social movements of our time, the *Movimento dos Sem Terra* of Brazil—and beyond, inspiring the admiration and solidarity of both the older generations and also of countless young people all over the world.

Surveying the last few decades of global developments, the change in the prevailing relation of forces would undoubtedly seem to favor capital. This is largely due not only to the ignominious capitulation of Gorbachev and his followers in the Soviet Union, after their pursuit of the totally unfounded strategy of "restructuring socialism" through the adoption of *glasnost* and *perestroika* (which turned out to be the active promotion of capitalist restoration, followed by the same kind of implosion in Eastern Europe), but also to a similar capitulatory transformation in the biggest Communist Parties of Western Europe, notably the French and the Italian. Thus, to take the latter only, precisely because it was once upon a time Gramsci's militant socialist party, the loudly proclaimed—but again totally unfounded—strategies of the "Italian road to socialism" and of the "great historic compromise," promised to better secure a future international socialist transformation, in actuality turned out to be unreserved capitulation to the U.S.-dominated imperialist forces of international capital, under the party flag of the so called "Democrats of the Left."

Yet, when we look at what has been actually achieved, the picture is very different. And that is by no means surprising. For *no lasting results can be built on capitulation.* As the annals of social, political, and military history amply prove, *capitulation can never be the basis of sustainable historical development.* It can only provide a one-sided gain and the corresponding temporary respite until the next round of antagonisms erupts on the historical stage, on a growing scale and asserting themselves with ever-greater intensity as a rule. Once it could be rationally maintained—as General von Clausewitz formulated it—that war was "the continuation of politics by other means." But the other side of the same equation—concerning the fateful reciprocity of politics and war—was never spelled out in the past, because its grievous implications for the total destruction of humanity were not clearly visible. Namely: that *politics (based on antagonisms) was the harbinger of necessary war,* because—in view of the unresolved nature of the antagonisms themselves—it had to end in the *capitulation of one side* and in the ultimately *explosive instability of the ensuing respite.*

Only a *substantively founded rationality*—in contrast to ephemeral "compromises" achieved in the name of either violently imposed or tactically rationalized "balancing acts"—could show a way out of this *vicious circle,* through the permanent removal of all forms of antagonistic adversariality. The great challenge and burden of our historical time is that *antagonistic adversariality* must be permanently consigned to the past in the interest of leaving behind forever also the fateful—and in our time unavoidably *fatal*—vicious circle of war and politics known to us up to the present. This means radically refounding politics on the basis of *substantive and historically sustainable rationality,* so as to be able to *consciously* manage all human affairs on the required *global scale.* This is why the viable institution of socialism in the "make or break" twenty-first century appeared on the historical agenda with great urgency, imposing the need to confront the failures of the past "with unmerciful thoroughness," as well as to explore all avenues of positive cooperation on the only feasible basis of *substantive equality.*

Nothing has been resolved in a durable way by the implosion of the Soviet-type system, nor indeed by the collapse of some of the biggest former communist parties anywhere in the world. The temptation for labor to follow the *line of least resistance, favoring capital's established order,* undoubtedly played and continues to play an important role in these developments. This is so because the establishment of the socialist reproductive order, as a viable alternative to the existing one, is an immense historical enterprise. But the line of least resistance is not going to secure the future of capital. For that line is incapable of delivering anything other than *ever diminishing returns* to labor under the present circumstances of our deepening historical crisis, and ultimately *no returns at all* as the destructive constituent of capital's reproductive order is bound to run out of control.

As to the falsely claimed successes of capital itself in its historical phase of structural crisis, in reality we see its dominant countries engaged in genocidal wars while cynically preaching democracy and liberty. Indeed, what we witness in the Middle East and elsewhere are conflagrations on an ever-more destructive scale, instead of lasting solutions to the grave internal and international problems of capital's social metabolic order of control.

Many of the ultimately self-destructive achievements of imperialism were built in the past on genocide in North and Latin America. Today the situation is even graver. For global hegemonic imperialism is driving humanity toward extermination. There must be another way. The uncompromising examples of Antonio Gramsci, Attila József, and Che Guevara show us that way.

—Rochester, England
January 1, 2007

1. The Tyranny
of Capital's Time Imperative

1.1 The Time of the Individuals and the Time of Humanity

No individual and no conceivable form of society today or in the future can avoid the objective determinations and the corresponding burden of historical time, together with the responsibility necessarily arising from them. In general terms, perhaps the greatest indictment of our given social order is that it degrades the inescapable burden of meaningful historical time—the life-time of both the individuals and of humanity—into the tyranny of capital's reified time-imperative, irrespective of the consequences.

Capital's historically unique mode of social metabolic reproduction must degrade time because the most fundamental objective determination of its own form of human interchange is the irrepressible drive to continued self-expansion, defined by the intrinsic characteristics of this mode of societal interchange as necessary *capital-expansion,* achievable in commodity society only through the exploitation of labor-time. Thus capital must become blind to all dimensions of time other than that of maximally exploitable surplus-labor and the corresponding labor-time.

This is why all possible value and meaning potentially arising from historically created relations must be obliterated from capital's equations, other than those directly linked to the systemic imperative of capital-accumulation. This is so whether the potential meaning and values involved are concerned with the personal relations of the individuals among themselves as separate individuals, or with the social groups of which the particular individuals form a part, or indeed with humanity in general when that relationship can be and must be consciously grasped, under determinate historical circumstances, like our own historical time today. Meaning and values become legitimate concerns in this reproductive system only if they are readily reducible to the capitalistically idealized *cash nexus* (as regards the isolated individuals), or to the imperative of *profitability* in general, when the issue at stake is the accumulation-securing class relation of structural domination and exploitation in the established social order.

Naturally, our interest in this context is *human historical time,* and not some "metaphysical" or "cosmological" considerations of time. For us the time relations linked to the question of "cosmological contingency"—regarding, for instance, the possibility of other earth-like planets which might be capable of supporting advanced forms of life in far away solar systems: a well-known part of some ongoing astrophysical enquiry today—are totally irrelevant. But focusing on human historical time does not mean that any form of *relativism* is acceptable in our assessment of meaningful time relations. On the contrary, the question of *historical necessity* is a vital issue here, although it must be evaluated in a qualitatively different way from those who, with hostile ideological intent, try to ascribe a crude mechanical deterministic view to the Marxian—profoundly dialectical—conception of historical time. For the core meaning of human historical necessity is precisely that it is *only historical,* which means that it is an ultimately *disappearing necessity* (*eine verschwindende Notwendigkeit* in Marx's words[1]), and should not be treated on the model of *naturalistic determinations.*

As we shall see in Chapter 9, through the arrival of human history in the natural order a radically new dimension of time enters the picture. From that time onwards the question of *meaning* appears on the horizon, even if it must take a very long historical development before the emancipatory objectives implicit in it can be turned into reality and *consciously* pursued by people as historically articulated human projects. The meaning in question is the potentially *meaningful lifetime of individuals,* arising in its close linkage to the productive development of humanity that progressively extricates individuals from the brutish constraints of their earlier "hand-to-mouth" existence and establishes for them the power of making *genuine choices.*

The potentiality of meaningful life for the social individuals aris-es because historically developing—and through its productive activi-ty self-mediating—humankind is a *unique* part of the natural order. Accordingly, human beings do not constitute a simple animal-like *genus* but a complex *social body* made from a multiplicity of *real indi-viduals.* To be sure, like the animals, human beings have their *limited* lifespan. But—quite unlike the animal "genus individuals"—they are also capable of consciously setting themselves *particular objectives* to pursue both on *distinct* occasions, in limited contexts, and also with some kind of *interconnected and overall coherence,* covering a more or less extensive part of their life-time and thereby conferring meaning upon it.

Moreover, it is also highly relevant here that the most comprehen-sive social body to which the individuals belong is *historically develop-ing humanity,* with its incomparably more extensive lifespan than that of the particular individuals. In this sense the historical time of humanity *transcends* the time of the individuals—bringing with it the most fundamental dimension of value—but remaining at the same time in a dialectical sense inseparable from it. Accordingly, only through the closest interrelationship between the individuals and humanity can a proper value system be established and further devel-oped—both expanded and intensified—in the course of history. Hu-manity is not acting on its own, but through the intervention of par-ticular individuals in the historical process, inseparably from the social groups to which the individuals belong as social subjects.

It is the objectively existing relationship between humanity and the individuals that makes possible the positing and actualization of values well beyond the *constraining immediate horizon* of the particu-lar individuals themselves. Not just in the sense that the increasing amount of *free time* made available for the individuals by productive-ly developing humanity—even if for the duration of class societies only in a most iniquitous way—is the necessary condition for their expanding alternative choices (and the associated values), in sharp contrast to their "hand-to-mouth" existence in the more remote past. What is directly relevant here is that the objective difference between the time of the individuals and the time of humanity constitutes the objective foundation of *value and counter-value.* For the *potentialities of humanity* are never *identical* to those of the always much more con-strained individuals. What we can really talk about regarding this relationship is a reciprocally enriching *interchange* between humanity and the individuals through which the real potentialities of both can fully unfold on a continuing basis. For the individuals can adopt as their own aspirations the values pointing in the direction of the realization of humanity's *positive potentialities,* and thereby also positively develop themselves; or, on the contrary, they can make choices acting against humanity's positive potentialities and historically reached attainments. In the latter case they become, of course, the more or less conscious carriers of *counter-value,* even if their actions are in reality intelligible on the basis of retrograde class determinations, rather than purely personal motivations, as frequently depicted in abstract philosophical and religious moral discourse.

To be sure, the positive potentialities of humanity can develop only through the activities of the individuals in their inseparability from the social groups to which they belong. But the positing of value, based on the objective relationship between the radically different time scale of the particular individuals and humanity, is an essential part of this process of historical progression. In this sense, the *assertion and contestation of value* is and shall always remain a vital organ of humanity's self-development.

Understandably, the complex problems involved in these relations—and in the first place the insurmountable fact itself that the historical time of humanity *transcends* the time of the individuals—is reflected for a long time in social consciousness as *religious transcendentalism,* assuming at the same time the form of religiously articulated *moral prescriptions.* The true consciousness that the vital underlying determination is the objective relationship between humanity and the particular individuals appears very late in history.

In a more general philosophical and literary form it arises in the second half of the eighteenth century (e.g., with Kant and Goethe), and in a much more broadly diffused variety, addressed to everyday consciousness in a non-religious form, as late as the twentieth century. Indeed, by the time the consciousness of the actuality of humanity is clearly pushed to the forefront of attention in the twentieth century it is increasingly associated with the awareness that what is depicted with growing concern is not simply the contingent situation of humanity but the fate of *gravely endangered humanity.* In other words, what appears on the horizon are the ever more tangible threats affecting the very survival of humanity, due to the ongoing—increasingly more dangerous—social and economic developments inseparable from the imposition of the most extreme form of *counter-value*. Thus, the *role of morality*, in its ability to fight for the realization of humanity's positive potentialities and against the structurally entrenched forces of counter-value inherent in capital's deepening structural crisis has never been greater than it is today. Only the most dogmatic kinds of philosophy (and associated politics) can ignore or explicitly deny that.

When Kant himself depicted the relationship between individuals and humanity, he identified with profound insight a most important aspect of development in the significance of human productive activity itself by underlining that historical advancement happens to be so determined that everything "should be achieved by *work* . . . as if nature intended that man should owe all to himself."[2] At the same time, however, he fully adopted the standpoint of political economy—corresponding to the vantage point of capital—in its version propounded by Adam Smith's idealized "commercial spirit." Accordingly, Kant had to set up an *insurmountable dichotomy* between individuals and the human species by insisting on more than one occasion that in his scheme of things "those natural faculties which aim at the use of reason shall be fully developed in the *species,* not in the *individual.*" [3]

Inevitably, this dichotomous conclusion had imposed on him further dilemmas. For he had to stipulate that in the rational administration of civil society the reconciliation of egotism and justice represented an *insoluble* problem. As he had put it: "The task involved is therefore most difficult; indeed, a complete solution is *impossible.* One cannot fashion something absolutely straight from wood which is as crooked as that of which man is made."[4] As to the Kantian characterization of human beings, it was very similar to that of all the major theoreticians of "civil society," representing the *"antagonism of men in society"* as directly arising from *human nature* itself and therefore equally insoluble. To quote Kant again: "I mean by antagonism the *asocial sociability* of men, i.e., the propensity of men to enter into a society, which propensity is, however, linked to a *constant mutual resistance* which threatens to dissolve this society. This propensity apparently is *innate in men.*"[5] Thus, the enlightened elements in the Kantian historical approach were undermined by capital's social imperative of domination and subordination of "civil society" and its matching state, ending up with the most unenlightened *explicit justification of substantive inequality.*[6]

In the various conceptions of "civil society" the place of the real social individuals—together with their class determinations and ultimate inseparability from humanity (which transcended them only in their strictly constrained particularity, without venturing into the realm of religious transcendentalism)—was replaced by the image of the *isolated individuals* and their *genus-determined* fixed "human nature." This kind of conceptualization was made in order to enable the isolated individuals to become fit for the role of eternalizing and spuriously legitimating the established antagonistic and adversarial relations of "asocial sociability." The consequence of this way of depicting capital's reproductive order was that the *social ground* of actual value-positing had to be represented even in the greatest and the most enlightened of such conceptions of "civil society," like, for instance, the Kantian philosophy, as the mysterious separate "intelligible world" of *ethical transcendentalism*.

Moreover, by the time we reached the twentieth century, when the close relationship between the individuals and society—to the no-longer deniable extent of directly depending for their very survival on one another—by that time anyway of clinging to the conception of isolated individuality, in the interest of continued capital-apologetics, became totally untenable. And yet, we were offered even by some major intellectual figures, like Max Weber, an extreme individualistic conception of social and moral relations, with a most deplorable irrationalist account of the isolated individuals' arbitrary ethical decisions, glorifying their unaccountable "private demons,"[7] and thereby undermining all claims to rationality of the Weberian philosophy.

Assuming "asocial sociability" as the nature-determined ground of establishing values can only be self-defeating. For it must ultimately deny the possibility of *real alternative choices* if they conflict—as they inevitably do—with the destructive determinations of the prevailing adversarial and conflictual "eternal present." It is the unfounded assumption of capital's "eternal present" which carries with it the circularly postulated permanence of "asocial sociability." To be sure, "sociability" can be not only "asocial" but even *most destructively anti-social,* as we know only too well. However, actually known sociability can be profoundly and responsibly *social* as well, assuming the form of *genuine co-operation.* It all depends on the value-positing orientation of the social individuals who may side with humanity's positive potentialities, or on the contrary, go along with capital's increasingly more dangerous counter-values—as they choose from among the available real alternatives—in confronting or evading the challenge and burden of their historical time.

If we really want to get out of capital's vicious circle of self-sustaining adversariality, we must question the system's prevailing practical premises and necessary assumptions. A closer look at the conceptual structure of the theories of "civil society" reveals that their *conclusions*—predicating the impossibility to create something straight from what is by its nature crooked—*coincide* with their *assumptions*. We can see this in our earlier quoted example from Kant's philosophy in the form in which the assumption and conclusion of the fateful affinity between human nature and the wood—which is supposed to be crooked by its original determination—is presented. For nothing establishes the postulated relationship between the two, other than the peremptory assertion contained in the claimed conclusive assumption itself.

A radical departure from such conceptions is vital for facing the urgency of resolving our grave problems of this historical time. In this respect, the actual given time of twentieth and twenty-first century history has caught up with both the individuals and the species. All the more because some powerful productive technologies and the potential use to which they may be put bring with them the necessity to make extremely difficult and perhaps even irreversibly dangerous decisions, directly involving the question of time.

To take an obvious example, the essential energy requirements of human productive activity have put on the agenda the prospect of using *nuclear power plants* for this purpose already today, not to mention the likely multiplication of such requirements in the more distant future. But even if we disregard the immense danger of *nuclear weapons proliferation,* easily achievable in close conjunction with the same technology, the mind-boggling *timescale itself* of the relevant productive processes and their unavoidable residues—their potentially lethal radiation time counted in *many thousands of years,* i.e., covering the life-time of countless generations—appear absolutely prohibitive. There are, of course, people, who for the sake of short-term profit, would not hesitate for a moment to tamper with the perilously long-term scale of nuclear radiation time. Others, instead, might simply run away from the problem itself by rejecting on some *a priori* ground the possibility of nuclear power production even if the need for it becomes overwhelming.

However, the real question concerns the nature of the productive system itself in which the decisions must be made, together with the ability or likely failure of the system in question to cope with the appropriate time-scale of the operations involved. As we know from all our historical experience, the capital system, even in its historical phase marked by recurrent *conjunctural crises* only, in contrast to its grave *structural crisis* in our time, is characterized by an *extreme short-term perspective,* covering no more than a few years in its usual cycle of reproduction, and by no means many thousands of years with the required reliable foresight. Moreover, even those few years under capital's customary reproductive processes are covered only in an adversarial and conflictual as well as *post festum* way, because of the systemic imperative of capital accumulation and its associated cycle of amortization. How much more problematic this relationship to historical time must become under the conditions of the system's *structural crisis?* For such a crisis can only aggravate the issue. In any case, within the framework of capital's social metabolic control, under all circumstances, *planning* for thousands of years ahead is totally inconceivable. Yet, without fully conscious and responsible planning on the most comprehensive and longest-term time-scale, based on the proper understanding of the unavoidable relationship in our historical time between the value-positing choices of the social individuals and the fate of humanity, there can be no viable solution at all to these problems.

"Asocial sociability" is the historical predicament of human beings only under determinate social and economic circumstances, and not their absolute ontological predestination. As *self-mediating* beings, and not *genus-individuals,* they are not only the sufferers of the antagonistic conditions of asocial sociability but also their makers. Yet, what is historically created by human beings—even if in its origins under the conditions of structurally embedded social antagonisms—can be also historically altered and ultimately consigned to the past. But the necessary precondition of success in that respect is that the social individuals should engage in the task of overcoming the antagonisms in question through the institution of a radically different and historically viable social order: the only conceivable way in which deep-seated structural antagonisms can be superseded.

Naturally, the historical time of the individuals can never be *identical* to the time of humanity. But from their difference does not follow that the two should constitute an *antagonistic* relationship, superimposing thereby the "unconscious condition of mankind" on the individuals in the form of blind material determinations, as experienced in the historical past. Nor is it more than a very poor consolation prize to come to terms with such a state of affairs—while remaining captive within the framework of the apparently irreconcilable antagonisms of the actually existing world—under the "other-worldly" halo of *religious transcendentalism.*

In truth, the historical time of individuals need not always conflict with the objective determinations of humanity's historical time. It is also capable of being brought into *harmony* with the time of humanity. This is achievable today if social individuals consciously adopt the positive alternatives that point in the direction of humanity's sustainable future. The specificity and urgency of our historical time is that they not only *can* but also *must* do so.

1.2 Human Beings Reduced to "Time's Carcase"

Naturally, the relationship between the individuals and humanity always depends on the way in which the necessary interaction between human beings and nature is mediated under the given circumstances by a historically determinate set of social relations. The grave and in principle insurmountable problem for the capital system is that it *superimposes* on the unavoidable *first-order mediations* between humanity and nature a set of *alienating second-order mediations,* creating thereby an *"eternalized"*—and even by the greatest thinkers of the bourgeoisie in that way conceptualized—*vicious circle* from which there cannot be any escape by sharing capital's vantage point.

To indicate the fundamental difference between the always unavoidable first-order, and the capitalistically specific second-order, mediations very briefly,[8] we must bear in mind that *none* of the first order mediatory requirements between human beings and nature prescribe the obvious *class relations of domination and subordination* inseparable from capital's second-order mediations, contrary to the theoretical misrepresentations conceived from capital's self-serving vantage point adopted even by the greatest of the classical political economists, like Adam Smith. The primary mediations between humanity and nature required for social life itself may be summed up as follow:

1. The necessary, more or less spontaneous, regulation of *biological* reproductive activity and the size of the sustainable population, in conjunction with the available resources;

2. The regulation of the *labor process* through which the given community's necessary interchange with nature can produce the goods required for human gratification, as well as the appropriate working tools, productive enterprises, and knowledge by means of which the reproductive process itself can be maintained and improved;

3. The establishment of *suitable exchange relations* under which the historically changing needs of human beings can be linked together for the purpose of optimizing the available natural and productive—including the culturally productive—resources;

4. The organization, *coordination,* and control of the *multiplicity of activities* through which the material and cultural requirements of the successful social metabolic reproduction process of progressively more complex human communities can be secured and safeguarded;

5. The *rational allocation* of the available material and human resources, fighting against the *tyranny of scarcity* through the economic (in the sense of *economizing) utilization* of the given society's ways and means of reproduction;

6. The *enactment* and administration of the *rules and regulations* of the given society *as a whole,* in conjunction with the other primary mediatory functions and determinations.

The ideologically most revealing theoretical misrepresentations of the actual historical developments operate in such a way that capital's second-order mediations—characteristic of the now dominant reproductive processes—are *assumed* to be the ontologically irreplaceable *first-order* mediations of social metabolic interaction as such. In this way, they are depicted as the vital *practical premises* not only of the historically created and changeable specific social order but of all conceivable social life in general. Thus, the *tendentiously assumed practical premises* of the capitalist mode of societal reproduction are presumed to offer the firm grounding of the required *conclusions*—in the case of the "assumptions and conclusions" from which the postulated "conclusive assumptions" were derived—which irretrievably close capital's systemic circle.

Inevitably, therefore, in order to overcome the paralyzing constraints of capital's vicious circle, as constituted in the form of the system's second-order mediations, it is necessary to oppose *in their entirety* the practical premises themselves which cannot be conveniently compartmentalized for illusory reformist purposes. The clamorous historical failure of all attempts aimed at reforming the capital system—whether they were once genuinely so intended or used primarily for the purpose of ideological mystification—find their painful explanation in the forbidding circularity between the structurally prejudged practical premises themselves and the absolutely necessary mode of operation of capital's social metabolic order which is already anticipated as a set of *reproductive imperatives* in those practical premises.

If we compare the first-order mediations with the well-known hierarchical structural determinations of capital's second-order mediations, we find that everything is altered with the rise of capitalism almost beyond recognition. For all of the primary mediatory requirements must be modified in such a way that they should suit the self-expansionary needs of a fetishistic and alienating system of social reproductive control which must subordinate absolutely everything to the imperative of capital accumulation. This is why, to take only one example, the single-mindedly pursued aim of reducing the material and living labor "costs of production" in the capital system, on the basis of the ruthless application of capital's *time accountancy,* and the concomitant fight against scarcity, show tremendous achievements on one plane. However, all that is done, self-contradictorily, only to completely nullify the claimed achievements on another plane through the creation of the most absurd "artificial appetites" and the associated ever-increasing scarcities, in the service of the most wasteful reproduction of the established mode of social metabolic control.

As a result of these developments, *use-value* corresponding to need can acquire the right to existence only if it conforms to the aprioristic imperatives of *self-expanding exchange-value.* It is therefore doubly ironical that one of the principal philosophies of capital's epoch should consider itself the champion of *"utilitarianism"* at a time when all genuine concern for *non-profitable utility* is ruthlessly obliterated and replaced by the universal commodification of objects and human relations alike. This process unfolds thanks to the apparently irresistible forward march of the idealized "commercial spirit" whose triumph the self-same philosophy wholeheartedly approves.

The ideological rationalization of these developments, fully in tune with capital's second-order mediations and practical premises, takes the form of *conflating* some important conceptual lines of demarcation. The way of fallaciously submerging *use-value* into *exchange-value*, so as to claim productive achievement when the diametric opposite is clearly in evidence—as in the case of capital's escalating *wastefulness* and *destructiveness* spuriously idealized by its ideologists as "productive destruction"—is a prominent example of this kind of mystifying conflation.

In the same way, significantly, the key problem concerning the one-sided expropriation of the *means of production* by the system's willing personifications is *conflated* into the vague generality of "accidents distributing the *means of subsistence* unequally," removing thereby the dimension of *class conflict.* As a result, it is conveniently obfuscated that *distribution* in capitalist society means first of all the *distribution of human beings into antagonistic social classes,* from which the domination of production in a hierarchically ordered way necessarily follows. In this context it should not come as a surprise that even the great dialectical thinker, Hegel, *conflates* the *means of production* with the means of *subsistence,* as well as *work* in general with *socially divided labor,* so as to be able to glorify what he calls "*universal permanent capital.*"[9]

One of the most degrading aspects of capital's social order is that it reduces human beings to a reified condition, so as to be able to fit them into the narrow confines of the system's *time accountancy:* the only kind of—extremely dehumanizing—accountancy compatible with capital's social order. This type of impoverishing social development is theoretically justified in the form of an ideologically revealing abstraction operated by the political economists who directly link *abstract individuality* (the isolated individuals) and *abstract universality* (the prevailing capitalist division and fragmentation of labor decreed to be the timeless universal rule created by nature itself). The extreme reductive theoretical procedure of the political economists—which abstracts from all human qualities—is based on capital's underlying practical reductionism, exposed by Marx by bringing into focus the objective relationship between *simple* and *compound labor* and the alienating subordination of human beings to the rule of *quantity and time* under capital's prevailing imperatives. In Marx's words:

Competition, according to an American economist, determines how many days of simple labour are contained in one day's compound labour. Does not this *reduction* of days of compound labour to days of simple labour suppose that simple labour is itself taken as a *measure of value?* If the mere quantity of labour functions as a measure of value regardless of quality, it presupposes that simple labour has become the pivot of industry. It presupposes that labour has been equalized by the *subordination of man to the machine or by the extreme division of labour,* that men are *effaced by their labour,* that the pendulum of the clock has become as accurate a measure of the relative activity of two workers as it is of the speed of two locomotives. Therefore we should not say that one man's hour is worth another man's hour, but rather that one man during an hour is worth just as much as another man during an hour. *Time is everything, man is nothing; he is at the most time's carcase. Quality* no longer matters. *Quantity* alone decides everything; hour for hour; day for day.[10]

Thus, within the framework of the existing socioeconomic system a multiplicity of potentially dialectical interconnections are reproduced in the form of perverse practical dualisms, dichotomies, and antinomies, *reducing human beings to a reified condition* (whereby *they* are brought to a common denominator with, and become replaceable by, "locomotives" and other machines) and to the ignominious status of *"time's carcase."* And since the possibility of practically manifesting and realizing the *inherent worth* and human specificity of the individuals through their essential productive activity is blocked off as a result of this process of *alienating reduction* (which makes "one man during an hour worth just as much as another man"), *value* as such becomes an extremely *problematical concept.* For, in the interest of capitalist *profitability,* not only can there be no room left for the actualization of the individuals' specific worth but, worse still, *counter-value* must unceremoniously prevail over value and assert its absolute domination as the one and only admissible practical value-relation.

The alternative *socialist accountancy* cannot prevail unless it succeeds in radically reorienting the process of societal reproduction in its entirety by breaking the tyranny of capital's dehumanizing time imperative. The fundamental categories of the social reproduction process, as inherent in the vital first-order mediations of a sustainable dialectical interaction between humanity and nature on an indefinite historical timescale, have been subverted in the course of development, especially in the last three centuries under the fetishistic imperatives of capital's social metabolic control. Thus the all-important achievement of humanity in the form of potentially emancipatory *free time*, embodied in society's productively expanding *surplus-labor*—which happens to be both the precondition as well as the promising storehouse of all future advancement, once extricated from its alienating capitalist integument—has been forced into the ultimately suffocating *strait-jacket of surplus-value*, under the corollary imperative of reducing *necessary labor-time* to the minimum, so as to be managed by the system's not only dehumanizing but also in historical terms increasingly more anachronistic *time accountancy*.

Accordingly, everything that cannot be *profitably* accommodated within such confines must be ruled at best to be irrelevant or non-existent, or indeed must be destroyed if it appears to present active resistance to capital's crippling design for containment, as all attempts aimed at instituting a genuine socialist alternative, at whatever scale, must do. If the *individuals' human worth* is categorically ruled out of consideration, because *counter-value* much better secures profitability while masquerading as the only viable producer of economic efficiency and value—and doing so by ruthlessly enforcing the reduction of labor-time to the minimum, disregarding the socially destructive consequences of chronic unemployment—in that case how could the regulator and measure of the objects to be produced arise from the individuals' *qualitatively determined human needs*, as *use-values* corresponding to such needs?

Profitable counter-value—at all cost—must dictate both the *measure* in tune with the historically prevailing type of capitalist time-accountancy, wedded to the increasingly anachronistic requirement of *reducing* necessary labor-time to the minimum, and doing that inseparably from the alienating *reduction of human beings themselves to time's carcase* who can fit into such productive parameters, on the one hand, and the kind of products—the profitably marketable commodities which acquire their *raison d'être* in virtue of their total conformity to capital's reductive time-accountancy—on the other. Thus, there can be no question of evaluating in relation to the qualitatively determined needs of the social individuals the question of *what kind of objects* must be produced, consciously determining at the same time also the *time dedicated to each product*, justified not by a blind economic mechanism but on the basis of freely made choices arising from human need. The *economic determinism* of capital's reductive time-accountancy—which happened to constitute in its own time a major productive advancement, but beyond a certain point is turned into a dangerous historical anachronism—is supposed to be sufficient for dictating everything, and also for *justifying by definition everything it can successfully dictate.* Not for nothing did Hegel spell out the ultimate formula of capital's fully completed circle from which no escape should be even contemplated, by saying in a tone of consenting resignation that *"what is rational is actual and what is actual is rational."*[11]

This is why the concept of *free time* is totally meaningless to capital. It must be subverted—and bastardized—by its conversion into idle "leisure," in order to be exploitatively subsumed under the overall imperative of capital-accumulation. By contrast, socialist accountancy must put into the forefront of its attention the task of always making the best use of society's available free time, as well as of optimally expanding it in the interest of all. This is how it becomes possible to enrich social individuals in a meaningful way through the process of creatively exercising their personally available free time—the individual's *disposable time* which is of necessity totally neglected in capitalist society—simultaneously also increasing thereby the positive potentialities of humanity itself as the basis of individual and social development in the future.

Productively expanding surplus-labor and creatively used free time are the important orienting concepts of socialist accountancy, in contrast to the narrow time horizon of surplus-value. The history of class societies was always characterized by the *forced extraction of surplus-labor,* whether its modality was *political* or *economic,* or indeed a combination of the two. The profitable extraction of surplus-labor as surplus-value, characteristic of capital's social order, did not alter the substance of the age-old exploitative relationship, but only its modality: by making structurally dominant the economically enforced expropriation of surplus- labor, reducing human beings—in the service of ever-accumulating surplus-value—to time's carcase. The historical challenge is to consign to the past this vicious circle of forced extraction through the rationally determined allocation of free time for the purposes consciously chosen by social individuals.

1.3 The Loss of Historical Time Consciousness

Surveying the theoretical developments of the last century and a half we find that the enlightened historical conception of the bourgeois philosophical tradition leaves its place to progressively more pervasive skepticism and pessimism from the decades that follow Hegel's death to our own time. Ranke and Alexis de Tocqueville set the tone, preaching the "equidistance" of everything from God as well as the desolateness of our inescapable predicament.

The celebrated historian, Sir Lewis Namier, sums up with pessimistic skepticism—tempered with the self-assured dogmatism of those who know that their class holds the reins of power—the antihistorical "philosophy of history" which predominates in the bourgeois ideologies of the twentieth century. As he puts it, in favor of describing "intersecting *patterns*," after rejecting the viability of investigating "envenomed *struggles*" (because "such inquiry would take us into *inscrutable depths* or into an *airy void*"): "there is no more sense in human history than in the changes of the seasons or the movements of the stars; or if sense there be, it escapes our perception."[12]

With the adoption of such views, all genuine achievements of the Enlightenment tradition in the field of historical theory are completely overturned. For the outstanding figures of the Enlightenment attempted to draw a meaningful line of demarcation between nature that surrounds *homo sapiens* and the manmade world of societal interaction, in order to make intelligible the rule-governed specificities of sociohistorical development which emerge from the pursuit of human objectives. Now, in complete contrast, even the rationality and legitimacy of such reflections is denied with categorical firmness. Thus, historical temporality is radically suppressed and the domain of human history is submerged into the cosmic world of—in principle "meaningless"—nature.

We are told that we can only understand history in terms of the immediacy of *appearance*—so that the question of taking control of the underlying *structural determinations* by grasping the *socioeconomic laws* at work cannot even arise—while resigning ourselves to the paralyzing conclusion that "if sense there be," it cannot be found any more in historically produced and historically changeable social relations, shaped by human purpose, than in cosmic nature, hence it must forever "escape our perception."

Naturally, the pessimistic skepticism of theories of this kind—which, however, do not hesitate to be stern castigators of all "overall conceptions" (exemplified also by the "postmodern" tirades against "grand narratives")—need not oppose social practice in general in the name of the otherwise stipulated necessary "withdrawal from the world." The need for the latter arises only when major structural change—with reference to some *radical* overall conception—is implicit in the advocated action.

So long as everything can be contained within the parameters of the established order, the "unity of theory and practice" need not be condemned as one of Marx's many alleged "confusions." On the contrary, under such circumstances it can be praised as a highly positive aspect of the intellectual enterprise. Just as we find it, in fact, in Sir Lewis Namier's observation according to which "it is remarkable how much *perception is sharpened* when the work serves a *practical purpose* of absorbing interest," with reference to his own study, "The Downfall of the Habsburg Monarchy," the fruit of work "in Intelligence Departments, first under, and next in, the Foreign Office."[13]

Thus, historical skepticism, no matter how extreme, is quite selective in its diagnoses and in the definition of its targets. For if the subject at issue involves the possibility of envisaging major structural transformations, then it preaches the "meaninglessness" of our predicament and the unavoidability of the conclusion that "if sense there be, it escapes our perception." On the other hand, however, when the question is: how to sustain with all the necessary means and measures the established order, despite its antagonisms, and how to divide the spoils of (or how to move into the vacuum created by) the dying Habsburg Empire, such "practical purpose of absorbing interest," in the service of the Intelligence Departments of another doomed Empire, the British, will miraculously "sharpen perception" and lay to rest the troublesome nuisance of skepticism.

Sadly, this is how the emancipatory quest of the Enlightenment tradition ends in modern bourgeois historiography. The great representatives of the bourgeoisie in the ascendant attempted to found historical knowledge by elucidating the power of the human historical subject to "make history," even if they could not consistently carry through their inquiry to the originally intended conclusion. Now, every single constituent of their approach must be liquidated.

The very idea of "making history" is discarded, with undisguised contempt for all those who might still entertain it, since the only history that should be contemplated is the one *already* made, which is supposed to remain with us to the end of time. Hence, while it is right and proper to chronicle the "Downfall of the Habsburg Empire," the intellectual legitimacy of investigating the objective trends and antagonisms of historical development which foreshadow the necessary dissolution of the British and French Empires—or, for that matter, also of the politically and militarily much more mediated and diffused postwar structures of overwhelmingly U.S.–dominated imperialism—all this must be *a priori* ruled out of court.

In the same way, the reluctant acknowledgement of the individuals' limitations in imposing the adopted state policy decisions "of absorbing interest" on historical development does not lead to a more realistic grasp of the dialectical reciprocities at work between individuals and their classes in the constitution of the historical subject, nor to the recognition of the inescapable *collective* parameters of historically relevant action. On the contrary, it brings the skeptical dissection and complete elimination of the historical subject, with devastating consequences for the theories which can be constructed within such horizons. For once the historical subject is thrown overboard, not only the possibility of *making* but also of *understanding* history must suffer the same fate, as the great figures of the Enlightenment had correctly recognized while trying to find solutions to the problems confronting them.

And finally, the ironical outcome of all this for the historians concerned is that their own enterprise, too, completely loses its *raison d'être*. A predicament which they bring upon themselves in the course of attempting to undermine the ground of those who refuse to give up the closely interconnected concepts of "historical subject," "making history," and "understanding history," thereby also necessarily breaking all links with the positive aspects of the philosophical tradition to which they belong.

In the end, what is left to them as a "way out" is the arbitrary generalization and idealization of a dubious intellectual stance which must turn in its search for skeptical self-assurance not only against its social adversary but even against its own ancestry.

They try to hide the contradictions of the solutions they end up with behind the ideology of universal "meaninglessness," coupled with the apparently self-evident viability of presenting, instead, "patterns" with descriptive "completeness": a hopelessly self-defeating aspiration, if ever there was one. And they justify their programmatic evasion of comprehensive issues—from which the question of how to make intelligible the trends and necessities that emerge from the individuals' pursuit of their socially circumscribed ends cannot be eliminated—on the ground that they properly belong to the "inscrutable depths" of cosmic mysteries.

If we look for the reasons behind the depressing trajectory of this radical reversal—from the Enlightenment's preoccupation with human meaning and its progressive realization in history, to the apotheosis of cosmic pessimism and universal meaninglessness—one particular factor stands out, more than anything else, with its weighty and irreversible significance, directly affecting the philosophical tradition in question in its qualitatively altered phases of development. It concerns the objectively given conditions and possibilities of emancipation, as well as the varying social constraints involved in their conceptualizations under different historical circumstances.

In truth, already the emancipatory quest of the great historical tradition of the Enlightenment suffers from the constraints which induce its major representatives to leave the question of the historical subject nebulously and abstractly defined (or undefined). This is due partly to the individualistic presuppositions of the philosophers who belong to this tradition, and partly to the potentially antagonistic heterogeneity of the social forces to which they are linked at the given phase of historical confrontations. Thus, what we encounter here, even under circumstances most favorable to the articulation of bourgeois historical conceptions, is the—at first latent, but inexorably growing—presence of untranscendable social antagonisms which find their way to the structuring core of the respective philosophical syntheses.

Understandably, therefore, the closure of the historical period in question, in the aftermath of the French Revolution and the Napoleonic wars, brings to light a truly ambivalent achievement. On the one hand, it gives rise to the greatest bourgeois conceptualization of the historical dynamics, at the highest level of generalization, magisterially anticipating within the abstract categorical confines of its horizons the objective logic of capital's global unfolding, coupled with truly epoch-making insights into the key role of labor in historical development. On the other hand, however, it also produces the formerly unimaginable expansion of the *mystifying arsenal* of ideology.

Significantly, the two are combined in the internally torn and even in its own terms extremely problematical synthesis of the Hegelian system; with its "identical Subject and Object" and its "cunning of Reason" in place of the real historical subject; with the reduction of the historical process to the "circle of circles" of the self-generating "progress of the Concept only," in his construction of the categorial edifice of *The Science of Logic* as well as in the claimed "true Theodicy" of *The Philosophy of History;* and with the suppression of historical temporality at the critical juncture of the present, self-contradictorily ending up with the biggest lie of all in a theory that purports to be historical—namely that "Europe is *absolutely the end of history*"[14]—after defining the task of Universal History as the demonstration of "how Spirit comes to a *recognition and adoption of the Truth.*"[15]

In this sense, hand in hand with the consolidation of the social order after the French Revolution go some highly significant conceptual transformations. At first, the sociohistorical substance and the explanatory value of "*class struggles*" is recognized by bourgeois historians, even if they try to insert this concept into an increasingly more conservative overall framework. Later, however, all such categories must be completely discarded as nineteenth-century concepts, characteristically ascribing them to Marx (although Marx himself never claimed originality in this respect) in order to be able to get rid of their own intellectual heritage without embarrassment. The Enlightenment's quest for emancipation suffers the same fate of being relegated to the remote past in all its major aspects, more and more being referred to—at best—as a "noble illusion."

When, "from the standpoint of political economy" (which represents the vantage point of capital's established order), the question is how to *prevent* that history be made by the subordinate classes in furtherance of a new social order, the historical pessimism of "growing meaninglessness," and the radical skepticism that tries to discredit the very idea of "making history," are perfectly in tune with the dominant material and ideological interests. At the same time, however, the social forces engaged in the struggle for emancipation from the rule of capital cannot give up either the project of "making history" or the idea of instituting a new social order. Not on account of some perverse inclination towards messianic "holism," but simply because the realization of even their most limited *immediate objectives*—like food, shelter, basic healthcare, and education, as far as the overwhelming majority of humankind is concerned—is quite inconceivable without radically challenging the established order whose very nature consigns them, *of necessity,* to their powerless position of structural subordination in society.

1.4 Free Time and Emancipation

Human emancipation is feasible only on the basis of a historical conception that rejects not only any idea of *mechanical materialistic determinism* but also the kind of idealist philosophical *closure of history* that we encounter in the monumental Hegelian vision of the world. For when Hegel declares in a tone of consenting resignation that *"what is rational is actual and what is actual is rational"* (as we have seen above), in order to justify his acceptance of the necessary *reconciliation with the present,* equating at the same time the claimed "rational actuality" of the existent with *positivity,* he takes to an arbitrary closure the historical dynamics itself in the aprioristically anticipated *"eternal present"* of his speculative system, parting thereby company also with his original emancipatory quest conceived in the spirit of the Enlightenment.

In contrast to both mechanistic determinism and speculative idealism, the socialist advocacy of real emancipation would not make any sense at all without asserting the *radical openness of history.* For what would be the point of emphasizing the positive emancipatory potential of humanity's productively developing *free time,* as put to creative use by the social individuals in the course of historical development, if the *overall process* of historical transformation was fatefully prejudged by the narrow confines of mechanistic determinism (or "naturalistic determinism"), or indeed by the grandiloquent *a priori* projections of "self-realizing World Spirit" amounting to the same thing?

This is why Marx insists, in his *dialectical* conception of the radical openness of history, set against all forms of deterministic ideological closure, that any specific process and stage brought about by *historical* determination is *only* historical and therefore must leave its place in due course to a more advanced—and for the social individuals also potentially more enriching and fulfilling—stage of development, increasingly in tune with humanity's productively underpinned emancipation. Thus, contrary to tendentious misrepresentations of

Marx's views—falsely condemned on account of their alleged "economic determinism," which happens to be in fact the theoretical approach of the political economists sharply criticized by Marx—when he underlines the overbearing power of the material base he does that with very clear qualifications. For he puts into relief that the material base of social transformation reaches its paradoxical dominance *under the historically determinate conditions* of capital's social order, when—thanks to humanity's productive development—some major emancipatory potentialities open up at the horizon, even if they are frustrated and undermined by capital's destructive inner antagonisms. And precisely in the interest of setting free those positive productive potentialities, Marx counterposes to capital's antagonistic structural determinations the socialist emancipatory alternative as a mode of social metabolic control aimed at *consciously superseding* not only the power of capital's historically specific material base, articulated in the form of the universally reifying determinations of commodity society, but aimed also at overcoming the age-old preponderance of the material base in general. This is the meaning of the Marxian discourse on humanity's *real history* and its *"realm of freedom"* as contrasted with "the realm of necessity" overwhelmingly dominant in what he calls humanity's *pre-history*.

The tyranny of *capital's time imperative* finds its appropriate completion on the all-embracing scale of development in the arbitrary closure of history. Thus, there can be no success in breaking capital's time imperative without forcefully asserting—not only in alternative theoretical conceptions but above all through the comprehensive practical strategy of revolutionary transformation—the radical openness of history by consciously challenging the established hierarchical framework of structurally predetermined and entrenched social relations. In this sense the tyranny of capital's *time imperative*, practically enforced in the societal reproduction process by means of the system's alienating *time-accountancy*, and the tyranny of capital's *historical closure*, stand or fall together.

The historically created *radical openness of history* is itself inseparable from the unique condition of humanity's *self-mediation* with nature across history. It is very real in the sense that there can be no way of *predetermining* on a permanent basis the forms and modalities of human self-mediation, precisely because it is *self*-mediation. The complex dialectical conditions of this self-mediation through produc-

tive activity can only be satisfied—since they are constantly being created and recreated—in the course of this self-mediation itself. This is
why all attempts at producing neatly self-contained and conveniently
closed systems of historical explanation result either in some arbitrary
reduction of the complexity of human actions to the crude simplicity
of mechanical determinations, or in the idealistic superimposition of
one kind or another of *a priori transcendentalism* on the *immanence* of
human development.

Through the production of humanity's *free time* in the course of
history, on an increasing scale, it becomes possible to bring about the
real emancipation and substantive equality of social individuals. Thus
individuals do not have to resign themselves to the idealistic consolation prize of "the *form* and not the *matter* of the object regarding
which they may possess a right,"[16] as stipulated by Kant in an earlier
quotation: a nobly conceived but by its very nature utterly illusory
consolation prize. One which is bound to remain illusory because it is
emptied of all intended significance by the dehumanizing actuality of
capital's mode of societal reproduction not only regarding its *matter*
but also its *form*. This must remain the case for as long as the capital
system survives.

In the course of humanity's development *natural necessity* progressively leaves its place to *historically created necessity,* whereas in due
course *historical necessity* itself becomes *potentially unnecessary necessity* through the vast expansion of society's productive capacity and
real wealth. Thus, representing the seminal condition of actually feasible emancipation we find that historical necessity is indeed "a *merely
historical* necessity": a necessarily disappearing or "vanishing necessity"[17] which must be conceptualized as inherently *transient,* in contrast
to the absoluteness of strictly natural determinations, like *gravity*. The
progressive displacement of natural necessity by historically created
necessity opens up the possibility of universal development of the productive forces, involving the *"totality of activities"*[18] which in their turn
always remain the pivot of exchange relations (as the necessary
exchange of activities), in contrast to the fetishistic view of *commodity
exchange* smuggled back into even the most remote corners of past
history, as well as gratuitously projected into the timeless future, by the
capital-apologetic Hayeks of this world.

The "universalizing tendency of capital," transferring the objective
conditions of production to the plane of *global* interchanges, within

the framework of the international division of labor and the *world market,* distinguishes the capital system "from all previous stages of production."[19] Since, however, the conditions of production are as a result outside the particular industrial enterprise—outside even the most gigantic transnational corporations and state monopolies—capital's "universalizing tendency" turns out to be a very mixed blessing indeed. For while on the one hand it creates the genuine *potentiality of human emancipation,* on the other it represents the greatest possible of all complications—implying the danger of even totally destructive collisions—in that the necessary conditions of production and control happen to be *outside,* thus, *nightmarishly everywhere and nowhere.* In view of that, the biggest nightmare would be to expect that the *"invisible hand"* should sort out all of the chaotically interlocking contradictions and destructive antagonisms of the *globally intertwined capital system* when it failed to do what it was supposed to do, despite the boundless confidence conferred upon it by Adam Smith, Kant, Hegel and many others, on a much more modest scale in past centuries.

The sobering truth is that capital's universalizing tendency can *never* come to fruition within its own framework, for capital must decree that the barriers which it cannot transcend—namely its innermost structural limitations—are the insurmountable limits of all production in general. At the same time, what should indeed be recognized and respected as an inviolable limit and vital condition of ongoing development—that is, nature in all its complexity as the foundation of humanity's very existence—is totally disregarded in the systematic subjugation, degradation, and ultimate destruction of nature. This is so because the ultimately blind interest of capital expansion must overrule even the most elementary conditions of human life as directly rooted in nature. Consequently on both counts, i.e., both in relation to what capital refuses to acknowledge: its own structural limits, and with regard to its incorrigibly destructive impact on nature: the vital substratum of human life itself, a *conscious break* must be made from the self-serving determinations of the capital system.

The same considerations apply to the mythology of *"globalization,"* promoted with missionary zeal by capital's ideologists as a more palatable version of the "invisible hand" for our time. When they project the supposedly all-round global benefits, in conjunction with the world market, they ignore or deliberately misrepresent that what actually exists—and existed for a very long time—is far from being universally and equitably beneficial but, on the contrary, it is an *imperialistically dominated "world market."* It was established as a set of most iniquitous *power relations,* working always to the advantage of the stronger and always producing the ruthless domination—if need be even the direct military subjugation—and exploitation of the weaker. A "globalized" order constituted on such a basis, under the overall command structure of the modern state, could make matters only worse. This is why, also in this respect, without a *conscious break* with capital's mode of social metabolic control the far-reaching *positive emancipatory potential* of humanity's global reproductive interchanges cannot come to real fruition. Only the creative use of free time by the social individuals, in pursuit of the objectives freely chosen by them, can bring about the much-needed beneficial result.

The production of *free time* in the course of history, as the necessary condition of emancipation, is a great collective achievement. As such it is inseparable from the progressive development of humanity, in the same way in which *knowledge*—and the historically cumulative *scientific knowledge* directly relevant to the societal reproduction process—is also unthinkable without the collective subject of humanity, extending over the whole of history. Yet, capital expropriates to itself the storehouse of all human knowledge, arbitrarily granting legitimacy only to those parts of it which can be profitably exploited—even in the most destructive way—through its own fetishistic mode of reproduction.

Naturally, capital relates to humanity's historically produced free time in the same way. Thus, only that fraction of it which happens to be directly subsumable under the exploitative determinations of the "leisure industry" can be activated by being inserted into the process of profitable capital expansion. However, the free time of humanity is not a speculative notion but a very real and by its very nature inexhaustible potentiality. It exists as the virtually unlimited—because generously renewable and expandable—*disposable time* of the social individuals, capable of being put to creative use by them as self-realizing individuals, provided that the meaningful purposes which their actions serve emerge from their own autonomous deliberations. That is the only way to turn the emancipatory potentials of humanity into the liberating actuality of everyday life.

2. The Uncontrollability and Destructiveness of Globalizing Capital[1]

We live in an age of unprecedented historical crisis. Its severity can be gauged by the fact that we are not facing a more or less extensive cyclic crisis of *capitalism*, as experienced in the past, but the deepening structural crisis of the *capital system* itself. As such, this crisis affects—for the first time ever in history—the whole of humankind, and demands fundamental changes to the way in which the social metabolism is controlled if humanity is to survive.

2.1 The Extraction of Surplus-Labor in Capital's "Organic System"

Constitutive elements of the capital system (like monetary and merchant capital, as well as original sporadic commodity production) go back thousands of years in history. However, for most of those thousands of years they all remained subordinate parts of the specific systems of social metabolic control which historically prevailed at the time, including the slave-owning and feudal modes of production and distribution. Only in the last few centuries, under the bourgeois capitalist form, could capital successfully assert its rule as an all-embracing "organic system." To quote Marx:

> It must be kept in mind that the new forces of production and relations of production do not develop out of nothing, nor drop from the sky, nor from the womb of the self-positing Idea; but from within and in antithesis to the existing development of production and the inherited, traditional relations of property. While in the completed bourgeois system every economic rela-

> tion presupposes every other in its bourgeois economic form, and everything
> posited is thus also a presupposition, this is the case with every *organic sys-*
> *tem*. This organic system itself, as a totality, has its presuppositions, and its
> development to its totality consists precisely in subordinating all elements of
> society to itself, or in creating out of it the organs which it still lacks; this is
> historically how it becomes a totality.[2]

In this way, by extricating its age-old organic constituents from the
shackles of earlier organic systems, and by demolishing the barriers
that prevented the development of some vital new constituents,[3] capital as an all-embracing organic system could assert its rule in the last
three centuries as generalized commodity production. By reducing
and degrading human beings to the status of mere "costs of production," as "necessary labor-power," capital could treat even living labor
as nothing more than a "marketable commodity," just like any other,
subjecting it to the dehumanizing determinations of economic compulsion.

Earlier forms of productive interchange of human beings among
themselves and with nature were on the whole oriented toward production for *use*, with a large degree of *self-sufficiency* as their systemic
determination. This imposed on them a great vulnerability to capital's
sharply contrasting reproductive principles which were already operative, even if at first on a very small scale, within the confines of the old
systems. For not one of the constitutive elements of capital's dynamically unfolding organic system was ever in *need* of, nor indeed *capable*
of, confining itself to the structural constraints of self-sufficiency.
Capital as a system of social metabolic control could emerge and triumph over its historical antecedents only by abandoning all considerations of human need as tied to the limitations of non-quantifiable
use-values, superimposing on the latter—as the absolute prerequisite
for their legitimacy as acceptable production targets—the fetishistic
imperatives of both quantifiable and *ever-expanding exchange-value*.
This is how the historically specific form of the capital system, its *bour-*
geois capitalist variety, came into being. It had to adopt the overwhelmingly *economic* mode of extracting surplus-labor as strictly
quantified *surplus-value*—in contrast to both the *pre-capitalist* and the
Soviet type *postcapitalist*, primarily *political*, forms of controlling the
extraction of *surplus-labor*—which was at the time by far the most
dynamic way of realizing the expansion-imperative of the victorious

system. Moreover, thanks to the perverse circularity of capital's fully completed organic system—in which "every economic relation presupposes every other in its bourgeois economic form" and "everything posited is also a presupposition"—the world of capital could also assert its claims to being an "iron cage" from which no escape could or should be contemplated.

However, the absolute necessity to successfully meet the requirements of expansion without constraint—the secret of capital's irresistible advance—had brought with it an insurmountable historical limitation as well. This it did not only for the sociohistorically specific form of bourgeois *capitalism*, but altogether for the viability of the *capital system* in general. For this system of social metabolic control either had to succeed in imposing on society its ruthless and ultimately irrational expansionary logic, no matter how devastating the consequences; or it had to adopt some rational constraints which directly contradicted its innermost determination as an uncontrollable expansionary system. The twentieth century had witnessed many failed attempts that aimed at overcoming the systemic limitations of capital, from Keynesianism to Soviet type state interventionism, together with the political and military conflagrations that they gave rise to. And yet, all that such attempts could achieve was only the "hybridization" of the capital system, compared to its classical economic form—with extremely problematical implications for the future—but not structurally viable solutions.

2.2 Unreformability, Uncontrollability, and Destructiveness

It is highly significant in this respect that, as a matter of fact—and notwithstanding all the triumphalism which has celebrated in recent years both the mythical virtues of an idealized "market society" and the "end of history" under the never again challengeable hegemony of liberal capitalist principles—the capital system could not be completed as a *global* system in its proper *capitalist* form; i.e., by making the overwhelmingly *economic* mode of extraction and appropriation of surplus-labor as surplus-value *universally* prevail. Capital in the twentieth century was forced to respond to ever-more extensive crises (which brought with them even two formerly unimaginable world wars) by accepting "hybridization"—in the form of an ever-greater intrusion of the state into the socioeconomic reproduction process—as a way out of its difficulties, ignoring the longer term dangers of the adopted remedy for the viability of the system. Characteristically, attempts to turn back the clock (even as far back as the age of a grossly misrepresented Adam Smith) are prominent among the uncritical defenders of the capital system. Thus the representatives of the "Radical Right" continue to fantasize about "rolling back the boundaries of the state," although in reality the opposite trend is clearly observable, due to the inability of the system to secure capital-expansion on the required scale without the administration of ever greater doses of "extraneous help" by the state in one form or another.

Capitalism may have gained the upper hand in the former Soviet Union and in Eastern Europe, but it is quite wrong to describe the present state of the world as successfully ruled by *capitalism* everywhere, even though it is certainly under the rule of *capital*. In China, for instance, capitalism is forcefully established in coastal "enclaves" only, leaving the overwhelming majority of the population (that is, well over one billion people) outside its framework. And even in those limited areas of China where capitalist principles prevail, the economic extraction of surplus-labor must be propped up by heavy political constituents, so as to keep the cost of labor artificially low. Similarly India—another country with an immense population—is only partially under the successful management of the capitalistically regulated socioeconomic metabolism, leaving the overwhelming majority of the population in a very different predicament so far.[4] Even in the former Soviet Union it would be quite inaccurate to talk about the successful restoration of capitalism everywhere, despite the complete dedication of the ruling political bodies to that task in no less than the last twelve years. Furthermore, the failed "modernization" of the so-called Third World in conformity to the prescriptions propagated for decades by "advanced capitalist" countries, underlines the fact that vast numbers of people—not only in Asia but also in Africa and Latin America—could not be brought into the promised land of the liberal capitalist millennium. Thus, capital could succeed in adjusting itself to the pressures emanating from the end of its "historical ascendancy" only by turning its back on its own progressive phase of development, abandoning altogether the liberal capitalist project, despite all self-serving ideological mystification to the contrary. This is why it should be more obvious today than ever before that the target of socialist transformation cannot be *capitalism* only, if it is to be of a lasting success; it must be the *capital system* itself.

This system in all of its capitalist or post-capitalist forms is (and must remain) *expansion-oriented* and driven by *accumulation*.[5] Naturally, what is at issue in this regard is not a process designed for the increasing satisfaction of human need. Rather, it is the expansion of capital as an end in itself, serving the preservation of a system which could not survive without constantly asserting its power as an extended mode of reproduction. The capital system is *antagonistic* to its inner core, due to the hierarchical structural subordination of labor to capital that totally usurps—and must always usurp—the power of decision making. This structural antagonism prevails everywhere, from the smallest constitutive "microcosms" to the "macrocosm," embracing the most comprehensive reproductive structures and relations. And precisely because the antagonism is *structural,* the capital system is—and must always remain—incapable of reform and *uncontrollable.* The historical failure of reformist social-democracy provides an eloquent testimony to the inability to reform the system; and the deepening structural crisis, with its dangers for the very survival of humanity, puts sharply into relief its uncontrollability. Indeed, it is inconceivable to introduce the fundamental changes required for remedying the situation without overcoming the destructive structural antagonism both in the reproductive "microcosms" and in the "macrocosm" of the capital system as an all-embracing mode of social metabolic control. And that can be achieved only by putting in its place a radically different form of social metabolic reproduction, oriented toward the qualitative redimensioning and the increasing satisfaction of human need; a mode of human interchange controlled not by a set of fetishistic material determinations but by the associated producers themselves.

2.3 The System's Threefold Internal Fracture

The capital system is characterized by a threefold fracture between:

1. Production and its control;
2. Production and consumption; and
3. Production and—both internal and international—circulation of the products.

As a result, it is an irremediably "centrifugal" system in which the conflicting and internally antagonistic parts pull in very different directions.

In the theories formulated from capital's standpoint in the past, remedies to the missing *cohesive* dimension were on the whole wishfully conceptualized. At first, by Adam Smith, as "the invisible hand," which was supposed to render political interventions by the state and its politicians—explicitly condemned by Smith as most harmful—quite superfluous. Later Kant offered a variation on Adam Smith's "Commercial Spirit," advocating the realization of "moral politics" and (rather naively) expecting from the agency of the Commercial Spirit not only universally diffused economic benefits but also a politically commendable reign of "perpetual peace," within the framework of a harmonious "League of Nations." Later still, at the peak of this line of thought, Hegel introduced the idea of the "cunning of Reason," attributing to it the fulfilment of a very similar function to Adam Smith's "invisible hand." However, in complete contrast to Smith—and reflecting the much more conflict-torn predicament of his own times—Hegel had directly assigned the totalizing and universalistic role of Reason in human affairs to the nation state, scornful of Kant's belief in the coming reign of "perpetual peace." Yet he also insisted "the Universal is to be found in the State, in its laws, its universal and rational arrangements. The State is the Divine Idea as it exists on Earth,"[6] since in the modern world "the State as the image and actuality of Reason has become objective."[7] Thus, even the greatest thinkers who conceptualized these problems from the standpoint of capital could only offer some idealized solutions to the underlying contradictions—i.e., to the ultimately irremediable threefold fracture mentioned above. They have, nevertheless, acknowledged at least by implication the existence of such contradictions, in contrast to the present-day apologists of capital—like the representatives of the "Radical Right," for instance—who would never admit the existence of anything in need of substantive remedy in their cherished system.

2.4 Capital's Failure to Create its Global State Formation

Given the centrifugal internal determination of its constitutive parts, the capital system could only find a—most problematical—cohesive dimension, in the form of its national state formations. The latter embodied the comprehensive and totalizing political command structure of capital, which proved itself adequate to its role throughout the system's historical ascendancy. However, the fact that this remedial cohesive dimension was historically articulated in the form of the far from mutually benevolent and harmonious nation states, with no desire whatsoever for conforming to the Kantian imperative of the coming "perpetual peace," meant that the state in its actuality was indeed "infected with contingency"[8] in more ways than one.

First, because the forces of destruction operating at the disposal of modern warfare have become absolutely prohibitive, thereby depriving the nation states of their ultimate sanction for resolving the most comprehensive international antagonisms in the form of yet another world war.

Second, because the end of capital's historical ascendancy had brought into prominence the system's irrational wastefulness and destructiveness also on the plane of production,[9] thereby intensifying the need for securing new outlets for capital's wares through hegemonic and imperialist domination under conditions when the traditional way of imposing it could no longer be considered a readily available option; not only for strictly military reasons but also on account of the grave implications of such steps on a potential global trade war.

And third, because the up-to-relatively recently veiled contradiction between the uncontrollable expansionary drive of capital (tending toward full global integration) and its historically articulated state formations—as competing nation states—had broken out into the open, underlying not only the *destructiveness* of the system but also its *uncontrollability.*

No wonder, therefore, that the end of capital's historical ascendancy in the twentieth century had carried with it also the profound crisis of all of its known state formations.

Nowadays, as an automatic solution to all of the encountered problems and contradictions, we are offered the magic wand of *"globalization."* This solution is presented as a complete novelty, as if the issue of globalization appeared on the historical horizon only in the last decade or two, with its promise of universal benevolence at par with the once similarly hailed and revered notion of the "invisible hand." Yet, in actuality, the capital system was inexorably moving toward "globalization" from its inception. Given the unconstrainability of its constituent parts, it cannot be envisaged as successfully completing itself in any other form than as an all-embracing global system. This is why capital had to attempt to demolish all obstacles that stood in the way of its full unfolding; and it must continue to do so for as long as the system survives.

That is where a massive contradiction becomes clearly visible. For whereas capital in its productive articulation—in our own time primarily through the agency of giant *national-transnational* corporations—tends toward a global integration (and in that sense truly and substantively toward globalization), the vital configuration of "total social capital" or "global capital" is to the present day totally devoid of its proper state formation. This is what sharply contradicts the intrinsic determination of the system itself as inexorably global and unrestrainable. Thus the missing "state of the capital system" as such demonstrates capital's inability to carry the objective logic of the system's unrestrainability to its ultimate conclusion. It is this circumstance that must put the sanguine expectations of "globalization" under the shadow of grievous failure, without removing, however, the problem itself—namely the necessity of a truly global integration of humanity's reproductive interchanges—to which only a socialist solution can be envisaged. For without a socialist solution the necessarily growing deadly antagonism and hegemonic confrontation of the principal competing powers for the required outlets can only result in a catastrophic threat to the survival of humankind. To take only one example, within two or three decades the economy of China (even at its present rate of development) is bound to far outweigh the economic force of the United States, with a military potential to match it. And in the good old tradition of "strategic thinking" in the United States, there are already "theories" anticipating the necessary solution of that immense economic and political challenge by some "preventive strike."

2.5 Chronic Insufficiency of "Extraneous Help" by the State

The structural crisis of capital is the sobering manifestation of the system's encounter with its own intrinsic limits. The adaptability of this mode of social metabolic control could go as far as the "extraneous help" compatible with its systemic determinations allowed it to do so. The very fact that the need for such "extraneous help" surfaced—and despite all mythology to the contrary continued to grow throughout the twentieth century—was always an indication that something rather different from the normality of capital's economic extraction and appropriation of surplus-labor had to be introduced in order to counter the severe "dysfunctions" of the system. Yet, for the greater part of our century, capital could digest the administered doses of remedy, and in the few "advanced capitalist countries"—but only there—it could even celebrate its most obviously successful expansionary phase of development during the postwar decades of Keynesian state interventionism.

The severity of the *structural* crisis of the capital system confronts socialists with a major strategic challenge, yet offering at the same time also some vital new possibilities for meeting that challenge. What needs to be stressed here is that no matter how abundant and how varied the forms of twentieth century "extraneous help"—quite unlike the early phases of capitalist development, when absolutist political "extraneous help" (as pointed out by Marx with reference to Henry VIII and others) was instrumental, nay vital, in establishing capital's normality and healthy functioning as an all-embracing system—all such help in our times proved to be *insufficient* for the purpose of securing the system's permanent stability and unchallengeable vitality. For twentieth-century state interventions could only intensify capital's "hybridization" as a social reproductive system, thereby piling up troubles for the future. In the years ahead of us the structural crisis of capital—asserting itself as the *chronic insufficiency of "extraneous help"* at the present stage of development—is bound to get deeper. It is also bound to reverberate across the globe, even in the most remote corners of the world, affecting every aspect of life, from the directly material reproductive dimensions to the most mediated intellectual and cultural concerns.

To be sure, historically viable change can only be a truly *epochal* one, setting the task to go *beyond capital* itself as a mode of social metabolic control. This means a move of much greater magnitude than the supersession of the feudal system by capital's own. For it is impossible to go beyond capital without radically overcoming the hierarchical structural subordination of labor to any alien controlling force whatsoever, as opposed to simply changing the specific historical *form* in which the extraction and appropriation of surplus-labor is perpetuated, as it always happened in the past.

The "personifications of capital" can assume many different forms, from the private capitalist variety to present-day theocracy, and from "Radical Right" ideologues and politicians to post-capitalist party and state bureaucrats. They can even present themselves as political transvestites, donning the attire of "New Labour"—as the Government today in Britain, for instance—so as to spread mystification in the interest of capital's continued rule with that much greater ease. All this, however, cannot resolve the system's structural crisis and the need for overcoming it through the hegemonic alternative of labor to capital's social metabolic order. This is what puts on the historical agenda the task for the radical rearticulation of the socialist movement as an uncompromising mass movement. To end the tragically self-disarming separation of labor's "industrial arm" (the trades unions) from its "political arm" (the traditional parties) and to embark on politically conscious direct action, as against the meek acceptance of the ever worsening conditions imposed on the producers by the pseudo-democratic rules of the parliamentary game, are the necessary orienting targets and transitional moves of a revitalized socialist movement in the foreseeable future. The continued submission to globalizing capital's globally destructive course of development is truly no option.

3. Marxism, the Capital System, and Social Revolution[1]

3.1 The Global View of Capital

Naghd: In your opinion which of the Marxian models can best explain the capitalist crises of the modern age?

1. The model of reproduction of total social capital?

2. The model of overproduction?

3. The tendency for the profit rate to fall?

4. Or can we combine all these models into one?

ISTVÁN MÉSZÁROS: Fundamentally you can combine them. But what takes precedence after all is a global view of capital. It is quite ironic that people have been recently discovering that we live in a world of "globalization." This was always self-evident to Marx, and I discussed it in the same way in my 1971 Isaac Deutscher Memorial Lecture ("The Necessity of Social Control," reprinted in Part IV of *Beyond Capital*). There I talk at length about "globalization"—not using that word, but the crucial equivalent categories of "total social capital" and the "totality of labor." The conceptual framework in which you can make sense of the capital system can only be a global one. Capital has absolutely no way of restraining itself, nor can you find in the world a counterforce that could restrain it without radically overcoming the capital system as such. So capital had to run its course and logic of development: it had to embrace the totality of the planet. That was always implicit in Marx.

The other things you have mentioned, like the declining rate of profit, etc., are in a way subsidiary to the globally expansionary logic of capital, so that you can incorporate all in the global vision. The capital system has a multiplicity of particular constituents, full of contradictions. You have a plurality of capitals, both nationally confronting one another as well as internal to any national community. In fact the plurality of capitals within particular national communities constitutes the theoretical basis of liberalism, deluding itself of being the champion of Liberty writ large. Capital is not a homogeneous entity. This carries with it great complications to the whole question of "globalization." The way it is customarily presented, "globalization" is a complete fantasy, suggesting that we are all going to live under a capitalistic global government, unproblematically obeying the rules of this unified global government. That is quite inconceivable. There can be no way of bringing the capital system under one big monopoly that would provide the material basis of such a global government. In reality, we have a multiplicity of divisions and contradictions, and "total social capital" is the comprehensive category that incorporates the plurality of capitals, with all their contradictions.

Now, if you look at the other side, also the "totality of labor" can never be considered a homogeneous entity for as long as the capital system survives. There are, of necessity, so many contradictions, which you find under the given historical conditions among sections of labor, opposing and fighting one another, competing against one another, rather than simply confronting particular sections of capital. This is one of the tragedies of our predicament today. And it cannot be simply wished out of existence. For, as Marx had put it a long time ago:

> Competition separates individuals from one another, not only the bourgeois but still more the workers, in spite of the fact that it brings them together. Hence every organized power standing over against these isolated individuals, who live in conditions daily reproducing this isolation, can only be overcome after long struggles. To demand the opposite would be tantamount to demanding that competition should not exist in this definite epoch of history, or that the individuals should banish from their minds conditions over which in their isolation they have no control.

These divisions and contradictions remain with us and ultimately they are all to be explained by the nature and functioning of the capital system itself. It is an insuperably contradictory system based on social antagonism. It is an adversarial system, based on the structural domination of labor by capital. So, there are of necessity all kinds of sectional divisions.

But we must also bear in mind that we are talking about a dynamically unfolding system. The dynamically unfolding tendency of the global capital system cannot help being a totally and inextricably intertwined, and at the same time deeply contradictory, system. This is why under the intrinsic determinations of globally unfolding "total social capital" and the corresponding "totality of labor," all those other models you have mentioned can be subsumed. This general framework has its own logic, in the sense of inexorably unfolding in accordance with its intrinsic structural determinations and limitations. There are some absolute—historically untranscendable—limitations to this system, which I have tried to spell out in Chapter 5 of *Beyond Capital*, entitled "The Activation of Capital's Absolute Limits."

3.2 Historical Limits of the Labor Theory of Value

Naghd: What is the validity of criticism regarding Marx's theory of the "conversion of value to price" and the Marxian model in response to that?

IM: I think it may be too technical to go into the details. You know the way in which modern economic theory was questioning these points. But I don't think that we can make much of it, in that the market system under which we operate makes it necessary to provide this conversion. This takes us back to the question of the "labor theory of value." The foundation of the Marxian conceptual framework is the labor theory of value, concerning the way in which surplus-value is generated and appropriated under the rule of capital. Since, under our present conditions of socioeconomic reproduction in most countries, we have a market framework in which the plurality of capitals, which I mentioned earlier, must adjust itself. You mentioned the profit rate which is also in the process of constant adjustment. But this adjustment cannot take place without the intermediary of conversion.

That is what has come to an end in the former Soviet Union, but by no means everywhere. Thus, when you think of the Chinese system, there you still find the predominance of the political control of surplus-labor extraction. Although many people talk about the market framework of the Chinese system, in reality—when you consider the totality of China's social metabolic reproduction—the market is very much subsidiary to it. So, primarily, in the Chinese system the political appropriation of surplus-labor is still going on, and indeed on a massive scale. In this sense, when you look at the problem of conversion from the angle of surplus-labor, rather than surplus-value—which must be present in a *particular* variety of the capital system—then you find that in the capitalistic variety (based on surplus-value) it is essential to operate with the intermediary of conversion whose particular details are historically contingent. They also depend on the historic phases of capitalistic developments. Thus, the more advanced monopolistic phases of capitalistic development must obviously operate in a significantly different way with respect to the conversion of surplus-value into prices, as compared to a much earlier phase of development known to Marx.

Naghd: Under what conditions would the "labor theory of value" not have any validity? Are such conditions technological, economic, or related to the human factor?

IM: The labor theory of value can cease to be operating only as a result of a radical socialist transformation. That is the first thing to stress. In order to do away with the labor theory of value, you have to do away with the extraction and allocation of surplus-labor by an external body of any sort, be that political or economic. But to do away with it, you have to change the whole system altogether. In other words, we can only speak about socialism when the people are in control of their own activity and of the allocation of its fruits to their own ends. This means the self-activity and self-control of society by the "associated producers," as Marx had put it. Naturally, the "associated producers" cannot control their activity and its objectives unless they also control the allocation of the socially produced surplus. It is therefore inconceivable to institute socialism if a separate body remains in control of the extraction and appropriation of surplus-labor. Under socialism the labor theory of value has absolutely no validity; there is no room for it.

Marx talks about the *"miserable foundation"* under which in the capital system the perverse extraction of surplus-labor must be the regulator of the social reproduction process. To be sure, in every society you need a way of dealing with the problem of how to allocate the resources. For what is the meaning of "Economy"? It is fundamentally a rational way of *economizing*. We do not have infinite resources to squander at will, as it happens—to our peril—under the capital system. We do not have an infinite amount of anything, whether you think of material resources or of human energy, at any particular time. Thus, we need a rational regulation of the social reproduction process. The important thing is the viability of the social reproduction process on a long-term basis, rather than within the irresponsibly myopic and thoroughly unsustainable confines of the capital system. This is why it is necessary to reorient societal interchange from the tyranny of surplus-value and from the expropriation of the surplus-labor of the producers by a separate body to a qualitatively different one. In the latter, where the "associated producers" are in control of both the production and the allocation of their products, there is absolutely no room for surplus-value to impose itself upon the social individuals. That is to say, there is no room for the imperatives of capital and capital accumulation.

Capital is not simply a material entity. We must think of capital as a historically determinate way of controlling social metabolic reproduction. That is the fundamental meaning of capital. It penetrates everywhere. Of course, capital is also a material entity; gold, banking, price mechanisms, market mechanisms, etc. But well beyond that, capital also penetrates the world of art, the world of religion and the churches, running society's cultural institutions. You cannot think of anything in our life that is not controlled by capital in that sense under the present circumstances. That is why the labor theory of value is valid for the historical period when capital is all embracing, when the regulation process itself is fundamentally irrational.

And this is by no means the end of the story. It is further complicated by the fact that in the difficult historical period of transition from the rule of capital to a very different system the labor theory of value and the law of value function in a very imperfect way. This is one of the reasons why the Soviet-type capital system was doomed. It was a transitional system that could go either in one direction, towards a socialist transformation of society, which it did not do; or it had to implode and embark on the road of capitalistic restoration sooner or later. This is what we have witnessed, because at a certain point in time the Soviet system was, so to speak, falling between two stools. It had no way of regulating the economy by some sort of economic mechanism like the market, the price system, and so on. Therefore, it could not have the kind of labor disciplining force that we actually have under the capitalist market system.

In our society, market forces settle so many things automatically; labor is ruthlessly subjected to the prevailing conditioning tyranny of the market. The crucial question in this regard is, precisely, the labor market. If you look back to the time when the Soviet system under Gorbachev collapsed, you will see that the system's demise coincided with the ill-conceived and futile attempt to introduce into it the labor market. That was the end of the much-advertised *perestroika*. For the labor market can properly work only under capitalist conditions. That is where the law of value successfully prevailed—not partially or marginally, but in principle as a matter of course—in the "expanded reproduction of capital." There were all kinds of limits beyond the capitalist world—namely the global framework—under which also the Soviet system had to operate. Under the conditions of twentieth-century development, many things that in the past could work within the framework of the economically regulated extraction of surplus-labor have become most problematical. Today the imperfections of the market and the far from unproblematical operation of the law of value are clearly in evidence also in our system in the capitalistically advanced countries of the West. The ever-greater role assumed by the state—without which the capital system could not survive today in our societies—puts very serious constraints on the law of value in our system. Here we are talking about potentially far-reaching limitations that are of course the system's self-contradictions.

It must be also added that it is one thing to *attempt* the full restoration of capitalism in the former Soviet Union, and quite another to succeed with it. Because *fifteen years* after Gorbachev had started the process of capitalist restoration one can only talk about *partial* successes, confined primarily to the mafia-ridden business circles of the major cities. The endemic and chronic crisis in Russia, strikingly manifest also in the form that many groups of workers—for instance the miners—do not have even their miserable wages paid for several months, sometimes up to a year and a half, which is inconceivable in a proper capitalistic framework where the fundamental regulator of surplus-labor extraction is economic and not political. This highlights a vital trend in twentieth century developments. It is a fact of world-historical significance that the capital system could not complete itself in the twentieth century in the form of its *capitalistic* variety, based on the economic regulation of surplus-labor extraction. So much so, that today approximately one half of the world's population—from China to India and to important areas of Africa, South East Asia and Latin America—do not belong to the world of capitalism proper, but live under some *hybrid* variety of the capital system, either due to chronically underdeveloped conditions, or to massive state involvement in regulating the socioeconomic metabolism, or indeed to a combination of the two. The endemic crisis in Russia—which may well end in total destabilization and potential explosion—can only be explained in this context. Understandably, the true significance of this world-historical fact—i.e., of the failure of capitalism to successfully impose itself everywhere, despite all self-complacent talk about "globalization"—is bound to take some time to sink in, given the mythologies of the past and the now predominant triumphalism. However, this cannot diminish the significance of the fact itself and of its far-reaching implications for the future that must arise from the deepening structural crisis of the capital system.

3.3 Ongoing Proletarianization and Its Wishful Denials

Naghd: Where is the proletariat today and what role does it play in social change? Where can we find the agency today?

IM: I think what you are really asking me about concerns the question of the social agency of transformation. For that is what the word "proletariat" summed up at the time of Marx, by which people often had meant the industrial proletariat. The industrial working classes are on the whole manual workers, from mining to various branches of industrial production. To confine the social agency of change to manual workers is obviously not Marx's own position. Marx was very far from thinking that the concept of "manual workers" would provide an adequate framework of explanation of what is required for a radical social change. You must recall that he was talking about how through the polarization of society ever-greater numbers of people are proletarianized. So, it is the process of proletarianization—inseparable from the global unfolding of the capital system—that defines and ultimately settles the issue. That is to say, the question is how the overwhelming majority of individuals fall into a condition whereby they lose all control over the possibilities of their life, and in that sense they become proletarianized. Thus, again, everything comes down to the question of "who is in control" of the social reproduction process when the overwhelming majority of individuals are proletarianized and degraded to the condition of utter powerlessness, as the most wretched members of society—the proletarians—were at an earlier phase of development.

There are degrees and possibilities of control, up to a certain point in capital's history, which means that some sections of the population are more in control than others. In fact, Marx in one of the chapters of *Capital* was describing the capitalist enterprise as almost a militaristic operation in which you have officers and sergeants, and the foremen like sergeants are overseeing and regulating the direct labor force on the authority of capital. Ultimately all of the control processes are under the authority of capital, but with certain leverages and possibilities of limited autonomy assigned to the particular overseeing sections. Now, when you talk about advancing proletarianization, it implies a leveling down and the negation of even the most limited autonomy some groups of people formerly enjoyed in the labor process.

Just think of the once sharply stressed distinction between "white-collar" and "blue-collar" workers. As you know, the propagandists of the capital system who dominate the cultural and intellectual processes like to use the distinction between the two as yet another refutation of Marx, arguing that in our societies blue-collar manual work altogether disappears, and the white-collar workers, who are supposed to enjoy a much greater job security (which happens to be a complete fiction), are elevated into the middle classes (another fiction). Well, I would say even about the postulated disappearance of blue-collar work: hold on, not so fast! For if you look around the world and focus on the crucial category of the "totality of labor," you find that the overwhelming majority of labor still remains what you might describe as blue-collar. In this respect it is enough to think of the hundreds of millions of blue-collar workers in India, for instance.

Naghd: Can I add something to it? Is Marx's distinction between productive and non-productive labor sufficient?

IM: Well, sufficient in the sense that you can make that distinction. When you consider the overall reproduction process, you find that certain constituents of the overall reproduction process are becoming more and more parasitic. Think of the ever-rising administration costs and insurance costs in this regard. The most extreme form of parasitism in our contemporary reproduction process is, of course, the financial sector, constantly engaged in global speculation, with very severe—and potentially extremely grave—repercussions on the production process properly so called. The dangerous parasitism of the speculative international financial sector—which, to add insult to injury, continues to be glorified under the propagandistic slogan of unavoidable and universally beneficial "globalization"—has an important bearing on the future prospects of social transformation. This takes us back to the vital question of the social agency of change. What decides the matter is not the historically changing relationship between blue-collar and white-collar workers, but the socially untranscendable fundamental confrontation between capital and labor. This is not confined to this or that particular section of labor but embraces the totality of labor as the antagonist of capital. In other words, labor as the antagonist of capital—i.e., of globally self-asserting "total social capital," can only be the "totality of labor," on a global scale—subsumes under itself all sections and varieties of labor, whatever their socioeconomic configuration at the present stage of history. We have witnessed what is going on in our societies; in the so-called advanced capitalist societies of the West. As it happened and continues to happen, vast numbers of white-collar workers were and are ruthlessly ejected from the labor process. Indeed, hundreds of thousands of them in every major country.

Look at this question in the United States. Once upon a time the white-collar workers had some sort of job security, accompanied by a relative little autonomy for their kind of activity. All this is now disappearing, going out of the window. Here the computerized advanced machinery and the question of technology very much enter the picture. But even in this context technology always takes the secondary place to the question of the imperative of capital accumulation. That is what ultimately decides the issue, using the "inevitable progress of technology" as its alibi for crushing human lives on a massive scale. So, we have the proletarianization of the once-upon-a-time more secure labor force. This is an ongoing process. Unemployment is endemic and ubiquitous; you cannot find today a single country that does not have it to an increasing degree. I mentioned in my introduction to the Farsi edition of *Beyond Capital* that in India there are 336,000,000 *(three-hundred-and-thirty-six million!)* people on the unemployment registers; and you can imagine how many more millions are not registered at all. This is the predicament of humanity today. Just look around, look at what is happening in Latin America, as well as the growing unemployment in Africa, and even in Japan: not so many years ago hailed as the "miracle" country. Now every month I read in Japanese publications about a new record of unemployment. In fact, Japan today has a considerably higher rate of unemployment than the United States. What an irony. For not so long ago the Japanese way of dealing with these problems used to be considered the ideal solution.

The cancerous growth of unemployment is affecting today every single country, including those that did not have it in the past. Take for instance Hungary. Now it has an unemployment rate higher than the very high rate in Germany. Here you can see the big difference between the capitalist and the Soviet-type post-capitalist system. There was no unemployment in the Soviet-type countries in the past. There were various forms of *underemployment,* but no unemployment. Now in Hungary unemployment is equivalent to something much higher than what we have not only in Germany but also in Britain and in Italy. You understand the gravity of unemployment. Look at what is happening in Russia. Russia once did not experience unemployment, and now its unemployment rate is massive. And, as mentioned earlier, even if you are employed in Russia, like the miners, you may not receive wages for months. You have to bear in mind all the time that we are talking about a dynamic process of unfolding and transformation. This process threatens humanity with devastation, and the social agency that can do something about it—indeed the only feasible agency capable of instituting an *alternative* way of controlling the social metabolism—is labor. Not particular sections of labor, but the totality of labor as the *irreconcilable antagonist of capital.*

3.4 The Necessary Renewal of Marxian Conceptions

Naghd: Before I start asking about the objective possibility or the real possibility of socialism, I would like to ask about Marx. What aspects of Marx's theory are vulnerable or need to be renewed? Which parts do you think need renewal—methodology, sociology, historical, or economic theory?

IM: The Marxian framework is always in need of renewal. Marx was writing in the middle of the nineteenth century and died in 1883.

Things have immeasurably changed since that time. The tendencies of transformation that we have witnessed in the recent past, with their roots going back to the first few decades of our century, are of such character that Marx could not even dream about them. Above all, this concerns the way in which the capital system could adjust and renew itself, so as to postpone the unfolding and maturation of its antagonistic contradictions. Marx was not in a situation in which he could have assessed the various modalities and the ultimate limitations of state intervention in prolonging the lifespan of the capital system. When you think of twentieth-century economic development, a key figure in it is John Maynard Keynes. The fundamental aim of Keynes was precisely how to save the system through the injection of massive state funds for the benefit of private capitalist enterprise, so as to regulate on a permanent basis within the framework of undisturbed capital accumulation the overall reproduction process.

Now, more recently we had "monetarism" and "neoliberalism" which pushed aside Keynes and indulged in the fantasy of doing away with state intervention altogether, envisaging rolling back the boundaries of the state in a most absurd way. Naturally, in reality nothing could correspond to such self-serving fantasies. In fact the role of the state in the contemporary capitalist system is greater than ever before, including the period of the postwar two-and-a-half decades of Keynesian developments in the capitalistically most advanced countries. All this kind of development is totally new as compared to what occurred in Marx's lifetime.

In the same way and even more, adding to the complications, is what happened in the former Soviet Union and in general to the Soviet-type system. When you have a revolution that wants to be socialist, with the objective of bringing about a socialist transformation of society, that is one thing. But when you look at the type of society that came out of it, you must say that it is quite something else. Because the rule of capital—even if in a very different way—continued also in the Soviet-type post-capitalist system. Looking at it more closely, we find an important connection with Marx. For Marx talks about the "personifications of capital," which is a very important category. Marx uses this category when he talks about the private capitalists, since there was no other form visible in his lifetime. But he perceives, with great insight, that what truly defines the commanding personnel of the capital system is that they are *personifications of capital.*

They have to operate under the objective imperatives of capital as such.

The ideologists and propagandists of capitalism like to perpetuate the mythology of the "enlightened capitalist" and the "benevolent caring capitalist" who are bound to take very good care of the workers as the general rule, referring to those who behave differently as "the unacceptable face of capitalism," to use a former Conservative British Prime Minister Edward Heath's expression. This is a grotesque fantasy, even when it is not voiced with complete cynicism, as admittedly it was not done so by Heath himself. For all capitalists have to submit to the objective imperatives emanating from the unalterable logic of capital expansion. If they do not do so, they will quickly cease to be capitalists, unceremoniously ejected from the overall reproduction process as viable commanding personnel by the self-same logic. It is inconceivable for the capitalist to function on the basis of being the helpers of working-class aspirations. That would be a contradiction in terms, given the necessary structural domination of labor by capital in all conceivable varieties of the capital system.

Now, that takes us back to the question of the personifications of capital as the connecting link with Marx's vision. For the personifications of capital must obey and impose on the workers the objective imperatives emanating from the logic of capital, according to the changing sociohistorical circumstances. And that is highly relevant to understanding the way in which you can have a variety of different personifications of capital that we have witnessed in the twentieth century. Marx knew only one—the ("single" or shareholding "combined") private capitalist—form of personification of capital. But we have seen several different ones, and may still see some new and quite unexpected permutations in the future, as the structural crisis of the global capital system unfolds.

One of the principal reasons why I wrote *Beyond Capital* was precisely to consider the future. It is the future we must bear in mind with critical eyes, in order to be active participants in the historical process, fully aware of and concerned about the fateful implications of capital's destructive power at the present stage of history. Capital has been with us for a very long time in one form or another; indeed in some of its more limited forms for thousands of years. Nevertheless, only in the last three to four hundred years in the form of capitalism which could fully work out the self-expansionary logic of capital, no matter how devastating the consequences for the very survival of humanity. This is what must be put in perspective. When we are thinking about the future, in the light of our painful historical experience, we cannot imagine a situation in which the overthrow of capitalism—in terms of which in the past we used to think about the socialist revolution—solves the grave problems confronting us. For capital is ubiquitous; it is deeply embedded in every single area of our social life. Consequently, if we are to have any success at all, capital must be eradicated from everywhere through a laborious process of profound social transformation. The aspirations of socialist change on a lasting basis must be related to that, with all its difficulties. It must be constantly watched that the potential personifications of capital do not impose themselves on the objectives of future socialist revolutions. Our perspective must orient itself toward devising and successfully asserting the necessary safeguards against the reappearance of the personifications of capital, in whatever new form.

The Marxian framework must be constantly renewed in that sense, so as to be able to cope with the bewildering twists and turns of "the cunning of history." There is no area of theoretical activity—and Marx would be the first to agree to this proposition; in fact he did it explicitly—which could escape the need for thoroughly renewing itself with every major historical change. And the fact is that from Marx's lifetime to our present conditions there has been a massive historical change.

Just to mention one more important consideration in conclusion to this question, Marx was to some extent already aware of the "ecological problem," i.e., the problems of ecology under the rule of capital and the dangers implicit in it for human survival. In fact he was the first to conceptualize it. He talked about pollution, and he insisted that the logic of capital—which must pursue profit, in accordance with the dynamic of self-expansion and capital accumulation—cannot have any consideration for human values and even for human survival. The elements of this discourse you can find in Marx. (His remarks on the subject are discussed in the 1971 lecture on "The Necessity of Social Control" mentioned earlier.) What you cannot find in Marx, of course, is the utmost gravity of the situation facing us. For us the threats to human survival are a matter of *immediacy*. We can today easily destroy humanity. The means and weapons are already at our disposal for the total destruction of humanity. Nothing of the kind was

on the horizon in Marx's lifetime. The underlying destructive imperatives can only be explained in terms of the mad logic capital applies to
the question of *economy*. As I stressed earlier, the true meaning of
economy in the human situation cannot be other than *economizing* on
a long-term basis. Today we find the exact opposite. The way in which
the capital system operates makes a mockery of the necessity of
economizing. Indeed, it pursues everywhere with utmost irresponsibility the opposite of economy: total *wastefulness*. It is this profit-seeking wastefulness that directly endangers the very survival of humanity,
presenting us with the challenge of doing something about it as a matter of great *urgency*. This was unthinkable under the conditions when
Marx had to write, although you can *project* the words on pollution
which he wrote in his critique of Feuerbach's ahistorical assessment of
nature, amounting to an idealization of nature taken completely out of
its social context and totally ignoring the impact on nature necessarily exercised by capital's labor process. You can find Marx's critical
remarks in *The German Ideology,* but obviously not a full development
of this complex of problems as they confront us in their immediacy
and urgency.

We were celebrating in March of 1998 the 150th anniversary of
The Communist Manifesto. The question is: has humanity got another
150 years to go? Certainly not if the capital system survives! What we
have to face is either total catastrophe, due to the capital system's monstrous wastefulness, or humanity must find a radically different way of
regulating its social metabolism!

3.5 The Objective Possibility of Socialism?

*Naghd: How do you describe the objective and real possibility of social-
ism?*

IM: For the moment this is a very difficult question, because of what
has happened in the recent past and in some ways is still happening.
What we have to bear in mind is that the great historical challenge for
present and future generations is to move from one type of social
metabolic order to a radically different one. It cannot be stressed
enough what an immense and difficult historic task this is. It never had
to be faced in the past with the dramatic urgency that is inescapable
today.

The social order of capital, which we are all familiar with, has culminated in an all-embracing and dominating system in the last three to four hundred years. In the twentieth century it has also succeeded in suffocating, undermining, or corrupting every major political effort aimed at going against and beyond it. But it would be a great illusion to assume that this means the end of socialism. This is how in the last few years neoliberal propaganda tried to describe what has happened, triumphantly shouting that "we have done away with socialism once and for all." Mrs. Thatcher, who was the Prime Minister of Britain for more than a decade, boasted that she had "seen off socialism for good." She was talking about the working-class movement, groups of workers and trade unionists, especially the miners. At the time, there was a miners' strike that had been defeated by the combined efforts of the capitalist state and the Labour Party leadership under Neal Kinnock. Mrs. Thatcher characterized the miners as "the enemy within." Despite its liberal pretences her side has no fear of, nor reservations about, talking of you and of all those who maintain their aspirations for the establishment of a socialist order as "the enemy" and "the enemy within."

At the present time, if you look around the world you find that capital has the upper hand everywhere. But is it able to solve the grave problems constantly created by the functioning of its own mode of social metabolic reproduction? Far from it. On the contrary, given its insuperable antagonistic contradictions, capital is unable to address these problems. Instead, it continues to generate them on an ever-increasing scale. This is what keeps on the historical agenda the question of socialism, despite even the most massive and concerted efforts aimed at doing away with it. Capital's success consists only in *postponing* the time when it becomes an unavoidable necessity to confront the grave problems of its system, which now continue to accumulate. There have been many social explosions in the past in response to the contradictions of the established social order, going back prominently to 1848 and 1871, and in some ways to the French Revolution of 1789 and its aftermath. Yet, to date the aspirations of people for a truly equitable social order were frustrated and on the whole even the most heroic attempts have been countered and repressed by the power of capital, in one way or in another. So many of the encountered problems remain perilously unsolved. What is in this sense quite untenable is precisely the kind of adversarial, antagonistic mode of social reproduction process that both continues to generate our grave problems and at the same time prevents their solution. For the adversarial structural determinations constitute an absolute necessity for the functioning and reproduction of the existing system, whatever the consequences might be. These determinations are ineradicable. Notwithstanding all triumphalism, they are not going to go away. The devastating consequences of such a structure will come back again and again. There can be only one kind of solution: the removal of the structural antagonism from our social metabolic reproduction. And that in its terms is conceivable only if the transformation embraces everything, from the smallest constitutive cells of our society to the largest monopolistic transnational corporations that continue to dominate our life.

Thus, although in a superficial sense capital is undoubtedly triumphant, in a much more fundamental sense it is in the gravest possible trouble. This may sound paradoxical. Yet, if you recognize the way in which capital can dominate the social reproduction process everywhere, you must also recognize that it is structurally incapable of resolving its problems and contradictions. Wherever you look you find that what appears to be—and is loudly advertised as—a rock-solid lasting solution, sooner or later crumbles into dust. For instance, just try to survey in your mind the ephemeral history of "economic miracles" we had in the postwar decades. What sort of "miracles" were they? We had the "German miracle" and the "Japanese miracle," followed by the Italian, Brazilian, and other "miracles." As we may well remember, the latest of them was the most tendentiously advertised miracle of the Asian tiger economies. And what happened to that "miracle?" Like all the others, it has evaporated, leaving its place to a severe crisis. Today you cannot find in the world one single country which is not facing some absolutely fundamental problems, including the recent calamities on the stock exchanges of Russia and several Eastern European countries. Well, if you now read the bourgeois newspapers, they are all in some sort of panic. Their headlines are frightening and self-frightening as to what is really going on. I remember that at the time when the "Asian miracle" was at its peak, the notion of this pretended "miracle" was also used as an overwhelming disciplinary argument against the working classes of the Western capitalist countries. "Behave yourself! Accept the standard of living and the work practices of the kind which the workers in the Asian tiger economies do, or you will be in deep trouble!" A system which claims to have resolved all its problems in the "post-industrial" Western "advanced capitalist" countries, and then has to rely for its continued health on such an authoritarian blackmailing message, does not promise much for the future even in its own terms of reference. Again, in this respect there is, and there can only be, one viable and sustainable solution. It is socialism. Socialism in the sense which I mentioned earlier; i.e., the elimination of the now-given adversarial and antagonistic framework in which one section of the population—a tiny minority—has to dominate the overwhelming majority as a matter of insurmountable structural determination. That is to say, a form of domination that totally expropriates for itself the power of decision-making. Labor as the antagonist of capital has absolutely no power of decision-making; not even in the most limited context. That is the vital and unavoidable question for the future. And in that sense, I am convinced, the chances for the revival of the socialist movement sooner or later are absolutely great and fundamental.

3.6 Political and Social Revolution

Naghd: What is the concept of "revolution" in your opinion?

IM: The concept of revolution remains very important and valid if we define it as a profound ongoing revolutionary transformation of all facets of our social life. One should not take the concept of revolution to mean "one big push that settles everything once and for all," nourishing the illusion that after cutting off a few heads you have won. For Marx's use of the concept of revolution was "social revolution." He said that the big difference between past revolutions and a socialist social revolution was that the revolutions of the past were essentially political in character, which meant changing the ruling personnel of society, while leaving the overwhelming majority of the people in their position of structural subordination. This is also the context in which the question of the personifications of capital must be considered. Breaking a smaller or greater number of heads—this you can do with relative ease, in the big push for overturning something; and all this usually happens in the political sphere. This is the sense in which the concept of "revolution" was defined even recently.

Now, we know from bitter experience that it did not work. To proceed in that way is not enough. So, we have to go back to what Marx was saying about the social revolution. I must also emphasize that this concept of the social revolution was not originally Marx's own idea. It is a concept that emerged from Babeuf and his movement way back during the turbulent aftermath of the 1789 French Revolution. Babeuf was executed at that time, accused with his group of conspiracy. In reality he was pressing for a society of equals. The same concept reappeared in the 1830s and during the revolutions of 1848. In such times of revolutionary upheaval the idea of social revolution was in the foreground of the most progressive forces, and Marx very rightly embraced it.

In a radical social transformation—we are talking about a Socialist Revolution—the change cannot be confined to the ruling personnel, and hence the revolution must be truly and all-embracingly social. That means that the transformation and the new mode of controlling the social metabolism must penetrate into every segment of society. It is in that sense that the concept of revolution remains valid; indeed, in the light of our historical experience, more valid than ever before. A revolution that not only eradicates but also implants. The eradication is as much a part of this process as what you put in the place of what has been eradicated. Marx says somewhere that the meaning of "radical" is to grasp matters at their roots. That is the literal meaning of being radical, and it retains its validity in the social revolution in the just mentioned sense of eradicating and implanting.

So much of what is firmly rooted today has to be eradicated in the future through the laborious processes of an ongoing—if you like "permanent"—revolutionary transformation. But the terrain on which this is done cannot be left empty. You have to put in the place of what has been removed something capable of taking deep roots. Talking about the social order of capital, Marx uses the expression "an *organic system.*" I quote a passage where he talks about it in the Introduction to the Farsi edition of *Beyond Capital.* The capital system under which we live is an organic system. Every part of it supports and reinforces the others. It is this kind of *reciprocal support* of the parts that makes the problem of revolutionary transformation very complicated and difficult. If you want to replace capital's organic system you have to put in its place *another organic system* in which the parts support the whole because the parts also reciprocally support each other. This is how the new system becomes viable, capable of standing firm, growing, and successfully moving in the direction that secures the gratification of every member of society.

Clearly, then, "revolution" cannot be simply a question of "overthrowing." Anything that can be overthrown can only be a very partial aspect of the *social revolution*. The historically known varieties of *capitalism* can be overthrown—in some limited contexts it has already happened—but *capital* itself cannot be "overthrown." It has to be eradicated, in the sense described above, and something must be put in its place. Likewise, the *capitalist state* can be overthrown. However, once you have overthrown the capitalist state, you have not removed the problem itself, because the *state as such* cannot be overthrown. This is why Marx is talking about the "withering away of the state," which is a fundamentally different concept. Moreover, the thorniest of these problems with regard to the task of revolutionary transformation is that *labor as such* cannot be "overthrown." How do you overthrow labor, together with capital and the state, one of the pillars of the capital system? For labor is the basis of the reproduction of society.

There have been all kinds of fantasies, especially in the last few decades, about the "information revolution" doing away for good with labor and allowing us to live happily ever after in the "post-industrial society." The idea of work becoming play has a respectable lineage, going back to Schiller. However, its capital-apologetic recent renewals constitute a complete absurdity. You can abolish by some decree *wage labor*, but that is very far from solving the problem of labor's emancipation, which is conceivable only as the *self*-emancipation of the associated producers. Human labor as productive activity always remains the absolute condition of the reproduction process. The natural substratum of the individuals' existence is nature itself which must be rationally and creatively *controlled* by productive activity—as opposed to being irresponsibly and destructively *dominated* by the irrational, wasteful and destructive imperatives of capital-expansion. The social metabolism involves the necessary interchange among individuals themselves and between the totality of individuals and recalcitrant nature. Even the original, non-apologetic idea of work as play in the eighteenth century was inseparable from the idealization of nature: the ignorance or denial of its necessary recalcitrance. But the recent capital-apologetic rejoinders defy all belief, given the overwhelming evidence of the wanton destruction of nature by capital that the proponents of such theories cynically ignore.

You must have read books and articles in the last two or three decades about the so-called post-industrial society. What the hell does that mean? "Post-industrial?" For as long as humanity survives, it must be industrious and industrial. It has to work to reproduce itself. It has to create the conditions under which human life not only remains possible but also becomes richer in human fulfillment. And that is conceivable only through industry in the most profound sense of the term. We will be always industrial, as opposed to the self-serving propagandistic fantasy according to which the "information revolution" will render all industrial work completely superfluous. Characteristically, at the same time when the champions of capital-apologetics were talking about the "post-industrial" paradise, they were also talking about transferring the smokestack industries to India, or to China, to the Philippines, or to Latin America. So the smokestack industries have to be removed from the advanced capitalist West! But where do the captains of industry put the poisonous smokestacks of Union Carbide? They are transferred to Bhopal in India, with catastrophic consequences, killing *fifteen thousand* people and blinding and injuring thousands more. Does that make society "post-industrial"? Far from it. Such transfers of technology only mean that the capitalist West sends its dirty linen to some "underdeveloped" part of the world—the so-called Third World. At the same time, with utmost cynicism, the ideologists and propagandists of the system also maintain that such transfers mean "modernization" on the American model, as a result of which in due course people everywhere will be rich and happy in a fully automobilized society.

The much-needed revolution means a fundamental change to all that. Nothing can be solved by overthrow alone. The overthrow or abolition of some institutions is a necessary *first step*. Radical political acts are necessary in order to remove one type of personnel and to make it possible for something else to arise in its place. But the aim must be a profound process of ongoing social transformation. And in that sense the concept of revolution remains absolutely fundamental.

3.7 Downward Equalization of the Differential Rate of Exploitation

Naghd: Western workers, having organized unions, try to adjust their Marx to the work situation in today's world. Their voice and struggle do not go beyond limited actions for welfare, higher wages, etc. In the East, on the other hand, because of dictatorship, delayed economic pressures, and lack of theoretical knowledge, the social movements aim at not only better life, but also at the overthrow of their capital system. Globalization and privatization have created opportunities for movements against capitalism. The radical movement seems to originate from the East rather than the West. What do you think?

IM: I think we have to examine the facts, and then you will find that some of what you say is right, but with historical qualifications. That is to say, what you describe reflects conditions of perhaps two or three decades ago, and less and less those of today. When you consider some crucial demands of the labor movement in Western capitalist countries, like France and Italy, they cannot be described as simply demands for improving wages. Take, for example, the demand for the 35-hour week without loss of pay, which has been granted by the French government. There was in France a law—implemented from 2000–2001—according to which the working week was reduced to 35 hours. This is not a wage demand. The same thing is happening in Italy, where there is a very important push for the realization of the same objective. I can perhaps find a quotation for you from one of the leading figures in the Italian movement for the 35-hour week, Fausto Bertinotti. He had to answer a question coming from a woman reader of the daily paper of *Rifondazione*. As you know, the condition of women workers in all capitalist societies is worse than that of men. (Not that it is rosy by any means for their male counterparts.) She asked the question: "If we have more hours for ourselves," as a result of the 35-hour workweek, "how shall we utilize them?" This was Bertinotti's answer:

> When we say that it is not only a matter of trade union objectives, but of civilization, we are referring precisely to the horizon of the question you are posing: the important question of time, and the relationship between worktime and life-time. First of all, we know, from Marx, that the theft of worktime, at a certain stage of historical development, becomes a very miserable foundation of production and wealth and organization of society: moreover we know that the struggle against exploitation can only go together, be intertwined and closely connected with, the struggle against alienation; that is to say, against that mechanism deeply inherent in the nature of capitalism, which not only takes away from each worker the product of 'living labour,' but induces estrangement, heterodirection, and the oppressive regulation of

life-time. In this sense, the 35 hours, beyond the benefits they will be able to trigger off from the point of view of employment, do come back to the central question of the betterment of one's own life: of the self-government of time, to put it in noncontingent political terms. Because there will not be a real social transformation without a project of collective self-government of working time and life-time: a real project, not a hypothesis elaborated from the outside of the social subject and of individual subjectivities. This too is a great challenge for politics and for our party.

Now that is where you can see that the fight for the 35-hour workweek is not simply a "trade union demand." It challenges the whole system of social metabolic reproduction, and therefore it would be most inaccurate to describe it as nothing more than a trade union demand.

You are right that for a long time economistic demands constituted the horizon of the labor movement in the capitalistically advanced countries. But this narrow orientation cannot be maintained any longer. This connects us with the question of the chances for socialism. The labor movement is now pushed in the direction that it has to raise the question of work-time and life-time. The reduction of work-time is only to a very limited extent a wage demand. The workers do not want simply an improvement in wages. True, they say: "we do not want to lose what we already have." But the objective logic of the situation is that they are losing it anyway for other reasons. One of the most important losses of the last thirty years of capitalistic development is what I call "the downward equalization of the differential rate of exploitation."[2] In Western capitalist countries, the working classes for a long time could enjoy the benefits of the *differential* rate of exploitation. Their conditions of existence and of work, were immeasurably better than what you had in the so-called Third World. (A concept that I always rejected as the self-serving propaganda of Western capitalism, because the Third World is an integral part of the one and only, profoundly interconnected world.)

Now, however, we find deteriorating conditions everywhere. The downward equalization is evidenced also in the most capitalistically advanced countries. Now workers have to face being threatened in their basic conditions of existence, because unemployment—often camouflaged as "flexible" casualization—is spreading everywhere. Fighting against unemployment cannot be considered simply a wage negotiation. The time has passed when you could treat "marginal unemployment"—at the peak of Keynesian expansion—in those terms. Thus, the working classes even in the most capitalistically advanced countries have to face up to this challenge.

You are, of course, right that the conditions are incomparably worse in the East. But it is important to stress that the countries concerned are an integral part of the system of "total social capital" and the "totality of labor." Anything that happens in one part has an impact on the conditions somewhere else. The conditions of the labor market are deteriorating everywhere, including the Western capitalist countries—in Canada as much as in the United States, or in England, Germany, France and Italy. The pressures are intensifying and, I may add, this means a necessary change in the orientation of the Western working-class movement. If you examine the history of the working-class movement in the 20th century, you will find that one of the great tragedies of this history was the internal division described as the separation of the so-called "industrial arm" of the movement (the trade unions) from the "political arm" (the political parties). This separation has meant the severe constraining of the labor movement, through confining its action to very narrow limits. The political parties are confined to a situation whereby the people they are supposed to represent have the chance to vote—to put a piece of paper into the ballot box once in every four or five years—and thereby renounce their power of decision-making in favor of whoever is in parliament.

Now what is significant about the ongoing changes is that it becomes necessary to make the trade-union movement itself (the "industrial arm") become directly political. This is now beginning to happen in some European capitalist countries (notably in France and Italy) as well as in Japan. And I trust that it will happen in the not too distant future also in Canada and the United States. This is the qualification I would add to your question. Things have been and are significantly changing under the impact of the tendential law of capital's development of the downward equalization of the differential rate of exploitation in the age of the *structural crisis* of the *capital system as such*, and not simply of *capitalism*. I discuss this problem in great detail in *Beyond Capital*. Under these conditions it is no longer possible to retain people in their submissive predicament.

I can mention to you the British miners who were waging a one-year-long struggle; not for wage improvement. It would be inconceivable to endure for a whole year the hardship, misery, discrimination, hostility, and repression of the state for the sake of improving their wages by ten, twenty, or even fifty dollars per week, when they were losing much more even in financial terms in the course of their struggle. The miners in Britain were eventually defeated through the concerted action of the state and, sadly, as mentioned already, also of the Labour Party, their presumed "political arm." And what happened to the labor force of the British miners? At the time of the strike their numbers were in the region of 150,000; today this number is down to less than 10,000! This is the reality of the situation. This is what the workers had to fight against—the extermination of their numbers, the transformation of their mining towns, and villages into the wasteland of unemployment. Thus, now more and more groups of workers in the capitalistically advanced countries are forced to proceed in the same way the British miners did. I can also mention to you another case, the Liverpool dockworkers, who endured the extreme hardship of strike not for one year but for two-and-a-half years. This kind of action, this kind of struggle, which is simultaneously industrial and political, is quite unthinkable within the narrow framework of "trade-union objectives."

Naghd: Thank you for accepting our interview. Would you like to add anything for the Persian reader?

IM: I can only wish great success to you all in our joint enterprise and struggle for a radical social transformation that we all badly need. And I trust that you will be moving in that direction.

4. Socialism or Barbarism: From the "American Century" to the Crossroads[1]

Foreword

We are about to leave the twentieth century, described by capital's most vocal apologists as "the American century." Such views are voiced as if the October Revolution of 1917, or the Chinese and Cuban Revolutions, and the colonial liberation struggles in the following decades had never taken place, not to mention the humiliating defeat directly suffered by the mighty United States in Vietnam. Indeed, the uncritical defenders of the established order confidently anticipate that not only the coming century but also the whole of the next millennium is destined to conform to the unchallengeable rules of *Pax Americana*. Yet, no matter how much the relation of forces has been realigned in capital's favor in the last decade, the plain truth is that the deep-seated causes beneath the major social earthquakes of the twentieth century mentioned above—to which one could add quite a few more, positive and negative alike, including two world wars—have not been resolved by subsequent developments. On the contrary, with every new phase of forced postponement the capital system's contradictions can only be aggravated, bringing with them an ever-greater danger for the very survival of humanity.

The chronic insolubility of our social antagonisms, coupled with capital's uncontrollability, may well continue to generate for some time the atmosphere of triumphalism as well as the disorienting illusions of permanency, as they did in the recent past. But in due course the accumulating and destructively intensifying problems must be confronted. For if the next century is really going to be capital's triumphant "American century," there will be no more centuries for humans afterwards, let alone a full millennium. Saying this has nothing to do with "anti-Americanism." In 1992 I expressed my conviction that:

> the future of socialism will be decided in the United States, however pessimistic this may sound. I try to hint at this in the last section of *The Power of Ideology* where I discuss the problem of universality.[2] Socialism either can assert itself universally and in such a way that it embraces all areas, including the most developed capitalist areas of the world, or it won't succeed.[3]

Given the present stage of development, with its gravely intertwined problems crying out for a lasting solution, only a universally viable approach can work. But despite its enforced "globalization," capital's incurably iniquitous system is structurally incompatible with universality in any meaningful sense of the term.

4.1 Capital—the Living Contradiction

4.1.1

Whatever claims are made for the ongoing process of "globalization," there can be no universality in the social world without substantive equality. Evidently, therefore, the capital system, in all of its historically known or conceivable forms, is totally inimical even to its own—stunted and crippled—projections of globalizing universality. And it is immeasurably more inimical to the only meaningful realization of socially viable universality which would fully harmonize the universal development of the productive forces with the all-round development of the abilities and potentialities of the freely associated social individuals, because it would be based on their consciously pursued aspirations. In place of this, the potentiality of capital's universalizing tendency is turned into the actuality of dehumanizing alienation and reification. As Marx phrased it:

> When the limited bourgeois form is stripped away, what is wealth other than the universality of individual needs, capacities, pleasures, productive forces, etc., created through universal exchange? The full development of human

mastery over the forces of nature, those of so-called nature as well as of humanity's own nature? The absolute working out of his creative potentialities, with no presupposition other than the previous historic development, which makes this totality of development, i.e., the development of all human powers as such the end in itself, not as measured on a predetermined yardstick? When he does not reproduce himself in one specificity, but produces his totality? Strives not to remain something he has become, but is in the absolute movement of becoming? In bourgeois economics—and in the epoch of production to which it correspond—this complete working out of the human content appears as a complete emptying-out, this universal objectification as total alienation, and the tearing-down of all limited, one-sided aims as sacrifice of the human end-in-itself to an entirely external end.[4]

The development of the—in principle universally applicable—functional division of labor constitutes the potentially liberating horizontal dimension of capital's labor process. However, this dimension is inseparable from the vertical or hierarchical division of labor within the framework of capital's command structure. The function of the vertical dimension is to safeguard the vital interests of the system by securing the continued expansion of surplus-labor on the basis of the maximum practicable exploitation of the totality of labor. Accordingly, the horizontal structuring force is allowed to advance at any given time only to the extent to which it is firmly controllable in capital's reproductive horizon by the vertical dimension.

This means that it can follow its own dynamic only to the extent to which the ensuing productive developments remain *containable* within the parameters of capital's imperatives (and corresponding limitations). Capital's demand for vertical ordering always constitutes the overriding moment in the relationship between the two dimensions. But whereas in the ascending phase of the system's development the horizontal and vertical dimensions complement one another through their relatively flexible reciprocal interchanges, once the ascending phase is left behind the formerly *overriding moment* of a dialectical complex is turned into an ultimately *disruptive one-sided determination.* This brings with it grave limitations to productive development, together with a major crisis of accumulation fully in evidence in our own time. This is why the once promised potential universality in the development of the productive forces must be aborted, in the interest of safeguarding capital's self-oriented partiality and insurmountable structural hierarchy.

The capital system is articulated as a jungle-like network of contradictions that can only be more or less successfully *managed* for some time but never definitively *overcome*. At the roots of all of them we find the irreconcilable antagonism between capital and labor, always necessarily assuming the form of the *structural and hierarchical subordination of labor to capital,* no matter how elaborate and mystifying the attempts aimed at camouflaging this structural subordination. To name only some of the principal contradictions, we are confronted by those between:

1. production and its control;
2. production and consumption;
3. production and circulation;
4. competition and monopoly;
5. development and underdevelopment (i.e., the "North/South" divide, both globally and within every particular country);
6. expansion pregnant with the seeds of crisis-producing contraction;
7. production and destruction (the latter often glorified as "productive" or "creative destruction");
8. capital's structural domination of labor and its insurmountable dependency on living labor;
9. the production of free time (surplus-labor) and its crippling negation through the imperative to reproduce and exploit necessary labor;
10. authoritarian decision-making in the productive enterprises and the need for their "consensual" implementation;
11. the expansion of employment and the generation of unemployment;
12. the drive for economizing with material and human resources wedded to the most absurd wastefulness of the same;
13. growth of output at all costs and the concomitant environmental destruction;
14. the globalizing tendency of transnational enterprises and the necessary constraints exercised by the national states against their rivals;
15. control over the particular productive units and the failure to control their comprehensive setting (hence the extremely problematical character of all attempts at planning in all conceivable forms of the capital system);

16. and the contradiction between the economically and the politically regulated extraction of surplus-labor.

It is quite inconceivable to overcome even a single one of these contradictions, let alone their inextricably combined network, without instituting a radical alternative to capital's mode of social metabolic control. An alternative based on *substantive equality* whose total absence is the common denominator and vitiating core of all social relations under the existing system.

What is also important to stress here is that—due to the *structural crisis* of the capital system as such, in contrast to the *periodic conjunctural* crises of capitalism witnessed in the past—the problems are fatefully aggravated at the present stage of development, putting on the historical agenda the need for a viable *overall control* of humanity's material productive and cultural interchanges as a matter of great urgency. Marx could still talk about the development of the capital system as one that, despite its own barriers and limitations, "enlarges the circle of consumption" and "tears down all the barriers which hem in the development of the forces of production, the expansion of needs, the all-sided development of production, and the exploitation and exchange of natural and mental forces."[5] In this spirit, he could characterize the full unfolding of the capital system as "the *presupposition* of a new mode of production."[6] Today, there can be no question of an "*all-sided development of production*" linked to the expansion of *human needs*. Thus, given the way in which capital's stunted globalizing tendency has been actualized—and continues to be enforced—it would be quite *suicidal* to envisage capital's destructive reality as the presupposition of the much needed new mode of reproducing the sustainable conditions of human existence. As things stand today, capital's concern cannot be the "enlargement of the consumption circle," to the benefit of the "rich social individual," that Marx talked about, but only its own enlarged reproduction at whatever cost. And the latter can be secured, at least for the time being, by various modalities of destruction. For from the perverse standpoint of capital's "realization process" *consumption and destruction are functional equivalents.* Once upon a time the enlargement of the consumption circle could go hand in hand with the overriding imperative of capital's enlarged self-realization. With the end of capital's historical ascendancy the conditions of the system's expanded reproduction have been radically and irretrievably altered, pushing into the foreground overwhelmingly the destructive tendencies and, as their natural companion, catastrophic wastefulness. Nothing illustrates this better than the *military-industrial complex* and its continued expansion despite the pretences of the "new world order" and its so-called "peace dividend" after the "end of the Cold War." (We return to this complex of problems in Section 4.2.7.)

<h2 style="text-align:center">4.1.2</h2>

In line with these developments the question of unemployment has also been significantly altered for the worse. It is no longer confined to the "reserve army of labor" waiting to be activated and brought into the framework of capital's productive expansion, as it used to be the case in the system's ascending phase, at times even to a prodigious extent. Now the grave reality of dehumanizing unemployment has assumed a chronic character, acknowledged even by the most uncritical defenders of capital—to be sure, in a self-justifying way, as if it had nothing whatever to do with the perverse nature of their cherished system—as "structural unemployment." By contrast, in the post-war decades of undisturbed expansion, the problem of unemployment was presumed to be permanently resolved. Thus one of the worst apologists of capital—Walt Rostow: a leading figure in President Kennedy's brain trust—arrogantly declared in a vacuous but massively promoted book that:

> There is every reason to believe, looking at the sensitivity of the political process to even small pockets of unemployment in modern democratic societies, that the sluggish and timid policies of the 1920s and 1930s with respect to the level of unemployment will no longer be tolerated in Western societies. And now the technical tricks of the trade—due to the Keynesian revolution—are widely understood. It should not be forgotten that Keynes set himself the task of defeating Marx's prognosis about the course of unemployment under capitalism; and he largely succeeded.[7]

In the same spirit, Rostow and a whole army of bourgeois economists confidently predicted not only that the "pockets of unemployment in Western democracies" would be soon and forever turned into an oasis of affluence and prosperity, but that thanks to their recipes and trade-tricks of universally applicable "modernization" also the Third World would reach the same level of "development" and happy fulfillment as our "Western democracies." For it was supposed to be in the preordained nature of the timeless universe that "underdevelopment" would be followed by capitalist "take-off," which in its turn inexorably brings with it a natural "drive to maturity," provided that the political forces of "Western democracies" prevent the evil deeds of troublemaking revolutionaries who are bent on interfering with this natural order.

This euphoria produced a generously financed industry of "development studies," going around in ever-enlarging circles and in the end running into the sands of total oblivion, like raindrops on a seashore, as—with the onset of capital's structural crisis—the tidal wave of neoliberal monetarism took over the ideological orienting positions up until then occupied by the high priests of Keynesian salvation. And when in the end it had to be admitted that the Keynesian tricks of the trade could never again regenerate the earlier "miracles" (that is, conditions described as "miracles" by those who at the time foolishly believed in them, not by their critical adversaries), the former propagandists of the Keynesian final solution of capital's defects simply turned their coats and, without the slightest murmur of self-criticism, invited all those who had not yet reached their own level of new transcendental enlightenment to wake up from their slumber and give their erstwhile hero a decent funeral.[8]

In this way the ideology of Third World modernization had to be—somewhat humiliatingly—abandoned. The issue was further complicated by the growing danger of ecological disaster and the obvious fact that if the catastrophic levels of wastefulness and pollution produced by the model country of "modernization," the United States, were allowed to prevail even just in China and India, that would bring devastating consequences also to the idealized "Western democracies." Besides, the self-serving solution newly advocated by the United States—to buy "pollution rights" from Third World countries—would be a self-destructive concept if it did not assume at the same time the permanency of Third World underdevelopment. Thus, from now on everywhere, including the Western democracies, the ideology of modernization had to be used as a new type of weapon, so as to clobber and disqualify "Old Labour" for refusing to be modernized by "New Labour"; that is, for failing to become modern by totally abandoning, as "New Labour" has, even its mildly social-democratic principles and commitments. The new universally commendable propaganda objectives were "*democracy and development:*" democracy as modeled on the U.S. political consensus between the Republicans and the Democrats, as a result of which the working class is unceremoniously and completely *disenfranchised* even in a limited parliamentary sense; and development meaning nothing more than what can be readily squeezed into the empty shell of the most tendentious definition of formal democracy, to be imposed all over the world, from the "newly emergent democracies" of Eastern Europe and the former Soviet Union to Southeast Asia and Africa as well as to Latin America. As a leading propaganda organ of the U.S.-dominated G7, the London *Economist* wrote with its inimitable cynicism:

> There is no alternative to the free market as the way to organize economic life. The spread of free-market economics should gradually lead to multi-party democracy, because people who have free economic choice tend to insist on having free political choice too.[9]

"Free economic choice" for labor as the antagonist of capital, in employment, can only amount to submission to the orders emanating from the system's expansionary imperatives; and for ever-increasing numbers of those not so "lucky," it means exposure to the indignities and the extreme hardship caused by chronic structural unemployment. The "free political choice" that can be exercised within the framework of "multi-party democracy" boils down, in reality, to the bitterly resigned acceptance of the consequences of an ever-narrowing political *consensus,* which made no less than *77 percent* of British voters—and almost the same percentage of voters in some other countries of the European Community—refuse to participate in such a meaningless ritual, when they were called upon to choose members of the European parliament at the last nationwide election.

Similar to what happened in the field of productive employment, as a result of capital's narrowing margins, we have witnessed dramatic reversals also in the field of political representation and management. In the domain of production, the ascending phase of capital's development brought with it a massive expansion of employment, leaving its place in our time to the dangerous trend of chronic unemployment. As to the political domain, we could see a move from the dramatic enlargement of the franchise, to the point of universal franchise and the corresponding formation of labor's mass parties, leading to a major reversal in the not formal but effective and complete disenfranchising of labor in its parliamentary political setting. It is enough to think in this respect of political formations like "New Labour" and its equivalents on the other side, operating the most peculiar form of "democratic decision-making" in tiny "kitchen cabinets," and ruthlessly imposing the wisdom of "there is no alternative" on any dissenting voice, even if it happens to surface by some accident in the rubber-stamping national cabinets.

4.1.3

The devastating trend of chronic unemployment now affects even the most advanced capitalist countries. At the same time, the people still in employment in those countries have to endure a worsening of their material conditions of existence, evidenced even by the official statistics. For the end of capital's historical ascendancy also brought with it a downward equalization of the differential rate of exploitation.[10]

The end of Third World modernization highlights a quite fundamental problem in the development of the capital system. It underlines the far-reaching historical significance of the fact that capital failed to complete its system as global capitalism, i.e., as the overwhelmingly economic regulation of the extraction of surplus-labor as surplus-value. Despite all past fantasies of "take-off" and "drive to maturity," today almost half of the world's population has to reproduce its conditions of existence in ways in sharp contrast to the idealized "market mechanism" as the overwhelmingly dominant regulator of the social metabolism. Instead of completing itself as a properly capitalist global system, capital, apart from the countries where its economic mode of controlling the appropriation of surplus-labor prevailed, also succeeded in creating *enclaves of capitalism,* with a more or less vast *non-capitalist hinterland.* India in this respect is an obvious example, China, by contrast, is a much more complicated one, in that its state cannot be qualified as capitalist. (Nevertheless, the country has some powerful capitalist enclaves, linked to a non-capitalist hinterland with well over one billion people.) This is in some way analogous to some past colonial empires, e.g., the British. Britain exercised an all-encompassing political and military control over India, fully exploiting its capitalist economic enclaves, leaving at the same time the over-whelming majority of the population to their own resources of pre-colonial and colonially aggravated hand-to-mouth existence. Nor is it conceivable, for a variety of reasons—including the untenable and ungeneralizable structural articulation of advanced capitalism, with its catastrophically wasteful decreasing rate of utilization as a major con-dition of its continued expansion—that this failure of capitalism will be remedied in the future. Thus, the failure of capitalist modernization of the Third World, despite all the efforts invested in it in the postwar decades of expansion, draws our attention to a fundamental structur-al defect of the whole system.

One more problem must be briefly mentioned in this context: the "hybridization" in evidence even in the capitalistically most advanced countries. Its principal dimension is the ever-greater direct and indi-rect involvement of the state in safeguarding the continued viability of capital's mode of social metabolic reproduction. Despite all protesta-tions to the contrary, coupled with neoliberal fantasies about rolling back the boundaries of the state, the capital system could not survive for a week without the massive backing it constantly receives from the state. I have discussed this problem elsewhere, and therefore a brief mention should suffice here. The point is that what Marx called the "extraneous help" given by Henry VIII and others to early capitalist developments has reappeared in the twentieth century in an unimaginably massive form, from common agricultural policies and export guarantees to immense state-financed research funds and to the insatiable appetite of the military-industrial complex.[11] What makes the problem much worse is that no amount of it is ever enough. Capital, at the present phase of historical development, has become totally dependent on an ever-increasing provision of extraneous help. In this respect, too, we are approaching a systemic limit in that we are confronted by the *chronic insufficiency of extraneous help* in regard to what the state is now capable of delivering. Indeed, the structural cri-sis of capital is inseparable from the chronic insufficiency of such extraneous help under conditions in which the defects and failures of this antagonistic system of societal reproduction call for an unlimited supply of it.

4.2 The Potentially Deadliest Phase of Imperialism

4.2.1

One of the weightiest contradictions and limitations of the system concerns the relationship between the globalizing tendency of transnational capital in the economic domain and the continued dominance of the national states as the comprehensive political command structure of the established order. The efforts of the dominant powers to make their own national states triumph over the others and thereby prevail as *the state* of the capital system as such have precipitated humankind in the course of such attempts into the bloodletting vicissitudes of two horrendous world wars in the twentieth century. Nonetheless, the national state remained the ultimate arbiter of comprehensive socioeconomic and political decisionmaking as well as the real guarantor of the risks undertaken by all significant transnational economic ventures. Obviously, this is a contradiction of such magnitude that it cannot be assumed indefinitely to endure, regardless of the endlessly repeated rhetoric pretending to resolve this contradiction through the discourse of "democracy and development" and its tempting corollary: "think globally, act locally." This is why the question of imperialism must be brought to the forefront of critical attention.

Many years ago Paul Baran rightly characterized the radical change in the postwar international power relationships in the capitalist world and "the growing inability of the old imperialist nations to hold their own in face of the American quest for expanded influence and power," insisting that "the assertion of American supremacy in the 'free' world implies the reduction of Britain and France (not to speak of Belgium, Holland and Portugal) to the status of junior partners of American imperialism."[12] He also quoted the bitterly sobering words of London's *The Economist,* pleading with characteristic subservience that "We must learn that we are not the Americans' equals now, and cannot be. We have a right to state our minimum national interests and expect the Americans to respect them. But this done, we must look for their lead."[13] A similar plea for the acceptance of American leadership—but perhaps not yet fully resigned to handing over to the United States, in some form or other, the British Empire—was expressed a quarter of a century earlier by the London *Observer,* saying with enthusiasm about President Roosevelt that "America has found a man. In him the world must find a leader."[14]

And yet, the end of the British Empire—together with all the others—was already foreshadowed in Roosevelt's First Inaugural Address, which made it absolutely clear that as President of the United States he "shall spare no effort to *restore world trade by international economic readjustment*."[15] And, in the same spirit, a few years later he advocated the right "to trade in an atmosphere of *freedom from unfair competition and domination by monopolies at home or abroad*."[16] Thus, the writing was on the wall for the British Empire from the beginning of Roosevelt's presidency, and the question of colonialism made the relationship with Churchill a very unhappy one for the latter. This was revealed in a partially off-the-record press briefing which Roosevelt gave on his return from the Yalta Conference with Churchill and Stalin. Concerning the question of French Indo-China, Roosevelt proposed a transitional trusteeship before independence as the solution, so as to:

> . . . educate them for self-government. It took fifty years for us to do it in the Philippines. Stalin liked the idea. China [Chiang Kai-Shek] liked the idea. The British don't like it. It might bust up their empire, because if the Indo-Chinese work together and eventually get their independence, the Burmese might do the same thing to England.
>
> INTERVIEWER: Is that Churchill's idea on all territory out there, he wants them all back, just the way they were?
> FDR: Yes, he is mid-Victorian on all things like that.
>
> INTERVIEWER: This idea of Churchill's seems inconsistent with the policy of self-determination?
> FDR: Yes, that is true.
>
> INTERVIEWER: Do you remember the speech the Prime Minister made about the fact that he was not made Prime Minister of Great Britain to see the Empire fall apart?
> FDR: Dear old Winston will never learn on that point. He has made his specialty on that point. This, of course, is off the record. [17]

Naturally, in the advocated "international economic readjustment"—a demand in the first place arising from the 1929–1933 great world crisis and rendered ever more imperative for America through the onset of another recession in the country just before the outbreak of the

Second World War—the whole of the British Empire was at stake. For Roosevelt believed that "India should be granted commonwealth status during the war and the choice of complete freedom five or ten years afterwards. The most galling suggestion, to old-line Britishers, was his proposal at Yalta that Hong Kong (as well as Dairen) be made into an international free port. His entire position seemed, in fact, naïve and wrongheaded from the British point of view. They felt that he misrepresented the aims and results of royal imperialism. More important, they warned that breakup of the Empire would weaken the West in a world of 'power politics.' It would leave dangerous areas of confusion and strife—[a] 'power vacuum' into which potential aggressors (the Reds) could move."[18]

With the appearance of an incomparably more powerful imperialist competitor, the United States, the fate of the British Empire was sealed. This was made even more pressing and in the colonies deceptively appealing because Roosevelt could present his policies aimed at achieving American international supremacy with the rhetoric of freedom for all, and indeed even with a claim to universally acceptable "destiny." He did not hesitate to declare: "a better civilization than any we have known is in store for America and by our example, perhaps, for the world. Here destiny seems to have taken a long look."[19] In no time at all, after deriding the transparently imperialist ideological justifications of "old-line Britishers," the propaganda slogans of the latter were fully adopted as their own by the Americans, justifying their military interventions in Indo-China and elsewhere in the name of preventing the generation of a "power vacuum" and blocking the possibility of the "domino effect" (produced by "the Reds"). This could only surprise those who continued to nourish illusions about the "end of imperialism."

4.2.2

To understand the seriousness of the present situation we have to put it in a historical perspective. The early modern imperialist penetration of various parts of the globe was of a rather different kind when compared with the incomparably more extensive—as well as intensive—penetration of some leading capitalist powers into the rest of the world in the last few decades of the nineteenth century. Harry Magdoff forcefully underlined the contrast:

> The same type of thinking that approaches the concept of economic impe-
> rialism in the restricted balance-sheet sense usually also confines the term to
> control (direct or indirect) by an industrial power over an underdeveloped
> country. Such a limitation ignores the essential feature of the new imperial-
> ism that arises in the late nineteenth century: the competitive struggle among
> the industrial nations for dominant positions with respect to the world mar-
> ket and raw material sources. The structural difference which distinguishes
> the new imperialism from the old is the replacement of an economy in which
> many firms compete by one in which a handful of giant corporations in each
> industry compete. Further, during this period, the advance of transportation
> and communication technology and the challenge to England by the newest
> industrial nations [like Germany] brought two additional features to the
> imperialist stage: the intensification of competitive struggle in the world
> arena and the maturation of a truly international capitalist system. Under
> these circumstances, the competition among groups of giant corporations
> and their governments takes place over the entire globe: in the markets of the
> advanced nations as well as in those of the semi-industrialized and non-
> industrialized nations.[20]

With the successful imposition of American hegemony in the postwar
world—with its roots in Roosevelt's first term, as we have seen
above—we have been subjected to a third phase in the development of
imperialism, with grave implications for the future. For now the catastrophic dangers that would go with a global conflagration, as experienced in the past, are self-evident even to the most uncritical defenders of the system. At the same time, no one in his or her right mind
could exclude the possibility of the eruption of a deadly conflict, and
with that the destruction of humankind. Yet, nothing is really done in
order to resolve the underlying massive contradictions that point in
that fateful direction. On the contrary, the continued enhancement of
the economic and military hegemony of the one remaining superpower—the United States—casts an ever-darkening shadow on the future.

We have reached a new historical stage in the transnational development of capital: one in which it is no longer possible to avoid facing
up to a fundamental contradiction and structural limitation of the system. That limitation is its grave failure to constitute *the state* of the
capital system as such, as complementary to its transnational aspirations and articulation, so as to thereby overcome the explosive antagonisms between national states that characterized the system in constantly aggravated form in the last two centuries.

Even at its best, capitalist rhetoric as successfully practiced by Roosevelt in a situation of emergency, can be no substitute in this respect. Roosevelt's rhetoric—nostalgically remembered by many intellectuals on the Left in the United States even today—was relatively successful precisely because it responded to a situation of emergency.[21] Although it greatly overstated the universal validity of the advocated actions and even more heavily understated or quite simply misrepresented the empire-building American elements, there was nevertheless some communality of interests both in addressing the symptoms of the world economic depression (even if not their *causes,* which tended to be reduced to "bad morals" equated with "bad economics" and to the actions of "blindly selfish men"[22]) and in the U.S. participation in defeating Hitler's Germany. Today, by contrast, instead of the best rhetoric of the New Deal years we are bombarded with the worst kind: a cynical camouflage of reality, which presents the most blatant U.S. imperialist interests as the universal panacea of *"multiparty democracy,"* and the tendentiously selective advocacy of *"human rights,"* The latter can happily accommodate, among many others, the Turkish genocide against the Kurds, the extermination of half a million Chinese in Indonesia at the time of installing Suharto, or the hundreds of thousands of people in East Timor later on by the same U.S. client regime. Further, what was once denounced as "domination by monopolies at home and abroad" is now presented in this discourse as the *"free market."*

Today, competition among groups of giant corporations and their governments has a major qualifier: the overwhelming power of the United States dangerously bent on assuming the role of *the state* of the capital system as such, subsuming by all means at its disposal all of the rival powers. The fact that this objective cannot be successfully accomplished on a lasting basis represents no deterrent to the forces ruthlessly pushing for its realization. And the problem is not simply some subjective misconception. As with every major contradiction of the given system, objective conditions make it imperative to pursue now the strategy of hegemonic domination by one economic and military superpower, at whatever cost, in order to try to overcome the structural cleavage between transnational capital and national states. However, the very nature of the underlying contradiction foreshadows the necessary failure of this strategy in the longer run. There have been many attempts to address the issue of potential conflagrations and the way of remedying them, from Kant's dream about the perpetual peace-producing League of Nations to the institutional establishment of such a League after the First World War, and from the solemnly declared principles of the Atlantic Charter to making the United Nations operational as an organization; they all proved to be woefully inadequate to the envisaged task. The failure of instituting a "world government" on the basis of the established mode of social-metabolic reproduction arises from the fact that here we are facing one of the absolute, untranscendable limits of the capital system itself. It goes without saying, in this regard, that the failure of labor's structural antagonist is very far from being a cause for comfort.

4.2.3

Imperialist domination is, of course, nothing new in America's history, even if it has been justified, in President Roosevelt's words, as "fifty years of educating the Filipino people for self-government," (not to mention, well over fifty years of "further education" through the agency of U.S. proxies like Marcos and his successors). As Daniel B. Schirmer emphasized in his penetrating and meticulously documented book on the short-lived anti-imperialist movement in the United States at the turn of the century:

> The Vietnam War is only the last, most prolonged and most brutal of a series of United States interventions in the affairs of other peoples. The invasion of Cuba sponsored by United States authorities failed at the Bay of Pigs, but intervention has been more effective on other occasions, as in the Dominican Republic, Guatemala, British Guiana, Iran and the Congo. Nor is the list complete; other colonial peoples (and some European as well) have felt the effects of aggressive American intrusion upon their domestic policies, whether or not in the form of outright violence. . . . Present-day policies of counter-insurgency and intervention have their source in events that occurred at the opening of the twentieth century. Then the United States defeated Spain in war and stripped her of colonies in the Caribbean and the Pacific, taking Puerto Rico outright, giving Cuba nominal independence, and annexing the Philippines after first suppressing a nationalist revolution in those islands by force. What particularly distinguishes modern foreign policy from the Mexican war and the Indian wars for most of their span is that it is the product of another era in American history and comes in response to decisively different social pressures. Modern foreign policy is associated with the rise of

the large-scale corporation, industrial and financial, as the dominant economic force in the country, exerting a most powerful influence upon the
government of the United States. The Spanish-American War and the war to
subdue Aguinaldo and the Philippine insurgents were the first foreign wars
conducted as a consequence of this influence, the first wars of modern corporate America.[23]

When President Roosevelt proclaimed the strategy of "international
economic readjustments" in his First Inaugural Address, his move
indicated a determination to work for the dissolution of all colonial
empires, not only the British. Like other major historical departures,
this approach had its predecessor several decades earlier. In fact, it was
closely connected with the "open door policy" declared at the turn of
the century. The so-called "open door" that was demanded from other
countries envisaged economic penetration (in contrast to direct colonial military occupation), keeping characteristically quiet about the
overwhelming political domination that went with it. No wonder,
therefore, that many people called the "open door policy" utterly hypocritical. When in 1899, in the name of such policy, the United States
declined to establish a colonial enclave in China, alongside the others
as their equal, this was not due to liberal enlightenment or to democratic compassion. The opportunity was turned down because—as the
most dynamic articulation of capital by that time—the United States
wanted the whole of China, in due course, for itself. Such design
became absolutely clear in the course of subsequent historical
developments, reaching down all the way into our own time.

However, accomplishing world domination through the "open
door" policy—given the relation of forces in the overall configuration
of the major imperialist powers—was hopelessly premature at the turn
of the century. The frightful bloodletting of the First World War was
needed, as well as the unfolding of the grave world economic crisis
after the short-lived period of reconstruction, before the Rooseveltian
version of the strategy could be announced. Moreover, it needed an
even greater bloodletting in the Second World War, coupled with the
emergence of the United States in the course of that war as by far the
greatest economic power, before the implementation of the Rooseveltian strategy could be forcefully attempted toward the end and in
the immediate aftermath of the Second World War. The only remaining major complication—the existence of the Soviet system (since the

additional complicating factor of China materialized with finality only in 1949)—was considered strictly temporary. This view was confidently asserted in the numerous declarations of Secretary of State John Foster Dulles concerning the policy of "rolling back communism."

Thus, in the course of twentieth-century developments, we have reached a point where the side-by-side existence—and competitive coexistence—of imperialist powers can no longer be tolerated, no matter how much lip service is paid to the so-called "plury-central world." As Baran rightly argued in 1957, the proud owners of former colonial empires had been cut down in size to play the role of "junior partners of American imperialism." When the future of imperial possessions was discussed toward the end of the war, British concerns were swept aside as the hopelessly "mid-Victorian" notions of "dear-old Winston." At the same time De Gaulle was not even consulted,[24] not to mention the Belgian, the Dutch and the Portuguese who did not even enter the picture. All talk about the "plury-central world," under the principle of some sort of inter-state equality, belongs to the realm of pure fantasy, if not to that of cynical ideological camouflage. Of course, there is nothing surprising about that. For "pluralism" in the world of capital can only mean the *plurality of capitals* and within such a plurality there can be no consideration of equality. On the contrary, it is always characterized by the most iniquitous pecking order of structural hierarchies and corresponding power relations, favoring always the stronger in their quest to gobble up the weaker. Thus, given the inexorability of capital's logic, it was only a question of time before the unfolding dynamism of the system had to reach the stage also at the level of inter-state relations when one hegemonic superpower had to overrule all of the less powerful ones, no matter how big, and assert its—ultimately unsustainable and for humanity as a whole most perilous—exclusive claim to being *the state* of the capital system as such.

4.2.4

Most significant, in this respect, is the attitude assumed in relation to the question of national interests. On the one hand, their legitimacy is forcefully asserted when the issues at stake affect, directly or indirectly, the presumed interests of the United States, not hesitating to use even the most extreme forms of military violence, or the threat of such violence, to impose their arbitrary decisions on the rest of the world.

On the other hand, however, legitimate national interests of other countries are arrogantly dismissed as intolerable "nationalism," and even as "ethnic pandaemonium."[25] At the same time, the United Nations and other international organizations are treated as a plaything of the United States, and defied with utmost cynicism when their resolutions are not palatable to the guardians of the more or less openly declared U.S. national interests. Examples are countless. About some, Noam Chomsky sharply commented: "The highest authorities explained with brutal clarity that the World Court, the UN, and other agencies had become irrelevant because they no longer follow U.S. orders, as they did in early postwar years . . . [U]nder Clinton the defiance of world order had become so extreme as to be of concern even to hawkish policy analysts."[26] To add insult to injury, the United States refused to pay its huge debt of UN membership arrears, while imposing its policies on the organization, including the cuts of funds for the chronically under-funded World Health Organization (WHO). This blatant obstructionism was noted even by such establishment figures as Jeffrey Sachs whose devotion to the cause of a U.S.-dominated "market economy" is beyond doubt. He wrote in a recent article: "The failure of the United States to pay its UN dues is surely the world's most significant default on international obligations...America has systematically squeezed the budgets of UN agencies, including such vital ones as the World Health Organization."[27]

It is necessary to mention here also the efforts—both ideological and organizational—invested in bypassing the national framework of decision-making. The superficially tempting slogan "think globally, act locally" is an interesting case in point. For obviously the people in general, who are deprived of all meaningful power of decision-making on a broader scale (other than the abdicating electoral ritual), might find it just feasible to intervene in some way at the strictly local level. Moreover, no one could deny the potential importance of appropriate local action. However, the "global" to which we are expected to pay uncritical attention—meekly subscribing to the theses about the "powerlessness of national governments" and the "inevitability of multinational globalization," which tendentiously misdescribe the *national transnational* corporations (heavily dominated by the United States) as "multinational" and thereby universally acceptable—is totally vacuous without its complex relations to the particular national communities. Besides, once the "global" is divorced from its manifold national setting, diverting attention from the intertwined contradictory inter-state relations, the call to act "locally" becomes utterly myopic and ultimately meaningless.[28] If "democracy" is thus confined to such decapitated "local action," the "global decision making and action" that inevitably affects the life of every single individual can be exercised in the most authoritarian fashion by the dominant economic and political forces—and of course predominantly the United States—in accord with the position occupied by them in the global pecking order of capital. The funds invested by the World Bank and other U.S.-dominated organizations in trying to enhance the "local" at the expense of the national, attempting to enlist the support of academic and other intellectual elites through well sponsored conferences and research projects (especially but not exclusively in the Third World), indicate a design to create a "world government" that effectively sidesteps the potentially most troublesome decision-making processes of the intermediary national level, with its unavoidable recalcitrance, and to legitimate the blatantly authoritarian domination of social life by a "world government" ruthlessly imposed from above in the name of the fictitious "democracy" synonymous with the pretended "local action" of "regular rubbish collections."

4.2.5

The manifestations of U.S. economic imperialism are too numerous to be listed here. I have discussed in the past some of the salient issues, including those against which even conservative politicians had to protest, like "technology transfer regulations, American protection laws, extra-territorial controls coordinated through the Pentagon and protected by Congress,"[29] and also "funds channeled into the largest and richest companies on earth [in such a way that if the ongoing process continues] unchecked it will buy its way through sector after sector of the world's advanced technologies."[30] I have also discussed in the same article "Industrial advantage from military secrecy," "Direct trade pressures applied by the U.S. legislative and executive," and "The real debt problem"[31] in the world: that is, the astronomical debt of the United States itself, imposed by the dominant imperialist power on the rest of the world, for as long as the latter can continue to pay for it.

Protests against "dollar imperialism," are often voiced, but to no avail. American economic imperialism remains secure for as long as the United States retains its overwhelmingly dominant position not only through the dollar as the privileged world economic currency, but also in ruling all of the international organs of economic interchange, from the IMF to the World Bank and from GATT to its successor, the World Trade Organization. Today, in France, many people protest against American economic imperialism on account of the punitive tariffs recently imposed on them by the United States under the pretended independent judgment of the WTO. The same kind of measures were unceremoniously imposed on Japan several times in the past, ending as a rule with the reluctant or willing submission by the Japanese authorities to the American dictates. If, in the last round of punitive tariffs imposed on Europe, Britain was treated somewhat more leniently, that was only as a reward for the total servility of the current British "New Labour" government toward all orders coming from Washington. But even so, skirmishes of an international trade war reveal a very serious trend, with far-reaching potential consequences for the future.

Similarly, the prepotent intervention of U.S. governmental agencies in the field of high technology, both military and civil, cannot be assumed to endure indefinitely. In a crucial area—computer technology, both hardware and software—the situation is extremely serious. To mention only one case, Microsoft enjoys an almost completely monopolistic position in the world, whereby its software carries massive implications also for the acquisition of the most suitable hardware. But well beyond that, it has been brought to light a short while ago that a secret code embedded in Microsoft software enables U.S. security and military services to spy on everybody in the world who uses Microsoft Windows and the Internet.

Also in another, literally vital, area—the production of genetically modified foods by giant transnational corporations, like Monsanto—the U.S. government is doing everything it can behind the scenes to ram down the throats of the rest of the world products whose adoption would compel farmers everywhere to buy nonrenewable seeds from Monsanto and would thus secure absolute domination for the United States in the field of agriculture. Attempts by U.S. corporations to patent genes serve a similar purpose.

U.S. attempts to impose "intellectual property rights"[32] on the rest of the world through the agency of the WTO—aimed at, among other things, securing the permanent domination of world cinema and television by the tenth-rate Hollywood products with which we are constantly flooded—have generated cries of "U.S. cultural imperialism." At the same time, the phenomenally well-financed "business culture imperialism," in the form of pushing the penetration of the U.S. army of "management consultancy" everywhere in the world, is part of the same picture.

But perhaps the most serious of the ongoing trends of economic and cultural domination is the rapacious and frightfully wasteful way the United States grabs for itself the world's energy and prime material resources: *25 percent of them for just 4 percent of the world's population*, with immense and relentlessly accumulating damage to environmental conditions. And that is not all. For, in the same vein, the United States continues its active sabotage of all international efforts aimed at introducing some form of control in order to limit, and perhaps by 2012 to some degree reduce, the ongoing catastrophic trend of environmental damage, no longer deniable even by the worst apologists of the system.

4.2.6

The military dimension of all this must be taken very seriously. It is no exaggeration to say—also in view of the formerly quite unimaginable destructive power of armaments accumulated in the second half of the twentieth century—that we have entered into the most dangerous phase of imperialism in all history. For what is at stake today is not the control of a particular, no matter how large, part of the planet, putting at a disadvantage but still tolerating the independent actions of some rivals, but the control of its totality by one hegemonic economic and military superpower, with all means—even the most extreme authoritarian and, if needed, violent military ones—at its disposal. This is what the ultimate rationality of globally developed capital requires, in its vain attempt to bring under control its irreconcilable antagonisms. The trouble is, though, that such rationality—which genuinely corresponds to the logic of capital at the present historical stage of global development—is at the same time the most extreme form of irrationality in history, including the Nazi conception of world domination, as far as the conditions required for the survival of humanity are concerned.

When Jonas Salk refused to patent his discovery, the polio vaccine, insisting that it would be like wanting "to patent the sun," he could not imagine that the time would come when capital would attempt to do just that, trying to patent not only the sun but also the air, even if that had to be coupled with dismissing any concern about the mortal dangers which such aspirations and actions carried with them for human survival. For the ultimate logic of capital in its processes of decision-making can only be of a *categorically authoritarian* "top-down" variety, from the "microcosms" of small economic enterprises to the highest levels of political and military decision-making. But how can one *enforce* patents taken out on the sun and the air?

There are two prohibitive obstacles in this regard, even if capital— in its drive to demolish its own untranscendable limits—refuses to acknowledge them. The first is that the *plurality of capitals* cannot be eliminated, no matter how inexorable and brutal the monopolistic trend of development manifest in the system. And the second, that the corresponding *plurality of social labor* cannot be eliminated, so as to turn the total labor force of humankind, with all its national and sectional varieties and divisions, into the mindless "obedient servant" of the hegemonically dominant section of capital. For labor in its insurmountable plurality can never abdicate its right of access to the air and the sun; and even less can it survive for capital's continued benefit— an absolute must for this mode of controlling social metabolic reproduction—without the sun and the air.

Those who say that today's imperialism does not involve the military occupation of territory, not only underrate the dangers we face but also accept the most superficial and misleading appearances as the substantive defining characteristics of imperialism in our time, ignoring both history and the contemporary trends of development. For one thing, the U.S. militarily occupies territory in no less than *69 countries* through its military bases: a number that continues to expand with the enlargement of NATO. Those bases are not there for the benefit of the people—the grotesque ideological justification—but for the sole benefit of the occupying power, so as to be able to dictate policies as it pleases.

In any case, the direct military occupation of colonial territories in the past could only be partial in extent. How otherwise could the small population of England rule the incomparably larger population and territories of its immense empire, above all India? Nor was such disproportionality an exclusive characteristic of the British Empire. As Renato Constantino reminded us in regard to the Philippines:

From its inception, Spanish colonization operated more through religion than through force, thus profoundly affecting consciousness. This enabled the authorities to impose tributes, forced labor and conscription despite the small military force. Without the work of the priests, this would have been impossible. The priests became the pillars of the colonial establishment; so much so that it became a clerical boast that 'in each friar in the Philippines the king had a captain general and a whole army.' The molding of consciousness in the interest of colonial control was to be repeated on another plane by the Americans who after a decade of massive repression operated likewise through consciousness, this time using education and other cultural institutions.[33]

China, another vitally important example, was never militarily occupied, except for a small part of its territory. Not even when the Japanese invaded it with massive military force. Yet, for a long time before that, the country was completely dominated by foreign powers. So much so in fact that the young Mao sarcastically commented that "when the foreigner farts it must be hailed as heavenly perfume." What mattered in all imperialist ventures was always the ability to impose dictates on the dominated country on a continuing basis, using punitive military interventions only when the "normal" way of ruling was challenged. The famous expression: "gunboat diplomacy" well encapsulated what was feasible and practicable with the available military resources.

The principal characteristics of such imperialist domination remain with us also today. The multiplication of the destructive power of the military arsenal available today—especially the catastrophic potential of aerial weapons—has to some extent modified the forms of imposing imperialist dictates on a country to be subdued, but not their substance. In all probability the ultimate form of threatening the adversary in the future—the new "gunboat diplomacy"—will be *nuclear blackmail*. But its objective would be analogous to those of the past, while its envisaged modality could only underline the absurd untenability of trying to impose capital's ultimate rationality on the recalcitrant parts of the world in that way. Also today, it is quite inconceivable to occupy the whole of China, with its 1,250 million people, and keep it occupied even by the largest economically sustainable outside military force. Not that such inconceivability would deter from their imperialist aims the most extreme adventurers who can envisage no alternative to their world domination; while the "more sober" ones—who in the end are not less dangerous—envisage strategic moves aimed at attempting to break up China, with the help of "free-market" ideology, into fragments controllable from the hegemonic center of global capitalism.

It is self-evident that military forces must be economically sustained, which makes them always confined to limited enterprises both in the size of the military machines themselves and in the timespan of their operations. The historical record of past imperialist ventures shows that by the time they are vastly extended—as the French first in Indo-China and then in Algeria, and later on the United States in Vietnam—the failure of the ventures in question stares them in the face, even if it may take quite some time to disengage from them. With regard to the countless U.S. military imperialist operations of the past, we have to recall not only the Philippines, as well as the failed large-scale war of intervention in Vietnam,[34] but also Guatemala, the Dominican Republic, British Guiana, Grenada, Panama and the Congo, as well as some military operations in other countries, from the Middle East and the Balkans to various parts of Africa.

One of the most favored ways of making U.S. imperial interests prevail has always been the overthrow of unpalatable governments and the imposition of dictators totally dependent on the new master, so as to rule the countries in question through these well-controlled dictators. Here we are talking about Marcos and Pinochet, Suharto and the Brazilian Generals, Somosa and the South Vietnamese puppet generals of the United States, not to mention the Greek colonels (called "sons of a bitch" by Lyndon Johnson and Mobutu (called in a curious sort of praise "our son of a bitch" by a high-ranking State Department official).[35] The contempt with which U.S. government figures ordered about their servants in the countries under their military domination, while cynically presenting them for public consumption as champions of the "free world," is clear enough in each case.

4.2.7

The onset of capital's structural crisis in the 1970s has produced important changes in the posture of imperialism. This is what made it necessary to adopt an increasingly more aggressive and adventurist stand, despite the rhetoric of conciliation, and later even the absurd propaganda notion of the "new world order," with its never maintained promise of a "peace dividend." Contrary to some assertions, it would be quite wrong to attribute these changes to the implosion of the Soviet system, although it is undoubtedly true that the Cold War and the presumed Soviet military threat was very successfully used in the past for justifying the unbridled expansion of what General Eisenhower, toward the end of his Presidency, warningly called "the military-industrial complex." The challenges calling for the adoption of a more aggressive—and ultimately adventurist—stand were there well before the collapse of the Soviet system. I described them in 1983 (i.e., eight years before the Soviet implosion) as follows:

1. the end of the colonial regime in Mozambique and Angola;
2. the defeat of white racism and the transfer of power to ZANU in Zimbabwe;
3. the collapse of the client regime of the United States run by the colonels in Greece and the subsequent victory of Andreas Papandreou's PASOK;
4. the disintegration of Somosa's lifelong, U.S.-backed rule in Nicaragua and the striking victory of the Sandinista Front;
5. armed liberation struggles in El Salvador and elsewhere in Central America and the end of the erstwhile easy control of the region by U.S. imperialism;
6. the total bankruptcy—not only figuratively but also in a literal sense—of 'metropolitan' inspired and dominated 'developmental strategies' all over the world, and the eruption of massive structural contradictions in all three principal industrial powers in Latin America: Argentina, Brazil, and even oil-rich Mexico;
7. the dramatic and total disintegration of the Shah's regime in Iran and with it a major defeat of long-established U.S. strategies in the region, calling into existence *desperately dangerous substitute strategies*—to be implemented *directly or by proxy*—ever since.[36]

What has changed after the collapse of the Soviet system was the need to find justification for the increasingly aggressive posture of U.S. imperialism in different parts of the world, especially after the disappointments encountered in trying to revitalize Western capital through the economically sustainable restoration of capitalism—in contrast to the relative but still unstable successes in manipulating the state political machinery through Western "aid"—in the former Soviet

Union. The "desperately dangerous substitute strategies implemented directly or by proxy" became prominent in the years preceding and following the Soviet implosion. But the appearance of such dangerous adventurist strategies could not be attributed, as some people think, to the fateful weakening of the Cold War adversary. Rather, the Soviet collapse itself is intelligible only as an integral part of the ongoing structural crisis of the capital system as such.

The Shah as an American proxy—as well as a presumed guarantor against the danger of a new Mossadeq—served his purpose by ruthlessly controlling his people and by buying massive quantities of arms from the West as the means to do so. Once he was gone, another proxy had to be found in order to destroy the antagonist who was talking about the "American Satan." Saddam Hussein's Iraq seemed to fit the bill, armed to the teeth by the United States and other Western countries. But Iraq had failed to destroy Iran and became disposable as an element of instability in a most unstable region of the world as defined by U.S. imperialist strategy. Moreover, Saddam Hussein as the former U.S. proxy now could serve a greater purpose: by being promoted to the status of the mythical all-powerful enemy who represents not only the danger attributed in Cold War days to the Soviet Union, but much more than that, threatening with chemical and biological warfare— and also with a nuclear holocaust—the whole of the Western world. Given this mythical enemy, we were expected to justify not only the Gulf War, but also several major military interventions in Iraq since then, as well as the callous killing of one million of its children through the sanctions imposed on the country as a result of U.S. dictates, shamefully accepted by our "great democracies" which continue to boast about their "ethical foreign policies."

But all this is not enough to scratch the surface of the chronic instability in the Middle East, let alone in the rest of the world. Those who think that present-day imperialism does not require territorial occupation should think again. Military occupation for an indefinite length of time is already in evidence in parts of the Balkans (also admitted to be an "indefinite commitment"), and who can show any reason why similar military territorial occupations should not follow in the future in other parts of the world? The ongoing trends are ominous and the deepening crisis of the system can only make them worse.

We have witnessed in the past two extremely dangerous developments in the ideology and organizational framework of U.S. imperialism. The first concerns NATO. Not simply its significant expansion toward the East, which may be considered by the Russian authorities a threat, if not today then some time in the future. But even more importantly, the aims and objectives of the organization have been radically redefined, in contradiction to international law, transforming it from what used to be claimed in the past to constitute a *purely defensive* military association into a potentially most aggressive *offensive* alliance, which can do what it pleases without any reference to a lawful authority—or, rather, it can do what the United States pleases and orders it to do. At the May 1999 North Atlantic Treaty Organization (NATO) summit in Washington NATO, under American pressure, "adopted a new strategic concept, by which they said they can resort to military action even outside the NATO area, without caring about the sovereignty of other countries and in disregard of the United Nations."[37] What is also highly significant in this respect is that the ideological justification of the new, unmistakably aggressive, posture—offered in the form of twenty four "*risk factors*"—is transparently shaky. It is even admitted that "out of the *twenty-four risk factors only five* can be considered to represent real military danger."[38]

The second dangerous recent development—almost completely ignored in the West, sadly even on the Left[39]—concerns the new Japan-U.S. Security Treaty, which has been characteristically railroaded through the Japanese houses of parliament (the Diet and the upper House of Counselors). In this regard, too, the new developments cynically defy international law, and also violate the Japanese Constitution. As an important Japanese political leader, Tetsuzo Fuwa commented: "The dangerous nature of the Japan-U.S. Security Treaty has evolved to the extent of possibly dragging Japan into U.S. wars, challenging the Japanese Constitution which renounces war. Behind this is the extremely dangerous *U.S. preventive strike strategy* by which the United States will interfere in another country and arbitrarily attack any country it dislikes."[40] It goes without saying, the intended position assigned to Japan in the "preventive strike strategy," in which the orders emanate from Washington, is to play the role of "*cannon fodder,*" generously contributing at the same time to the financial costs of military operations, as they were compelled to do also in the case of the Gulf War.[41]

One of the most sinister aspects of these developments came to light recently through the forced resignation of the Japanese Vice Defense Minister, Shingo Nishimura, for "jumping the gun" and agg-

ressively advocating that Japan should arm itself with nuclear
weapons. And he went even further, projecting in an interview the use
of military force, with reference to the disputed Senkaku Islands. He
declared: "Should diplomacy fail to settle the dispute, the Defense
Agency will tackle it." As an editorial article of the journal *Akahata*
pointed out:

> The real problem here is that a politician who openly argued for the nuclear
> armament of Japan and the use of military force as means to solve interna-
> tional disputes was given a cabinet seat. It is natural that other Asian nations
> have expressed grave concern over the matter. What is more, under a secret
> agreement with the U.S. government, LDP [Liberal Democratic Pary] gov-
> ernments have gutted the three non-nuclear principles (not to possess, man-
> ufacture, or allow nuclear weapons to be brought into Japan). Moreover, the
> recent 'emergency legislation' is aimed at giving military operations by the
> U.S. forces and the SDF [Self-Defence Force] priority in the event of war by
> mobilizing for war cooperation, commandeering commodities, land sites,
> buildings, and controlling ships, aircraft and electric waves. Such legislation
> will undermine the Constitution.[42]

Naturally, the new aggressive posture of the "U.S.-Japan Security
Treaty" is justified in the name of the necessities of Japanese defense.
In truth, however, the "Common Defense" claimed in the legitimating
report has nothing to do with "defending Japan" against a fictitious
"aggressor," but everything to do with the protection and enhancement of U.S. imperialist interests:

> The United States use[s] their bases in Japan, including those in Okinawa, to
> carry out military intervention in politically unstable situations in South East
> Asian countries, including Indonesia. In May last year, when the Suharto
> regime went down in Indonesia, U.S. Army Special Forces units suddenly
> returned to the U.S. Torii Station in Yomitan village, Okinawa, via U.S.
> Kadena Base in Okinawa. They had trained the special forces of the
> Indonesian Armed Forces (ABRI) which suppressed demonstrations in the
> country. The sudden return of the U.S. Army Special units Forces [sic] indi-
> cated the secret activity that U.S. Green Beret units in Okinawa had engaged
> in Indonesia.[43]

The way in which these dangerous policies and practices are imposed
on the countries whose "democratic" governments meekly submit to

all U.S. dictates speaks for itself. As a rule, the changes are not even discussed in the respective parliaments, they are bypassed, instead, through secret treaties and protocols. And in the same spirit of cynical evasion, when for some reason they appear on the parliamentary agenda, they are bulldozed through, dismissing in the most authoritarian fashion all opposition. The politicians who in this way continue to "sow dragon seeds" seem to be oblivious to the danger of real dragons appearing on the historical stage in due course. Nor do they seem to understand or admit that the devastating flame of the nuclear dragons is not confined to a given locality—the Middle or the Far East, for instance—but can engulf absolutely everything on this planet, including the United States and Europe.

4.2.8

The ultimate target of the projected U.S. preventive strikes strategy is, of course, China. Commenting on the aggressive noises and leaks in Washington against China in the aftermath of the bombing of the Chinese Embassy in Belgrade, Rear Admiral Eugene Carroll, of the Center for Defense Information(CDI), an independent think-tank, said: "There is a demonization of China going on here. I am not sure who is doing it, but these leaks are orchestrated to show China as the yellow peril."[44]

The bombing of the Chinese Embassy in Belgrade was at first presented and justified by NATO spokesmen as an "inevitable, even if regrettable, accident." When later it became undeniable that the Embassy was not hit by a stray bomb but by rockets from three different directions, hence a carefully targeted strike, Washington produced a fairy-tale explanation: the CIA could not obtain an up-to-date map of Belgrade, available to everybody else in any corner shop. But even then, it remained a complete mystery as to what was so important about the building that was once supposed to have occupied the space filled by the Chinese Embassy or what made it a legitimate target. We are still waiting for some credible answers, which will obviously never come. A rational explanation that could come to mind is that the operation was designed as a testing ground, in two respects. First, to test the way the Chinese government would respond to such acts of aggression, compelling it to swallow the humiliation that went with them. And second, perhaps more importantly, it was a test of world public opinion, which proved to be utterly meek and compliant.

The problems deeply affecting U.S.-China relations could not be more serious. In one sense they arise from the inconvenient fact that "*The party-state has still not found a place in the free-market world.*"[45] When global hegemonic imperialism uses as its ideological legitimation the concepts of "democracy" and "free market," any departure from such an ideology—backed by a major economic and military power—represents a serious challenge. And what makes the challenge quite intolerable is the prospect of economic developments to the disadvantage of the United States, given the comparable present rates of expansion, coupled with the fact that China's population is by a staggering *one thousand million* greater than that of the United States. As the same article puts it, reflecting great concerns about the ongoing developments: "*By 2020 China's economy alone would be three times that of the United States.*"[46] It is not too difficult to imagine the alarm raised by such prospects in U.S. ruling circles.

True to its apologetic role, *The Economist* tries to put a glaze of respectability on the advocated military readiness and preparedness to die for "democracy" and for the "free market." In an article on "The New Geopolitics" it calls for the acceptance of piling up "body bags." Not by the United States, of course, but by what *The Economist* calls the "*local assistants*" of the United States. With boundless hypocrisy, *The Economist* speaks of a necessary "*moral commitment*" to war by the democracies, asking them in the name of that morality to accept that "*war is a time of dying as well as of killing.*"

To be the devoted "local assistant" of the United States is the role assigned to Japan, justified in view of the projected Chinese threat. The serious opposition in the country to the redefined and dangerously expanded U.S.-Japan Security Treaty is characterized as "nervousness." Happily, China will make the Japanese come to their senses and strengthen their resolve. For "a growing China will also make a nervous Japan readier to cling on to its alliance with America." The same role of a devoted local assistant is assigned to Turkey and, expressing *The Economist*'s hope, also to India, arguing that "the armies of allied countries whose people do not mind their soldiers doing the *face-to-face work* [i.e., dying] may come to the rescue; this is why Turkey matters to the alliance,[47] and why one day it may be a good idea to ask for India's help." In this scheme of things Russia, too, will occupy an actively pro-American place, thanks to its projected unavoidable opposition to China. "Worried about the vulnerability of its eastern territories, Russia may at last choose to put some substance into its flimsy Partnership-for-Peace links with NATO." The characterization of countries as "nervous" and "worried"—if not today, then tomorrow—is all on account of their expected conflicts with "the rising giant of the East," China. In the "new geopolitics," China is presented as the common denominator of all trouble, and simultaneously also as the solution cementing all the "worried" and "nervous" into an "Alliance for Democracy" and a "Partnership-for-Peace," which "might even draw a democratic India [a traditionally non-aligned country] into a new, South Asian version of the Partnership-for-Peace" under the United States. We are not told, however, that we shall live happily ever after, or indeed live at all.[48]

Naturally, this kind of "doctrine," inspired by Washington, is not confined to London's *The Economist.* It had found its spokesmen also in the Far East, where Australia's Prime Minister, John Howard, proclaimed the "Howard Doctrine" according to which his own country should fulfill the role of the faithful United States' "local assistant." To the consternation of Southeast-Asian political opinion, he declared that "Australia will act as the United States' 'deputy sheriff' in regional peace-keeping."[49] Malaysia's opposition leader, Lim Kit Siang, responded to this idea by saying that "Mr Howard had done more than any previous Australian Prime Minister to damage Australia's relations with Asia since the 'White Australia' policy was abolished in the 1960s."[50] However, it was Hadi Soesastro, an American educated Indonesian academic who hit the nail on the head by pointing out that "It is always the deputy sheriff who gets killed."[51] Indeed. That is precisely the role of the U.S. "local assistants": to kill and to get killed for the cause handed down to them from above.

Marx wrote in his *Eighteenth Brumaire of Louis Bonaparte* that historical events often appear twice, in contrasting forms: first, as *tragedy,* and second as *farce.* The role assigned to Japan in the recently revised, unconstitutional U.S.-Japan Security Treaty could only produce a major tragedy in Southeast Asia, and an equally tragic devastation to Japan itself. The muscle-flexing "U.S. deputy sheriff" role proclaimed in the "Howard Doctrine," can be only described as the farce eagerly running ahead of the tragedy.

4.2.9

The history of imperialism shows three distinctive phases:

1. Early modern *colonial empire-building imperialism,* brought about through the expansion of some European countries in the relatively easily penetrable parts of the world;
2. *"Redistributive"* imperialism, antagonistically contested by the major powers on behalf of their quasi-monopolistic corporations, called by Lenin "the highest stage of capitalism," involving only a few real contenders, and some smaller survivors from the past hanging on to their coat-tails, coming to an end in the immediate aftermath of the Second World war; and
3. *Global hegemonic imperialism,* with the United States as its overpowering force, foreshadowed by Roosevelt's version of the "open-door policy," with its pretences of democratic equity. This third phase was consolidated soon after the Second World War and become sharply pronounced with the onset of the capital system's structural crisis in the 1970s, when the imperative to constitute an all-embracing political command structure of capital under a "global government" presided over by the globally dominant country became pressing.

Those who entertained the illusion that postwar "neocolonialism" had brought into being a stable system in which political and military domination had been replaced by a straightforward economic domination, tended to assign too much weight to the continued power of the former colonial imperialist masters after the formal dissolution of their empires, underrating at the same time the exclusionary aspirations of global U.S. hegemonic domination and the causes sustaining them. They imagined that by setting up institutes of development studies—for the purpose of "further educating" the postcolonial political and administrative elites of their former dependencies, inducing them into the adoption of the newly promoted theories and policies of "modernization" and "development"—the former colonial rulers could secure a substantive continuity with their old system. What had put an end to such illusions was not only the overwhelmingly greater power of penetration of the American corporations (forcefully backed by the U.S. government) but, even more so, the collapse of the whole "modernization policy" everywhere, as discussed above.

However, the fact that U.S. hegemonic imperialism proved to be so successful, and still continues to prevail, does not mean that it can be considered stable, let alone permanent. The envisaged "global government" under U.S. management remains wishful thinking, just like the "Alliance for Democracy" and the "Partnership for Peace," projected—at a time of multiplying military collisions and social explosions—as the solid foundation of the newest version of the "new world order." We have been there before, when—after the implosion of the Soviet system—such vision:

> . . . found favor in a Unites States anxious to keep the capitalist dynamo going at the end of the Cold War. Selective engagement with key 'emerging market' states provided an alternative foreign policy to the defunct containment strategy. The policy envisaged the United States at the hub of a 'One World' driving toward shared prosperity, democracy and better living conditions for all. Western corporations would pour technologies into the poorer regions of the world, where labor was abundant, cheap and talented. Global financial markets, no longer under political lock and key, would provide capital. Within a couple of decades, there would arise a huge transnational market for consumers.[52]

The greater part of the projected couple of decades is over, and we are in much worse condition than ever before, even in an advanced capitalist country like Britain, where—according to the latest statistics— *one in three children* lives below the poverty line, and in the last twenty years their numbers *multiplied threefold.* And no one should have illusions about how the structural crisis of capital affects even the richest country, the United States. For there also conditions greatly deteriorated in the last two decades. According to a recent report of the Congressional Budget Office—and no one could accuse that office of a "left-wing bias"—the richest *1 percent* of the population earns as much as the bottom *one hundred million* (i.e., nearly *40 percent*). And significantly, this appalling number has *doubled since 1977,* when the top 1 percent's income was equivalent to that of "only" *forty nine million* of the poorest, i.e., less than *20 percent* of the population.[53]

As to the rest of the optimistic projections quoted above, no longer are we treated to the mirage of "a huge transnational market" bringing "prosperity to all," including the people in the East. The Chinese Prime Minister, Zhu Rongji, is now praised for his "bold attempts to bring reform to the state sector, which now means *unemployment for millions of Chinese workers.*"[54] How many more millions of workers—or indeed hundreds of millions of them—must be made unemployed before it can be said that China has finally qualified "for a place in the free-market world"? For the time being the editorial of *The Economist* can only express its hope, and prognosticate its realization, that the Chinese system will be overthrown from inside,[55] and project the external military solution in other articles, as we have seen above. What is common to the two approaches is the complete absence of any sense of reality. For even if the Chinese system could be overthrown today or tomorrow, that would solve absolutely nothing as regards the total failure of the sanguine expectations once attached to the "emergent market states" and their projected impact "to keep the capitalist dynamo going at the end of the Cold War."

In the meantime, the contradictions and antagonisms, linked to ineradicable causes, continue to intensify. Under the rule of capital, which is *structurally* incapable of resolving its contradictions—hence its way of *postponing* the "moment of truth," until the accumulated pressures result in some kind of explosion—there is a tendency to misrepresent historical time, in the direction of both the past and the future, in the interest of eternalizing the present. The tendentious misreading of the past arises from the ideological imperative to misrepresent the present as the necessary structural framework of all possible change. For precisely because the established present must be timelessly projected into the future, the past must also be fictionalized—in the form of a projection backwards—as the domain of the system's eternal presence in another form, so as to remove the actual historical determinations and the time-bound limitations of the present.

As a result of the perverse interests at the roots of capital's relation to time, it can have neither a *long-term perspective*, nor a sense of *urgency* even when an explosion is about to take place. Enterprises are oriented toward, and their success is measured in, the fulfillment of projections conceived on the most myopic timescale. This is why the intellectuals who adopt the standpoint of capital like to argue that whatever worked in the past—encapsulated in the idealized method of doing "little by little"—is bound to work also in the future. This is a dangerous fallacy. For time is not on our side, given the accumulating pressure of our contradictions. The projection of *The Economist* about the happy alignment of all the "nervous" and "worried" countries with U.S. strategies is, at best, an arbitrary projection of the present into the future, if not a complete misrepresentation of present realities in order to make them suit the wishfully anticipated future. Even the present-day contradictions between the United States and Japan, as well as between Russia and the United States, are much greater than the adopted scheme of things allows for, not to mention their potential unfolding in the future. Nor should one ignore the objective conflicts of interest between India and the United States in order to transfigure them into perfect harmony on account of the postulated "nervousness" about China.

Moreover, even the apparently prevalent harmony of the United States with the European Union in the framework of NATO should not be taken for granted to persist in the future, given the clear signs of inter-imperialist conflicts both within the EU and between the EU and the United States.[56] At times even *The Economist* gives away its concern that not everything is going as it should in the conflict-ridden power relations of the West, insisting though that no one should even dream about challenging U.S. domination. As an editorial for *The Economist* puts it:

> Even the motives for a common foreign policy vary. Some Europeans want it as an expression of Europe's common political will; others as a rival to, and restraint upon, the United States. If it turned into nothing more than a form of anti-Americanism, it would be a disaster. For the foreseeable future, NATO, preferably in synch with the UN, will be the linchpin of western security. America must still take the lead in dealing with most of the world's danger zones. But in near-at-hand places like the Balkans, America will happily defer to Europe. And even in areas like the Middle East or Russia, Europe ought to be able to play a complementary role to America. Europe can and should exercise a greater influence in the world, but it will not be a superpower for many years yet.[57]

The meaningless phrase "Europe can and should exercise a greater influence in the world" (like what? and where?) is thrown in as an empty consolation prize, so as to legitimate in the eyes of the feeble-minded the absolute supremacy of the United States, propagandized by *The Economist*. In truth, however, the question is not at all: how long will it take for Europe to become a "superpower" matching the military might of the United States? Rather, in what form and with what intensity will the simmering inter-imperialist antagonisms erupt into the open in the by-no-means distant future?

As a matter of fact, the U.S. administration is already quite concerned about the prospects of European developments:

> Strobe Talbot, deputy Secretary of State, said, the last thing Washington wanted to see was a European defense identity 'which begins within NATO, but grows out of NATO, and then away from NATO.' The risk, he told a seminar at the Royal Institute of International Affairs, is of an EU defense structure that 'first duplicates the alliance and then competes with the alliance.' Mr Talbot's words . . . also touch America's basic ambivalence about greater European unity: that it is fine *so long as it does not threaten U.S. global pre-eminence.*[58]

Thus the American State Department misses no opportunity to hammer home the plain truth about its determination to keep the rest of the world subservient to the demands of its "*global preeminence.*" Naturally, the most subservient of all Western governments, the British, hastened to oblige and voice its unqualified reassurance at the same seminar of the Royal Institute of International Affairs. "Trying to allay U.S. anxieties, Lord Robertson, the outgoing Secretary of State for Defense who takes over at NATO from Mr. Solana next week, declared that the Atlantic alliance remains the cornerstone of British defense policy."[59] That may be so, for as long as the "Trojan horse" role assigned by the United States to the British government in Europe remains unquestioned. However, such reassurances are no more than whistling in the dark as regards the existing objective contradictions of interest among the Western powers, which are bound to intensify in the future, no matter how forcefully the U.S. State Department reminds the EU of who is really entitled to call the tune even when refusing to pay for it.

4.3 Historical Challenges Facing the Socialist Movement

4.3.1

As we have seen earlier, the anti-imperialist movement in the United States at the turn of the nineteenth to the twentieth century failed because of labor's "conciliation with the trusts and support for their foreign policy." The conclusion of Lincoln's former associate, George S. Boutwell, in 1902, that "the final effort for the salvation of the republic is to be made by the laboring and producing classes" sounds prophetic today. For the conditions of success remain the same, and only the American laboring and producing classes can bring to an end the destructive drive of global hegemonic imperialism. No political/military power on earth can accomplish from the outside what must be done from inside by a movement offering a positive alternative to the existing order in the United States.

Naturally, this does not mean that everyone else can sit back and wait until the required action is over, because it can never be completed in isolation. The problems and contradictions are so inextricably intertwined that their solution requires profound changes also in other parts of the world. The deep-seated causes of the explosive contradictions must be addressed everywhere, through the commitment of a truly international enterprise whose particular constituents confront their own share of capital's jungle-like network of contradictions, in solidarity with the "laboring and producing classes" in America and elsewhere in the world. American labor's "conciliation with the trusts and support for their foreign policy" at the turn of the century[60] was due, on the one hand, to the availability of outlets for imperialist expansion and thereby the postponing displacement of capital's contradictions; and on the side of labor, to the absence of the objective and subjective conditions[61] of a *viable hegemonic alternative* to capital's mode of controlling societal reproduction. Such an alternative is inconceivable without international solidarity oriented toward the creation of an order of substantive equality.

One does not have to be a militant socialist to realize the dangers we face. It is relevant to recall in this context the alarm raised in 1997 by Nobel Prize–winner Joseph Rotblat, concerning the profit-driven research activities pursued in the field of biotechnology, and specifically cloning. As we know, under the rule of capital such activities— entrapped by the system's expansionary imperatives, whatever the human and environmental consequences—represent a new dimension of humanity's potential self-destruction. This new dimension is now being added to the already existing arsenal of nuclear, chemical and biological weapons: each capable of inflicting on us a universal holocaust many times over.

In the same way as Joseph Rotblat—a distinguished liberal scientist who was most prominent in the protest movement which prevented Margaret Thatcher's election to the Chancellorship of Oxford University—acknowledged the danger of uncontrollability and potential human self-destruction, with regard to the way in which scientific knowledge in general is produced and utilized in our social order. He wrote in a recent paper on academic integrity:

> The structures of society—social, political, religious—are creaking heavily with our inability to absorb what we know into ethical and social systems that are capable of being widely accepted. The problem is *urgent*. . . . One possible outcome is, of course, a retreat into fundamentalism of various forms, which would certainly challenge academic integrity severely. The alternative is to acknowledge that there is an obligation on the part of the creators of this stockpile of knowledge to work out *how to disarm its ability to destroy us*.[62]

The social responsibility of scientists for fighting against such dangers cannot be overstated. Indeed, the scientists who took part in this enterprise in the twentieth century included some of our greatest. Thus Einstein, for instance, conducted for many years a struggle against the militarization of science and for the vital cause of nuclear disarmament. In a message he drafted for a planned—but, significantly, as a result of gross interference never actually convened—National Congress of Scientists, Einstein wrote:

> I am sincerely gratified that the great majority of scientists are fully conscious of their responsibilities as scholars and world citizens; and that they have not fallen victim to the widespread hysteria that threatens our future and that of our children. It is horrifying to realize that the poison of militarism and imperialism threatens to bring undesirable changes in the political attitude of the United States . . . What we see at work here is not an expression of the sentiments of the American people; rather, it reflects the will of a powerful minority which uses its economic power to control the organs of political life. Should the government pursue this fateful course, we scientists must refuse to submit to its immoral demands, even if they are backed by legal machinery. There is an unwritten law, that of our own conscience, which is far more binding than any bills that may be devised in Washington. And there are, of course, even for us, the ultimate weapons: non-cooperation and strike.[63]

Surely, Einstein's publicly declared belief in the consciously accepted social responsibility of the great majority of scientists was greatly disappointed by the cancellation of the planned vital meeting, scheduled for January 10–12,1946. Nevertheless, he continued his struggle until he died, defying threats and public denunciations. He knew very well that "men have never freed themselves from intolerable bondage, frozen into law, except by revolutionary action,"[64] and he insisted that "Deeds, not words are needed; mere words get pacifists nowhere. They must initiate action and begin with what can be achieved now."[65] Yet, despite his immense prestige and quite unparalleled access to heads of governments, as well as to the media, Einstein was in the end completely isolated and defeated by the political apologists of the growing military-industrial complex. They even called for his prosecution,[66] with a view to expulsion from the United States, thundering in Congress that, "this foreign-born agitator would have us plunge into another European war in order to further the spread of Communism throughout the world."[67]

Thus, even the protest of the century's greatest socially concerned and politically conscious scientist had to remain a cry in the wilderness. For it was not amplified by a mass movement which could confront and disarm the deeply entrenched destructive forces of capital through its own practically viable alternative vision of how to order human affairs. An alternative envisaged also by Boutwell, when he insisted that "The final effort for the salvation of the republic"—as against the empire-building, adventurist big corporations and their state—"is to be made by the laboring and producing classes." Boutwell uttered these words nearly a century ago, and their truth has been intensifying ever since. For the dangers have immeasurably increased for the whole of humanity not only compared to 1902, when Boutwell spoke, but even in comparison to Einstein's time. The megatons in the nuclear arsenal, which worried Einstein, have proliferated since the time of his death, despite all self-deluding talk about the "end of the Cold War." We were reminded of the real state of affairs quite recently when President Yeltsin tried to justify the "sovereign right" of his country's gruesome war against Chechnya by warning the rest of the world that Russia still possessed a full arsenal of nuclear weapons.

Today, in addition to the nuclear threat of Mutually Assured Destruction (MAD), the knowledge of how to employ chemical and biological weaponry in the service of mass extermination is at the disposal of all those who would not hesitate to use such weapons if the rule of capital was threatened. And that is by no means all. For by now environmental destruction, in the service of capital's blindly pursued interests, has assumed such proportions—dramatically illustrated by the terrible calamity inflicted in the dying days of the twentieth century on the people of Venezuela, as a result of irresponsible deforestation and speculative "development"—that even if the process is reversed tomorrow, it would take decades to produce any significant change in this respect by neutralizing capital's pernicious self-propelling and self-sustaining articulation which must pursue its "rational," and in immediate terms "economic," line of least resistance. Moreover, the potentially lethal implications of tampering with nature through recklessly used biotechnology, cloning, and through the uncontrolled genetic modification of food products, under the dictates of profit-seeking giant corporations and their governments, represent the opening of a new Pandora's box.

These are the clearly visible dangers on our horizon, as things stand today, and who knows what additional dangers will appear through capital's destructive uncontrollability for our children's tomorrow! However, what in the light of our historical experience is absolutely clear is that only a genuine socialist mass movement can counter and defeat the forces which are now pushing humankind toward the abyss of self-destruction.

4.3.2

The urgently needed constitution of the radical alternative to capital's mode of social metabolic reproduction cannot take place without a critical reexamination of the past. It is necessary to examine the failure of the historical Left to live up to Marx's optimistic projection in 1847 of trade unionist "combination" and ensuing political development of the working class in close parallel to the industrial development of the various capitalist countries. As Marx put it then:

> The degree to which combination has developed in any country clearly marks the rank it occupies in the hierarchy of the world market. England, whose industry has attained the highest degree of development, has the biggest and best-organized combinations. In England they have not stopped at partial combinations...they went on simultaneously with the political

struggles of the workers, who now constitute a large political party, under the name of the Chartists.[68]

Marx expected this process to continue in such a way that:

> The working class, in the course of its development, will substitute for the old civil society an association which will exclude classes and their antagonism, and *there will be no more political power properly so called*, since political power is precisely the official expression of antagonism in civil society.[69]

However, the historical development of the working class is characterized by partiality and sectionality. These characteristics were not confined to "partial combinations" and to the various trade unions that arose from them. Inevitably at first, partiality affected every aspect of the socialist movement, including its political dimension. So much so, in fact, that a century and a half later it still presents an immense problem, to be resolved some time in the hopefully not very distant future.

The labor movement could not help being sectional and partial in its beginnings. This was not simply a question of subjectively adopting the wrong strategy, as often claimed, but a matter of objective determinations. As mentioned earlier, the "plurality of capitals" could not and cannot be overcome within the framework of capital's social metabolic order, despite the overpowering tendency toward monopolistic concentration and centralization—as well as the transnational, but precisely in its *trans*national (and not genuinely *multi*national) character necessarily partial development—of globalizing capital. At the same time, the "plurality of labor," too, cannot be superseded on capital's ground of social metabolic reproduction, no matter how much effort is invested in trying to turn labor from capital's structurally irreconcilable antagonist into its uniformly compliant servant; attempts ranging from the mystifying and absurd propaganda of share-holding "people's capitalism" to the all-embracing direct political extraction of surplus-labor exercised by the post-capitalist personifications of capital who tried to legitimate themselves through their spurious claim to be the embodiment of the true interests of the working class.

The sectional and partial character of the labor movement was combined with its *defensive* articulation. Early trade unionism—from which the political parties later emerged—represented the tendentially authoritarian *centralization of sectionality,* and thereby the transfer of the power of decision-making from the local "combinations" to the trade-union centers, and subsequently to the political parties. Thus already the early trade-union movement as a whole was inevitably *sectional and defensive.* Indeed, due to the inner logic of development of this movement, the *centralization of sectionality* carried with it the *entrenchment of defensiveness* as compared to the sporadic attacks through which the local combinations could inflict serious damage on their local capital-antagonists. (The more distant Luddite relatives tried to do the same in a more generalized destructive, and therefore within a very short run of time quite unviable, form.) The entrenchment of defensiveness thus represented a paradoxical historical advance. For through its early trade union's labor became also the *interlocutor* of capital, without ceasing to be objectively its structural antagonist. From this new position of labor's generalized defensiveness certain advantages could be derived, *under favorable conditions,* for some sections of labor. This was possible so long as the corresponding constituents of capital could adjust themselves on a countrywide scale—in tune with the dynamic of potential capital-expansion and accumulation—to the demands conveyed to them by the defensively articulated labor movement. This movement operated within the structural premises of the capital system, as a legally constituted and state-regulated interlocutor. The development of the "welfare state" was the ultimate manifestation of this logic, workable in a very limited number of countries. It was limited both as regards the *favorable conditions* of undisturbed capital-expansion in the countries concerned, as the precondition of the welfare state's appearance, and in relation to its time scale, marked in the end by the radical Right's pressure for the complete liquidation of the welfare state in the last three decades, as a result of the structural crisis of the capital system as a whole.

With the constitution of labor's political parties—in the form of the separation of the "industrial arm" of labor (the trade unions) from its "political arm" (the social-democratic and the vanguard parties)—the defensiveness of the movement was further entrenched. For both types of parties appropriated for themselves the exclusive right of overall decision-making, which was already foreshadowed in the centralized sectionality of the trade-union movements themselves. This defensiveness was rendered worse still through the mode of operation adopted by the political parties, obtaining certain successes at the cost of derailing and diverting the socialist movement from its original objectives. For in the capitalist parliamentary framework, in exchange for the acceptance by capital of the legitimacy of labor's political parties, it became quite unlawful to use the "industrial arm" for political purposes.

This amounted to a severely constraining condition to which the parties of labor consented, thereby condemning the immense combative potential of materially rooted and potentially also politically most effective productive labor to total powerlessness. Acting in this way was all the more problematical since capital, through its structurally secured supremacy, remained the *extra-parliamentary force par excellence,* which could dominate parliament as it pleased from the outside. Nor could the situation be considered any better for labor in post-capitalist countries. For Stalin degraded the trade unions to the status of being what he called the "transmission belts" of official propaganda, exempting simultaneously the post-capitalist political form of authoritarian decision making from any possibility of control by the working class base. Understandably, therefore, in view of our unhappy historical experience with both main types of political parties, there can be no hope for the radical re-articulation of the socialist movement without *fully combining labor's "industrial arm" with its "political arm"*: by conferring the power of meaningful political decision making on the trade unions (thus encouraging them to be directly political), on the one hand, and by making the political parties themselves defiantly active in industrial conflicts as the uncompromising antagonists of capital, assuming responsibility for their struggle *inside and outside* parliament.

Throughout its long history, the labor movement remained sectional and defensive. Indeed, these two defining characteristics constituted a veritable vicious circle. Labor in its divided and often internally torn plurality could not break out of its paralyzing sectional constraints, in dependency to the plurality of capitals, because it was articulated defensively as a general movement; and *vice versa*, it could not overcome the grave limitations of its necessary defensiveness *vis-à-vis* capital, because up to the present time it remained sectional in its organized industrial and political articulation. At the same time, to make the vicious circle even tighter, the defensive role assumed by labor conferred a strange form of legitimacy on capital's mode of social metabolic control. For, by default, labor's defensive posture explicitly or tacitly consented to treating the established socioeconomic and political order as the necessary framework of, and the continuing prerequisite to, what could be considered "realistically feasible" out of the advocated demands, demarcating at the same time the only legitimate way of resolving the conflicts which would arise from the rival claims of the interlocutors. This amounted to a kind of *self-censorship,* much to the delight of capital's eager personifications. It represented a numbing self-censorship, resulting in a strategic inactivity which continues to paralyze today even the more radical remnants of the organized historical Left, not to mention its once-upon-a-time genuinely reformist but by now totally tamed and integrated constituents.

So long as the defensive posture of capital's "rational interlocutor"—whose rationality was *a priori* defined by what could be fitted into the practical premises and constraints of the ruling order—could produce relative gains for labor, the self-proclaimed *legitimacy* of capital's overall political regulatory framework remained fundamentally unchallenged. Once, however, under the pressure of its structural crisis, capital could not yield anything of significance to its "rational interlocutor" but, on the contrary, had to take back also its past concessions, ruthlessly attacking the very foundations of the welfare state as well as labor's defensive legal safeguards through a set of "democratically enacted" authoritarian anti-trade-union laws, the established political order had to lose its legitimacy, exposing at the same time the total untenability of labor's defensive posture.

The *crisis of politics* cannot be denied today even by the system's worst apologists. Of course, they try to confine it to the sphere of political manipulation and its unholy consensus, in the spirit of New Labour's "third way." But the crisis of politics represents a profound *crisis of legitimacy* of the established mode of social metabolic reproduction and its overall framework of political control. This is what has brought with it the *historical actuality of the socialist offensive,*[70] even if labor's pursuit of its own "line of least resistance" continues to favor for the time being the maintenance of the existing order, despite its more and more obvious failure to "deliver the goods"—even in the most advanced capitalist countries—as the ground of its once overwhelmingly accepted legitimacy. "New Labour" today, in all of its European varieties, is the facilitator for "delivering the goods" only to the entrenched capital interests, whether in the domain of finance capital—cynically championed by the Blair government even in conflict with some of its European partners—or some industrial and quasi-monopolistic commercial sections of it. At the same time, in order to defend the system under the conditions of capital's narrowing margin of reproductive viability, the concerns of the working class are totally ignored. Thus, capital's vital interests are facilitated by retaining all of the authoritarian anti-labor legislation of the recent past,[71] and by supporting, with the power of the state, capital's push for the massive *casualization* of the labor force, as a cynically deceptive "solution" to the unemployment problem. This is why the need for a socialist offensive cannot be removed from the historical agenda by any given or conceivable variety of labor's defensive accommodation.

It should be of no surprise that under the present conditions of crisis the siren song of Keynesianism is heard again as a wishful remedy, appealing to the spirit of the old "expansionary consensus" in the service of "development." However, today that song can only sound as something very faint, emerging through a long pipe from the bottom of a very deep Keynesian grave. For the type of consensus cultivated by the existing varieties of accommodated labor in reality has to make palatable the *structural failure* of capital's expansion and accumulation, in sharp contrast to the conditions which once enabled Keynesian policies to prevail for a very limited historical period. Luigi Vinci, a prominent figure in the Italian *Rifondazione* movement, rightly stressed that today the proper self-definition and autonomous organizational viability of the radical socialist forces is "often badly hindered by a vague and optimistic left-Keynesianism in which the central position is occupied by the magic word of 'development.'"[72] A notion of "development," which even at the peak of Keynesian expansion, could not bring one inch nearer the socialist alternative. For it has always taken for granted the necessary practical premises of capital as the orienting framework of its own strategy, firmly under the internalized constraints of the "line of least resistance."

It must be also stressed that Keynesianism is by its very nature *conjunctural*. Since it operates within capital's structural parameters, it cannot help being conjunctural, irrespective of whether the prevailing circumstances favor a shorter or a longer conjuncture. Keynesianism, even in its "left-Keynesian" variety, is necessarily situated within, and constrained by, capital's *stop-go logic*. Even at its best,

Keynesianism can represent nothing more than the 'go' phase of an expansionary cycle, which sooner or later must be brought to an end by the 'stop' phase. In its origins Keynesianism tried to offer an alternative to the stop-go logic, by managing both phases in a balanced way. However, it failed to do so, remaining instead tied to the one-sided 'go' phase, due to the very nature of its capitalist state-oriented regulatory framework. The quite unusual length of postwar Keynesian expansion—confined, significantly, to a handful of capitalistically advanced countries—was largely due to the favorable conditions of postwar reconstruction and to the dominant position assumed in it by the overwhelmingly state-financed military-industrial complex. On the other hand, the fact that the corrective 'stop' phase had to acquire the exceptionally harsh and callous form of neoliberalism (and monetarism, as its pseudo-objective ideological rationalization)— already under Harold Wilson's Labour government, whose monetarist financial policy was presided over by Denis Healy, as Chancellor of the Exchequer—was due to the onset of capital's (no longer traditionally cyclic) *structural crisis*, embracing an entire historical epoch. This is what explains the exceptional duration of the neoliberal 'stop' phase, by now much longer than the postwar Keynesian 'go' phase, with no end in sight yet, perpetuated under the watchful eyes of Conservative and Labour governments alike. In other words, both the anti-labor harshness and the frightening duration of the neoliberal stop phase, together with the fact that neoliberalism is practiced by governments which were supposed to be situated on the opposite sides of the parliamentary political divide, are in reality intelligible only as the manifestations of capital's structural crisis. The circumstance that the brutal longevity of the neoliberal phase is ideologically rationalized by some Labourite theoreticians as the "downward long cycle" of normal capitalist development, to be followed for certain by another "expansionary long cycle," only underlines the complete failure of reformist "strategic thinking" to grasp the nature of the ongoing trends of development. All the more so because the savagery of neoliberalism continues its course, quite unchallenged by accommodated labor, and we are now running out of the years predicated even by the fanciful notion of the coming "positive long cycle" as theorized by capital's Labourite apologists.

Thus, given the structural crisis of the capital system, even if a conjunctural shift could bring back for a while an attempt to institute some form of Keynesian state financial management, that could be only for an extremely limited duration, due to the absence of the material conditions which would favor its extension for a longer time even in the dominant capitalist countries. More importantly still, such limited conjunctural revival could offer absolutely nothing for the realization of a radical socialist alternative. For it would be absolutely impossible to build a viable strategic alternative to capital's mode of social metabolic control on an internal conjunctural way of managing the system; a way which needs the healthy expansion and accumulation of capital as the necessary precondition of its own mode of operation.

4.3.3

As we have seen in the last few pages, the sectional limitations and defensiveness of labor could not be overcome through the movement's trade unionist and political centralization. This historical failure is now strongly underlined by capital's transnational globalization to which labor does not seem to have any answer.

It must be recalled here that in the course of the last century and a half no less than *four Internationals* have been founded in an attempt to create the international unity of labor. However, all four of them failed even to approximate their stated objectives, let alone to realize them. This cannot be made intelligible simply in terms of personal betrayals. Even if correct in personal terms, this still begs the question and ignores the weighty objective determinations that must be kept in mind if we want to remedy the situation in the future. It remains to be explained *why* circumstances actually favored such derailments and betrayals over a very long historical period.

The fundamental problem is that the sectional plurality of labor is closely linked to the hierarchically structured conflictual plurality of capitals, both within every particular country and on a global scale. If not for the latter, it would be much easier to envisage the successful constitution of labor's international unity against unified or unifiable capital. However, given the necessarily hierarchical and conflictual articulation of the capital system, with its incorrigibly iniquitous internal and international pecking order, the global unity of capital—to which in principle the corresponding international unity of labor could be unproblematically counterposed—is not feasible. The much deplored historical fact that in major international conflicts the working classes of the various countries sided with their country-wide exploiters, instead of turning their weapons against their own ruling classes, as the socialists invited them to do, finds its material ground of explanation in the contradictory power relationship referred to here, and cannot be reduced to the question of "ideological clarity." By the same token, those who expect a radical change in this respect from the unification of *globalizing capital* and its "*global government*"—which would be combatively confronted by internationally united and fully class conscious labor—are also bound to be disappointed. Capital is not going to oblige and do such a "favor" to labor for the simple reason that it cannot do so.

The hierarchical and conflictual articulation of capital remains the system's overall structuring principle, no matter how large, indeed how gigantic even, its constitutive units might be. This is due to the innermost nature of the system's decision-making processes. Given the irreconcilable structural antagonism between capital and labor, the latter must be categorically excluded from all meaningful decision making. This must be the case not only at the most comprehensive level but even at the constitutive "microcosms," in the particular productive units. For capital, as the alienated power of decision making, cannot possibly function without making its decisions absolutely unquestionable (by the labor force) in the particular workshops, or by the rival production complexes at the intermediary level, in a given country, or even at the most comprehensive scale (by the commanding personnel in charge of other internationally competing units). This is why capital's mode of decision making—in all known and feasible varieties of the capital system—must be a *top-down authoritarian* way of managing the various enterprises. Understandably, all talk about labor "sharing power" with, or "participating" in the decision-making processes of capital belongs to the realm of pure fiction, if not to the cynical camouflage of the real state of affairs.

This structurally determined inability to share power explains why the wide-ranging twentieth century *monopolistic* developments had to assume the form of *takeovers*—"hostile" or "non-hostile" takeovers (ubiquitous today on a mind-boggling scale), but invariably takeovers, with one of the parties involved coming out on top, even when the ideological rationalization of the process is misrepresented as the "happy marriage of equals."

The same inability explains, for our time even more significantly, the important fact that the ongoing globalization of capital produced and continues to produce giant transnational corporations, but not genuine multinationals, despite the much-needed ideological convenience of the latter. No doubt in the future there will be many attempts to rectify this situation through the creation and operation of proper multinational companies. However, the underlying problem is bound to remain even in that circumstance. For the future "shared boardroom arrangements" of genuine multinationals are workable only *in the absence of significant conflicts of interest* among the particular national constituents of the multinationals in question. Once such conflicts arise, the former "harmonious collaborative arrangements" become unsustainable, and the overall decision-making process must revert to the customary authoritarian top-down variety, under the overpowering weight of the strongest member. For this problem is inseparable from the relationship of the particular national capitals to *their own labor force*, which remains always structurally antagonistic and conflictual. Accordingly, in a situation of major conflict no particular national capital can afford—and permit—to become disadvantaged by decisions that would favor a rival national labor force, and by implication its own rival national capital-antagonist.

The wishfully projected "world government" under the rule of capital would become feasible only if a workable solution could be found to this problem. But no government, and least of all a "world government," is feasible without a well-established and efficiently functioning material basis. The idea of a viable world government would imply as its necessary material base the elimination of all significant material antagonisms from the global constitution of the capital system, and thereby the harmonious management of social metabolic reproduction by *one* uncontested global monopoly, embracing *all facets* of societal reproduction with the happy cooperation of the global labor force—a veritable contradiction in terms—or the totally authoritarian and, whenever necessary, extreme violent rule of the whole world by one hegemonic imperialist country on a permanent basis: an equally absurd and unsustainable way of running the world order. Only a genuine socialist mode of social metabolic reproduction can offer a genuine alternative to these nightmare solutions.

Another vital objective determination we have to face, however uncomfortable it might be, concerns the nature of the political sphere

and the parties within it. For the centralization of labor's sectionality—a sectionality which its political parties were expected to remedy—was due to a large extent to the necessary mode of operation of
the political parties themselves, in their unavoidable opposition to
their *political* adversary within the capitalist state representing the
overall political command structure of capital. Thus all of labor's
political parties, including the Leninist party, had to appropriate for
themselves the comprehensive political dimension, so as to be able to
mirror in their own mode of articulation the underlying political
structure (the bureaucratized capitalist state) to which they were
subjected. What was problematical in all of this was that the politically necessary and successful mirroring of the adversary's political
structuring principle could not bring with it the practicable vision of
an *alternative* way of controlling the system. Labor's political parties
could not elaborate a viable alternative because they were centered in
their negating function exclusively on the adversary's *political dimension,* remaining thereby utterly *dependent on the object of their negation.*

The vital missing dimension, which political parties as such cannot supply, was capital not as *political command* (that aspect was
undoubtedly addressed) but as the *social metabolic regulator of the
material reproduction process,* which ultimately determines *also* the
political dimension, but much more than that besides. This unique
correlation in the capital system between the political and the material
reproductive dimension is what explains why we witness periodic
moves, at times of major socioeconomic and political crises, from the
parliamentary democratic articulation of politics to its extreme
authoritarian varieties, when the social metabolic processes in turmoil
require and permit such shifts, and back to the political framework
regulated by the *formal democratic rules of adversariality* in due course,
on capital's newly reconstituted and consolidated social metabolic
ground.

Since capital is *actually* in control of all vital aspects of the social
metabolism, it can afford to define the separately constituted sphere of
political legitimation as a strictly formal matter, thereby *a priori*
excluding the possibility of being legitimately challenged in its *substantive* sphere of socioeconomic reproductive operation. Conforming
to such determinations, labor as the antagonist of actually existing
capital can only condemn itself to permanent impotence. The post-

capitalist historical experience tells a very sad cautionary tale in this respect, regarding its way of misdiagnosing and tackling the fundamental problems of the negated social order.

The capital system is made up from incorrigibly *centrifugal* (conflicting and adversarial) constituents, complemented as their *cohesive* dimension under capitalism not only by the unceremoniously overruling power of the "invisible hand," but also by the legal and political functions of the modern state. The failure of post-capitalist societies was that they tried to counter the centrifugal structuring determination of the inherited system by *superimposing* on its particular adversarial constituents the *extreme centralized command structure* of an authoritarian political state. This they did in place of addressing the crucial problem of how to *remedy*—through internal restructuring and the institution of *substantive democratic control*—the adversarial character and the concomitant centrifugal mode of functioning of the particular reproductive and distributive units. The removal of the private capitalist personifications of capital therefore could not fulfill its role even as the first step on the road of the promised socialist transformation. For the adversarial and centrifugal nature of the negated system was in fact retained through the superimposition of centralized political control at the expense of labor. Indeed, the social metabolic system was rendered more uncontrollable than ever before as a result of the failure to productively replace the "invisible hand" of the old reproductive order by the voluntaristic authoritarianism of the "visible" new personifications of post-capitalist capital.

In contrast to the development of so-called actually existing socialism, what is required as the vital condition of success is the progressive reacquisition of the alienated powers of political—and not only political—decision-making by the individuals in their transition toward a genuine socialist society. Without the reacquisition of these powers neither the new mode of political control of society as a whole by its individuals nor the *non-adversarial,* and thereby *cohesive* and *plannable,* operation of the particular productive and distributive units by their self-managing associated producers is conceivable.

The reconstitution of the unity of the material reproductive and the political sphere is the essential defining characteristic of the socialist mode of social metabolic control. Creating the necessary mediations toward it cannot be left to some faraway future. This is where the defensive articulation and sectional centralization of the socialist movement in the twentieth century demonstrates its veritable historical anachronism and untenability. Confining the comprehensive dimension of the radical hegemonic alternative to capital's mode of social metabolic control to the political sphere can never produce a successful outcome. However, as things stand today, the failure to address the vital social metabolic dimension of the system remains characteristic of labor's organized political embodiments. This is what represents the greatest historical challenge for the future.

4.3.4

The possibility of meeting this challenge by a radically rearticulated socialist movement is indicated by four major considerations.

The first is a negative one. It arises from the constantly aggravated contradictions of the existing order that underline the vacuity of the apologetic projections of its absolute permanence. For destructiveness can be stretched very far, as we know only too well from our constantly worsening conditions of existence. The defenders of the system hail ongoing globalization the solution to the problems. In reality, however, it sets into motion forces that put into relief not only the system's uncontrollability by rational design but also its own inability to fulfill its controlling functions as the condition of its endurance and legitimacy.

The second consideration indicates the possibility—but only the possibility—of a positive turn of events. Nevertheless, this possibility is very real because the capital/labor relation is not a *symmetrical* one. That means in the most important respect that while capital's dependency on labor is *absolute*—in that capital is absolutely nothing without labor, which it must permanently exploit—labor's dependency on capital is *relative, historically created and historically surmountable.* In other words, labor is not condemned to remain permanently locked into capital's vicious circle.

The third consideration is equally important. It concerns a major historical change in the confrontation between capital and labor, bringing with it the necessity to look for a very different way of asserting the vital interests of the "freely associated producers." This is in sharp contrast to the reformist past that had brought the movement to a dead end, liquidating at the same time even the most limited concessions squeezed out of capital in the past. Thus, for the first time in history, maintaining the mystifying gap between *immediate aims* and *overall strategic objectives*—which made the pursuit of the reformist blind alley so dominant in the labor movement—has become quite untenable. As a result, the question of *real control of an alternative social metabolic order* has appeared on the historical agenda, no matter how unfavorable are the conditions of its realization for the time being.

And finally, as the necessary corollary of the last point, the question of *substantive equality* has also surfaced, in contrast to the *formal* equality and the most pronounced *substantive hierarchical inequality* of capital's decision making processes, as well as the way in which they were mirrored and reproduced in the failed post-capitalist historical experience. For the socialist alternative mode of controlling a *non-adversarial* and genuinely *plannable* social metabolic order—an absolute must for the future—is quite inconceivable without substantive equality as its structuring and regulating principle.

4.4 Conclusion

Following in Marx's footsteps, Rosa Luxemburg expressed in a striking way the dilemma we have to face: "Socialism or Barbarism." When Marx first formulated his early version of this idea, he situated it within the ultimate historical horizon of the unfolding contradictions. In his view, these contradictions were bound to confront individuals some time in the indeterminate future with the imperative to make the right choices about the social order to adopt, so as to save their very existence.

By the time Rosa Luxemburg talked about the stark alternative, the second historical phase of imperialism was in full swing, causing a vast destruction that was quite unimaginable at an earlier stage of development. But the timescale of how long the capital system could continue to assert itself in the form of its "productive destruction" and "destructive production" was still indeterminate in Rosa Luxemburg's lifetime. For no single power—not even all of them put together—were capable of destroying humankind at the time with their devastating conflicts.

Today the situation is qualitatively different, and for that reason Rosa Luxemburg's sentence has acquired a dramatic urgency. There are no escape routes for workable conciliatory evasions. Yet, even if it

can be asserted with certainty that the historical phase of global hegemonic imperialism, too, must fail, because it is incapable of resolving
or postponing forever the system's explosive contradictions, this can
promise no solution for the future. Many of the problems we have to
confront—from chronic structural unemployment to the major
international economic, political, and military conflicts indicated
above, as well as to the ever-more widespread ecological destruction
in evidence everywhere—require concerted action in the very near
future. The timescale of such action may be measured perhaps in a
few decades, but certainly not in centuries. We are running out of
time. Thus, only a radical alternative to the established mode of controlling social metabolic reproduction can offer a way out of capital's
structural crisis.

Those who talk about "the third way" as the solution to our dilemma, asserting that there can be no room for the revival of a radical
mass movement, either want to deceive us by cynically calling their
slavish acceptance of the ruling order "the third way," or fail to realize
the gravity of the situation, putting their faith in a wishfully non-con-
flictual positive outcome which has been promised for nearly a century but never approximated even by one inch. The uncomfortable truth
of the matter is that if there is no future for a radical mass movement
in our time, there will be no future for humanity.

If I had to modify Rosa Luxemburg's dramatic words, in relation
to the dangers we now face, I would add to "socialism or barbarism"
this qualification: "barbarism if we are lucky." For the *extermination of
humanity* is the ultimate concomitant of capital's destructive course of
development. And the world of that third possibility, beyond the alternatives of "socialism or barbarism," would be fit only for cockroaches,
which are said to be able to endure lethally high levels of nuclear radiation. This is the only rational meaning of *capital's third way*.

The now fully operative third and potentially deadliest phase of
global hegemonic imperialism, corresponding to the profound structural crisis of the capital system as a whole on the political and military
plane, leaves us no room for comfort or cause for self-assurance.
Instead, it casts the darkest possible shadow on the future, in case the
historical challenges facing the socialist movement fail to be successfully met in the time still within our reach. This is why the century in
front of us is bound to be the century of "Socialism or Barbarism."

Militarism and the Coming Wars
Postscript to *Socialism or Barbarism*[74]

1.

It is not for the first time in history that militarism weighs on the consciousness of the people as a nightmare. To go into detail would take far too long. However, here it should be enough to go back in history only as far as the nineteenth century, when militarism as a major instrument of policymaking came into its own, with the unfolding of modern imperialism on a global scale, in contrast to its earlier—much more limited—varieties. By the last third of the nineteenth century, the British and French were not the only prominent rulers of vast territories. The United States, too, had made a heavy imprint by directly or indirectly taking over the former colonies of the Spanish Empire in Latin America. Also, the United States undertook the bloody repression of a great liberation struggle in the Philippines, installing itself as ruler in that area in a way which still persists in one form or another today. Nor should we forget the calamities caused by "Iron Chancellor" Bismarck's imperialist ambitions and their aggravated pursuit later on by his successors, resulting in the eruption of the First World War and its deeply antagonistic aftermath, bringing with it Hitler's Nazi revanchism and thereby very clearly foreshadowing the Second World War itself.

The dangers and immense suffering caused by attempts to solve deep-seated social problems by militaristic interventions, on any scale, are obvious enough. If, however, we look more closely at the historical trend of militaristic adventures, it becomes frighteningly clear that they show an ever-greater intensification and an ever-increasing scale, from local confrontations to two horrendous world wars in the twentieth century, and to the potential annihilation of humankind in our own time.

It is most relevant to mention in this context the distinguished Prussian military officer and strategist, Karl Marie von Clausewitz (1780–1831), who died in the same year as Hegel; both of them killed by cholera. It was von Clausewitz, Director of the Military School of Berlin in the last thirteen years of his life, who in his posthumously published book—*Vom Kriege* [*On War*], 1833—offered a frequently quoted classic definition of the relationship between politics and war: "war is the continuation of politics by other means."

This famous definition was tenable until quite recently, but has become totally untenable in our time. It assumed the rationality of the actions that connect the two domains of politics and war as the continuation of one another. In this sense, the war in question had to be winnable, at least in principle, even if miscalculations leading to defeat could be contemplated at the instrumental level. Defeat by itself could not destroy the rationality of war as such, since after the—however unfavorable—new consolidation of politics, the defeated party could plan another round of war as the rational continuation of its politics by other means. Thus, the absolute condition of von Clausewitz's equation, to be satisfied, was the winnability of war in principle, so as to recreate the "eternal cycle" of politics leading to war, and back to politics leading to another war, and so on *ad infinitum*. The actors involved in such confrontations were the national states. No matter how monstrous the damage inflicted by them on their adversaries, and even on their own people (just remember Hitler!), the rationality of the military pursuit was guaranteed if the war could be considered winnable in principle.

Today, the situation is qualitatively different—for two principal reasons. First, the objective of the feasible war in the present phase of historical development, in accordance with the objective requirements of imperialism—world domination by capital's most powerful state, in tune with its own political design of ruthless authoritarian "globalization" (dressed up as "free exchange" in a U.S.-ruled global market)— is ultimately unwinnable, foreshadowing, instead, the destruction of humankind. This objective by no stretch of imagination could be considered a rational objective in accord with the stipulated rational requirement of the "continuation of politics by other means" conducted by one nation, or by one group of nations, against another. Aggressively imposing the will of one powerful national state over all of the others—even if for cynical tactical reasons the advocated war is absurdly camouflaged as a "purely limited war" leading to other "open-ended limited wars"—can therefore be qualified only as total irrationality.

The second reason greatly reinforces the first. For the weapons already available for waging the war or wars of the twenty-first century are capable of exterminating not only the adversary but the whole of humanity. Nor should we have any illusion that the existing weaponry marks the very end of the road. Others, even more instant-ly lethal ones, might appear tomorrow or the day after tomorrow. Moreover, threatening the use of such weapons is by now considered an acceptable strategic device of the state. Thus, put reasons one and two together, and the conclusion is inescapable: envisaging war as the mechanism of global government in today's world underlines that we find ourselves at the precipice of absolute irrationality from which there can be no return if we accept the ongoing course of development. What is missing from von Clausewitz's classic definition of war as the "continuation of politics by other means" is the investigation of the deeper underlying causes of war and the possibility of their avoidance. The challenge to face up to such causes is more urgent today than ever before. For the war of the twenty-first century looming ahead of us is not only "not winnable in principle"—worse than that, it is in principle unwinnable. Consequently, envisaging the pursuit of war, as the American administration's September 17, 2002 strategic document does, makes Hitler's irrationality look like the model of rationality.

2.

Since September 11, 2001, Washington has been imposing its aggressive policies on the rest of the world with open cynicism. The justification given for the pretended change of course from "liberal tolerance" to what is now called the "resolute defense of freedom and democracy" is that on September 11, 2001, the United States became the victim of international terrorism: in response to which it is deemed imperative to wage an undefined and indefinable—but in fact arbitrarily defined—"war on terror." The military venture in Afghanistan is admitted to be only the first of an unlimited series of "preventive wars" to be embarked upon in the future, and indeed in the very near future, in Iraq itself, America's long-favored ally, in order to appropriate for the United States the Middle East's vast and strategically crucial oil resources.

However, the chronological order of current American military doctrine is presented completely upside down. In reality, there can be no question of a "change of course" after September 11, 2001, purportedly made possible by the dubious election of George W. Bush to the presidency in place of Al Gore. For President Clinton was pursuing the same kind of policies as his Republican successor, even if in a little more camouflaged form. As for former Democratic Presidential Candidate Al Gore, he declared in December 2002 that he fully supported the war against Iraq, because such a war "would not mean a regime change" but simply the "disarming of a regime which possesses weapons of mass destruction." Can one get more cynical and hypocritical than that?

I have been firmly convinced for a long time that the onset of capital's structural crisis at the end of the 1960s or the beginning of the 1970s marked a qualitatively new phase of imperialism, with the United States as its overwhelmingly dominant force. I called it "the new historic phase of global hegemonic imperialism" in my book *Socialism or Barbarism: From the "American Century" to the Crossroads.*

The critique of U.S. imperialism—in contrast to the fashionable fantasy of "deterritorialized imperialism," which is not supposed to carry with it the military occupation of other nations' territories—constitutes the book's central theme. The chapter entitled "The Potentially Deadliest Phase of Imperialism," was written two years before September 11, 2001, and delivered as a public lecture in Athens, Greece, on October 19, 1999. I strongly stressed that "the ultimate form of threatening the adversary in the future—the new 'gunboat diplomacy'—will be nuclear blackmail." Since the time of publishing these lines, first in March 2000 in a Greek periodical, and then the whole book in Italian in September 2000, the predicted gruesome military strategic shift to the ultimate nuclear threat—which could initiate a military adventure precipitating the destruction of humankind—has become openly professed official U.S. policy. Nor should one imagine that the declaration of such a strategic doctrine is an idle threat against a rhetorical "axis of evil." After all, it was the United States that actually used the atomic weapon of mass destruction against the people of Hiroshima and Nagasaki.

When we consider these extremely grave issues, we cannot be satisfied with any suggestion pointing to a particular and shifting political conjuncture. Rather, we must set them against their background of deep-rooted structural—economically as well as politically necessary—development. This is most important if we want to envisage a viable strategy to counter the forces responsible for our perilous state of affairs. The new historic phase of global hegemonic imperialism is not simply the manifestation of the existing relations of big-power politics, to the overwhelming advantage of the United States, against which a future realignment among the most powerful states, or even some well-organized demonstrations in the political arena, could successfully assert itself. Unfortunately, it is much worse than that. For such eventualities, even if they could come about, would still leave the underlying causes and structural determinations untouched.

To be sure, the new phase of global hegemonic imperialism is preponderantly under the rule of the United States, while the other would-be imperialist powers on the whole seem to accept the role of hanging on to the American coattails, though of course by no means for eternity. One can indeed unhesitatingly envisage, on the basis of the already visible instabilities, the explosion of weighty antagonisms among the major powers in the future. But would that by itself offer any answer to the systemic contradictions at stake, without addressing the causal determinations at the root of imperialistic developments? It would be very naïve to believe that it could.

Here I only wish to underline a central concern, namely that the logic of capital is absolutely inseparable from the imperative of the domination of the weaker by the stronger. Even when one thinks of what is generally considered the most positive constituent of the system, competition resulting in expansion and advancement, its necessary companion is the drive to monopoly and the subjugation or extermination of the competitors who stand in the way of self-asserting monopoly. Imperialism, in turn, is the necessary result of capital's relentless drive to monopoly. The changing phases of imperialism both embody and more or less directly affect the changes of ongoing historical development.

With regard to the present phase of imperialism, two closely connected aspects are of paramount importance. The first is that the ultimate material and economic tendency of capital is for global integration, which, however, it cannot secure at the political level. This is due, to a large extent, to the fact that the global capital system unfolded in the course of history in the form of a multiplicity of divided and indeed antagonistically opposed national states. Not even the most violent imperialist collisions of the past could produce a lasting result in this respect. They could not impose the will of the most powerful national state on a permanent basis on its rivals. The second aspect of our problem, which is the other side of the same coin, is that despite all efforts capital failed to produce *the state* of the capital system as such. This remains the gravest of complications for the future, notwithstanding all the talk about "globalization." U.S.-dominated global hegemonic imperialism is an ultimately doomed attempt to superimpose itself on all of the other, sooner or later recalcitrant, national states as the "international" (global) state of the capital system as such. Here, too, we are confronted by a massive contradiction, for even the recent, most aggressive and openly threatening U.S. strategic documents try to justify their advocated "universally valid" policies in the name of "American national interests."

3.

Here we can see the contradictory relationship between a historical contingency—American capital finding itself in its preponderant position at the present time—and the structural necessity of the capital system itself. The latter can be summed up as capital's irrepressible material drive to monopolistic global integration at whatever cost, even if it means directly endangering the very survival of humanity. Thus, even if one can successfully counter on the political plane the force of the now prevalent American historical contingency—which was preceded by other imperialist configurations in the past and may well be followed by others in the future (if we can survive the present explosive dangers)—the structural or systemic necessity emanating from capital's ultimately global monopolistic logic remains as pressing as ever before. For whatever particular form a future historical contingency may assume, the underlying systemic necessity is bound to remain the drive to global domination.

The issue is, therefore, not simply the given militaristic ventures of some political circles. That is, militaristic ventures that could be tackled and successfully overcome at the political and military level. The causes are much more deep-seated and cannot be countered without introducing quite fundamental changes in the innermost systemic determinations of capital as a mode of social metabolic control—of overall reproduction—which embraces not only the economic, political, and military domains but also the most mediated cultural and ideological interrelations. Even the expression "military-industrial complex"—introduced in a critical sense by President Eisenhower who knew a thing or two about it—clearly indicates that what we are concerned with is something much more firmly grounded and tenacious than some direct political and military determinations (and manipulations) which could be in principle reversed at that level. War as the "continuation of politics by other means" will always threaten us within the present framework of society, with total annihilation. It will threaten us for as long as we are unable to confront the systemic determinations at the root of political decision making, which made necessary in the past the adventure of wars. Such determinations trapped the various national states in a vicious circle of politics leading to wars, and the wars bringing with them intensified antagonistic politics that had to explode in more and ever bigger wars. Take away from the picture, for the sake of argument rather optimistically, the historical contingency of today's American capital, and you are still left with the systemic necessity of capital's ever-more destructive production order, which brings to the fore the changing but increasingly more perilous specific historical contingencies.

Militarist production, today primarily embodied in the "military-industrial complex," is not an independent entity, regulated by autonomous militaristic forces that are then also responsible for wars. Rosa Luxemburg was the first to put these relations in their proper perspective, in 1913, in her classic book *The Accumulation of Capital,* published in English fifty years later. She prophetically underlined ninety years ago the growing importance of militarist production, pointing out that:

> "Capital itself ultimately controls this automatic and rhythmic movement of militarist production through the legislature and a press whose function is to mould so-called 'public opinion.' That is why this particular province of capitalist accumulation seems capable of infinite expansion." [73]

We are, thus, concerned with a set of interdeterminations which must be viewed as parts of an organic system. If we want to fight war as a mechanism of global government, as we must in order to safeguard our very existence, we have to situate the historical changes that have taken place in the last few decades in their proper causal framework. The design of one overpowering national state controlling all of the others, following the imperatives emanating from capital's logic, can only lead to humanity's suicide. At the same time it must be also recognized that the seemingly insoluble contradiction between national aspirations—exploding from time to time in devastating antagonisms—and internationalism can only be resolved if regulated on a fully equitable basis, which is totally inconceivable in capital's hierar-chically structured order.

In conclusion, in order to envisage a historically viable answer to the challenges posed by the present phase of global hegemonic impe-rialism, we must counter the systemic necessity of capital for globally subjugating labor through whichever particular social agency can assume the role assigned to it under the circumstances. Naturally, this is feasible only through a radically different alternative to capital's drive to monopolistic and imperialist globalization, in the spirit of the socialist project, embodied in a progressively unfolding mass move-ment. For only when it becomes an irreversible reality that *patria es humanidad*, to say it with José Marti's beautiful words, only then can the destructive contradiction between material development and humanly rewarding political relations be permanently consigned to the past.

—Rochester, England
December 10, 2002–January 6, 2003

5. Unemployment and "Flexible Casualization"

5.1 The Globalization of Unemployment

Socialists in several European countries—as well as in North and South America—are fighting for the objective of reducing labor-time to thirty-five hours per week without loss of pay. This important strategic demand is by no means free from its difficulties. For it highlights both the pressing problem of unemployment all over the world, and the contradictions of the socioeconomic system which by its own perverse necessity imposes on countless millions the hardship and suffering that goes with unemployment.

Thus the fight for the "35-hour week," if it is to succeed at all, cannot be a traditional trade unionist demand, confined to the long-established machinery of wage negotiations. On the contrary, it has to be fully aware not only of the magnitude of the task and the long-term implications of the issues at stake, but also of the unavoidably tenacious resistance of the socioeconomic order which must follow its own imperatives in order to nullify whatever concession might be made in the legal and political sphere under conditions temporarily favorable to trade unions and to their left-wing political representatives. Understandably, therefore, in Italy for instance, *Rifondazione*, in its way, underlines the concern with increased employment and improved conditions of living (*"per l'occupazione & per migliorare la vita"*) and the necessity of *changing society* (*"per cambiare la società"*) simultaneously in order to secure the envisaged objective of shortened working time on a viable social foundation. For lasting success in this matter is feasible only through a sustained interchange—a dialectical reciprocity—between the fight for the immediate objective of significantly reduced labor-time and the progressive transformation of the established social order which cannot help resisting and nullifying all such demands.

Those who deny the legitimacy of these demands, extolling instead the virtues of their cherished system, continue to idealize the U.S. model for solving the unemployment problem as well as all the social evils inseparable from it. Yet, even a cursory examination of the actual state of affairs reveals the purported success of the U.S. model to belong to the realm of fantasy. For, as an editorial in *The Nation* stressed:

> The poverty rate last year, 13.7 percent, was higher than in 1989, despite seven years of nearly uninterrupted growth. Approximately 50 million Americans—19 percent of the population—live below the national poverty line. Those in poverty include one in four children under the age of 18, one in five senior citizens and three of every five single parent households. In constant dollars, average weekly earnings for workers went from a high of $315 in 1973 down to $256 in 1996, a decline of 19 percent. Last year the poorest fifth of families saw their income decline by $210, while the richest 5 percent gained an average of $6,440 (not counting their capital gains). . . . The number of Americans without health insurance stood at 40.6 million in 1995, an increase of 41 percent since the mid-seventies. In 1995, almost 80 percent of the uninsured were in families where the head of household held a job.[1]

This is how rosy the American model really looks once you are willing to open your eyes. We may also add here a most significant figure supplied recently by the Budget Office of the U.S. Congress, an unobjectionable source even to capital's worst apologists. It tells us that the income of the richest *1 percent* of the population is equivalent to that of the bottom *40 percent.* Even more importantly, it also transpires that this appalling figure has actually *doubled* in the last two decades, as the consequence of capital's *structural crisis.* Thus, no amount of cynical camouflage of the deteriorating conditions of work, no matter how eagerly misrepresented as blessed "flexibility," can hide the serious implications of this trend for the future of capital's expansion and accumulation.

Naturally, unemployment statistics can be fiddled with, or quite arbitrarily defined and redefined, not only in America but also in every single country of so-called advanced capitalism. In Britain, for instance, even the professional apologists of the capital system—the editors of *The Economist*—had to admit that the unemployment figures have been "revised" thirty-three times by the government in order to make them look better. Not to mention the fact that anybody who works for sixteen hours per week in Britain is counted as enjoying *full-time employment*. And even more strikingly in Japan—a country until recently hailed as a paradigm case of "dynamic advanced capitalism"—"anybody who works for wages for over *one hour* in the *last week* of the month is not included in the unemployment statistics."[2] Ultimately, such devices of economic and political manipulation fool no one. For no matter how concerted and devious the misrepresentation of the existing state of affairs, the potentially very grave challenge of unemployment cannot be avoided in even the most advanced capitalist countries. Thus, whatever the apologetic statistical figures might suggest, it is now no longer possible to conceal alarm about the constantly rising record of unemployment in Japan and the deepening economic recession that goes with it.

In reality, the dramatic rise in unemployment in the advanced capitalist countries is not a recent phenomenon. It appeared on the horizon—after two-and-a-half decades of relatively undisturbed postwar capital-expansion—with the onset of the *structural crisis of the capital system* as a whole. It appeared as the necessary and ever-worsening feature of this structural crisis. Accordingly, I argued way back in 1971 that under the unfolding conditions of unemployment:

> . . . the problem is no longer just the plight of unskilled laborers but also that of large numbers of *highly skilled* workers who are now chasing, in addition to the earlier pool of unemployed, the depressingly few available jobs. Also, the trend of 'rationalizing' amputation is no longer confined to the 'peripheral branches of ageing industry' but embraces some of the *most developed* and modernized sectors of production—from ship-building and aviation to electronics, and from engineering to space technology. Thus we are no longer concerned with the 'normal,' and willingly accepted, by-products of 'growth and development,' but with their driving to a halt; nor indeed with the peripheral problems of 'pockets of underdevelopment' but with a fundamental contradiction of the capitalist mode of production as a whole which turns even the latest achievements of 'development,' 'rationalization' and 'modernization' into paralyzing burdens of chronic underdevelopment. And

most important of it all, the human agency which finds itself at the receiving end is no longer the socially powerless, apathetic and fragmented multitude of 'underprivileged' people but *all* categories of skilled and unskilled labor: i.e., objectively the *total labor force* of society. [3]

Since the time when these lines were written we have witnessed a striking increase in unemployment in Britain and elsewhere. As things stand today, even according to the "official" figures, there are more than *forty million* unemployed in the industrially most developed countries. Of this figure, Europe accounts for more than *twenty million*, and Germany—once eulogized for producing the "German miracle"—has passed the *five million* mark. As I have stressed before, India—a country highly praised in the traditional organs of economic wisdom for its achievement as a healthily developing country—has no less than *336 million* people on its unemployment register,[4] and many more millions without proper work who should be counted but are not registered. Moreover, International Monetary Fund (IMF) intervention in "developing" countries, true to the organization's U.S.-dictated mandate, worsens the plight of the unemployed while pretending to improve the economic conditions of the countries concerned. As an editorial in *The Nation* put it:

> Mexico's economy may appear to be great, but its people are hurting. Since the IMF bailout, the middle class has been crushed; 25,000 small businesses have gone belly up; two million workers have lost their jobs over the same time. In dollar terms, wages have plummeted 40 percent. The IMF had to destroy the domestic economy in order to save it.[5]

At the same time, the former post-capitalist countries belonging to the Soviet-type system, from Russia to Hungary—which in the past did not suffer unemployment, though they had run their economies with high levels of underemployment—had to accommodate themselves, often under direct IMF pressure, to the dehumanizing conditions of massive unemployment. Hungary, for instance, has been congratulated by the IMF[6] for "stabilizing" unemployment at about 500,000. In reality the figure is considerably higher, and still increasing. But even 500,000, in terms of the relatively small Hungarian population, represents a much higher level of unemployment than what happens to be the case all over Western Europe. In the Russian Federation the situation is just as bad, and getting worse all the time, including such out-rages as not paying the wages of miners and other workers for many months. Vietnam presents a particularly tragic example, for after the heroic victory of its people over the long and devastating intervention-ist war of U.S. imperialism, the peace is being lost under the pressure of capitalist restoration.[7] And even China is no exception to the gener-al rule of rising unemployment, despite the very special way in which its economy is politically controlled. A confidential but leaked report prepared by its Ministry of Labor warns the Chinese government that within a few years unemployment in the country is bound to reach the staggering figure of *268 million*—pointing also to the danger of major social explosions to go with it—unless appropriate (but not specified) measures are adopted to counter the present trend.[8]

We have reached a point in our historical development in which unemployment is a dominant feature of the capital system as a whole. In its new modality, it constitutes a close network of interrelations and interdeterminations. As a result of this, it is now impossible to find partial remedies and solutions to the unemployment problem in lim-ited areas, in sharp contrast to the postwar decades of development in a few privileged countries where liberal politicians could speak about *Full Employment in a Free Society.*[9]

In recent years there has been a great deal of talk extolling the uni-versally beneficial virtues of "globalization," which misrepresents the trend of capital's global expansion and integration as a radically new phenomenon destined to resolve all our problems. The great irony of the real trend of development—inherent in capital's logic from the first constitution of its system centuries ago, reaching its maturity in our own time in a form inextricably tied up with the system's structur-al crisis—is that the productive advancement of this antagonistic mode of controlling the social metabolism throws an ever-increasing portion of humanity into the category of *superfluous labor.* Already in 1848, in the *Communist Manifesto,* Marx insisted that:

> In order to oppress a class, certain conditions must be assured to it under which it can, at least, continue its slavish existence. . . . [But] the bourgeoisie is unfit any longer to be the ruling class in society, and to impose its condi-tions of existence upon society as an overriding law. It is unfit to rule because it is incompetent to assure an existence to its slave within his slavery, because it cannot help letting him sink into such a state, that it has to feed him, instead of being fed by him.[10]

Ironically, the development of by far the most dynamic productive system in history culminates by rendering an ever-growing number of
human beings superfluous to its machinery of *production,* although—
true to the system's incorrigibly contradictory character—far from
superfluous as *consumers.* The historical novelty of the type of unemployment in the globally completed system is that the contradictions
of any specific part complicates and aggravates the problem in other
parts and, consequently, in the whole. For the need for unemploy-
ment-producing "downsizing," etc., necessarily arises from the antagonistic profit- and accumulation-seeking productive imperatives of
capital which it cannot conceivably renounce, so as to restrain itself in
accordance with rational and humanly gratifying principles. Capital
either maintains its inexorable drive toward its self-expansionary targets, no matter how devastating the consequences, or it ceases to be
capable of controlling the social metabolism of reproduction. There
can be no halfway house or even the slightest attention paid to human
considerations. This is why, for the first time ever in history, a dynamic—and in its ultimate implications dynamically destructive—system
of self-expansionary social metabolic control arises that ruthlessly
ejects, if necessary, the overwhelming majority of humankind from
the labor process. This is the deeply disturbing meaning of "globalization" today.

When capital reaches this stage of development, it has no way of
addressing the *causes* of its structural crisis; it can only fiddle with
effects and surface manifestations. Accordingly, since capital "cannot
feed its slave any longer," the "personifications" of its system (to use
Marx's expression) try to resolve the problem by rolling back even the
limited benefits conceded to labor in the form of the "welfare state,"
during the postwar period of undisturbed capital-expansion. Thus in
the United States, the unemployed are compelled to submit to the dictates of *"work-fare,"* if they want to receive any social benefits. And true
to form, in Britain the same shift is being attempted, *from "welfare" to
"work-fare,"* by the government of a party which once considered itself
socialist. Accordingly, when an eight-column headline of a British liberal newspaper (which happens to be very friendly to the government
of "New Labour") announces "Jobless told: join Army or lose benefit"
that headline gives a foretaste of the measures in store for unemployed
youth.[11] This, again, underlines the fact that the now fully accomplished globalization of unemployment and casualization cannot be

redressed without the radical supersession of the capital system itself. Not so many years ago it was confidently anticipated that all known social evils, even in the most "underdeveloped" parts of the world, would be overcome by universal "modernization," in conformity with the U.S. model. Characteristically, however, we are now confronted by the diametrical opposite of the projected rosy picture. For the conditions once confined, in the tales of "development theory" and governmental wisdom, to the allegedly temporary difficulties of "underdevelopment" are now becoming clearly visible even in the most developed capitalist countries.

5.2 The Myth of "Flexibility" and the Reality of Precarization

On May 19, 1998 the French Parliament passed a law reducing the working week to thirty-five hours. Similar legislation has been instituted also in Italy. It would be very naïve, however, to think that this is the end of the story. For in Paris the move was immediately "described by many economists and business leaders as *economic suicide*,"[12] In Italy, even before any legislative move the leader of the Confederation of Italian Industry *(Confindustria)*, Giorgio Fossa made absolutely clear the intention of his organization to nullify all such legislation.[13] Moreover, Confindustria President Fossa (whose name in Italian means, most appropriately, "grave") also unashamedly declared (as if it should not be obvious to everyone who knows his organization) that they intend to bury the law, if enacted in Parliament, with the help of a "grand coalition" which would include the supporters of even the extreme right-wing parties.[14] And with customary cynicism, the London *Economist* pontificated:

> So who really wants Lionel Jospin's 35-hour working week? Certainly not France's employers, who claim it will increase labor costs and reduce their competitiveness. Nor the taxpayer, who suspects he will have to pay higher taxes to finance the scheme. Nor, increasingly, the unions, who fear it will lead to lower wages and fewer workers' rights. Nor even the workers, most of whom expect to continue working as much as before, but with more awkward shifts and unsocial hours. Even the unemployed, the scheme's supposed beneficiaries, are wondering how many jobs, if any, it will actually create. . . . Mr Jospin finds himself saddled with a scheme not even he—it is whispered—believes in.[15]

Naturally, there are serious difficulties that must be faced by the labor movement in its struggle for a real reduction in the working week without loss of pay. But they are of a very different order as compared with the frightening tales devised by *The Economist* and by other spokesmen of the ruling order. The real obstacles confronting labor in the present and in the near future can be summed up with two words: *"flexibility"* and *"deregulation."* These are two of the most cherished slogans of capital's personifications in business as well as in politics today. They are meant to sound very attractive and progressive. In truth though, they encapsulate the most aggressive anti-labor aspirations and policies of neoliberalism, claimed to be as commendable to every rational being as motherhood and apple pie. For "flexibility" with regard to labor practices—to be facilitated and enforced through various kinds of "deregulation"—amounts in reality to the ruthless *casualization* of the labor force. It is often coupled with authoritarian anti-labor legislation—from Reagan's suppression of the U.S. air controllers to Margaret Thatcher's long series of vicious anti-labor laws— retained by Tony Blair's "New Labour" government. And the same people who call the diffusion of the most precarious labor conditions of casualization universally beneficial *"flexibility"* also have the nerve to call the practice of authoritarian anti-labor legislation *"democracy."*

Flexibility is expected to take care of the concession of thirty-five hours, if for the sake of political contingency it becomes unavoidable, as seems to be the case in France and Italy. Thus, in France "some ministers talk of making the labor market *more flexible*, notably by letting employers vary the working week in accordance with seasonal demand, so that the number of hours worked weekly would be calculated as an average over the year."[16] The same ploy is expected to do the trick in Italy. At the time of its introduction, Italy's Prime Minister Romano Prodi—later rewarded with the Presidency of the European Commission—reassured his critics that appropriate flexibility should be able to counter the negative effects of the law.

The real concern of the personifications of capital is to promote "labor flexibility" and to fight in every possible way against "rigid labor markets." Thus a prominent article in *The Financial Times* insists that "In both Japan and Europe, companies are gearing up to shed jobs faster than rigid labor markets can create them," indicating approvingly that *"deregulation* may force the pace" and adding for the sake of propagandistic reassurance that "optimists believe deregulation will eventually lead to the creation of sufficient jobs in new markets to absorb much of the excess labor. But for this to happen, Japan will need the kind of *labor mobility* that operates in the United States."[17] (The story of Renault's takeover of Nissan, bringing with it the sacking of 30,000 Nissan workers, must please the advocates of such remedies, in that it shows that Japan is moving in the "right direction.") Similarly, an IMF staff paper—enthusiastically reviewed by *The Economist*—asserts: "Studies suggest that in Europe real wages are only *half as flexible* as those in America, and that Europe's workers are much less likely to *move around* in search of work than American ones." They say this while blissfully forgetful of John Kenneth Galbraith's complaint many years earlier that workers in the United States can only blame themselves for their unemployment because they refuse to move around as a result of their "homing instinct," which ties them to the place of their upbringing. Nothing seems to change over decades either in diagnosis or in remedial wisdom.

The authors of this IMF staff paper display an automatic Pavlovian reflex in the form of neoliberal capital's wishful "should be" projections:

> Suppose, for instance, that a government cuts unemployment benefits. Workers now have a sharper incentive to seek work and so unemployment *should* fall. An increase in the number of job-seekers will also put downward pressure on wages. Lower wage costs *should*, in turn, boost employment.[18]

Naturally, as a result of this wonderful shrinking of the wage bill, we shall live happily ever after. And on the other hand, if—despite the very real sacrifices of the workers—the fictitious expectations of "should be" do not materialize, that could in no way invalidate the shared theory of the IMF and *The Economist*. It would only reveal that the proverbial pigs of the well-known English adage stubbornly refuse to grow wings, to look like giant bumblebees, in order to fly toward capital's wishfully projected optimistic future.

In the meantime, the real savagery of the system continues unabated, not only in ejecting more and more people from the labor process but, with a characteristic contradiction, also *lengthening* the time of work, wherever capital can get away with it. To mention a very important example, in Japan the government has introduced a parliamentary bill "to raise the upper limits of the working day, from *9 hours to 10*, and the work week, from *48 to 52 hours*. Such a provision will allow a company to compel employees to work longer hours when the company is busy as long as the total hours worked in a year do not exceed the fixed limit."[19] Moreover, the same bill also intends to extend so-called *"discretionary work schedules"* in order to "allow a company to *pay its white-collar workers for just eight-hours* work even though they may have worked longer."[20] Some frightening examples of the inhuman destructive effects of such "discretionary work" are reported from the fields where they are already operative, now to be extended. For instance a young computer programmer died of heavy overwork, according to the judgment of the Tokyo District Court. We read that "his average annual working time was over 3,000 hours. In the three months just before his death, he worked 300 hours a month. At that time he was engaged in developing a computer software system for banks."[21] Another young man who died of heart failure due to gross overwork, "in the two weeks prior to his death worked on average *16 hours and 19 minutes* a day."[22] In the words of another Japanese journal even today:

> . . . employers impose strict quotas on workers, which means long working hours and unpaid work put upon the shoulders of the workers. . . . A train conductor, for example, working for East Japan Railways Co., Japan's biggest railroad company, actually performed his duties for 14 hours and 5 minutes while he was kept in the workplace for 24 hours and 13 minutes, and the company did not pay him for the rest of the 10 hours and 8 minutes, saying that these hours are 'neither working hours nor rest periods.'[23]

Significantly, in the age of capital's structural crisis even this level of exploitation is not enough. It must be extended as far as the labor movement can put up with. In Japan, a present bill before parliament "is the *biggest attack in the postwar period against workers' rights*."[24] No wonder that some Japanese trade unions are envisaging for themselves a much more directly political role in the future, compared to their traditional line in the past. To quote Kanemichi Kumagai, secretary general of the Japanese National Confederation of Trade Unions: "This year's spring struggle will not just follow what has been done in the past but will aim to *change the trends of politics* and the labor movement, including how Japan's policies and economy should be. For this we attach greater importance to achieving *workers and trade unions taking actions* to have influence over society."[25]

Japan is a particularly important example, because we are not talking about a so-called Third World country about which even the most callous and ruthlessly exploitative labor practices were always taken for granted as a matter of course. On the contrary, Japan represents the second-most powerful economy in the world: a paradigm of capitalistic advancements. And now, even in such a country unemployment is perilously rising and the conditions of work must be made worse than ever under the long period of capital's postwar development and expansion, including not only the great intensification of exploitative work schedules in the name of "flexibility," but also the—to many people quite incomprehensible—imperative of a longer working week.

At the roots of this baffling and in some ways self-contradictory advocacy of "flexibility," coupled with *rigid authoritarian* labor legislation, we find the vitally important tendential law of the *downward equalization of the differential rate of exploitation,* which becomes sharply pronounced through capital's ever more destructive globalization in the period of the system's structural crisis. This is why I wrote in 1971 that:

> The working classes of some of the most developed 'post-industrial' societies are getting a foretaste of the real viciousness of 'liberal' capital. . . . Thus, the real nature of the capitalist production relations: the ruthless domination of labor by capital is becoming increasingly more evident as a *global* phenomenon. . . . The understanding of the development and self-reproduction of capital's mode of production is quite impossible without the concept of *total* social capital . . . Similarly, it is quite impossible to understand the manifold and thorny problems of nationally varying as well as socially stratified labor without constantly keeping in mind the necessary framework of a proper assessment, namely the irreconcilable antagonism between *total* social capital and the *totality* of labor.
>
> This fundamental antagonism is inevitably modified in accordance with: (1) the local socioeconomic circumstances; (2) the respective positions of particular countries in the global framework of capital production; and (3) the relative maturity of the global sociohistorical development. Accordingly, at different periods of time the system as a whole reveals the workings of a complex set of objective differences of interest on *both* sides of the social antagonism. The objective reality of *different rates of exploitation*— both within a given country and in the world system of capital—is as unquestionable as are the objective differences in the *rates of profit* at any par-

ticular time . . . All the same, the reality of the different rates of exploitation and profit does not alter the fundamental law itself: i.e., the *growing equalization of the differential rates of exploitation* as the *global trend* of development of world capital.

To be sure, this law of equalization is a long-term trend as far as the global system of capital is concerned. . . . Let it now suffice to stress that 'total social capital' should not be confused with 'total national capital.' When the latter is being affected by a relative weakening of its position within the global system, it will inevitably try to compensate for its losses by increasing its specific rate of exploitation over against the labor force under its direct control—or else its competitive position is further weakened within the global framework of 'total social capital.' . . . There can be no way out, other than the intensification of the specific rates of exploitation, which can only lead, both locally and in global terms, to an explosive intensification of the fundamental social antagonism in the long run. Those who have been talking about the 'integration' of the working class—depicting 'organized capitalism' as a system which succeeded in radically mastering its social contradictions—have hopelessly misidentified the manipulative success of the differential rates of exploitation (which prevailed in the relatively 'disturbance-free' historic phase of postwar reconstruction and expansion) as a basic *structural remedy*.[26]

As a necessary concomitant of the ongoing globalization of productive and distributive relations, the downward equalization of the differential rate of exploitation affects every single advanced capitalist country, even the richest ones. There can be no more room for paternalistically manipulated labor relations, however "traditional" and "deeply rooted" they are supposed to be, nor indeed for permanently avoiding the severe negative impact of the ubiquitous structural crisis through relative trade and technological advantages. (Remember *The Nation*'s revealing figures quoted above.) Indeed, as an appeal by some distinguished intellectuals in an Italian newspaper stressed, what makes the situation grave is that casualization and insecurity ("*la precarietà e l'insicurezza*") are growing everywhere in the world of labor: "unsafeguarded and underpaid work is spreading like pools of oil, while even the most stable work undergoes a pressure toward an intensification without precedent of its performance, and toward full availability to a submission to the most diversified working hours."[27]

To put it in another way, here we have to face an extremely significant and far-reaching tendency: the return of *absolute surplus-value*, to an increasing extent, in the societies of advanced capitalism in the last few decades. Professor Augusto Graziani spoke most eloquently in February 1998, at the *Convegno of Rifondazione* in Milan dedicated to the issue of the 35-hour week, about the labor conditions of the *Mezzogiorno* in general and about the frightful exploitation of female labor in Calabria in particular. His intervention is most relevant to the question of "absolute surplus-value" in an advanced capitalist country, like Italy, in that some of the highly exploitative labor practices can be identified also in the industrially most developed North of the country. In England, at the same time, a TV documentary illustrated the widespread diffusion of child labor, although it is clearly against the law. Naturally, the law is not in the least enforced. On the contrary, all kinds of phony arguments are promoted in order to indirectly justify such unlawful practices. Thus, business interests conduct a vociferous campaign against the minimum wage in general, with the excuse that its introduction would make the unemployment of young people much worse. Another way of manipulating the same issue—as is done by the Confederation of British Industry, the Institute of Directors, and various "think-tank" organizations of business—is to press for the "exemption of the young" from the minimum-wage legislation, or the concession of much lower minimum wage only. Moreover, the worsening labor conditions of people of all ages in countless "sweatshops"—legal or illegal immigrants as well as a far from negligible portion of the English, Scottish, Welsh and Irish labor force—speak loudly enough about the reappearance of the drive for absolute surplus-value, as a most retrograde tendency in the twentieth century development of capital, in one of the most privileged of the advanced capitalist countries. Needless to say, both the ruthless pursuit of absolute surplus-value in general and its particularly obnoxious manifestation in the form of child labor were *always prominent* (and, of course, so they remain today) in Third World countries.

Paradoxically, the global crisis of capital-accumulation in the age of advanced globalization creates some major new difficulties, instead of solving the long-contested iniquities of the system, as the "optimistic" spokesmen of globalization want us to believe. For the *margins* of capital's productive viability are diminishing (hence the drive also for absolute surplus-value), despite all efforts of the capitalist states—individually or in concert, like the G7/G8 jamborees—to expand, or to keep steady at least, the system's productive margins. In actuality, there can be only one way for attempting to enlarge the *shrinking margins of*

capital-accumulation: at the expense of *labor.* This is a strategy actively promoted by the state—indeed, because of this need, *the interventionist role of the state has never been greater*[28] than in our own time,
despite all neoliberal mythology to the contrary—and the strategy is
objectively underpinned in our time by the tendency for the downward equalization of the differential rate of exploitation. In the end,
however, the strategy is bound to fail, provided that the labor movement succeeds in radically rearticulating its own strategies and forms
of organization, to be oriented toward the creation of a genuine mass
movement, in order to face up to the historical challenge. For not even
the most optimistic theorists of the IMF and of the other generously
funded organs of capital-apologetics have managed to invent so far,
nor are they likely to do so in the future, a device through which it
would be possible to squeeze out the required ever-increasing purchasing power and the corresponding capital-accumulation from the
ever-worsening economic conditions and "casualized wage packets" of
the labor force.

5.3 From the Tyranny of "Necessary Labor Time" to Emancipation Through "Disposable Time"

How can labor—the structural antagonist of capital—counter the
deteriorating trend inseparable from the narrowing margin of capital's
productive viability?

This question takes us back to the third element of *Rifondazione*'s
quest for securing the 35-hour week quoted at the beginning of this
chapter: "changing society" *("per cambiare la società").* For today—
because of capital's need to unceremoniously roll back even its past
concessions[29]—it is quite impossible to realize even the most immediate and limited objectives of traditional trade unionism without
embarking on the road that leads to a fundamental social transformation. The radical reconstitution of the socialist movement is a
vitally important part of this process.[30]

Some of capital's more intelligent representatives, like Dean
Witter—the chief economist and director of global economics for
Morgan Stanley—are willing to confess that the ongoing trends are
much more problematic than usually depicted in the propaganda
organs of neoliberalism. In an article published in the *Sunday New
York Times,* entitled "The Worker Backlash," he rejects the explanation

that recent successes were the result of "deregulation and increasing productivity." His own, far more conflict-conscious and less reassuring explanation is that there has been:

> . . . a dramatic realignment of the nation's economic pie, with a much larger slice going to capital and a smaller one going to labor. Call it a labor-crunch recovery, one that flourished only because corporate America puts unrelenting pressure on its workforce.[31]

In truth, not only does corporate America put unrelenting pressure on its workforce but so too do the personifications of capital *everywhere*. For the reformist achievements of the past were premised on the continuing *growth of the pie*—which appeared under favorable economic conditions as capital's concessions, although there could *never* be a question of realigning the pie in favor of labor, since capital must always appropriate the lion's share for itself. Now, due to capital's structural crisis and to the narrowing margin of the system's productive viability, it becomes absolutely necessary to *realign the nation's economic pie* more than ever in capital's favor, so as to secure a *labor-crunch recovery*, thanks to the passivity and resignation of the labor force. But what happens when labor refuses to go along with such a ruthless realignment of the economic pie, because it can no longer afford to do so, as a result of the increasing hardship imposed by the traditional or newly invented forms of labor-crunch economy? The possibilities of realigning even a stationary pie, let alone a shrinking one, have well-definable limits. Not to mention the fact that the resignatory inactivity of the labor movement cannot be simply taken for granted forever in any country, as a matter of natural necessity. Not even in the most advanced capitalist ones. No wonder, therefore, that today even the chief economist of Morgan Stanley has to speak about "The Worker Backlash" in the United States, voicing his worries about a possible "raw power struggle between capital and labor," and adding that "gone are the days of a docile labor force that once acquiesced to slash-and-burn corporate restructuring."[32]

Naturally, from capital's standpoint there can be no answers to the question: what kind of alternative to the labor-crunch economy should be pursued in order to avoid the raw power struggle between capital and labor. Whatever his misgivings and worries might be, the chief economist of Morgan Stanley must continue to advise his firm about the best ways of exploiting the opportunities of global financial speculation, or else he will be quickly dispatched to more restful pastures with a forceful golden handshake. From the standpoint of capital there can be truly "no alternative" to crunching labor as much as possible—and more so in situations of emergency—even if one perceives some of the dangers implicit in the pursued socioeconomic course. For in the end there is always the lure of authoritarian solutions, not only in the U.S. client country of General Suharto, but also in the "advanced capitalist democracies" of the West which helped to put Suharto in power in the first place, supporting him in every possible way for thirty-two years, including his savage military repression of the people, and trying to save his wretched regime with massive IMF funds even in the last minute before his demise.

The general promise of solving the crying iniquities and contradictions of the system has been for a long time—and on the whole remains today—that through the benefits of ever-increasing and globally integrated "free trade" the condition of workers will greatly improve all over the world, thanks to the return of the economy to a situation of undisturbed capital-expansion, free from the defects of the postwar decades which ended in inflation and stagnation. The actual signs and economic indicators, however, point in the opposite direction, a fact at times acknowledged even by "mainstream" economists who retain their belief in the insuperable virtues of the capital system. Thus, to quote a review of a recent book by such an economist:

> [Dani] Rodrick argues [in *Has Globalizaion Gone Too Far?*] that trade in general, not just low-wage imports, worsens income distribution. Increased international competition, he writes, translates into greater 'elasticity' of the domestic demand for labor. In lay terms, this means that a worker is now competing with a much larger labor supply. As a result, a small shift in foreign workers' wages or in the global demand for a product or service can cause big shifts in the domestic demand for workers. Labor's greater vulnerability to market fluctuations undercuts its bargaining position vis-à-vis capital. Therefore, concludes Rodrik, 'The first-order effect of trade appears to have been a redistribution of the enterprise surplus toward employers rather than the enlargement of the surplus.' The evidence, therefore, tells us that the critics of free trade have been right; trade is not enlarging wealth, but redistributing it upward. [33]

And yet, when it comes to the question of alternatives, we get from Rodrick only pious preaching. Thus, to continue our quote:

> Rodrick's politics are at best naïve. He lectures labor and government to be more responsible, but has nothing to say to multinational corporate business. . . . Rodrick writes, 'Labor should advocate a global economy that carries a more human face,' but he is silent about the fiercely organized efforts of multinational business and finance to prevent humane policies from even being considered by the International Monetary Fund, the World Bank, the World Trade Organization, and other rule-setters for the global marketplace. This suggests a point of view that is, to put it mildly, out of touch with the realities of the global political economy.[34]

Indeed, adopting the standpoint of capital—not only in its blindly uncritical and most aggressive neoliberal form, but also in its wishfully liberal reformist varieties—has meant for a very long time "losing touch with the realities of the global political economy."

The radical novelty of our time is that the capital system is no longer in a position of conceding to labor anything whatsoever, in contrast to the reformist acquisitions of the past. The depressing accommodation, and even wholesale capitulation, of some former working-class parties to the demands of big business interests—for instance in Britain and in several European countries, but by no means in Europe alone—to the extent of not only retaining the authoritarian anti-labor legislation of the last few decades but also giving key cabinet posts in Britain's "New Labour," in the Italian "Democratic Left" governments and elsewhere to prominent representatives of corporate capital, speak unequivocally on this score. (Lord Simon, Lord Sainsbury, Geoffrey Robinson, etc. in Britain, and similar figures in Germany, France and Italy.) This is why in the present historical period even the *limited* and modest objectives of labor—like the 35-hour week—can only be realized by "changing society," since *objectively* they contest the established socioeconomic and political order (in other words: the whole system of decision making) under which "the nation's economic pie" is produced and distributed.

Under the conditions of capital's structural crisis this is the objectively unavoidable nature of the socioeconomic contestation, even if for the time being many representatives of labor do not conceptualize or articulate it in such terms. And this is also the reason why liberal and social-democratic reformism, which once upon a time had a powerful ally in capital's expansionary dynamism, is now condemned to the futility of pious preaching—from Professor John Kenneth Galbraith's sermons about "The Culture of Contentment" (quickly echoed, without the slightest remedial effect, by Bishops and Archbishops in the Church of England) to the notion of a "labor and government-inspired global economy with a human face" quoted above. A preaching to which the personifications of capital cannot possibly listen.

The demand for a significant reduction of the working week has a fundamental strategic importance. Not only because the underlying issue profoundly affects and therefore directly concerns every single worker, manual and intellectual alike, whatever might be the color of their collars. Equally, because the issue of facing up to this challenge is not going to fade away. On the contrary, it is growing in importance with the passing of every day, and the imperative to do something meaningful about it cannot be legislated out of existence by capital's parliamentary personifications in the advanced capitalist countries, nor indeed repressed by naked force on the periphery of capital's global order. In other words, this is a vital strategic demand for labor because it is non-negotiable: i.e., it cannot be integrated into the manipulated pseudo-concessions of the existing order. For it directly concerns the question of *control*—an *alternative system of social metabolic control*—to which capital is and must be inimically opposed.

Naturally, the 35-hour week—even if it could be genuinely conceded and not deviously nullified in many different ways, as it is cynically planned already—could not resolve the monumental and grave unemployment problem. Thus the question that legitimately arises: why thirty-five and not twenty-five or twenty hours per week? That is the question that takes us to the heart of the matter.

The radical incompatibility between the existing social order and one in which human beings are in control of their life-activity, including their "free time," liberated by a significant reduction of the working week, was graphically and painfully illustrated in Britain through the destruction of the mining industry. In 1984 the British coal miners waged a heroic struggle, not for money but in defense of their jobs: a one-year-long strike that was defeated through the combined efforts of the government of Mrs. Thatcher—who called the miners "the enemy within"—and Neal Kinnock's Labour Party which stabbed them in the back. As a result, the miners' workforce, at the time over 150,000, has been decimated to the present figure of less than 10,000, and the towns and villages of many mining communities have been turned into the wasteland of dehumanized unemployment. At the time of the miners' strike the coal mines were still "nationalized," which meant being run with the most ruthless capitalist criteria of "efficiency" and authoritarian control by the National Coal Board, becoming subsequently "privatized" in a fraction of their original size. What was highly characteristic of the Coal Board's way of dealing with the problem of "greater efficiency," while talking about the absolute need for "rationalizing" the work requirements of the coal industry, was the fact that the state-run Board imposed on the miners an almost insane *seven-day work schedule* at the same time when it was savagely cutting the labor force under its control. For capital is quite incapable of human considerations. It knows only one way of managing work-time: *maximally exploiting the "necessary labor-time" of the workforce in employment,* totally ignoring the available *"disposable time"* in society at large, because it cannot squeeze profit out of it.

This is what sets insurmountable limits to capital in its way of addressing the unemployment problem. There is something rather paradoxical, indeed profoundly contradictory about this. For capital's productive system *de facto* creates "superfluous time" in society as a whole, on an ever-increasing scale. Yet it cannot conceivably acknowledge the *de jure* existence (i.e., the legitimacy) of such socially produced surplus-time as the potentially most creative *disposable time* we all have, which could be used in our society for the satisfaction of so much of the now cruelly denied human needs—from education and health service requirements to the elimination of famine and malnutrition all over the world. On the contrary, capital must assume a *negative, destructive, and dehumanizing* attitude towards it. Indeed, capital must callously disregard the fact that the concept of "superfluous labor," with its "superfluous time," in reality refers to *living human beings* and possessors of *socially* useful—even if *capitalistically* redundant or inapplicable—productive capacities.

The concept of disposable time, taken in its positive and liberating sense, as an aspiration of socialists, appeared well before Marx, in an anonymous pamphlet entitled *The Source and Remedy of the National Difficulties,* published in London almost fifty years before Marx's *Capital,* in 1821. In some passages, quoted by Marx, this pamphlet offered a remarkable dialectical grasp of both the nature of the capitalist productive process and—by focusing attention on the vitally important categories of "disposable time," "surplus-labor," and the "shortened working day"—the possibilities of escaping from its contradictions. To quote:

> Wealth is disposable time and nothing more. . . . If the whole labor of a country were sufficient only to raise the support of the whole population, there would be no surplus-labor, consequently nothing that can be allowed to accumulate as capital. . . . Truly wealthy a nation, if there is no interest or if the working day is six hours rather than twelve.[35]

We are slowly catching up with the demand, advanced by our ancestors in 1821, for the six-hour working day, but we are still very far from organizing society on the basis of the immeasurably greater wealth-producing potential of disposable time. Without the latter, there can be no question of emancipating the working individuals from the tyranny of fetishistic determinations and crying iniquities. The realization of even our limited objectives will require mass mobilization[36] of the employed and unemployed people, guided by solidarity with the problems we are all bound to share, if not today then tomorrow.

The strategic long-term perspective, which makes feasible also the realization of immediate demands, is inseparable from our awareness of the viability and, indeed, the ultimate necessity of adopting the mode of controlling our social metabolic reproduction on the basis of disposable time. This is the objective to which our resources need to be dedicated if we care about the unemployment problem. Only a radical socialist mass movement can adopt the strategic alternative of regulating social metabolic reproduction—an absolute must for the future—on the basis of disposable time. For due to the insurmountable constraints and contradictions of the capital system, any attempt at introducing disposable time as the regulator of social and economic interchanges—which would have to mean putting at the disposal of individuals great amounts of free time, liberated through the reduction of work-time well beyond the limits of even a twenty-hour working week—would act as social dynamite, blowing the established reproductive order sky high. For capital is totally incompatible with free time autonomously and meaningfully utilized by freely associated social individuals.

6. Economic Theory and Politics —Beyond Capital[1]

6.1 Alternative Economic Approaches

I would like to start with two contrasting cases that illustrate the—not so fortunate—fortunes of some influential economic theories.

The first case arises from a quotation taken from a recent editorial in *The Economist*. It reads as follows:

> It is daunting to consider just how much turns on the question of American productivity. Stock market valuations, dizzy even now by historical standards; global financial stability; the outlook for living standards not just in the United States but worldwide; the long-term prospects for combining low inflation and high employment—all these and more depend on whether growth in American productivity really did shift on to a new and faster track, as was widely supposed, during the late 1990s. Over the past year many of the claims of the new economy have been exposed as *false:* the notion that the business cycle was dead; that spending on information technology was recession-proof; that classic methods of valuing shares were henceforth irrelevant; and so forth. Now, however, the most important pillar of the new economy has been if not demolished at least badly dented.[2]

And in conclusion, *The Economist*'s editorial tells readers that in due course a price will have to be paid for all those false assumptions. Accordingly, the "new-economy fanatics ... may regret that they bet so much not on a solid, plausible improvement, but on a *miracle that now turns out not to have happened.*"[3]

Thus, in this case, we can clearly see the fragility of half-baked assumptions, denounced now unhesitatingly as *false* by *The Economist* itself. The trouble is, though, that all such assumptions are in their heyday eagerly proclaimed to be the solid pillars of the most up-to-date theoretical edifices. As such, they sing the praises of nothing less than "*the new economy*"—which in its turn is supposed to warrant massive investment in the latest South Sea bubble. As we know, the sums involved in the recent implosion of "the new economy" were so mind-boggling that in *one year* NASDAQ's losses were *two-and-a-half times* the total amount of tax reductions announced—for the entire coming *decade*—by President George W. Bush, thereby making the NASDAQ losses in one year *thirty times* higher than the corresponding intended annual tax savings. The fact that *The Economist*'s recent editorial wisdom is "being wise after the event" need not concern us too much in the present context. After all, the journal's theoretical arsenal is much the same as those which its lead writers now belatedly criticize, made up always from a very short-term perspective. This is why *The Economist* can readily shift its position—to take as an example something by no means of negligible importance—from the long-pursued idealization of "*the economy of scale*" to its diametrical opposite, denouncing it as "*the diseconomy of scale*" when the earlier advocated panacea fails to work, and back to advocating again "the economy of scale" when the latter seems to be more convenient.

The second case indicated at the beginning of this paper concerns me much more closely than the first. For it refers to a conception of organizing the productive system—under the guiding principles of the *planned economy*—and intended to provide a viable alternative to the accident-prone character of the capitalist market economy.

The case I wish to recall actually happened, even if today it might seem quite incredible that such an event could ever take place. Yet it did. At the time when I learned about it, in the Summer of 1954 (not from the press, where such matters could not be mentioned, but in a hospital room, from a suffering subject of the case: my neighbor), I exposed in public at the earliest opportunity the absurdity of what I called a "real-life satire" whereby in a small county of southwest Hungary "*some mindless bureaucrats added the date—1952—multiplied by 100 kilos, to the county's compulsory consignment of pork meat to the state.*"[4] What was particularly absurd in this case was not that it happened at all, but more so the fact that it proved quite impossible to redress the situation—by canceling the astronomical addition to the obligations of a relatively small economic entity—even after the obvious error came to light and it had to be acknowledged by the relevant authorities that something had gone badly wrong, with serious consequences for the already precarious economic conditions of one of the poorest counties of Hungary, the county of Zala. Instead, the authorities arbitrarily decreed that no reduction was permissible because in the meantime the inflated obligation had become a legally sanctioned part of the National Plan, and therefore had to be fulfilled. This is why I argued under the circumstances that:

> it is clear that behind such accidents we find the inhumanity of bureaucracy. Indeed, this would be the social content and characterizing force of the event, even if such an astonishing deed were not committed by a born bureaucrat but quite accidentally by a subjectively well-meaning simpleton. For the deed itself has its *objective* inner logic, which points its accusing finger against the bureaucracy.[5]

True to form, the county of Zala had to deliver the insanely inflated quantity of pigs to the state, purchasing them wherever it could in order to fulfill its "nationally planned" obligations. For the total number of pigs in Zala could not even remotely match the "lawful figure" imposed on it. Accordingly, to be able to conform to the law the county of Zala—a hilly region where oxen were used as agricultural traction force, instead of horses which were far less suitable for the job—had to exchange for pigs in the neighboring counties many of its oxen, and borrow money on top of even that, taking on thereby further economic hardship for the future.

Not surprisingly, such an arbitrary economic planning process—one from which the people who had to suffer its consequences were excluded from directing—had generated resentment and even hostility in every country under the Soviet-type socioeconomic system. A Russian author, O. I. Antonov, in a book published in 1965, described in this way the practically negating attitude of the workers who had to conform to the arbitrarily imposed "norms" and corresponding labor discipline:

> Two workers who were employed to unload bricks quickly from trucks did so by throwing them on the ground, usually breaking some 30 percent of them. They knew that their actions were both against the interests of the country and against simple common sense, but their work was assessed and paid on

the basis of a time indicator. Therefore they would be penalized—indeed would not be able to make their living—if they were to arrange the bricks carefully on the ground. Their way of doing the job was bad for the country, but, on the face of it, good for the plan! So they acted against their consciences and intelligence, but with a deep feeling of bitterness against the planners: 'You don't want it done in a way good husbandry would have it, you keep pressing only for quicker and quicker! Bang! Bang!' Thus, all over the country, decent and responsible citizens, perfectly rational beings, acted in wasteful, almost criminal ways.[6]

Thus the sharp and apparently irreconcilable contradiction between the planning process and the needs of the people which the legally enforced National Plan was supposed to serve, had to end sooner or later in the implosion of the Soviet-type socioeconomic system, instead of remedying, as it was promised, the defects of capitalism.

6.2 The Need for Comprehensive Planning

However, it would be quite wrong to conclude, as many intellectuals both in the East and in the West did after the collapse of Gorbachev's *perestroika*, that planning as such could not have any future, and therefore there could be no alternative to the "market economy." Under the name of the market economy, for a while some people, including Gorbachev's ideologists,[7] tried to postulate an economic system that was not just compatible with socialism but ideally suited to it. They promised the institution of "market socialism," saying that its unique advantage was that it coexisted in full harmony with democracy; and indeed more than that, namely that in their view it was a "guarantee of socialism and democracy." Soon, however, it became clear that all talk about the insuperable virtues of market society was at best only a shy way of advocating the absolute permanence of capitalism.[8]

We shall have to return to the importance of planning for humanity as a whole in the future, after exploring some related issues. But already at this point it must be stressed that the blind hostility to planning that we are all familiar with leaves out of account some embarrassing but undeniable historical facts. Thus, for instance, it willfully ignores the unavoidability of planning under certain circumstances even for the richest and most powerful capitalist countries. To quote from a firsthand account by Harry Magdoff, who—as a governmental planning official—was himself a distinguished participant in such an enterprise:

> The necessity for central planning was shown in the United States during the Second World War when the national priorities were crystal clear (e.g., military airplanes vs. civilian autos, tanks vs. home refrigerators, barracks vs. civilian homes). Central planning was the only way an industrial miracle was achieved. In short order the armaments, transportation facilities, food, clothing, and housing for military forces fighting on two continents were supplied. Authorities in Washington in effect dictated what to produce and what not to produce (not in every detail but with sufficient direction to assure that the most urgent priorities would be met), what sort of new productive capacity was to be built, and how to distribute the insufficient output of metals, industrial supplies, metal-working machinery, etc. One of the saddest misconceptions these days arises from equating the Soviet method with national planning. The failures of Soviet-style planning are then taken to prove that national planning is bound to fail. But there is no good reason to assume that the Soviet model is the only possible one. It is a system that evolved in given historic circumstances. If anything, its failures need to be exhaustively studied in order to avoid repeating its errors. . . . [I]n the Soviet Union, production for production's sake, rather than production for use, replaced production for profit. Although the logic of accumulation in the post-revolutionary societies differed markedly from that of capitalism, the direction of their productive activity, including the spoilation of the environment, largely resembled the patterns of capitalist development.[9]

The kind of imperative that induced the United States to undertake central planning is by no means confined to the quite *extraordinary* circumstances of a world war. It applies to all great historical emergencies—like, for instance, the perilous ecological conditions of survival already foreshadowed, as a matter of *normality*, for our own future.

This is so for the simple reason that the mode of functioning of a system made up from a multiplicity of capitals—which happens to be, by definition, always characteristic of the private capitalist system, no matter how underdeveloped or advanced—cannot help being *centrifugal*, pulling its constituent microcosms in different directions, irrespective of whether such centrifugality produces positive or negative consequences. Clearly, though, under the conditions of a great historical emergency, like the potential ecological devastation just referred to, the *centrifugal inner determination* of the system, tending to disruption and to the intensification of the dangers, must be countered by some form of cohesion-inducing, and if necessary forcefully *overruling*, authority whose power of intervention must depend on the nature and size of the problems generated by the necessarily centrifugal mode of operation of the capitalist system. The kind of central planning practiced in the United States during the Second World War was only one specific instance of the variety of possible forms that are bound to arise from the general determinations and imperatives of great emergencies under very different historical circumstances. It is therefore salutary to bear in mind at least these considerations, when we try to put in perspective the blind prejudice against comprehensive planning which has become quite fashionable, particularly in the last decade.

6.3 Capital's Hierarchical Command Structure

There are some very good reasons for adopting a more critical position *vis-à-vis* the self-complacent message of the dominant neoliberal economic theories of the last few decades, particularly in order to have a more realistic view of the future, capable of envisaging a viable alternative to the ongoing developments. For, after all, even the customary reassurances of *The Economist* now seem to be pushed into the background by the journal's leading theoreticians. Instead, they invite us to contemplate the far from reassuring fact that "America's industrial production fell again in July, for the tenth consecutive month—the longest period of decline since 1983. Output is now *more than 4 percent below its peak*. However, America is not alone. *Industrial production is falling around the world*."[10] What makes this turn of events even worse, according to *The Economist*, is that the no longer deniable recessionary trend of the advanced capitalist countries—uniformly bad in every one of them, for the first time since the 1990s—cannot be alleviated today by a countervailing trend in the so-called emerging economies, in contrast to 1990 and its immediate aftermath. "In 1990 growth remained relatively brisk in emerging economies, propping up exports from the rich world. This time, however, the emerging world is also in trouble, with industrial production tumbling by 10 percent or more over the past year in several East Asian economies."[11]

Naturally, even in these circumstances, when the existence of serious problems all over the world must be publicly admitted, the theoretical vantage point of *The Economist* remains captive to the journal's hopelessly short-term perspective. Accordingly, *The Economist* notes: "When America's Federal Reserve meets to set interest rates on August 21st, it will have more than the weakness of the American economy to worry about."[12] This is not a very convincing line to follow, in view of the recent past. For expecting remedies to the deepening problems of the worldwide recessionary trend to come from the *seventh intervention* of America's Federal Reserve, after its painfully obvious failure to produce significant improvements to the sluggish economy through six previous interventions in the United States alone, is not much better than believing in witchcraft. After all, the strategy of producing a wishfully postulated positive solution by means of the reduction of the key interest rate had resulted in no improvement whatsoever in the world's second-most powerful economy, Japan, where the Central Bank of the country instituted the astonishing *zero rate of interest*, leaving the economy at the same time to stagnate at the dangerously high *8 percent rate of industrial recession*. The severe problems which we are experiencing today emanate from a much deeper level of socioeconomic and political determination than what could be reached by the instruments of monetary and fiscal adjustments.

The great difficulty is that in order to envisage a significantly different and viable alternative to the troubled order of today we must adopt a much longer-term perspective. It is not enough to think of partial adjustments—in the spirit of the famous advice of doing "little by little"—to the given socioeconomic conditions. Indeed, it is not enough even to think in terms of "overthrowing capitalism" in favor of a society matching the structural parameters of the now defunct Soviet-type post-capitalist order. That has been tried, at great human sacrifice, and failed conclusively, ending its days with a dramatic implosion not only in the former Soviet Union but all over Eastern Europe as well. In order to produce the required changes it is necessary to think of an incomparably more difficult undertaking: the historic task of overcoming the objective logic of *capital as such*, by a sustained attempt to go *beyond capital itself*.[13] For the overthrow of the capitalist state and of the private capitalist personifications of capital cannot create by itself anything other than a fatefully *unstable* system, which sooner or later must revert to the capitalist order if it fails to move beyond capital.

Capital is not simply a set of economic mechanisms, as its nature is often conceptualized, but a multi-faceted and all-embracing mode of social metabolic reproduction, deeply affecting every single aspect of life, from the directly material and economic to the most mediated cultural relations. Consequently, *structural change is feasible only by challenging the capital system in its entirety as a mode of social metabolic control,* instead of introducing partial adjustments into its framework.

As twentieth-century historical experience tells us, the target of socialist transformation was set by both wings of the labor movement—the social-democratic and reformist and the Stalinist post-revolutionary—well within the overall strategic confines of the established order, and as a result failed to challenge the systemic determinations of capital and its logic of self-reproduction. Social-democratic reformism had to fail because it wanted to reform capitalism while uncritically accepting its structural constraints. Thus, in a self-contradictory way it wanted to institute a reformist transformation of capitalism—at first even to the point of turning it, as time went by, into socialism (under the Bernsteinian slogan of "evolutionary socialism")—without changing its capitalist substance. Likewise, the post-revolutionary socioeconomic system remained trapped by the alienating structural constraints of capital as such, even though it instituted a *post-capitalist mode of extracting surplus-labor by direct political means* at an enforced rate, bringing into existence a *new type of enforcer of capital's time-imperative* (in place of the earlier, market-imposed one), as it befits the capital system in all of its feasible forms. This is also why all of the post-Stalin reform attempts had to fail, including Gorbachev's programmatically restructuring *perestroika.* The *self-contradiction* of such post-revolutionary reform attempts was no less acute than what characterized their social-democratic counterparts in the West. For they tried to "restructure" the existing order without changing its hierarchical and exploitative command structure at all.[14]

Thus, if the crucial question of capital's social metabolic controlling power is not addressed in a sustained way, in the form of all-embracing and consistently pursued strategic transformations (in contrast to more or less isolated reactive measures), in that case even the most radical political intervention in a situation of major crisis—be such intervention as far-reaching as the historically already experienced overthrow of the capitalist state in several countries—is bound to remain "one-dimensionally" unstable and ultimately endangered. To be able to produce the desired socialist transformation of society it is necessary to change the *hierarchical command structure of capital.* This is required because there can be no successful reorientation of the economy in the spirit of *production for use* without doing so. However, we are talking about a much more fundamental issue than the conquest of the levers of control over the top levels of the political state. For every single constituent—no matter how large or small—of capital's mode of social metabolic control has its own self-serving and deeply embedded command structure, traditionally oriented toward securing *expansion* (without concern for real human need and use) and driven by *accumulation* (which favors the adoption of its most easily achievable modalities, even if extremely damaging in environmental and other respects). This is the vicious circle that must be broken if there is to be any hope of success for socialist aims. But to be able to do so, *the inherited hierarchical command structure* of even the smallest social metabolic microcosms of capital must be replaced by a productively viable alternative.

6.4 From Predictions Based on "Economic Laws Working Behind the Backs of the Individuals" to Anticipations of a Controllable Future

We are accustomed to think of expansion and accumulation as inseparable from one another, accepting thereby the *paralyzing vicious circle* of our historically created and historically alterable conditions of socioeconomic existence as a *natural* determination. However, once we do that, it clearly follows that there can be *no alternative* to the capital system. For it would be self-defeating to renounce the idea of matching the expansion of human needs with a corresponding production potential for their satisfaction; and, indeed, for helping the enrichment of human needs by society's productive development as well. Utopian conceptions of the past are easily dismissed, and even ridiculed, as they fall into the trap of giving up on the idea of instituting a successfully expanding productive system, which would be fully in tune with the demands raised by richly expanding human needs. Unfortunately, they avoid challenging the vicious circle of inseparability just mentioned.

In truth, however, the presumed relationship of "natural" inseparability only holds under the capital system. For under the rule of capital the imperative of accumulation boils down, with historical arbitrariness and finality, to *capital accumulation*. Even the long-term accumulation of human knowledge must become, most selectively and restrictively, an attribute of capital, in the sense that in order to be socially acknowledged and appropriated, as well as productively utilized, it must first acquire its legitimacy as a capital asset. And this vitiating relationship works also the other way around, for under the rule of capital, the only kind of expansion that can be considered genuine expansion (the usually unqualified "growth") is the one that carries with it the accumulation of capital assets. This is why the alternative to our troubled socioeconomic order which we have to envisage means: breaking the vicious circle in question by going beyond capital itself, and insisting at the same time on the necessary separation of expansion (properly defined) from the unavoidable limitations and constraints of capital accumulation.

Naturally, the necessary redefinition of economic theory and politics "beyond capital" involves some major changes, as compared to their traditional forms. For the material ground of quasi-natural determinations on which they have been erected from the time of their birth cannot be assumed to persist under such radically different conditions.

Modern economic theory was originally conceived, quite properly, as a theoretical approach with its own appropriate orienting principles. In the eighteenth century, a legitimate concern was expressed by some classical economists, and most explicitly by Adam Smith, aiming to safeguard the new science of political economy against the interference of individual politicians and even of entire political bodies, stipulating in the latter respect that "no council or senate whatever" should try to tamper with the objective framework of spontaneously beneficial economic development.[15] The chaotic multiplicity of individual economic interactions was idealized in this conception, with reference to the celebrated "*invisible hand*" as the mysterious but thoroughly benevolent guide of individual decisions.[16] Thus, Adam Smith recognized, even if in an idealized form, that the *centrifugal* character of capitalist society needed vital correctives, if the chaotic multiplicity of economic interactions by "individuals"—in his picture characteristically confined to *capital-possessing individuals*, who in Smith's words "employ their capital in the support of domestic industry"—was not to fall to pieces by its constituents pulling in very different directions.

In reality the centrifugal determinations of the capitalist reproduction process do not simply arise from the diverging intentions of individuals, but simultaneously also from the irreconcilable interests of antagonistic classes made up by society's individuals. There are two vital correctives to the capitalistic system's otherwise dangerously destructive centrifugality. The first is the market whose importance is almost universally acknowledged. However, this is not so in the case of the second essential corrective: the more or less extensive role of intervention undertaken by the capitalist state. In this regard even the most vociferous—and wildly exaggerating—champions of "the market," like Hayek and his followers, assume a totally unrealistic position, inviting neoliberal and conservative believers to "roll back the boundaries of the state," when in reality without its diametrical opposite, i.e., the ever-greater propping up role exercised by the state, the capitalist system could not survive for a day.

To be sure, the acknowledgement of the basic antagonism between capital and labor could not be an integral part of Adam Smith's picture. Partly for this reason, he could still more or less ignore the major corrective role of the state; and he could do so partly also because the capitalist state in his day played a considerably less pronounced interventionist role than it does in our own time. Nevertheless, in some ways, the functions Smith assigned to the "invisible hand" fulfill the role of both correctives, even if not clearly separated out. Indeed, the rather mysterious characterization of the "invisible hand" was the consequence of the need to merge the vaguely perceived dual corrective functions into one, while also wanting to protect the spontaneous capitalist economic processes from the interfering "folly and presumption" of politicians. The cohesion-producing role of the market appeared obvious enough in the way in which the "invisible hand" was supposed to guide the intentions of the individuals and promote at the same time their particular interests. But the beneficial and efficacious nature of the "invisible hand" was not exhausted by that alone. For the individuals were also said to be guided "to employ their capital in the support of domestic industry," which happens to be one of the capitalist state's most important corrective functions.

In the twentieth century, it was no longer possible to leave the corrective and protective role of the state vaguely defined. A stand had to be taken by economists *for or against* state intervention in the market. Hayek's attempt to, ahistorically, idealize Adam Smith's "invisible hand" and demonize at the same time state intervention as "*The Road to Serfdom*"—as the title of his famous book put it—served an eminently conservative purpose. But even such hostility could not deny the objective character of the condemned trend. Keynes, by contrast, assumed a thoroughly positive attitude in this respect. Contrary to his neoliberal detractors who accuse him of *anti-liberal* intent—though he spoke out in fact only against the persistence of *laissez-faire* fantasies—he took a positive view of state involvement in economic management, unreservedly in the interest of the survival of private capitalism, even if some of his followers tried to use his approach for more left-oriented reformist purposes (on the whole not more successfully than some postwar Tory ministers in Britain). But it was very clear to Keynes that changes in the objective conditions and determinations of twentieth century economic and political development made necessary a corresponding adjustment of overall economic policy, in contrast to the bygone age of *laissez-faire* capitalism.[17] This position was forcefully expressed in an important passage of his *General Theory of Employment, Interest, and Money:*

> Whilst the enlargement of the functions of government, involved in the task of adjusting to one another the propensity to consume and the inducement to invest, would seem to a nineteent-century publicist or to a contemporary American financier to be a terrific encroachment on individualism, I defend it, on the contrary, both as the only practicable means of avoiding the destruction of existing economic forms in their entirety and as the condition of the successful functioning of individual initiative. . . . The authoritarian state systems of today seem to solve the problem of unemployment at the expense of efficiency and of freedom. It is certain that the world will not much longer tolerate the unemployment, which, apart from brief intervals of excitement, is associated—and in my opinion inevitably associated—with present-day capitalistic individualism. But it may be possible by a right analysis of the problem to cure the disease whilst preserving efficiency and freedom.[18]

Thus the major theoreticians who adopted the vantage point of the capitalist economy formulated their conceptions on the ground of the objective—indeed quasi-natural—determinations of their favored system. If Keynes was utterly naïve in his prognostication that "the world will not much longer tolerate the unemployment which is associated with present-day capitalistic individualism" (parroted later without much conviction by Walt Rostow and others), that was not simply his fault as a thinker. The Keynesian wishful projection was genuinely intended to counter an objective *structural defect of the sys-*

tem. A defect which came to the fore with a vengeance—defeating with utmost brutality the kind of remedial interventions compatible with the explicit defense of the "existing economic forms" made by Keynes—at a later stage of development, irrepressibly asserting itself with the onset of the structural crisis of the capital system in general.

The quasi-natural determinations manifest under the rule of capital are quasi-natural precisely because they "work behind the backs of the individuals," including among them the economic and political decision makers. This applies also to the way in which the correctives mentioned above can be introduced, no matter how "conscious" the designs of the decision makers might be. The blindness emanating from the determinations which work behind the backs of the individuals affect not only the decision makers directly concerned with their often frustrated anticipations within the domain of the market, but also the managers of the various modalities of state intervention. Of course, this circumstance does not diminish the objective character of the ongoing processes. If anything, it tends to intensify them in that it confers upon the determinations, which the individuals have to confront with their consciousness, the most problematic objectivity of reification. This is why the greatest thinkers who picture the world from the standpoint of capital, like Hegel, dream about the "identical Subject and Object" which would in principle overcome the obstacles towering in front of consciousness.

Paradoxically, the economic theories conceived within the framework of such objectivity, which imposes itself "behind the backs of the individuals," are to a considerable extent helped by the quasi-natural determinations of the system's functioning. Even if we think of this relatively helpful objectivity only as a crutch, it is nevertheless important for enabling the thinkers concerned to identify—although often quite one-sidedly—some weighty objective trends, and base advocated policies, as the ground of decision making, on them. Once, however, we envisage the conditions arising beyond capital, the formerly available crutch—for the kind of economic theorizing that we are familiar with—disappears from view. Consequently, something qualitatively different must take the place of the quasi-natural determinations as the orienting framework of economic theory and of the corresponding practical processes of autonomous policy-making.

The difference becomes clear when we consider the question of *predictability.* Under the conditions of capitalism, the objective determinations of development manifest themselves as identifiable economic *tendencies*—and in that specific sense "economic laws" (for this reason it is necessary to introduce the qualification stressing the *quasi*-natural character of such determinations), in contrast to the much firmer laws of the natural sciences, with their incomparably more precise and reliable form of predictability—which can form the basis of *probabilistic anticipations* of future consequences. This asset, which is simultaneously also a limitation, circumscribes for better or worse the predictive possibilities of *critical theories* as well, not just those produced by the uncritical believers in the virtues of the established system. The conclusions and policy recommendations of the critical and the uncritical theories may indeed be very different. But they both must base their evaluations on the quasi-natural determinations of ongoing developments. In this way, expansionary trends or recessions can be anticipated in order to adopt measures judged appropriate for facing them.

All this is very different when we think of the economic theories feasible beyond capital. Once the limitations arising from the quasi-natural determinations that assert themselves "behind the backs of the individuals" are successfully overcome, the deterministic consequences—which follow from them and constitute the framework of the earlier, probabilistic anticipations—disappear with them. Accordingly, in the new theories, anticipations of the future cannot be considered *predictions* in the former sense. They become *stipulations* with regard to the future, which arise from policy decisions made in a determinate context, on the basis of some objectives consciously set by the individuals concerned, in relation to the available material and human resources. In other words, this kind of "prediction" is analogous to a sporting body, like the Football Association, for instance, stipulating and anticipating that a particular game shall and will begin on Saturday afternoon at 3pm It must be, in principle, within the power of the individuals concerned.

Thus, the fact that in the society *beyond capital* "economic determinism" is left behind, carries with it the necessary consequence that under the new circumstances economic theory must find a very different way of relating the *future* to the present. The conceptualization of the *inertia of the past* as the *conditioning force of the present* and of the *future* cannot play its traditional role any longer. Accordingly, the practical redefinition of the temporal relationships of societal interaction means that conscious decision making with regard to the future, tangibly embodied in the objectives set by individuals, becomes the *controllable guiding force* of the present, in contrast to the same role once rather uncontrollably played by the inertia of the past.

6.5 Objective Preconditions for the Creation of Non-Deterministic Economic Theory

Naturally, without the realization of some objective preconditions there can be no question of articulating a new type of—non-deterministic—economic theory, in conjunction with a corresponding framework of conscious political decision-making.

The root of the problem is that non-deterministic economic theory, as a guide to conscious decision-making, is conceivable only when the conditions to which it refers, as the basis of evaluation of the pursued objectives, are *transparent.* Theories envisaging a solution through the "invisible hand" try to get rid of this problem by decreeing the *a priori impossibility of transparency.* Such theories can assume extremely conservative forms, attempting to make a moral virtue out of a role that confines individuals to unquestioningly subordinating themselves to the imperatives of the capital system. Hayek's crusading zeal is a prominent example of this way of assessing the issues. He writes in an article programmatically entitled "The Moral Imperative of the Market":

> In order to enable people to *adapt themselves to a structure which they do not know (and the determinants of which they do not know),* we have to allow the spontaneous mechanism of the market to tell them what they *ought to do.* . . . Our modern insight is that prices are signals which inform people of what they *ought to do* in order to *adjust themselves to the rest of the system.* . . . People must be willing to *submit to the discipline constituted by commercial morals.*[19]

Thus, Hayek wants us to believe that by conferring the status of a fictitious "morality" on the capitalist imperative of submitting individuals to the structural determinations of a system, which in his words they do not know and in principle cannot know, and by fallaciously using "*ought to do*" in place of *must do*, his authoritarian message (according to which the reluctant individuals[20] have to "*adjust* themselves to the rest of the *system*") becomes synonymous with the defense of freedom. And Hayek pursues this line of reasoning, asserting the *a priori* impossibility of transparency in the name of the "spontaneous mechanism of the market" (which, under the conditions of advancing monopolistic trends and the corresponding most iniquitous power relations, is neither a simple mechanism nor is it spontaneous), even though he has to admit that the principles which he advocates "*have never been rationally justified.*"[21] At the same time, not in the slightest worried about the absence of rational justification, Hayek warns us that the unreserved adoption of his "commercial morals" (which curtly dismiss the idea of *social justice* as a "*mirage*"[22] and make it a moral duty "to learn the *taut discipline of the market*") is "a crucial question for the future preservation of civilization which must be faced before the arguments of socialism return us to a primitive morality."[23]

In truth, the fundamental reason for the lack of transparency in our time is not the *unalterable* fact that society is made up of individuals, but the *radically alterable* condition that they are subsumed under hierarchically structured and antagonistic forces. The basic difficulties confronting economic theory and political decision making do not arise from the diverging intentions of particular individuals—for which reason the good services of the "invisible hand" must be invoked, while keeping silent about, or tendentiously misrepresenting, the well "visible hand" of the state—but from the antagonistic nature of the prevailing social relationships. The power of individuals *as particular individuals*—and not as personifications of social forces acting in accord with the imperatives of their "station in life"—is greatly exaggerated, in order to prejudge the issue in favor of the "invisible hand." However, the main reason why decision-making is incorrigibly vitiated by the opacity of social determinations can be pinpointed in their *adversarial* character. Thus, if we want to replace the *opacity of reified objectivity* by the *transparency of controllable social relations* we have to overcome the fateful inertia of *adversariality*.

The viability of conscious economic and political decision making "beyond capital" is feasible only on this basis. Submission to an *external discipline*—be that in the name of the fictitious morality, which advocates the "*taut discipline of the market,*" or the imposition of the *politically enforced* extraction of surplus-labor—is a non-starter in this respect. The only discipline compatible with the conception we are talking about (that is, a new type of—non-deterministic—economic theory, developed in conjunction with a corresponding frame-work of conscious political decision making) is the *internal discipline* adopted by individuals on the basis of the shared objectives which they have set themselves in a non-adversarial way, without the pressure of conflicting irreconcilable determinations. Otherwise, the consciousness of individuals is incorrigibly distorted and turned into varieties of *false consciousness*. For they are induced to rationalize and justify decisions imposed upon them, as if they were *their own*, autonomous decisions.

Non-deterministic economic theory presupposes a qualitatively different relationship between economy and politics in two senses. The first concerns the direct connection between the two domains, which might be called their *internal* relationship. This follows from the fact that since the preponderance of material and economic imperatives and determinations is left behind, the traditional political decision making processes can be significantly redefined in a much less one-sided form. The second sense, closely connected with the first, refers to the question of overcoming alienation both in economics and in politics. For the way the two domains function under the rule of capital can only be characterized as the alienation of the power of decision making from individuals; *all individuals,* who have to conform to the alienated role assigned to them as *personifications of capital, or person-ifications of labor.* This is why the notion concerning the "sovereign individuals who assert their intentions and pursue their particular interests in the one and only sustainable market society"—in full harmony with the interest of society as a whole, thanks to the benevolent "invisible hand"—is so hopelessly out of character with the actual state of affairs.[24] Decision making in both politics and in the domain of the economy is, in reality, grossly constrained and distorted by the alienating imperatives of capital-accumulation and expansion. At the same time, individuals are denied the power of decision making, in that their "decisions" are predetermined for them by "the power of things," in tune with alienation and reification. Thus, the qualitative change in the relationship between economics and politics in the second sense means the *restitution* of the power of decision making to individuals as consciously acting *social individuals.* This is the only possible way to reconstitute the unity of politics and economics, together with the harmonization of individual and social decision making in a meaningful sense of the term.

All this has far-reaching implications for society's productively usable time, not only in the earlier mentioned sense that the practical redefinition of societal interaction with regard to the *future* becomes the guiding force of the *present*, in contrast to the role once played in this respect by the *inertia of the past*. Equally important is the change that takes place in the time directly controllable by individuals as social individuals. As we know, under the rule of capital the "*necessary time*" required for expanding production and capital-accumulation is externally imposed on the individuals—through the "taut discipline of the market" or by means of the post-capitalist modalities of extracting surplus-labor—as the system's unchallengeable *time-imperative*. However, the more advanced a society's productive potential, the more wasteful it becomes to manage in this way its productive relations. For well beyond the extraction and appropriation of strictly regulated and externally controlled surplus-labor (under capitalism restrictively equated with surplus-value), in a productively advanced society, we find also the vast positive potentiality of the individuals' *disposable time* which cannot be readily utilized by capital's mode of social metabolic control with externally manageable "economic efficiency."

Naturally, there is no reason whatsoever for individuals to feel *internally and positively motivated*—the vital condition for activating this dimension of wealth—to put their disposable time into the common pool of their productive and distributive practices, if they are not in full control of their life-activity as social individuals. This is why, under conditions of adversariality and the necessary absence of transparency, the potentially immense—though due to its very nature, and to capital's displeasure, only *qualitatively* definable—wealth of the individuals' disposable time must be wasted in our societies, where the need for its creative deployment is painfully growing every day. Regrettably, even when we consider the unsustainable prodigality of our social metabolic order, we tend to focus on the question of poorly utilized energy and prime material resources, and forget altogether about this vital dimension of the problem. By contrast, non-deterministic economic theory and a corresponding framework of political decision making, based on the active involvement of all, are not feasible without realizing the great positive potentiality of the individuals' disposable time.

6.6 Socialist Accountancy and Emancipatory Politics

Returning to the question of planning, it is the importance and the great difficulty of instituting comprehensive planning that need to be underlined in the first place.

We have already seen that during the Second World War even the government of the most powerful capitalist country, the United States, had to adopt central planning, in order to secure the material conditions required for victory over Hitler. To be sure, this occurred under the extreme conditions of a state of emergency. Without it the social and historical determinations of the capitalist system render most problematical all attempts at comprehensive planning. However, the promoters of market-idolatry misrepresent this issue as if the opposition between "central planning" and "individual choice" was a timeless metaphysical one. Yet, "individual choice"—and the associated idea of "local autonomy"—mean absolutely nothing if the "autonomous" choices made by individuals or groups of individuals at a local level are nullified by the material imperatives of the economic system and the authoritarian directives of its overall command structure. Without introducing the appropriate historical qualifications the much-favored opposition between "planning or individual choice"—just like "growth or no-growth"—can only be a self-serving, *false opposition.*

Under normal circumstances, in the capitalist variety of our social reproductive order there can be no *comprehensive* planning. This must remain the case even when the quasi-monopolistic giant corporations adopt a problematical form of—necessarily truncated—planning. Their kind of planning must be truncated because they themselves can only be *quasi*-monopolistic, no matter how giant, since they can never corner the global market even in their own relatively restricted branch of productive activity, let alone its totality. The fact that incorrigibly truncated corporate planning is at times idealized as in every sense fully viable planning, as John Kenneth Galbraith has done,[25] is of course not surprising. But such an assessment of the problem amounts to nothing more than wishful thinking. Indeed, in Galbraith's case, the grossly overstated notion of big corporate planning was even wedded to the idea that—due to both the Soviet economy as a whole and the giant corporations of the United States allegedly sharing the same planning process—the two systems were actually *converging* into something qualitatively different from both capitalism and socialism.

Nothing could be further from the truth than the wishful projection of the "convergence" of the two societies, as the dramatic implosion of the Soviet system and the subsequent restoration of capitalism all over Eastern Europe clearly demonstrated.

The necessary frustration of planning under capitalism[26] came to the fore in Britain under Harold Wilson's government, formed after the Labour Party's electoral victory in 1964. At that time, Wilson was still talking about "conquering the commanding heights of the economy," and invented a new economic Ministry for Lord George Brown, the Deputy Leader of the Labour Party. This Ministry was supposed to introduce some important changes into the management of the British economy, in tune with the advocated planning process. As it turned out, however, this attempt was a complete failure, and the venture had to be brought to an end. Instead of the government "conquering the commanding heights of the economy," the diametrical opposite came about: the "commanding heights" of big business conquered the government, compelling it to abandon altogether the old ideas of social-democratic reform, foreshadowing thereby the transformation of the Labour Party into the "friend of business," in the proud words of its present leader.

In the course of capital's historical development, and particularly in the decades following the Second World War, the original meaning of *economy, as economizing,* has been completely obliterated by the imperative of the system's ever-expanding self-reproduction process. As mentioned earlier, expansion under the rule of capital was always subordinated to the imperative of capital-accumulation to which— from the standpoint of the system—there could be no admissible limit. Failure to achieve "growth" in this stunted sense, as the "expansion of further expandable capital assets," is considered with utter gloom, as the violation of the system's inner logic. The idea of consciously introducing regulatory constraints with regard to capital-accumulation, in the interest of sustainable development, was—and always must be—ruled out as an absolute non-starter. The quasi-natural systemic determinations of capital would not stand for that. Thus, "economy" becomes synonymous with "whatever is conducive to ongoing expansion and accumulation," irrespective of the human and environmental consequences. This rules out *economizing,* which is viewed as a useless and even hostile concept. This is why comprehensive planning as a necessary corrective must be categorically rejected, even if such an *a priori* rejection is ideologically embellished—from Ludwig von Mises[27] to Frederick von Hayek and his followers—as unchallengeable "common sense."

Clearly, however, without rediscovering the original meaning of economy, as the necessary economizing of good husbandry in a world of finite resources, and without its only feasible conscious application through comprehensive planning, the destructive consequences of capital's reproduction process[28] cannot be redressed. The extreme wastefulness of our existing mode of social metabolic control—with regard to both the utilization of nonrenewable material resources and to the perilous impact of capital's production processes on the global environment—is getting worse as time goes by, without any evidence of addressing the underlying determinations on the required scale. Even the most limited attempts to plan some improvement, in a single domain: the reduction of harmful emissions into the atmosphere, through the "good intentions" of the Kyoto protocols, are unceremoniously overruled by the most powerful capitalist country.

The trouble is that talking about the need for comprehensive planning is not simply a question of *scale* (partial in its application to certain branches of industry by some corporations, for instance, in contrast to embracing the national territory as a whole), or even that of the *duration* of the process (necessarily *temporary* under capitalism, in that it must be confined to states of emergency, however great). More importantly, commitment to comprehensive planning unavoidably puts on the agenda the challenge of envisaging an *alternative* mode of social metabolic reproduction, at least by implication. For, given the conditions under which the issue itself can arise, even the positive partial measures of regulatory intervention—which are bound to be predominantly *counter-measures* to capital's quasi-natural determinations in the first place—remain constantly endangered, under the threat of complete reversal and even full-scale capitalist restoration, unless they are successfully extended in such a way that they add up to being the building blocks of a *radically different* way of managing the interchange of the individuals among themselves and with nature. The implosion of the Soviet-type system, with its authoritarian planning process, contested in rather unorthodox ways by the producers, provides an eloquent proof of the truth of this proposition.

Naturally, there can be no economy, in the meaningful sense of economizing, without a practically viable form of accountancy. In contrast to capital's narrowly quantifying "economic accountancy"—which claims to be the only "economically acceptable," indeed the ideal "allocator of scarce resources," although in reality it favors even the most extreme form of waste, in conformity to the imperatives of capital-accumulation—the *socialist accountancy* of comprehensive planning must operate on the basis of restoring in social practice the *dialectic of quantity and quality*, destroyed through the universal unfolding of commodification, alienation, and reification. In this sense, socialist accountancy must be *quality-oriented*, even when it has to assess the quantities available for allocation among alternative activities and legitimately different purposes.

There is no time to properly explore here the great variety of rather complicated and often, for ideological reasons, distorted issues[29] of the necessary quality-orientation of socialist accountancy. Nevertheless, a very brief mention of at least some of them is in order.

The first concerns the question of *production for need*, in sharp contrast to the now prevailing submission and widely diffused overruling of even the most elementary needs of the overwhelming majority of humanity, in the service of the self-serving dictates of "economically viable" production. The determination of the distribution and consumption process is thus working the wrong way round. Instead of reaching out from need-based real demand toward the determination of productive targets, the capitalistically adopted objectives press frustrated human aspirations into their procrustean bed. People must content themselves with whatever they can get, if can they get anything. And to add insult to injury, all this is done in conjunction with the laughable ideology of "consumer sovereignty."

Another aspect of our problem can be spelled out as *production of use-values* as against the dominance of *exchange-values*, which are easily amenable to mechanical quantification and profit-accounting. Here, too, the pre-established grooves of the production system must prevail, irrespective of how wasteful it is to manage in this way the husbandry of human and material resources. Moreover, in the last few decades the situation has actually been getting worse in this respect, with the unfolding of capital's structural crisis. This is why we have been witnessing a *decreasing rate of utilization* of products, services, and productive machinery, although the need for the exact opposite—i.e., for *increasing the rates of utilization*, in order to meet the demand arising from countless millions who have to survive on less than *one dollar per day*—is quite undeniable.

It is also necessary to mention in this context, perhaps, the most immediate and urgent problem, threatening everywhere social destabilization and potentially even explosion: the cancer of growing *unemployment.* Capital's strictly quantifying approach cannot even perceive the real nature of the problem, let alone solve it. At best it can turn a portion of unemployment into varieties of *underemployment,* which cannot possibly work in the longer run. This is why all of the projected solutions turned out to be illusory and unsustainable, as for instance the program, conceived in the Keynesian spirit, of *"Full Employment in a Free Society"* that was advanced by the "father of the Welfare State," Lord Beveridge.[30] In a world in which labor must be considered a quantifiable "cost of production," remedies can only be temporary and conjunctural, subject to the imperatives of—at least relatively undisturbed—capital-accumulation, as experienced during the two-and-a-half postwar decades of expansion. The recent attempt to solve the unemployment problem by *casualization*—which is really the most callous *precarization* of living human beings—can only camouflage a failure whose impact is bound to get much more serious in the near future.

Evidently, in all these respects nothing commensurate to the importance of the issues themselves can be achieved without drastically reorienting social accountancy toward *quality,* within the comprehensive planning framework of consciously agreed and managed objectives, working in harmony with the people—the "freely associated producers"—who are most actively involved in managing their own affairs. Here, we have to consider also the famous Marxian principle of distribution, which asserts that in an advanced socialist society individuals will work in accordance with their *abilities* and receive from the overall social product *according to their need.*[31] This principle is often interpreted with bureaucratic one-sidedness, disregarding the emphasis laid by Marx on the *individuals' self-determination,* without which "working according to their *abilities"* means very little, if anything. Thus, both of the key terms of the Marxian definition—i.e., *individual ability* as well as *need*—can only acquire their true meaning in a framework of *qualitative accountancy.* This is what sets the parameters of a practically viable comprehensive planning process, feasible only in a long-term perspective.

Naturally, stressing the importance of a long-term perspective does not mean that we can ignore *the here and now*. On the contrary, the reason why we must concern ourselves with a much broader horizon than is customary is to be able to conceptualize realistically a *transition*[32] to a different social order from the determinations of the present. The long-term perspective is necessary because the real target of transformation can only be set within such horizons. Besides, without identifying the proper target, the journey is bound to be without a compass, and therefore the people involved can become easily diverted from their vital objectives. On the other hand, the understanding of the objective and subjective determinations of the here and now is just as important. For the task of instituting the necessary changes defines itself already in the present, in the sense that unless its realization is begun in *right here and now*, even if for the time being in a modest way—in full awareness of the existing constraints as well as of the difficulties in sustaining the journey within its more distant time horizon—we will not get anywhere. While no one should encourage hasty and premature action, the risk of being premature, when dedicated to an enterprise as fundamental and difficult as instituting a major structural change, cannot be excluded even when the individuals concerned act in a most responsible way. The truth of the matter is that nothing can be achieved by waiting for "*the favorable conditions*" and for "*the right moment.*"

People advocating a major structural change must be constantly aware of the constraints they have to face. At the same time, they must be watchful not to permit the weight of such constraints to become frozen into the paralyzing force of some fictitious "objective law" which is allowed to divert them from their professed aims. The planning process feasible in the here and now is a prominent case in point. As Harry Magdoff rightly emphasized both in relation to the unavoidable objective difficulties and their fetishistic transfiguration:

> Obviously, the size and skills of the labor force, the amount and quality of arable land, the potential supply of raw materials, the available tools and other equipment, the transportation and communication facilities—all these set severe constraints on what can be accomplished at any given time. Every step in planning, at the national and local levels, must take into account practical limitations. An aluminum plant without an adequate source of electric power would be useless. A chemical factory usually needs lots of water. A steel

plant must have reachable sources of coking coal and iron ore. At the higher levels of planning, various balances and proportions have to be constantly taken into consideration—for example, between industry and agriculture, producer and consumer goods, extracting and manufacturing industries, transportation and distribution requirements, consumer income and the supply of consumer goods. But what do objective limits have to do with 'objective economic laws' of socialism? Here we come to the heart of the matter. The effect of confusing limits and constraints with laws obscures, one might even say covers up, the basic problems and policy issues of a socialist transition.[33]

To be sure, the constraints and difficulties associated with the historic attempt to bring a largely underdeveloped society of 1,300 million people (that is: fifty-five Venezuelas!) to the level of production attained by the industrially most advanced countries is quite staggering by any standard. It is understandable, therefore, that the historical record shows advances punctuated by major reversals and disappointments. Many things must be tried out, under severe constraints and in the midst of outside hostility of which there are likely to be possibly even greater ones in the future.

Observing these developments from a distance, they might at times appear rather baffling. It is worth recalling in this context an old adage, quoted with approval by the late Chinese leader Deng Hsiao Ping, according to which "*the color of the cats*" does not matter—meaning that one need not worry whether they are capitalist or socialist—"*so long as they catch the mouse.*"

On the face of it, this may be considered fair enough. However, we may also be tempted to ask the question: what if the adopted policies end up with a giant rat infestation, in the form of *massive structural unemployment*, instead of happy mouse catching? Calling the undeniable constraints and dangers at work "the objective laws of socialism," as the article criticized by Magdoff did, offers no reassurance whatsoever in this respect.[34] It takes the most peculiar logic of *The Economist* to concede, on the one hand, that rural migration into China's cities would cause "an unemployment crisis with far-reaching social and political consequences," and, on the other hand, to advocate in the same paragraph the adoption of such a potentially explosive policy, insisting that "China needs to keep its labor costs low by letting its rural population find work freely in urban areas."[35]

The pursuit of the socialist strategic aim of comprehensive planning, as the way to overcome the ecological and other perils humanity faces—not in the distant future but already today—remains more valid than ever before. No one can deny that the changes required for the much-needed transition toward a society beyond capital are almost prohibitively difficult to make. Economic theory, respectful of the weight of objective constraints but refusing to submit to their fetishistic determinations, and thus working hand in hand with emancipatory politics, can make a vital contribution to the success of this enterprise.

7. The Challenge of Sustainable Development and the Culture of Substantive Equality[1]

7.1 Farewell to "Liberty-Fraternity-Equality"

Two, closely connected, propositions are at the center of this intervention. The first is that if development in the future is not sustainable development, there will be no significant development at all, no matter how badly needed; only frustrated attempts to try to square the circle, as in the last few decades marked by ever more elusive "modernizing" theories and practices, condescendingly prescribed to the so-called Third World by the spokesmen of former colonial powers. And the corollary, second proposition is that the condition inseparable from the pursuit of sustainable development is the progressive realization of substantive equality. It must be also stressed, in this context, that the obstacles to be overcome could hardly be greater. For up to our own day, the culture of substantive inequality remains dominant, despite the usually half-hearted efforts to counter the damaging impact of social inequality by instituting in the political sphere some mechanism of strictly formal equality.

We may well ask the question: what happened in the course of subsequent historical development to the noble ideas of *Liberty-Fraternity-Equality* proclaimed at the time of the French Revolution and genuinely believed by many long afterwards? Why were *Fraternity* and *Equality* discarded altogether, often with undisguised contempt, and *Liberty* reduced to the fragile skeleton of "the democratic right to vote," exercised by a skeptically diminishing number of people in the countries which like to describe themselves as "models of democracy"?[2] And that is far from the sum total of the bad news. For, as twentieth-century history amply demonstrates, even the meager measures of formal equality are often considered an unaffordable luxury, and are unceremoniously nullified by corrupt and authoritarian political practices, or indeed by openly pursued dictatorial interventions.

After more than a whole century of promises of eliminating—or at least greatly reducing—inequality, through "progressive taxation" and other state legislative measures, and thereby securing the conditions of socially viable development all over the world, reality turned out to be characterized by ever growing inequality not only between the "developed North" and the "underdeveloped South," but even within the most advanced capitalist countries. A recent report of the U.S. Congress (which could not be accused of left-wing bias) admitted that the income of the top *1 percent* of the American population now exceeds the bottom *40 percent*;[3] a figure, which in the last two decades *doubled* from "only" 20 percent, scandalous as it was even at that lower figure. These regressive developments went hand in hand with first stipulating a false opposition between "equality of outcome" and "equality of opportunity," and then abandoning even the lip-service once paid to the (never realized) idea of "equality of opportunity." Not that this kind of end result could be considered surprising. For once the socially challenging "outcome" is arbitrarily eliminated from the picture and opposed by "opportunity," the latter becomes devoid of all content and, in the name of the totally vacuous term of objectless (and worse: *outcome-denying*) "equality," it is turned into the ideological justification of the effective practical negation of all real opportunity to those who need it.

Once upon a time, the progressive thinkers of the rising bourgeoisie optimistically predicted, as indeed a great figure of the Scottish historical school of the Enlightenment, Henry Home, did that the domination of one social being by another will be remembered in the future as a bad dream, because, "reason, resuming her sovereign authority, will banish persecution altogether, and within the next century it will be thought strange that persecution should have prevailed among social beings. It will perhaps be even doubted, whether it ever was seriously put into practice."[4] Ironically, however, in the light of the way things actually turned out, what now seems to be rather hard to believe is that the intellectual representatives of the bourgeoisie in the ascendant could once reason in such terms. For a giant of eighteenth-century French Enlightenment, Denis Diderot, did not hesitate to assert with great social radicalism that *"if the day-worker is miserable the nation is miserable."*[5] Equally, Rousseau, with utmost radicalism and biting sarcasm, described the prevailing order of social domination and subordination in this way:

> The terms of the social compact between these two estates of man may be summed up in a few words: 'You have need of me, because I am rich and you are poor. We will therefore come to an agreement. I will permit you to have the honor of serving me, on condition that you bestow on me the little you have left, in return for the pains I shall take to command you.'[6]

In the same spirit, the great Italian philosopher, Giambattista Vico, insisted that the culmination of historical development is "the age of men in which all men recognized themselves as *equal in human nature.*"[7] And a long time earlier Thomas Münzer, the Anabaptist leader of the German peasant revolution, pinpointed in his pamphlet against Luther the root cause of the advancing social evil in quite tangible terms, diagnosing it as the cult of universal commodification and alienation, concluding his discourse by saying how intolerable it was "that every creature should be *transformed into property*—the fishes in the water, the birds of the air, the plants of the earth."[8] This was a far-sighted identification of what was to unfold with all-engulfing power in the course of the next three centuries. As befits the paradoxical achievements of premature utopian anticipations, it offered from the vantage point of the far less settled structures of early capitalistic developments a much clearer vision of the dangers to come than what became visible to the participants directly involved in the vicissitudes of the more advanced phases. For once the social trend of universal commodification triumphs, in tune with the inner requirements of capital's social formation, what appeared to Münzer as the gross violation of the natural order (and, as we know, what in the longer run endangers the very existence of humankind), to the thinkers who unreservedly identify themselves with the historically created (and in principle likewise removable) constraints of capital's fully developed social order seem to be self-evidently natural, unalterable and acceptable. Thus, many things become opaque and obfuscated by this shift in historical vantage point. Even the crucial term of "liberty" suffers a reduction to its alienated core, hailed as the conquest of "the power to freely sell oneself" through the presumed "contract between equals," in opposition to the political restrictions of the feudal order but ignoring, and even idealizing, the grave material and social constraints of the new one. Accordingly, the original meaning of both "liberty" and "equality" is changed into abstract and circularly self-sustaining determinations,[9] making thereby the idea of "fraternity"—the third member of the once solemnly proclaimed noble aspirations—utterly redundant.

7.2 The Failure of "Modernization and Development"

It is this kind of spirit that must be now confronted, unless we are willing to resign ourselves to the acceptance of the *status quo* and with it the prospect of continuing social paralysis and ultimate human self-destruction. For those who are the beneficiaries of the now prevailing system, with its gross inequality between the "developed" and the "underdeveloped" parts of the world, do not hesitate to impose, with utmost cynicism, the impact of their self-serving irresponsibility—as they have done quite recently in the arbitrary dismissal of the Kyoto protocols and other environmental imperatives—by insisting that the countries of the "South" should remain stuck at their present level of development. They have the nerve to speak in the name of equality! At the same time they also refuse to see that the North/South divide is a major structural defect of the whole system, affecting every single country, including their own, even if for the time being in a less extreme form than in the so-called Third World. Nevertheless, the tendency in question is far from reassuring even for the most advanced capitalist countries. As an illustration, we may add here to the earlier quoted U.S. figure of the income of the top 1 percent outstripping that of bottom 40 percent, the alarming rise in child poverty in Britain; in the last two decades, according to the most recent statistics, the number of children living below the poverty line has multiplied *threefold* in the United Kingdom and continues to increase every year.

The difficulty for us is that viewing these matters from a *short-term* perspective, as the dominant cultural and political organs necessarily portray them, carries with it the temptation to follow "the line of least resistance," leading to no significant change. The argument associated with this way of assessing the issues at stake is that "the problems worked themselves out in the past; they are bound to do so also in the future." Nothing could be more fallacious than this line of reasoning, even if it is most convenient to the beneficiaries of the *status quo* who cannot face up to the explosive contradictions of our predicament in the longer-run. Yet, as concerned scientists of the ecological movement keep reminding us: the "longer-run" is by no means that long by now, since the clouds of an environmental catastrophe are visibly getting darker on our horizon. Shutting our eyes offers no solutions. Nor should we allow ourselves to be deceived by the illusion that the danger of devastating military collisions belongs irretrievably to the past, thanks to the good offices of the "new world order." The perils in this respect are as great as ever, if not greater, in that not even a single one of the underlying contradictions and antagonisms has been resolved through the implosion of the Soviet system. The recently announced abandonment of even the fragile and limited arms agreements of the past, and the adventurist pursuit of the nightmare project of "the son of Star Wars," with the lamest possible justification of installing such weaponry "against rogue states," represent a stark reminder in this respect.

For a very long time we were expected to believe that all our problems will be happily solved through socially neutral "development" and "modernization." Technology was supposed to overcome by itself all conceivable obstacles and difficulties. This was at best an illusion imposed on all those who, for want of any outlet for their own active role in decision making, went on hoping that major improvements in their conditions of existence will be realized in the promised way. They had to find out by bitter experience that the technological panacea was a self-serving evasion of the contradictions by those who held the levers of social control. The "green revolution" in agriculture was supposed to resolve once and for all the world problem of famine and malnutrition. Instead, it created monster corporations like Monsanto, entrenching their power all over the world in such a way that major grassroots action is required in order to eradicate it. Yet, the ideology of strictly technological remedies continues to be propagandized to the present despite all the failures. Recently some heads of governments, including the British, have started to preach sermons about the coming *"green industrial revolution,"* whatever that might mean. What is clear, nevertheless, is that this new-fangled technological panacea is intended, again, as a way to run away from the inerad-

icable social and political dimension of the ever-intensifying environmental dangers.

Thus, it is no exaggeration to say that in our time the interests of
those who cannot even imagine an alternative to the short-term perspective of the given order, and to the fanciful projection of strictly
technological correctives compatible with it, directly collide with the
interest of human survival. In the past the magic term for judging the
health of our social system was *"growth,"* and still today it remains the
framework in which solutions must be envisaged. What is evaded by
the unqualified praise of "growth" is precisely the question of *what
kind of growth* and *to what end?* Especially since the reality of unqualified growth under our conditions of social metabolic reproduction
happens to be *extreme wastefulness* and heaping up problems for
future generations to face, as they must one day deal with the consequences of nuclear power—peaceful and military alike—for instance.

The cousin of "growth": the concept of "development" must be
also subjected to the same kind of critical scrutiny. Once upon a time,
it was embraced without hesitation by virtually everybody, and major
institutional resources were mobilized in the service of spreading the
gospel of U.S. type "modernization and development" in the so-called
underdeveloped world. It took some time before it could be realized
that there was something fatefully defective about the recommended
model. For if the U.S. model—whereby *4 percent* of the world population wastes *25 percent* of world energy and strategic material resources,
and pollutes the world by the same *25 percent*—were to be followed
everywhere else, we would be all suffocated in no time at all. This is
why for us it became necessary to qualify all future development as *sustainable development,* in order to fill the concept with actually feasible
and socially desirable content.

7.3 Structural Domination and the Culture
of Substantive Inequality

The great challenge of sustainable development, which we now have to
face, cannot be properly addressed without removing the paralyzing
constraints of the *adversarial* character of our social reproduction
process. This is why the question of *substantive equality* cannot be
avoided in our time, in contrast to the past. For *sustainability* means
being really *in control* of the vital social, economic, and cultural

processes through which human beings can not merely survive but can also find fulfillment, in accordance with the designs which they set themselves, instead of being at the mercy of unpredictable natural forces and quasi-natural socioeconomic determinations. Our existing social order is built on the structural antagonism between capital and labor, and therefore it requires the exercise of *external control* over all recalcitrant forces. *Adversariality* is the necessary concomitant of such a system, no matter how much waste of human and economic resources must be paid for its maintenance.

Yet, the imperative for eliminating waste has clearly surfaced on our horizon, as a major requirement of *sustainable* development. For "economy" in the longer-run must go hand-in-hand with rational and humanly meaningful *economizing,* as befits the core of its concept. But the meaningfully economizing way of regulating our social metabolic reproduction process, on the basis of *internal and self-directed,* as opposed to the now prevailing *external and top-down* control, is radically incompatible with *structural inequality and adversariality.* The Soviet-type system had its own form of adversariality that ultimately resulted in its implosion. But no one should nourish the illusion that our type of capital system is immune to such contradictions, just because for the time being it can manage wastefulness and inequality in a more effective way.

In our societies, the structurally entrenched and safeguarded determinations of material inequality are greatly reinforced by the dominant *culture of inequality,* mentioned earlier, through which individuals *internalize* their "station in society," more or less consensually resigning themselves to their predicament of subordination to those who make the decisions over their life-activity. This culture was constituted parallel to the formation of capital's new structures of inequality, on the iniquitous foundations inherited from the past. There was a *reciprocal interaction* between the material reproductive structures and the cultural dimension, creating a vicious circle, which trapped the overwhelming majority of individuals in their strictly restrained domain of action. If we now envisage a qualitative change for the future, as we must, the vital role of cultural processes cannot be overstated. For there can be no way to break out from the now dominant vicious circle, unless we succeed in operating the same kind of interaction—but this time in a positive emancipatory direction—which characterized social development in the past. From the present, in the longer-run quite untenable, mode of social reproduction to one no longer burdened with the destructive tendencies of the adversarial confrontations of our time, no instant change can be envisaged. Success will require the constitution of a *culture of substantive equality,* with the active involvement of all, and the *awareness* of one's own share of *responsibility* implicit in the operation of such a—non-adversarial—mode of decision-making.

Understandably, in the creation of the long-established culture of substantive inequality, even the greatest and most enlightened thinkers of the bourgeoisie in the ascendant, as children of their time and station, were implicated. Let me illustrate this point with Goethe's lifelong struggle with the meaning of the Faust legend, intended to represent humanity's quest for realizing its destiny. As we know, according to the pact of the restless Faust with the devil, he is bound to lose his wager (and his soul) the moment he finds fulfillment and satisfaction in life. And this is how Faust greeted that fateful moment:

> Such busy, teeming throngs I long to see,
> Standing on freedom's soil, a people free.
> Then to the moment could I say:
> Linger you now, you are so fair!
> Now records of my earthly day
> No flight of aeons can impair—
> Foreknowledge comes, and fills me with such bliss,
> I take my joy, my highest moment this.

However, with supreme irony, Goethe shows that Faust's great excitement is misplaced. For what he greets (when blinded by Sorge) as the great work for conquering land from the swamps, in fulfillment of his own plan, is in reality the noise made by the lemurs digging his grave. And only celestial intervention can, in the end, save Faust, rescuing his soul from the clutches of the devil. The greatness of Goethe is evident in the way he also indicates why Faust's quest must end in irony and insoluble ambiguity, even if Goethe cannot distance himself from the world view of his hero, trapped by the conception of "enlightened inequality." This is the summation of the Faustian vision:

> Only *the master's word* gives action weight,
> And what I framed in thought I will fulfill.

> Ho, you my people, quickly come from rest:
> Let the world see the fruit of bold behest.
> Man all the tools, spade, shovel, as is due,
> The work marked out must straight be carried through.
> Quick diligence, firm discipline,
> With these the noblest heights we win.
> To end the greatest work designed,
> A thousand hands need but one mind.

Clearly, the destination of the overwhelming majority of humankind to the role of *"hands,"* asked to *"man all the tools,"* in the service of *"one mind,"* and obeying *"the master's words"* with *"quick diligence and discipline,"* is quite untenable in the longer run, no matter how closely it resembles the now dominant actual state of affairs. How could we consider the human beings confined to such role to be *"Standing on freedom's soil, a people free"*? The instructions given by Faust to the Overseer as to the way to control the workers, faithfully realistic for our predicament today, reflect the same, untenable, spirit:

> Use every means, and strive
> To get more workers, shift on shift enroll,
> With comforts spur them on, and good control.
> Pay them, cajole them, use a press-gang drive,
> A fresh report you'll bring me daily, showing
> How my projected locks and dykes are growing.

And what meaning can we give to Faust's "great plan on behalf of humanity," when capital's social order is radically incompatible with the *comprehensive planning* without which the very survival of humanity cannot be secured? Goethe's Mephistopheles describes the prospects ahead of us with brutal realism:

> What matters our creative endless toil,
> When, at a snatch, oblivion ends the coil?

"A thousand hands" in the service of "one mind" obviously cannot offer us any solution. Nor can the mystical Chorus of Angels in the last scene of Goethe's *Faust* counter the Mephistophelian threat of *oblivion* looming at the end of the road.[10]

In a somewhat more conflict-torn age, Balzac, in one of his great novellas, *Melmoth Reconciled*, takes up the Faust theme, rescuing in a very different way Melmoth (Faust)—who, thanks to a pact with the devil, enjoys unlimited wealth throughout his life. There is no need for divine intervention in this case. On the contrary, the solution is offered with extreme irony and sarcasm. Melmoth cleverly saves his own soul—when he feels death approaching and wants to get out of his pact with the devil—by making a deal with another man, Castanier, in trouble for embezzlement. Melmoth exchanges his imperiled soul with Castanier, who doesn't hesitate to enter into a deal that confers unlimited wealth upon him. Castanier's words, when he in turn hits on the idea of how to get out of ultimate trouble, by obtaining still another soul in exchange for his own devil-plighted soul, sum up in a striking way Balzac's sarcasm, which brings up-to-date Thomas Münzer's prophetic diagnosis of all-encroaching alienation. Castanier goes to the stock exchange, absolutely convinced he will succeed in finding someone whose soul he can obtain in exchange for his own, saying that on the stock exchange *even the Holy Spirit has its quotation* (*Il Banco di Santo Spirito)* in the list of the great banks.[11]

However, it is enough to follow even for a few days the threatening disturbances on our stock exchanges in order to realize that Melmoth's solution is no more realistic today than Goethe's celestial intervention. Our historical challenge for securing the conditions of sustainable development must be solved in a very different way.

Extricating ourselves from the culture of substantive inequality and progressively replacing it with a viable alternative is the road we need to follow.

8. Education—Beyond Capital[1]

Learning is our very life, from youth to old age, indeed to the brink of
death; no one lives for ten hours without learning.
—Paracelsus

*Se viene a la tierra como cera—y el azar nos vacía en moldes
prehechos. Las convenciones creadas deforman la existencia verdadera
. . . Las redenciones han venido siendo formales; es necessario que sean
esenciales. La libertad política no estará asegurada, mientras no se
asegura la libertad spiritual. . . . La escuela y el hogar son las
dos formidables cárceles del hombre.*
—José Martí

The materialist doctrine concerning the changing of
circumstances and upbringing forgets that circumstances are changed
by men and that the educator must himself be educated. This doctrine
must, therefore, divide society into two parts, one of which [the edu-
cators] is superior to society. The coincidence of the changing of
circumstances and of human activity or self-change can be
conceived and rationally understood only
as revolutionary practice.
—Marx

I have chosen three epigraphs, in order to anticipate some of the main
points of this lecture. The first is from the great sixteenth-century
thinker, Paracelsus; the second is from José Martí; and the third is from
Marx. The first says, in sharp contrast to the nowadays customary but
tendentiously narrow conception of education, that "Learning is our

very life, from youth to old age, indeed to the brink of death; no one lives for ten hours without learning."[2] José Martí writes, in the same spirit as Paracelsus, when he insists that "*La educación empieza con la vida, y non acaba sino con la muerte.*" ("Education begins with our life, and it is brought to its end only with our death.") But he adds some crucial qualifications, forcefully criticizing the remedies attempted in our societies and also summing up the massive task ahead. This is how he puts in perspective our problem: "One arrives on this earth as wax—and chance pours us into prefabricated moulds. Existing conventions deform real existence. . . . Redemptions are made only in a formal sense; it is necessary that they should become substantial. . . . School and the home are the two formidable prisons of human beings."[3] And the third epigraph, from Marx's "Theses on Feuerbach," puts into relief the dividing line that separates utopian socialists, like Robert Owen, from those who must in our time overcome the grave structural antagonisms of our society. For these antagonisms block the road to the absolutely necessary change, without which there can be no hope for the very survival of humanity, let alone for improving its conditions of existence. These are Marx's words: "The materialist doctrine concerning the changing of circumstances and upbringing forgets that circumstances are changed by men and that the *educator must himself be educated.* This doctrine must, therefore, divide society into two parts, one of which is *superior to society.* The coincidence of the changing of circumstances and of human activity or *self-change* can be conceived and rationally understood only as *revolutionary practice.*"[4] The point I wish to stress is that all three of these quotations, across a time-span of almost five centuries, underline the imperative for instituting—and at the same time making irreversible—a radical structural change. That is, a change taking us *beyond capital* in a genuine and educationally viable sense of the term.

8.1 Capital's Incorrigible Logic and Its Impact on Education

Not many people would wish to deny today that the educational and the broader social processes of reproduction are closely intertwined. Accordingly, a significant reshaping of education is inconceivable without a corresponding transformation of the social framework in which society's educational practices must fulfill their vitally important and historically changing functions. But beyond agreement about this simple fact the roads sharply divide. If the given mode of societal reproduction itself is taken for granted as the necessary framework of social interchange, then in the name of reform only minor adjustments are admissible in all domains, including education. Changes under such *a priori* prejudging constraints are admissible for the legitimate purpose of mending some defective detail of the established order, so as to keep the fundamental structural determinations of society as a whole intact, in conformity to the unalterable requirements of the given reproductive system's *overall logic.* One is allowed to adjust the ways in which a multiplicity of conflicting particular interests are supposed to conform to the pre-established *general rule* of societal reproduction, but in no way to change the *general rule itself.*

This logic excludes, with categorical finality, the possibility of legitimating the contest of the *fundamental rival hegemonic forces* of the given social order as *viable alternatives* to one another, whether in the field of material production or in the cultural and educational domain. It would be, therefore, quite absurd to expect the formulation of an educational ideal from the standpoint of the feudal ruling order which would envisage the dominance of the serfs, as a class, over the lords as the well-entrenched dominant class. Naturally, the same goes for the fundamental *hegemonic alternative* between capital and labor. Not surprisingly, therefore, even the noblest educational utopias, formulated in the past from the standpoint of capital, had to remain strictly within the confines of perpetuating capital's dominance as a mode of social metabolic reproduction. The objective interests of the class had to prevail even when the subjectively well-meaning authors of those utopias and critical discourses sharply perceived and pilloried the inhuman manifestations of the dominant material interests. Their critical stance could reach only as far as wanting to use the *educational reforms* proposed by them in order to remedy the worst *effects* of the established capitalist reproductive order, without, however, removing their deep-seated antagonistic *causal foundations.*

The reason why all past efforts intended for instituting major changes in society by means of enlightened educational reforms, reconciled with the standpoint of capital, had to come to grief was—and remains today—the fact that the fundamental determinations of the capital system are *unreformable.* As we know, from well over one hundred years of failed reformist strategy—beginning with Edward Bernstein[5] and his associates, who promised the gradual transformation of the capitalist order into a qualitatively different, socialist one—capital is unreformable because it is by its very nature, as a systemic regulative totality, quite *incorrigible*. It either succeeds in imposing on the members of society, including the "caring" personifications of capital, the structural imperatives of its system as a whole, or it loses its viability as the historically dominant regulator of the well-established mode of all-embracing social metabolic reproduction. Consequently, in its fundamental structural parameters capital must always remain *uncontestable*, even if all kinds of strictly marginal correctives are not only compatible with its rule but also beneficial, and indeed necessary, to it in the interest of the system's continued survival. Confining radical educational change to capital's self-serving corrective margins means abandoning altogether, knowingly or not, the objective of qualitative social transformation. By the same token, however, looking for margins of *systemic reform* within the framework of the capital system itself is a *contradiction in terms*. This is why it is necessary to *break capital's logic*, if we want to envisage the creation of a meaningfully different educational alternative.

For reasons of limited time I can refer here only to two major figures of the enlightened bourgeoisie, to illustrate the insurmountable objective limits even when wedded to the best of subjective intentions. The first is one of the greatest political economists of all times, Adam Smith; and the second, the outstanding utopian social and educational reformer—who also tried to practice what he preached, until he went bankrupt—Robert Owen.

Adam Smith, despite his profound commitment to the capitalist way of organizing economic and social reproduction, condemned in no uncertain way the negative impact of the system on working people. Talking about the "Commercial Spirit," as the cause of the trouble, he insisted that it:

> . . . confines the views of men. Where the division of labor is brought to perfection, every man has only a simple operation to perform; to this his whole attention is confined, and few ideas pass in his mind but what have an immediate connection with it. When the mind is employed about a variety of objects, it is somehow expanded and enlarged, and on this account a country artist is generally acknowledged to have a range of thoughts much above a city one. The former is perhaps a joiner, a house carpenter, and a cabinetmaker, all in one, and his attention must of course be employed about a number of objects of very dif-

ferent kinds. The latter is perhaps only a cabinetmaker; that particular kind of work employs all of his thoughts, and as he had not an opportunity of comparing a number of objects, his views of things beyond his own trade are by no means so extensive as those of the former. This must be much more the case when a person's whole attention is bestowed on the seventeenth part of a pin or the eightieth part of a button, so far divided are these manufactures. . . . These are the disadvantages of a commercial spirit. The minds of men are contracted, and rendered incapable of elevation. Education is despised, or at least neglected, and heroic spirit is almost utterly extinguished. To remedy these defects would be an object worthy of serious attention.[6]

This sharp observer of the conditions of England under the triumphantly advancing "Commercial Spirit," can find no remedy other than a moralizing denunciation of the degrading *effects* of the underlying forces, blaming the working individuals themselves rather than the system which imposes upon them their unhappy predicament. In this spirit, Smith writes:

When the boy is grown up he has *no ideas with which he can amuse himself.* When he is away from his work, he must therefore betake himself to *drunkenness and riot.* Accordingly we find that, in the commercial parts of England, the tradesmen are for the most part in this despicable condition; their work through half the week is sufficient to maintain them, and through *want of education they have no amusement for the other but riot and debauchery.*[7]

Thus the capitalist exploitation of "leisure time" brought to perfection today, under the rule of the more up-to-date "Commercial Spirit," would seem to be the solution, without altering in the slightest the alienating core of the system. The consideration that Adam Smith would have liked to have instituted something much more elevating than the ruthless and callous exploitation of the "leisure time" of the young, does not alter the fact that even the discourse of this great figure of the Scottish Enlightenment is quite incapable of addressing the *causes* but must remain trapped within the vicious circle of the condemned *effects.* The objective limits of capital's logic prevail even when we are talking about the greatest figures who conceptualize the world from capital's standpoint, and even when they are subjectively trying to express, in an enlightened spirit, a genuinely held humanitarian concern.

Our second example, Robert Owen, half a century after Adam Smith, does not mince his words when he denounces profit-seeking and the power of money, insisting that "The employer regards the employed as *mere instruments of gain*."[8] Yet, in his practical educational experiment, he expects the cure from the impact of "reason" and "enlightenment," preaching not to "the converted" but to the "unconvertible" who cannot think about labor in any other term than as "mere instruments of gain." This is how Owen argues his case:

> Shall we then longer withhold national instruction from our fellow-men, who, it has been shown, might easily be trained to be industrious, intelligent, virtuous, and valuable members of the State?
>
> True, indeed, it is that all the measures now proposed are only a compromise with the errors of the present system; but as these errors now almost universally exist, and must be overcome solely by the force of reason; and as reason, to affect the most beneficial purposes, makes her advance by small degrees, and progressively substantiates one truth of high import after another, it will be evident, to minds of comprehensive and accurate thought, that by these and similar compromises alone can success be rationally expected in practice. For such compromises bring truth and error before the public; and whenever they are fairly exhibited together, truth must ultimately prevail. . . . It is confidently expected that the period is at hand, when man, through ignorance, shall not much longer inflict unnecessary misery on man; because the mass of mankind will become enlightened, and will clearly discern that by so acting they will inevitably create misery to themselves.[9]

What makes this discourse extremely problematical, notwithstanding the author's best intentions, is that it must conform to capital's crippling limits. This is why Owen's noble practical utopian experiment at Lanark was condemned to failure. For he tried to accomplish the impossible: the reconciliation of a conception of liberal and reformist utopianism with the ruthless dictates of capital's structurally incorrigible order.

Owen's discourse reveals the close interrelationship between liberal utopianism and the advocacy of proceeding "by slow degrees," "by compromises alone," and of wanting to overcome the existing problems "solely by the force of reason." Since, however, the problems at stake are *comprehensive* ones, corresponding to the unalterable requirements of structural domination and subordination, the contradiction between the all-embracing *global* character of the criticized social phenomena and the *partiality and gradualism* of the proposed remedies—which alone are compatible with the standpoint of capital—must be fictitiously superseded by the sweeping generality of some utopian "ought to be." Thus, we see in Owen's characterization of "what is to be done?" a shift from the originally well pinpointed specific social phenomena—e.g., the deplored condition that the "employer regards the employed as *mere instruments of gain*"—to the vague and timeless generality of "error" and "ignorance," so as to circularly conclude that the problem of "truth versus error and ignorance" (which is said to be a question of "reason and enlightenment") can be solved "solely by the force of reason." And, of course, the assurance we receive for the success of the Owenite educational remedy is, again, a circular one: the assertion that "truth must ultimately prevail, because the mass of mankind will become enlightened."

At the roots of the vague generality of Owen's remedial conception we find that his utopian gradualism is, revealingly, motivated by the fear of, and anguish about, the emerging socio-historical hegemonic alternative of labor. In this spirit, he insists that under the conditions in which the workers are condemned to live they "acquire a gross ferocity of character, which, if legislative measures shall not be judiciously devised to prevent its increase, and ameliorate the conditions of this class, *will sooner or later plunge the country into a formidable and perhaps inextricable state of danger.* The direct object of these observations is to affect the amelioration and *avert the danger.*"[10]

When thinkers castigate "error and ignorance," they should also indicate the ground from which the criticized intellectual sins arise, instead of assuming them as their own, irreducible ultimate foundation to which the question of "why?" cannot and should not be addressed. In the same way, also the appeal to the authority of "reason and enlightenment," as the unfailing future solution of the analyzed problems fallaciously evades the question: "Why did reason and enlightenment not work in the past?" And if they did not, "What is the guarantee that they will do so in the future?" To be sure, Robert Owen is by no means the only thinker who offers "error and ignorance" as the ultimate explanatory ground of the denounced phenomena, to be happily rectified by the almighty power of "reason and enlightenment." He shares this characteristic, and the associated—far from securely founded—positive faith, with the liberal enlightenment tradition as a whole. This makes the underlying contradiction that much more significant and difficult to overcome. Accordingly, when we object to the circularity of such final diagnoses and declarations of faith, which insist that beyond the assumed explanatory point one cannot possibly go, we cannot satisfy ourselves with the idea, far too often encountered in philosophical arguments, that these dubious answers arise from the criticized thinkers' "error" which must be corrected in its turn by "proper reasoning." To do so would mean committing the same sin as one's adversary.

Robert Owen's critical discourse and his educational remedy have nothing to do with "logical error." The watering down of his social diagnosis at a crucial point, and the circularity of the vague and timeless solutions offered by Owen, are *necessary practical derailments*, due not to the defectiveness of the author's formal logic, but to the *incorrigibility of capital's perverse logic*. It is the latter which categorically denies him the possibility of finding answers in a genuine communal association with the social subject whose potentially "gross ferocity of character" he fears. This is how he ends up with the—not logical but fundamentally practical—contradiction of wanting to change the established dehumanized relations while rejecting, as nothing more than acute danger, the only feasible social hegemonic alternative to them. The insoluble contradiction resides in Owen's conception of *significant change* as the *perpetuation of the existent*. The circularity we have seen in his reasoning is the necessary consequence of *assuming* an "outcome": triumphant "reason" (proceeding safely "by small degrees") that *prescribes* "error and ignorance" as the suitably distilled problem, which reason is supposed to be eminently suitable to solve. In this way, even if unconsciously, the relationship between the problem and its solution is actually *reversed*, thereby ahistorically redefining the former in order to fit the—capitalistically permissible and—conceptually preconceived solution. This is what happens when even an enlightened social and educational reformer, who honestly tries to remedy the alienating and dehumanizing *effects* of the "power of money" and "profit seeking" which he deplores, cannot escape from the straitjacket of capital's self-imposing *causal determinations*.

The impact of capital's incorrigible logic on education has been great throughout the system's development. Only the *modalities* of imposing capital's structural imperatives in the educational domain have changed from the bloody days of "primitive accumulation" to the present, in tune with altered historical circumstances, as we shall see in the next section. This is why the meaning of radical educational change today cannot be other than shredding the straitjacket of the system's incorrigible logic: by devising and consistently pursuing the strategy of *breaking the rule of capital* with all available means, as well as with those which have yet to be invented.

8.2 Remedies Cannot Be Just Formal; They Must Be Essential

Paraphrasing the epigraph taken from José Martí, we can say with him, "remedies cannot be just *formal;* they must be *essential.*"[11]

Institutionalized education, especially in the last century and a half, has served—on the whole—the purpose of not only supplying the know-how and the personnel needed by the capital system's expanding productive machinery, but also of generating and transmitting a framework of values which *legitimate* the dominant interests, as if there could be no alternative whatsoever to running society in the form of either "internalized" (i.e., by the suitably "educated" individuals accepted) or ruthlessly enforced hierarchical structural domination and subordination. History itself had to be utterly misrepresented, and indeed often blatantly falsified, for the purpose. Fidel Castro, talking about the falsification of Cuban history in the aftermath of the war of independence from Spanish colonialism, gives a striking example:

> ?Qué nos dijeron en la escuela? ?Qué nos decían aquellos inescrupulosos libros de historia sobre los hechos? Nos decían que la potencia imperialista no era la potencia imperialista, sino que, lleno de generosidad, el gobierno de Estados Unidos, deseoso de darnos la liberdad, había intervenido en aquella guerra y que, como consequencia de eso, éramos libres. Pero no éramos libres por cientos de miles de cubanos que murieron durante 30 años en los combates, no éramos libres por el gesto heroico de Carlos Manuel de Céspedes, el Padre de la Patria, que inició aquella lucha, que incluso prefirió que le fusiliaran al hijo antes de hacer una sola concesión; no éramos libres por el esfuerzo heroico de tantos cubanos, no éramos libres por la predica de Martí, no éramos libres por el esfuerzo heroico de Máximo Gómez, Calixto García y tanto aquellos próceres ilustres; no éramos libres por la sangre derramada por las veinte y tantas heridas de Antonio Maceio y su caída heroica en Punta Brava; éramos libres sencillamente porque Teodoro Roosevelt desembarcó con unos quantos rangers en Santiago de Cuba para combatir contra un ejército agotado y prácticamente vencído, o porque los acorazados americanos hundieron a los 'cacharros' de Cerveza frente a la bahia de Santiago de Cuba. Y esas monstruosas mentiras, esas increíbles falseades eran las que se enseñaban en nuestras escuelas.[12]

What did they tell us in our schools? What did those history books without scruple tell us about the facts? They said that the imperialist power was not really the imperialist power but, full of generosity, the government of the United States, in its desire to give us freedom, intervened in that war, and that, as a result, we became free. But we did not become free thanks to hundreds of thousands of Cubans who died in 30 years of the struggle; we did not become free thanks to the heroic sacrifice of Carlos Manuel de Céspedes, the Father of our Homeland, who initiated that struggle, who even preferred that they shoot dead his son, rather than make a concession; no, we did not become free thanks to the preeching of Martí, nor through the heroic efforts of Máximo Gómez, Calixto García and many other illustrious ancestors; no, we did not become free through the blood flowing from the twenty and more wounds suffered by Antonio Maceio and through his heroic fall at Punta Brava; we became free simply because Theodor Roosevelt disembarked with some *rangers* in Santiago de Cuba in order to combat against an exhausted and practically defeated army, or because the American troops had found the bier in the 'old crock' on the bay of Santiago de Cuba. And these monstrous lies, these unbelievable falsehoods were what they have been teaching in our schools.

Misrepresentations of this kind are the normality, when the stakes are really high, and particularly so when they are directly concerned with the rationalization and legitimating of the established social order as the supposedly unalterable "natural order." History, then, must be rewritten and propagandized in a most distorted form not only in the broadly diffused organs of political opinion formation, from mass newspapers to radio and television channels, but even in supposedly objective academic theories. Marx offers a devastating characterization of how a vital question of capitalist history, known as the *primitive or original accumulation of capital,* is treated by the science of political economy. He writes in a powerful chapter of *Capital*:

Primitive accumulation plays in political economy about the same part as original sin in theology. Adam bit the apple, and thereupon sin fell on the human race. Its origin is supposed to be explained when it is told as an anecdote about the past. In times long gone by there were two sorts of people; one, the diligent, intelligent and above all frugal élite; the other, lazy rascals, spending their substance, and more, in riotous living. . . . Thus it came to pass that the former sort accumulated wealth, and the latter sort finally had nothing to sell except their own skins. . . . Such insipid childishness is every day

preached to us in the defense of property. . . . In actual history, it is a notorious fact that conquest, enslavement, robbery, murder, in short, force, play the
greatest part. In the tender annals of political economy, the idyllic reigns
from time immemorial. . . . As a matter of fact, the methods of primitive
accumulation are anything but idyllic. . . . The proletariat created by the
breaking-up of the bands of feudal retainers and by the forcible expropriation of the people from the soil, this 'free' [*vogelfrei*, i.e., 'free as a bird'] proletariat could not possibly be absorbed by the nascent manufactures as fast as
it was thrown upon the world. On the other hand, these men, suddenly
dragged from their wonted mode of life, could not as suddenly adapt themselves to the discipline of their new condition. They were turned en masse
into beggars, robbers and vagabonds, partly from inclination, in most cases
from stress of circumstances. Hence at the end of the 15th and during the
whole of the 16th centuries, throughout Western Europe a bloody legislation
[was instituted] against vagabondage. The fathers of the present working-
class were chastised for their enforced transformation into vagabonds and
paupers. Legislation treated them as 'voluntary' criminals, and assumed that
it depended on their own good will to go on working under the old conditions which in fact no longer existed. . . . Out of the poor fugitives, of whom
Thomas More says that they were forced to thieve, '72,000 great and petty
thieves were put to death' in the reign of Henry VIII.[13]

Naturally, not even the highly respected thinkers of the ruling class
could adopt a stance dissenting from the most cruel way of subduing
those who had to be kept under the strictest form of control in the
interest of the established order. Not until the changing conditions of
production itself created the need for a—greatly enlarged—labor force
under the expansionary conditions of the industrial revolution.

By the time John Locke was writing, there was a greater demand
for profitably employable people than at the time of Henry VIII, even
if still very far from what came about during the industrial revolution.
Thus, the significantly diminishing "surplus population" did not have
to be physically exterminated as before. Nevertheless, it had to be treated in the most authoritarian fashion, rationalizing at the same time the
commended brutality and inhumanity in the name of high-sounding
morality. In the last decades of the seventeenth century, in conformity
to capital's standpoint of political economy at the time, the great idol
of modern liberalism, John Locke—an absentee landowner in
Somersetshire as well as a most generously paid government official—
preached the same "insipid childishness" as described by Marx. Locke

insisted that the cause of "the growth of the poor . . . can be nothing else but the relaxation of discipline and corruption of manners; virtue and industry being as constant companions on one side as vice and idleness are on the other. The first step, therefore, towards the setting of the poor on work . . . ought to be a restraint of their debauchery by a strict execution of the laws provided against it [by Henry VIII and others]."[14]

Receiving annually the astronomical remuneration, for the time, of around £1,500 for his services to government (as a Commissioner at the Board of Trade, one of his several offices), Locke did not hesitate to praise the prospect of the poor earning "a penny per diem,"[15] i.e., a sum approximately *1,000 times lower* than his own income from just one of his governmental offices. Not surprisingly, therefore, "The value of his estate at death—nearly £20,000, of which £12,000 was in cash—was comparable to that of a well-to-do London merchant."[16] Quite an achievement for someone whose principal source of revenue was milking the—admittedly more than willing—state!

Moreover, being a true gentleman, with a very high stake to protect, he also wanted to regulate the movements of the poor through the draconian measure of passes, proposing: "That all men begging in maritime counties without passes, that are maimed or above fifty years of age, and all of any age so begging without passes in inland counties nowhere bordering on the sea, shall be sent to the next house of correction, there to be kept at hard labor for three years."[17] And while the brutal laws of Henry VIII and Edward VI wanted to slice off only "half the ear" of the second offenders, our great liberal philosopher and state official—one of the leading figures of early English Enlightenment—suggested an improvement on such laws by solemnly recommending the loss of both ears, to be administered already to first offenders.[18]

At the same time, in his "Memorandum on the Reform of the Poor Law," Locke also proposed the institution of workhouses for the children of the poor from a very early age, arguing:

> The children of laboring people are an ordinary burden to the parish, and are usually maintained in idleness, so that their labor also is generally lost to the public til they are twelve or fourteen years old. The most effectual remedy for this that we are able to conceive, and which we therefore humbly propose, is, that, in the fore-mentioned new law to be enacted, it be further provided that working schools be set up in every parish, to which the children of all such as

demand relief of the parish, above three and under fourteen years of age . . . shall be obliged to come.[19]

Not a religious man himself, Locke's chief concern was how to combine severe work discipline and religious indoctrination with the maximum of state and municipal financial frugality. He argued: "Another advantage also of bringing children thus to a working school is that by this means they may be *obliged to come constantly to church* every Sunday, along with their schoolmasters or dames, whereby they may be brought into some sense of religion; whereas ordinarily now, in their idle and loose way of breeding up, they are as utter strangers both to *religion and morality* as they are to *industry.*"[20]

Obviously, then, the measures that had to be applied to the "laboring poor" were radically different from those the "men of enlightenment" considered suitable for themselves. In the end, it all boiled down to naked power relations, enforced with utmost brutality and violence in the course of early capitalist developments, irrespective of how they were rationalized in the "tender annals of political economy," in Marx's words.

Naturally, the institutions of education had to be adapted as time went by, in accordance with the changing reproductive determinations of the capital system. In this way, utmost brutality and legally enforced violence as educational means—once not only unquestioningly accepted but even actively promoted by early enlightenment figures, like Locke, as we have just seen—had to be left behind. They were abandoned not because of humanitarian considerations, even if they were frequently rationalized in such terms, but because maintaining the machinery of strict enforcement proved to be economically wasteful or at least superfluous. And this was true not only of the formal institutions of education but also in some fields indirectly connected with educational ideas. To take only one significant example, the initial success of Robert Owen's experiment was due not to the paternalistic humanitarianism of this enlightened capitalist, but to the relative productive advantage at first enjoyed by the industrial enterprise of his utopian community. For thanks to the reduction of the absurdly long working-day prevailing as a general rule at the time, the Owenite approach to work resulted in a much greater *intensity* of productive achievement during the reduced hours. Once, however, similar practices were more broadly diffused, as they had to be under the rules of capitalist competition, his enterprise became doomed and went bankrupt, notwithstanding the undoubtedly advanced views of Robert Owen on educational matters.

Capital's overall determinations deeply affect *every single* domain that has a bearing on education, and by no means only the formal educational institutions. The latter are closely integrated in the totality of the social processes. They cannot function properly, unless they are in tune with the *comprehensive educational determinations of society* as a whole.

Here the crucial issue, under the rule of capital, is to secure the adoption of the objectively feasible reproductive aims of the system by the particular individuals as "their own ends." In other words, in a truly comprehensive sense of the term *education*, this is a need for an *"internalizing"* by individuals of the legitimacy of the station assigned to them in the social hierarchy, together with their "proper" expectations and the "right" forms of conduct more or less explicitly stipulated on that ground. So long as *internalization* can do its good work, securing the overall reproductive parameters of the capital system, brutality and violence can be pushed into the background (though by no means permanently abandoned) as wasteful modalities of value-enforcement, as indeed happened in the course of modern capitalistic developments. Only in periods of *acute crisis* is the arsenal of brutality and violence brought back to prominence for the purpose of value-enforcement, as the tragedy of many thousands of *desaparecidos* in Chile and in Argentina demonstrated in recent times.

To be sure, the formal institutions of education are an important part of the overall system of internalization. But they are only one part of it. Whether or not the individuals are participating in the formal educational institutions, they must be induced into the active (or more or less resigned) acceptance of the dominant reproductive orienting principles of society itself, as befits their station in the social order, and in accordance with the reproductive tasks assigned to them. Under the conditions of slavery or feudal serfdom this is, of course, a very different problem from what must prevail under capitalism, even when the working individuals are formally not at all, or very little, educated in the formal sense of the term. Nevertheless, by internalizing the ubiquitous outside pressures, they must adopt the overall perspectives of commodity society as the unquestionable limit of their own aspirations. Only the *most conscious collective action* can extricate them from this paralyzing predicament.

Viewed in this perspective, it is very clear that formal education is not the *primary* ideological cementing force of the capital system; nor is it capable of providing, *on its own*, a radical emancipatory alternative to it. A main function of formal education in our societies is to produce as much conformity or "consensus" as it is capable of within and through its own institutionalized and legally sanctioned limits. To expect from commodity society the active enactment—or even the mere toleration—of a mandate given to its formal educational institutions which would invite them to fully embrace the great historic task of our time: that is, the task of *breaking capital's logic in the interest of human survival*, would be a monumental miracle. This is why remedies, also in the educational field, "cannot be *formal*; they must be *essential*." In other words, they must embrace the totality of educational practices of established society.

Formal educational remedies, even some major ones, and even when they are enshrined in law, can be completely *reversed*, so long as capital's logic remains intact as the orienting framework of society. In Britain, for instance, the main debate on education, for several decades, centered on the question of *"Comprehensive Schools,"* to be instituted in place of the long established elitist school system. In the course of those debates, the British Labour Party not only adopted as a key electoral program the general strategy of replacing the former privileged system of learning by the Comprehensive Schools, but in fact also legally codified that policy after successfully forming the government, although even then it did not dare to touch the most privileged sector of education, the so-called "Public Schools."[21] Today, however, the British government of "New Labour" is bent upon *dismantling* the comprehensive school system, by not only refurbishing the old elitist educational institutions but also by instituting a new variety of middle-class-favoring "academies" in addition to them, despite all criticism even among its own supporters about the establishment of a "two-tier system" in the field, just like the two-tier-system is in the course of being established and reinforced by the government in the British National Health Service.

Thus, one cannot escape even from the "formidable prison" of the established school system (condemned in these words by José Martí) by simply reforming it on its own. For what was there before such reforms will surely be restored sooner or later, due to the utter failure to challenge, by any isolated institutional change, the self-asserting

overall logic of capital itself. What needs to be confronted and fundamentally altered is the *entire* system of *internalization*, with all of its
visible and hidden dimensions. Breaking capital's logic in the field of
education is therefore synonymous with replacing the ubiquitous and
deeply entrenched forms of mystifying internalization with a comprehensive *positive* alternative.

This is the question we must now turn to.

8.3 "Learning is Our Very Life, From Youth to Old Age"

Paracelsus was absolutely right in his day, and he is no less right today:
"Learning is our very life, from youth to old age, indeed to the brink of
death; no one lives for ten hours without learning."

The big question is: what is it that we learn in one way or another? Is it conducive to the self-realization of individuals as humanly
"rich social individuals" (in Marx's words), or is it in the service of perpetuating, knowingly or not, capital's alienating and ultimately uncontrollable social order? Is it the knowledge that is required for turning
into reality the ideal of human emancipation, together with the individual's sustained determination and dedication to see humanity's
self-emancipation through to its successful conclusion, despite all
adversity? Or is it, on the contrary, the adoption of modes of behavior
by the particular individuals that favor only the realization of capital's
reified ends? In this broadest and deepest meaning of education,
which includes in a prominent way all moments of our working life,
we can agree with Paracelsus that so much (nearly everything) is
decided, for better or worse—not only for ourselves as individuals but
simultaneously also for humanity—in all those inescapable hours
which we cannot spend "without learning." This is so because "learning is, truly, our very life." And since so much is decided in this way for
better or worse, success hinges on making this process of learning, in
the Paracelsian all-embracing sense, a *conscious* one, in order to maxi-
mize the *better* and minimize the *worse*.

Only the broadest conception of education can help us pursue the
aim of a truly radical change, by providing the levers through which
capital's mystifying logic can be broken. That way of approaching matters is, indeed, both the hope and the guarantee of feasible success. By
contrast, falling for the temptation of formal institutional tinkering—
"little by little," as the reformist wisdom goes from time immemori-

al—means remaining trapped within the institutionally articulated and safeguarded vicious circle of capital's self-serving logic. The latter way of looking both at the problems themselves and at their "realistic" solutions is carefully cultivated and propagandized in our societies, whereas the genuine and far-reaching real alternative is *a priori* disqualified and bombastically dismissed as "gesture politics." This kind of approach is incurably *elitist*, even when it pretends to be democratic. For it defines both education and intellectual activity in the narrowest possible way, as the only right and proper form of preserving "civilized standards" by those destined to educate and govern, against anarchy and subversion. It excludes at the same time the overwhelming majority of humankind from the field of acting as *subjects*, and condemns them forever to being only acted upon as *objects* (and manipulated in the same sense), in the name of the presumed superiority of the elite—"meritocratic," "technocratic," "entrepreneurial," or whatever else.

Against the tendentiously narrow conception of education and intellectual life, which is of course intended to keep labor "in its proper place," Gramsci forcefully argued:

> There is no human activity from which all intellectual intervention can be excluded—*homo faber* cannot be separated from *homo sapiens*. Also every man, outside his own job, develops some intellectual activity; he is, in other words, a 'philosopher,' an artist, a man of taste, he shares a conception of the world, he has a conscious line of moral conduct, and so *contributes towards maintaining or changing a conception of the world*, that is, towards encouraging new modes of thought.[22]

As we can see, Gramsci's position is profoundly democratic. It is the only tenable one. His conclusion is twofold. First, he insists that *every* human being contributes to the formation of the prevailing conception of the world in one-way or another. And second, he underlines that such contribution can fall into the contrasting categories of "maintaining" and "changing." It can be not simply one or the other but simultaneously also both. Which of the two is more accentuated, and to what degree, will obviously depend on the way in which the conflicting social forces clash with one another and assert their important alternative interests. In other words, the dynamic of history is not some mysterious external force but the intervention of the great multiplicity of human beings in the actual historical process, on the line of "maintaining and/or changing"—in a relatively static period much more "maintaining" than "changing," or vice versa at the time of a major upsurge in the intensity of antagonistic hegemonic confrontations—the given conception of the world, and thereby delaying or hastening the arrival of a significant social change.

This puts into perspective the elitist claims of self-appointed politicians and educators. For they cannot change at will the "conception of the world" of their age, no matter how much they would like to do so, and no matter how massive might be the propaganda apparatus at their disposal. An inescapably *collective process* of elemental proportions cannot be expropriated for good even by the cleverest and most generously financed political and intellectual operators. If it was not for this inconvenient "brute fact," put so forcefully into relief by Gramsci, the dominance of narrow formal institutional education could reign forever in capital's favor.

No amount of *manipulation from above* can turn the immensely complex process of shaping the general world view of our times— made up of countless particular conceptions constituted on the basis of objectively irreconcilable alternative hegemonic interests, irrespective of how conscious the individuals involved might be of the underlying structural antagonisms—into a *uniform and homogeneous* device, functioning as the *permanent* promoter of capital's logic. Not even the aspect of "*maintaining*" can be considered a *passive* constituent of the individuals' prevailing conception of the world. Even if in a very different way from the aspect of "changing" the worldview of the age, it is nevertheless *active*, and beneficial to capital only while it remains active. This means that "maintaining" has (and must have) its own ground of rationality, no matter how problematical it is as regards labor's hegemonic alternative. That is, it must be not only produced at some point in time by the structurally dominated classes of individuals, but must be *constantly reproduced* as well by them, subject to the permanence (or not) of its original ground of rationality. When a significant majority of the population—something approaching 70 percent in many countries—turns away with disdain from the "democratic process" of the electoral ritual, having fought for the right to vote for decades in the past, that shows a real shift in attitude toward the ruling order; one might say a crack in the thick layers of plaster carefully deposited over the "democratic" facade of the system. However, by no means could or should that be interpreted as a radical withdrawal from *maintaining* the now dominant conception of the world.

Naturally, the conditions are much more favorable to the attitude of "changing" and to the emergence of an alternative conception of the world in the midst of a revolutionary crisis, described by Lenin as the time "when the ruling classes cannot rule the old way, and the subordinate classes do not want to live the old way." These are quite extraordinary moments in history, and they cannot be prolonged as one would wish, as the failure of voluntaristic strategies has demonstrated it in the past.[23] Thus, with regard to both "maintaining" and "changing" the given conception of the world, the fundamental issue is the necessity to modify, in an *enduring* way, the historically prevailing mode of *internalization*. Breaking capital's logic in the field of education is quite inconceivable without that. And, more importantly, this relationship can and must be expressed also in a *positive* way. For through a radical change in the now overbearing mode of internalization, which sustains the dominant conception of the world, the rule of capital can and will be broken.

One cannot stress enough the strategic importance of the broadest conception of education, expressed in the phrase: *"learning is our very life."* Thankfully, much of our continued process of learning lies outside of formal educational institutions. Thankfully, these processes cannot be readily manipulated and controlled by the legally safeguarded and sanctioned formal educational framework. They embrace everything, from our budding critical responses *vis-à-vis* the more or less deprived material surroundings of our early childhood, as well as from our first encounter with poetry and art, all the way through our manifold work experiences, subjected to reasoned scrutiny by ourselves and by the people with whom we share them, and, of course, to our involvement in many different ways in conflicts and confrontations throughout our life, including the social, political, and moral disputes of our days.

Only a very small part of all this is directly connected with formal education. Yet, it has a great importance not only in our early formative years but throughout our life, when so much must be constantly reassessed and brought into a coherent, organic, workable unity without which we could not possess a personality, but would fall to fragmentary pieces—good for nothing, defective even for the service of authoritarian sociopolitical ends. The nightmare of Orwell's *1984* is unrealizable precisely because the overwhelming majority of our constitutive experiences remain—and shall always remain—outside the domain of formal institutional control and enforcement. To be sure, many schools can do a great deal of damage, fully deserving thereby Martí's severe strictures as "formidable prisons." But even their worst network cannot prevail uniformly. Young people can find intellectual, moral, and artistic nourishment elsewhere.

I was personally most fortunate to encounter, at the age of eight, a very great teacher. Not in school but almost by chance. He has been my companion ever since, every day. His name is Attila József—a giant of world literature. Those who have read the epigraph of my book, *Beyond Capital*, know his name already. But let me quote a few lines from another of his great poems, chosen as the epigraph of my present book. They read in Spanish like this:

> *Ni Dios ni la mente, sino*
> *el carbón, el hierro y el petróleo,*
>
> *la materia real nos ha creado*
> *echhándonos hirvientes y violentos*
> *en los moldes de esta*
> *sociedad horrible,*
> *para afincarnos, por la humanidad,*
> *en el eterno suelo.*
>
> *Tras los sacerdotes, los soldatos y los burgueses,*
> *al fin nos hemos vuelto fieles*
> *oidores de las leyes:*
> *por eso el sentido de toda obra humana*
> *zumba en nosotros*
> *como el violón profundo.*[24]

Neither god nor reason:

> real matter created us,
> coal, iron and petrol,
> thrown us into the mould
> of this horrible society,
> ardently and untrammelled,
> to make our stand for humanity
> on the eternal soil.

After priests, soldiers and burghers,
thus we became at last the faithful
listeners to the laws:
this is why the sense of all
human work throngs in us
like the deep viola.

These lines were written seventy-one years ago, in 1933, when Hitler
seized power in Germany. But they speak to all of us today with greater
intensity than ever before. They invite us to "listen attentively and
faithfully to the laws," and proclaim them everywhere loud and clear,
since today nothing less than the very survival of humanity is at stake.
No formal mis-educational practices can extinguish the enduring
validity and power of such influences.

Yes, "learning is our very life," as Paracelsus put it nearly five centuries ago, and in his footsteps many others too who have never even
heard his name. But to make this truth self-evident, as it should be, we
have to reclaim the full domain of lifelong education, in order to be
able to put the formal part of it in perspective, in the interest of instituting a radical reform also there. This cannot be done without challenging the now dominant forms of *internalization,* greatly reinforced
in capital's favor by the formal educational system itself. In fact, the
principal function of formal education is to act as an *ex officio author-
itative* watchdog over inducing a general *conformism* in the given
modes of internalization, so as to subordinate them to the requirements of the established order. That formal education cannot succeed
in creating *universal conformity* does not alter the fact that on the
whole it is oriented towards that end. The teachers and pupils who
rebel against such design do so with the ammunition they acquire
both from their fellow rebels within the formal domain, and from the
broadest field of educational experience "from youth to old age."

What we badly need, then, is a coherent and sustained activity of
"counter-internalization" which does not exhaust itself in *negation—*
no matter how necessary that is as a *phase* in this enterprise—but
defines its fundamental aims as the creation of a comprehensive *positively sustainable* alternative to the existent. Nearly thirty years ago, I
was editing and introducing a volume of essays by the outstanding
Filipino historian and political thinker, Renato Constantino. He was
kept at the time under the most severe authoritarian constraints by the

U.S. client regime of General Marcos. At some point he succeeded to pass on to me the message that he would like to have the volume entitled: *Neo-Colonial Identity and Counter-Consciousness*.[25] Fully aware of the enslaving impact of the internalization of colonial consciousness in his own country, Constantino always tried to put the accent on the historic task of producing an enduring alternative system of education, with all means at the people's disposal, well beyond the formal educational domain. "Counter-consciousness" thereby acquired a positive meaning. In relation to the past, Constantino pointed out that "From its inception, Spanish colonization operated more through religion than through force, thus profoundly affecting consciousness. . . . The molding of consciousness in the interest of colonial control was to be repeated on another plane by the Americans who after a decade of massive repression operated likewise through consciousness, this time using education and other cultural institutions."[26] And he made it clear that the constitution of decolonized counter-consciousness directly involved the popular masses in the critical enterprise. This is how he defined the meaning of a "philosophy of liberation" which he advocated: "It is itself a growing thing depending on accretions of consciousness. . . . It is not contemplative; it is active and dynamic and encompasses the objective situation as well as the subjective reaction of the people involved. It cannot be the work of a select group, even if this group regards itself as motivated by the best interests of the people. It needs the participation of the *backbone of the nation*."[27] In other words, the advocated educational approach had to embrace the totality of cultural, educational, and political practices in the broadest conception of emancipatory transformations. This is how a strategically conceived counter-consciousness, as the necessary alternative to colonially dominated internalization, could fulfill its great educative mandate.

Indeed, the role and the corresponding responsibility of the educators could not be greater. For, as José Marti made it clear, the pursuit of culture, in the proper sense of the term, involves the highest stake in that it is inseparable from the fundamental objective of liberation. He insisted that "*Ser cultos es el único modo de ser libres.*" And he summed up, in a beautiful way, the *raison d'être* of education itself: "*Educar es depositar en cada hombre toda la obra humana que le ha antecedido: es hacer a cada hombre resumen del mundo viviente hasta el dia en que vive . . .*"[28] ["To educate is to deposit in every human being all human work which had preceded him: to make every human being the sum of the living world up to the time when he lives . . ."] This is quite impossible within the narrow confines of formal education as it is constituted, under all kinds of heavy constraints, in our time. Martí himself felt that the whole process of education must be remade in every respect, so as to transform the "formidable prison" into a site of emancipation and genuine fulfillment. This is why he single-handedly also wrote and published a monthly periodical for the young in 1889, entitled *La Edad De Oro*.[29]

This is the spirit in which all dimensions of education can be brought together. The orienting principles of formal education must be in this way extricated from their integument with capital's conformity imposing logic, moving instead towards an active and positive interchange with the broadest educational practices. Without a conscious progressive interchange with the all-embracing processes of education as "our very life," formal education cannot fulfill its much-needed *emancipatory aspirations*. If, however, the progressive elements of formal education succeed in redefining their task in a spirit oriented towards the perspective of a hegemonic alternative to the existing order, they can make a vital contribution to breaking capital's logic, not only in their own more limited domain but also in society as a whole.

8.4 Education as the "Positive Transcendence of Labor's Self-Alienation"

We live under conditions of dehumanizing alienation and of a fetishistic overturning of the real state of affairs in consciousness (often characterized as "reification"), because capital cannot exercise its social metabolic functions of enlarged reproduction in any other way. To change these conditions requires a conscious intervention in all domains and at all levels of our individual and social existence. This is why, according to Marx, human beings must change "from top to bottom the conditions of their industrial and political existence, and consequently *their whole manner of being*."[30]

Marx also stressed that—if we are looking for the Archimedean point from which the mystifying contradictions of our social order can both be made intelligible and transcended—we find at the roots of all varieties of alienation the historically unfolding *alienation of labor*, a process of enslaving *self-alienation*. But precisely because we are concerned with a *historical* process, imposed not by a mythical outside agency of metaphysical predestination (characterized as the inescapable "human predicament")[31], nor indeed by an unchangeable "human nature"—the way in which this problem is often tendentiously depicted—but by labor itself, it is possible to *overcome alienation* through a *radical restructuring* of our long-established conditions of existence, and thereby "our whole manner of being."

Consequently, the necessary conscious intervention in the historical process, oriented by the adopted task of overcoming alienation through the new social reproductive metabolism of the "freely associated producers," this kind of strategically sustained action cannot be only a question of *negation*, no matter how radical. For in Marx's view all forms of negation remain *conditioned by the object of their negation*. As bitter historical experience has amply demonstrated, the *conditioning inertia* of the negated object tends to grow in power as time goes by, imposing at first the pursuit of "the line of least resistance" and subsequently—with greater and greater intensity—the "rationality" of going back to the "well tried practices" of the *status quo ante* which are bound to survive in the un-restructured dimensions of the previous order.

This is where education—in the most comprehensive meaning of the term as discussed above—comes to the fore. Inevitably, the first steps of a major social transformation in our age involve the need to bring under control the hostile political state, which opposes, and by its very nature must oppose, any idea of an all-embracing societal restructuring. In this sense, the *radical negation* of the overall political command structure of the established system must assert itself, in its unavoidable predominant negativity, at the *initial phase* of the intended transformation. But even at that phase, and indeed prior to the conquest of political power, the necessary negation is appropriate to its assumed role only if it is positively informed by the *overall target* of the envisaged social transformation, as the *compass* of the whole journey. Thus, the role of education is vitally important right from the beginning for breaking the prevailing internalization of the political choices confined to the "democratic constitutional legitimation" of the capitalist state. For also this "counter-internalization" (or "counter-consciousness") requires the anticipation of the comprehensive positive outlines of a radically different way of managing the overall decision-

making functions of society, well beyond the long-established expropriation of the power of taking all of the fundamental decisions, as
well as of their unceremonious imposition on individuals, by politics
as the form of alienation *par excellence* under the existing order.

However, the historic task we have to face is immeasurably greater
than the negation of capitalism. The concept of going *beyond capital* is
an inherently *positive* one. It envisages the realization of a social metabolic order, which *positively sustains itself,* without any self-justifying
reference to the evils of capitalism. This must be the case because the
direct negation of the various manifestations of alienation is still con-
ditional on what it negates, and therefore remains vulnerable in virtue
of that conditionality.

The reformist strategy of defending capitalism is in fact based on
trying to postulate a gradual change in society through which the *particular defects* are removed, so as to undermine the ground on which
the claims of an *alternative system* can be articulated. This is feasible in
tendentiously fictionalized theory only, since the postulated remedial
"reforms" are structurally unrealizable in practice within the established framework of society. In this way, it becomes clear that the real
object of reformism is not at all what it claims for itself—namely, the
actual remedy of the undeniable particular defects, even if their magnitude is deliberately minimized, and even if the projected way of dealing with them is admitted to be very slow. The only term which has an
actually intended referent in this discourse is *"gradual,"* and even that
happens to be wildly inflated into an overall strategy, which it cannot
be. For the particular defects of capitalism cannot be even superficially surveyed, let alone genuinely remedied, without examining the *system as a whole* which necessarily produces and constantly *reproduces*
these defects.

The reformist refusal to address the contradictions of the existing
system, in the name of the assumed legitimacy of dealing with *particular manifestations only*—or in their "postmodern" varieties, the *a priori* rejection of so-called *grandes narratives* in the name of arbitrarily
idealized *petits récits*—is in reality only a peculiar way of rejecting
without a proper analysis the possibility of any rival system, and an
equally *a priori* way of eternalizing the capitalist system. The real
object of reformist argument is, rather mystifyingly, the ruling system
as such, and not the *parts* of either the rejected or of the defended system, notwithstanding the alleged reforming zeal explicitly stated by the

advocates of "gradual change."[32] The necessary failure to bring out into the open the real concern of reformism arises from its inability to sustain the *timeless validity* of the established socioeconomic and political order. It is in reality quite inconceivable to sustain the timeless validity and permanence of anything *historically created*. This is what makes it unavoidable, in all varieties of sociopolitical reformism, to try and divert attention from the *systemic* determinations—which ultimately define the character of all vital issues—to more or less haphazard disputes over particular *effects* while leaving their incorrigible *causal ground* not only unchallengeable and permanent but even unmentioned.

All this remains hidden by the very nature of the reformist discourse. And precisely because of the mystifying character of such a discourse whose fundamental constituents often remain hidden even to its leading ideologists, it does not matter at all to the believers in this creed that at a certain point in history—as with the arrival of "New Labour" in Britain and of its brother and sister parties in Germany, France, Italy and elsewhere—the very idea of any meaningful social reform is completely abandoned, and yet the claims to a pretended "advancement" (leading absolutely nowhere really different) are disingenuously reasserted. Thus, even the former differences between the main parties are conveniently obliterated in the now dominant U.S. style "two-party" (*one-party*) system, no matter how many "subparties" we can still find in the particular countries. What remains constant is the more or less concealed defense of the actual *systemic determinations* of the existing order. The pernicious axiom which asserts that *there is no alternative*—talking not simply about the given political institutions but about the established social order in general—is as acceptable to the British Conservative Party's former Prime Minister, Margaret Thatcher (who championed and popularized it), as to the so-called "New Labour" of current Prime Minister Tony Blair, as well as to many others in the worldwide parliamentary political spectrum.

In view of the fact that the process of radical restructuring must be oriented by the strategy of a comprehensive *positive* reshaping of the entire system in which individuals find themselves, the challenge that must be faced has no parallels in history. For the fulfillment of this novel historic task simultaneously involves a qualitative change of the objective conditions of societal reproduction, in the sense of regaining full control from capital itself—and not simply from particular types of personifications of capital who assert the system's imperatives as devoted capitalists—and the *ongoing transformation of consciousness* in response to the necessarily changing conditions. Thus, the role of education is paramount both for elaborating appropriate strategies to change the objective conditions of reproduction, and for the *conscious self-change* of the individuals called upon to realize the creation of a radically different social metabolic order. This is what is meant by the envisaged "*society of freely associated producers*." It is not surprising, therefore, that in the Marxian conception the "*positive transcendence of labor's self-alienation*" is characterized as an inescapably educational task.

Two key concepts must be kept in the forefront of our attention: the *universalization of education* and the *universalization of labor (work) as self-fulfilling human activity*. In fact, neither is viable without the other. Nor is it possible to think of their close interrelationship as a problem for a rather distant future. It arises *here and now*, and it is relevant to every level and degree of socioeconomic development. We can find a prominent example of it in a speech made by Fidel Castro in 1983, regarding the problems Cuba had to face by accepting the imperative of *universalizing education*, despite the apparently prohibitive difficulties not only in economic terms but also in providing the required teachers. This is how he summed up the problem:

> A la vez habíamos llegado ya a una situación en que el estudio se universalizaba. Y para universalizar el estudio en un país subdesarrollado y no petrolero— digamos –, desde el punto de vista económico era necesario universalizar el trabajo. Pero aunque fuésemos petroleros, habría sido altamente conveniente universalizar el trabajo, altamente formativo en todos los sentidos, y altamente revolucionario. Que por algo estas ideas fueron planteadas hace mucho tiempo por Marx y por Martí.[33]

> We reached a situation where study was *universalized*. And to universalize study in an underdeveloped country without petrol–to say so–from the standpoint of the economy it was necessary to *universalize work*. But even if we had petrol, it would have been most appropriate to universalize work, which is *highly formative* in every sense, and *highly revolutionary*. In any case, these ideas have been advocated a long time ago, by Marx and by Martí.

The outstanding educational achievements in Cuba, from the speedy and total elimination of illiteracy to the highest levels of creative scientific research[34]—in a country which had to struggle not only against the massive economic constraints of *subdesarrollo* but also against the grave impact of forty-five years of hostile encirclement—is understandable only against this background. This achievement also demonstrates that there can be no justification for waiting for a "favorable time" to arrive, in the indefinite future. Embarking on the road of a qualitatively different approach to education and learning can and must begin *here and now*, if we want to achieve the necessary changes in due course.

There can be no positive solution to labor's self-alienation without consciously promoting the conjoined universalization of work and education. However, there was no real chance for that in the past, due to the structural hierarchical subordination and domination of labor. Not even when some great thinkers tried to conceptualize these problems in a most progressive spirit. Thus Paracelsus, a model for Goethe's *Faust*, tried to universalize work and learning in this way:

> *Although man was created whole as regards his body, he was not so created as regards his 'art.' All the arts have been given him, but not in an immediately recognizable form; he must discover them by learning. . . . The proper way resides in work and action, in doing and producing; the perverse man does nothing, but talks a great deal. We must not judge a man by his words, but by his heart. The heart speaks through words only when they are confirmed by deeds. . . . No one sees what is hidden in him, but only what his works reveal. Therefore man should work continually to discover what God has given him.*[35]

Indeed, Paracelsus insisted that labor [*arbeit*] should be the general ordering principle of society. He went as far as actually advocating the expropriation of the wealth of the idle rich, in order to compel them to lead a productive life.[36]

The idea of universalizing work and education, in their inseparability from one another, goes back very far in our history. It is, therefore, all the more significant that this idea had to remain a most frustrated idea only, because its realization necessarily presupposes the *substantive equality* of all human beings. The grave fact that the dehumanizing *working-time* of individuals is also the greater part of their *lifetime*, had to be callously disregarded. The *controlling* functions of social metabolic reproduction had to be separated from, and opposed to the overwhelming majority of humankind, assigned to the implementation of subordinate tasks in the given socioeconomic and political system. In the same spirit, not only the control of structurally subordinated labor but also the control dimension of education had to be kept in a separate compartment, under the rule of the personifications of capital in our time. Changing this relationship of structural domination and subordination is impossible without the realization of true—*substantive*, and not only *formal* (which is always deeply affected, if not completely nullified by the actually existing substantive dimension of)—*equality*. This is why only within the perspective of going *beyond capital* can the challenge of universalizing work and education, in their inseparability from one another, appear on the historical agenda.

In the long dominant conception of education, the political rulers and the ruled, as well as the educationally privileged (whether the individuals employed as educators or as administrators in control of the educational institutions) and those who have to be educated, appear in separate, almost watertight, compartments. A good example of this vision is expressed in an article on education published in the reputedly last scholarly edition of the *Encyclopaedia Britannica*. It reads as follows:

> The action of the modern state cannot stop short at elementary education. The principle of 'the career open to talent' is no longer a matter of abstract humanitarian theory, a fantastical aspiration of revolutionary dreamers; for the great industrial communities of the modern world it is a cogent practical necessity imposed by the fierce international competition which prevails in the arts and industries of life. The nation that is not to fail in the struggle for commercial success, with all that this implies for national life and civilization, must needs see that its industries are fed with a constant supply of workers adequately equipped in respect both of general intelligence and technical training. On political grounds, too, the increasing democratization of institutions renders a wide diffusion of knowledge and the cultivation of a high standard of intelligence among the people a necessary precaution of prudent statesmanship, especially for the great imperial states which confide the most momentous issues of world policy to the arbitrament of the popular voice.[37]

Even in its own terms of reference this—undoubtedly in its historical survey impressive—scholarly article is most defective, as a result of clearly identifiable ideological reasons. For it greatly exaggerates the beneficial effects of the "fierce international competition" of national capitals on the education of the working people. Harry Braverman's insightful book on "*The Degradation of Work in the Twentieth Century*"[38] gives an incomparably better assessment of the alienating and brutalizing forces at work in the modern capitalist enterprise. They cast a sharply negative light on the wishful misrepresentation of the "struggle for commercial success," which the author of this article postulates as having a "civilizing" impact, where in reality often the diametrical opposite is the necessary outcome. And even as regards the particular industrial enterprises, the so-called scientific management of Frederic Winslow Taylor gives away the secret of how high the educational and intellectual requirements of capitalist firms are supposed to be for running a competitively successful operation. As F.W. Taylor, the founder of this system of authoritarian managerial control, writes with undisguised cynicism:

> . . . one of the first requirements for a man who is fit to handle pig iron as a regular occupation is that he shall be so stupid and so phlegmatic that he more nearly resembles in his mental make-up the ox than any other type. . . . The workman who is best suited to handling pig iron is unable to understand the real science of doing this class of work. He is so stupid that the word 'percentage' has no meaning for him.[39]

Very scientific indeed! As to the proposition according to which "a wide diffusion of knowledge and the cultivation of a high standard of intelligence" is the happily adopted aim of the modern capitalist state—"*especially for the great imperial states which confide the most momentous issues of world policy to the arbitrament of the popular voice*"—it is too laughable and too obviously apologetic in character to be considered even for a moment a serious argument in favor of the claimed causes of democratically inspired and politically enlightened improvement in education under the conditions of capital's rule over society.

Education *beyond capital* envisages a qualitatively different social order. It is now not only feasible to embark on the road leading to that order but also necessary and urgent as well. For the incorrigible destructive determinations of the existing order make it imperative to counterpose to the capital system's irreconcilable structural antagonisms a sustainable *positive alternative* for regulating social metabolic reproduction, if we want to secure the elementary conditions of human survival. The role of education, oriented by the only positively viable perspective of going beyond capital, is absolutely crucial in this respect.

Sustainability equals the *conscious control* of the social metabolic process of reproduction by the freely associated producers, in contrast to the untenable, structurally entrenched *adversariality* and ultimate destructiveness of capital's reproductive order. It is inconceivable to bring about this conscious control of the social processes—a form of control that also happens to be the only feasible form of *self-control*: the necessary requirement to being *freely associated producers*—without fully activating the resources of education in the most comprehensive sense of the term.

The grave and unsurpassable defect of the capital system consists in the *alienating second order mediations* it must impose on all human beings, including the personifications of capital. In fact, the capital system could not survive for a week without its second-order mediations: principally the state, the market-oriented exchange relation, and labor in its structural subordination to capital. They are necessarily interposed between individuals, as well as between particular individuals and their aspirations, turning the latter upside down and inside out, in order to be able to subordinate them to the fetishistic imperatives of the capital system. In other words, these second-order mediations impose an *alien form of mediation* on humanity. The *positive alternative* to this way of controlling social metabolic reproduction can only be *self-mediation*, in its inseparability from *self-control* and *self-realization through substantive freedom and equality*, in a social reproductive order consciously regulated by the associated individuals. It is also inseparable from *values* chosen by the social individuals themselves, in accordance with their real needs, instead of being imposed on them— in the form of thoroughly *artificial appetites* by the reified imperatives of profitable capital-accumulation, as happens to be the case today. *None* of these emancipatory aims are conceivable without the most active intervention of education as conceived in its positive orientation toward a social order beyond capital.

We live in a social order in which even the minimal requirements of human fulfillment are callously denied to the overwhelming majority of humankind, while the production of waste has assumed prohibitive proportions, in accordance with the shift from the claimed capitalist *"productive destruction"* in the past to the ever more dominant actuality of *destructive production* today. The crying social inequalities in evidence today, and even more pronounced in their already unfolding development, are well illustrated by the following figures:

> According to [the] United Nations' Human Development Report, the world's richest 1 percent receive as much income as the poorest 57 percent. The income gap between the richest 20 percent and the poorest 20 percent in the world rose from 30 to 1 in 1960, to 60 to 1 in 1990, and to 74 to 1 in 1999, and is projected to reach 100 to 1 in 2015. In 1999-2000, 2.8 billion people lived on less than $2 a day, 840 million were undernourished, 2.4 billion did not have access to any form of improved sanitation services, and one in every six children in the world of primary school age were not in school. About 50 percent of the global nonagricultural labor force is estimated to be either unemployed or underemployed.[40]

What is at stake here is not simply the *contingent deficiency* of available economic resources, to be overcome sooner or later, as gratuitously promised, but the *necessary structural deficiency* of a system that operates through its *vicious circle of waste and scarcity.* It is impossible to break out of this vicious circle without the positive intervention of education, capable of both *setting priorities* and defining *real needs* with the full and free deliberations of the individuals concerned. Otherwise scarcity can and will be reproduced on an ever-growing scale, in conjunction with the utterly wasteful generation of artificial needs, as done today, in the service of capital's insanely oriented self-enlargement and counter-productive accumulation.

A positively articulated rival conception of education *beyond capital* cannot be confined to a limited number of years in the life of individuals but, due to its radically changed functions, embraces all of them. The "self-education of equals" and the "self-management of the social reproductive order" cannot be separated from one another. The self-management—by the freely associated individuals—of the vital functions of the social metabolic process is an *ongoing*—and inevitably *changing*—enterprise. The same goes for the educational practices, which enable the individuals to fulfill those functions as constantly redefined by themselves, in accord with the changing requirements of which they are the active agents. Education, in this sense, is truly *"continuing education."* It can be neither "vocational" (which means in our society the confinement of the people involved to narrowly predetermined utilitarian functions, deprived of any power of decision making), nor "general" (which is supposed to teach the individuals, in a patronizing way, the "skills of thinking"). These notions are the arrogant presumptions of a conception based on a totally untenable separation of the practical and the strategic dimensions. Thus "continuing education," as a necessary constituent of the regulating principles of a society beyond capital, is inseparable from the meaningful practice of *self-management*. It is an integral part of the latter both as representing at first the *formative phase* in the life of the individuals, and, on the other hand, in the sense of enabling a *positive feedback* from the educationally enriched individuals, with their appropriately changing and equitably redefined needs, to the overall determination of society's orienting principles and objectives.

Our historical predicament is defined by the *structural crisis* of the *global capital system*. It is fashionable to talk, with utter self-complacency, about the great success of capitalist globalization. A recently published and devotedly propagandized book has the title: *Why Globalization Works*.[41] However, the author, who is the Chief Economics Commentator of London's *The Financial Times*, forgets to ask the really important question: *For whom does it work?* if it does. It certainly works, for the time being, and by no means that well, for the decision makers of transnational capital, but not for the overwhelming majority of humankind who must suffer the consequences. And no amount of "jurisdictional integration" advocated by the author— that is, in plain English, tighter direct control of the deplored "too many states" by a handful of imperialist powers, especially the biggest one of them—is going to remedy the situation. Capitalist globalization in reality does not work and cannot work. For it cannot overcome the irreconcilable contradictions and antagonisms manifest through the global structural crisis of the system. Capitalist globalization itself is the contradictory manifestation of that crisis, trying to overturn the *cause-and-effect* relationship in a vain attempt to cure some negative effects by other *wishfully projected effects*, because it is structurally incapable of addressing their *causes*.

Our epoch of capital's *global structural crisis* is also the historical epoch of *transition* from the existing social order to a qualitatively different one. These are the two fundamental defining characteristics of the social and historical space within which the great challenges of *breaking capital's logic*, and at the same time also elaborating the strategic outlines of *education beyond capital,* must be met. Our education-al task is therefore simultaneously also the task of a comprehensive social emancipatory transformation. Neither of the two can be put in front of the other. They are inseparable. The required radical social emancipatory transformation is inconceivable without the most active positive contribution of education in its all-embracing sense, as depicted in this lecture. And vice versa: education cannot work sus-pended in the air. It can and must be properly articulated and con-stantly reshaped in its dialectical interrelationship with the changing conditions and needs of the ongoing social emancipatory transforma-tion. The two succeed or fail, stand or fall together. It is up to us *all*—because we know full well that "the educators must also be educat-ed"—that they should stand and not fall. The stakes are far too high for contemplating the possibility of failure.

In this enterprise, the *immediate* tasks and their overall *strategic framework* cannot be separated from, and opposed to, one another. Strategic success is unthinkable without accomplishing the immediate tasks. In fact, the strategic framework itself is the overall synthesis of innumerable, ever renewed and expanded, immediate tasks and chal-lenges. But the solution of the latter is feasible only if the tackling of immediate challenges is informed by the synthesizing strategic frame-work. The mediatory steps toward the future—in the sense of the only viable form of *self-mediation*—can only start from the *immediate,* but illuminated by the space it can legitimately occupy in the overall strat-egy oriented by the envisaged future.

9. Socialism in the Twenty-First Century

The question of socialism presents itself in the twenty-first century both as the need for a critical evaluation of the past and as the unavoidable challenge for identifying the fundamental requirements that must be incorporated in the envisaged strategies of radical change. This must be done under conditions in which the urgency to counter the ongoing destructive trends of development can only be denied by the worst apologists of the established social metabolic order.

In the present chapter, the principal aims and characteristics of the necessary socialist transformation can only be briefly indicated as *orienting principles* for the elaboration of viable strategies for our future. The order in which the particular points are here presented is not meant to be an order of their importance to which the subsequent ones must be subordinated. By the very nature of the issues at stake it would be artificial and distorting to rank them in that way. For the defining characteristics of a genuine socialist transformation constitute a closely integrated whole. All of them are, in a sense, *Archimedean points* which sustain themselves and one another through their reciprocal determinations and all-round implications. In other words, *all* of them are of equal importance in the sense that *none* should be neglected or omitted in the longer-run from the overall strategy, whatever might be their *immediate* relevance at the outset of the journey.

Nevertheless, the reason why they have to be presented as separate points is twofold. First, for analytical purposes it is helpful to group the relatively homogeneous elements together under the same heading when the complex interconnections of the whole could be established only by bringing into play a series of more distant and somewhat contrasting mediations, with their own specific contexts. And second, the *temporal* dimension of realizing the particular characteristics and requirements of a truly enduring socialist transformation cannot be assumed to be the same. Naturally, some of the advocated changes are feasible considerably earlier than some others. However, even the most difficult aims, whose realization is unavoidably more remote in time, must be acknowledged right from the beginning as vital for the success of the necessary radical transformation in its entirety, otherwise sooner or later the whole enterprise is bound to be derailed or undermined. For without identifying the *overall destination* of the journey, together with the *strategic direction* and the necessary *compass* adopted for reaching it, there can be no hope of success. The disastrous historical failure of social democracy all over the world, thanks also to its false panacea of "the aim is nothing, the movement is everything"—which greatly contributed to transforming its erstwhile reformist program into the reactionary defense of even the most untenable aspects of the ruling order—offers a powerful reminder and warning in this respect.

To be sure, the *radical negation* of the established system of destructive social metabolic control is only one side of what needs to be done. The undoubtedly necessary negation of the capital system can only succeed, if the positive side of the whole enterprise complements it. That is, the progressive creation of an *alternative*—from its inception humanly commendable and *viable*, as well as, even in the longest historical perspective, truly *sustainable*—social reproductive order. This approach indicates an unavoidably complex and intertwined social *process* which defines every single aim and requirement of the socialist transformation as an integral part of an *open-ended* historical undertaking, contrary to the self-serving accusations leveled against socialism as a "utopian closed system," and as such destined to failure because it could only be temporarily imposed on reality by untenable dictatorial measures. In truth, on the contrary, the inherently *processual* determination of socialist aims and requirements means that the particular objectives at any time in focus simultaneously always refer, explicitly or not, to an overall design and become strengthened, as well as deepened and enriched, through their unfolding inter-determinations with one another and thereby in an organic way with the developing whole. With these qualifications, the principal aims and requirements of socialist transformation in the twenty-first century may be characterized as follows.

9.1 Irreversibility: The Imperative of a Historically Sustainable Alternative Order

9.1.1

Past history testifies to many instances of not only noble efforts dedicated to introducing significant social changes in order to overcome some major contradictions but also to some partial successes in the originally envisaged direction. All too often, however, the successes have been sooner or later rolled back by the subsequent restoration of the dependency relations of the earlier *status quo*. The primary reason for such developments was the fateful inertia of *structural inequality* reproduced in one form or another throughout history, despite some change in personnel from time to time at the apex of society. For structural inequality acted as an anchor, with shorter or longer chains attached to it, invariably dragging the ship back to a position from which there seemed to be no possibility of further progress in the journey, no matter how well intentioned might have been some of the personnel of the ship during a major historical tempest. And to make things worse, this historically determinate and humanly alterable predicament of the people dominated by the existing order was on a regular basis conceptualized and ideologically rationalized as a *fatality of nature,* even when it had to be conceded that the prevailing structural inequality was very far from being an all-round beneficial one.

The necessary corollary of this kind of rationalization—and justification of the unjustifiable—was that social iniquity as an allegedly unalterable determination of nature (said to be well in tune with "human nature") is permanent and tenable. But what if the notion of permanence as such is put into question by evidence of a clearly identifiable and menacing historical change? For as soon as it must be admitted that human historical time is not measurable in terms of the permanence of nature, not to mention the fact that the lasting temporality of nature itself on our planet is being catastrophically undermined by the ongoing destructive intervention in nature by perverse socioeconomic forces, the whole reasoning of anti-historical justi-

fication collapses. At that point, it becomes imperative to orient ourselves well within the potentialities and limitations of real historical
time, with a view to radically overcoming the perilous social antagonisms that point in the direction of putting an end to human history.
At that point in time, exactly where we stand today, the elaboration of
the required remedies in the form of a sustainable alternative social
order, together with appropriate safeguards to make that order irreversible, becomes an unavoidable historical challenge. For without
successfully meeting that challenge, given the urgency of a unique
historical time when the survival of humanity is at stake—under the
shadow of both the apparently uncontrollable accumulation and
deployment of the "real" and not cynically and self-servingly fictionalized weapons of mass destruction, and of capital's devastating
encroachment on nature—humankind cannot risk relapsing into an
ever more destructive social order, as if we had the infinity of time at
our disposal before we have to undertake some corrective action.

9.1.2

Given the capital system's grave structural crisis, today the stark alternative is *socialism or barbarism*, if not the complete annihilation of
humankind. This burdensome historical fact calls for the pursuit of a
set of coherent strategies which cannot be reversed at the first opportune moment, in contrast to past failures due to the acceptance of the
"line of least resistance" and the concomitant *defensiveness* of the socialist movement. At the same time, the *target* of sustainable socialist transformation must be firmly reoriented from the *"overthrow of capitalism"*—manageable only on a strictly temporary basis—to the *complete
eradication of capital* from the social metabolic process. Otherwise, the
old structures of the inherited system will surely be revitalized, as we
witnessed in Soviet-type societies in the twentieth century. And such
revitalization brings with it potentially devastating consequences not
only for the societies directly concerned, where capitalism has been
actually restored, but also for the whole of humanity. Indeed, it brings
such consequences for the whole of humanity, on account of the socialist forces being held back by the ideological paralysis caused by internalizing beyond all proportion the relative success of capitalist restoration in some areas while ignoring the much more fundamental conditions of the deepening structural crisis of the capital system as a whole.

Marx warned us about capital's ability to reemerge stronger than before from its partial defeats, characterizing—in contrast to such restorative power—the necessary orientation of proletarian revolutions by saying that they:

> . . . criticize themselves constantly, interrupt themselves continually in their own course, come back to the apparently accomplished in order to begin it afresh, deride with unmerciful thoroughness the inadequacies, weaknesses and paltriness of their first attempts, seem to throw down their adversary only in order that he may draw new strength from the earth and rise again, more gigantic, before them, and they recoil again and again from the indefinite prodigiousness of their own aims, until a situation has been created which makes all turning back impossible, and the conditions themselves cry out:
> Hic Rhodus, hic salta! [Here is Rhodes, leap here!][1]

Naturally, Marx could not anticipate in 1851, when he wrote these lines, that the unavoidable imperative of "Here is Rhodes, leap here!" would arise under the conditions of a grave social and historical emergency, when the threat of humanity's potential self-destruction would be clearly on the horizon. Nevertheless, he succeeded in identifying the two principal considerations that must be kept in mind when assessing the viable perspective of an irreversible socialist transformation. First, the acknowledgement of capital's ultimately most threatening ability to "draw new strength from the earth and rise again," as Anteus did in Greek mythology, so that appropriate strategic measures should be elaborated in order to overcome on a *permanent* basis the power of the ever-more-destructive historical adversary. Especially when the dominant capitalist states undertake genocidal wars in order to prove the "productive viability" of their system. And second, the realization that in the course of historical development there comes a time when the pursuit of the *"line of least resistance"* is no longer tenable, and attempting to leap becomes unavoidable. The historical emergency of our time modifies Marx's second consideration only in the sense that pursuing the "line of least resistance" today is not merely "no longer tenable" but must be brought into the foreground of social consciousness as *suicidal.*

9.2 Participation: The Progressive Transfer
of Decision Making to the Associated Producers

9.2.1

It is inconceivable to make the alternative social order irreversible without the full participation of the associated producers in decision-making at all levels of political, cultural, and economic control. For that is the only way in which the great masses of people can acquire an enduring stake in their society, thereby truly identifying themselves with the aims and modalities of reproducing the conditions of their social existence, determined not only to defend them against all restoratative attempts but also to constantly expand its positive potentialities.

Up to the present time, very few ideas have been used with greater effectiveness for the purpose of ideological mystification than the pretended offer of "participation" in decision making. Even some sizable capitalist enterprises claim to have opened the doors wide to the "democratic participation" of their workforce in their affairs, while in reality keeping the workers as far away as ever before—just like the "sovereign" non-voting shareholders—from all of the really important matters, in the spirit of "good business practice." Social-democratic reformist wishful thinking adopted the same line of approach, often successfully disarming waves of unrest on the Left-syndicalist base by means of utterly meaningless "concessions," allegedly obtained from the industrial leaders in particular enterprises, so as to be able to tie the hands of the workforce that much more tightly, and as a rule behind its back. A bitterly ironical rejection of this practice by popular wisdom was expressed at times in political debates by conjugating the verb "to participate" in the form of finishing the conjugation not with "we participate, you participate, they participate" but *"they profit,"* or, in another version: "we participate, you participate—*they decide."*

That was indeed the mystifying substance of this much-favored reformist strategy. For, notwithstanding all pretenses to the contrary, there could be absolutely no question of moving in the direction of progressively transforming the associated producers into the *subject of power.* Not even by the smallest of the idealized "small degrees." What had to remain an absolute taboo was in fact the *direction* of the transformative journey, leading to a qualitative change. An issue cynically misrepresented as if it was a question of the *size* of the particular steps to be taken: "gradual" or "piecemeal," as opposed to strategically comprehensive. However, the idealized piecemeal method was very far from being without its own strategic direction. For in reality its well hidden ideological orientation was to lead *nowhere* out of the maze of the sharpening contradictions, prudently locked into the vicious circle of the established order. And precisely that sensible apologetic way of going around in pre-established circles was—and remains—its principal function.

Without the overall strategy of *progressively transferring the power of decision making to the associated producers* (that is to say, transferring it at all levels, including the highest of them) the concept of participation has no commendable rationality. This means that the false dichotomies which oppose the "small" to the "large scale," or the "local" to the "global," have no place in a viable socialist strategy, whatever might be the good intentions with which the road to preserving the capital system's hell is paved. The power to be transferred to the associated producers cannot be confined to the *local* level, not even when the bitter pill of continued powerlessness is sugar-coated by slogans like "small is beautiful" and "think globally, act locally."

It is a paralyzing illusion of bourgeois legality that decision-making power can be suitably *divided* and *shared out* in an all-round beneficial way between *hegemonic alternatives.* In truth, however, no real power of decision-making is shared in capital's social order among the competing *social classes,* despite the ideology of the "division of powers" under a claimed "democratic constitutionality." For all significant—as opposed to strictly marginal—powers are possessed by capital itself. Capital, by its very nature, is an all-embracing *extra-parliamentary force* that *also* must rule over parliament, leaving to the forces of parliamentary opposition a narrowly circumscribed margin of action. It cannot be stressed enough, to envisage a very different relationship to the power of decision making in our society, it is necessary to radically challenge capital as the *overall controller* of social metabolic reproduction.

The fact that in the course of radical transformation the required all-embracing changes in the envisaged transfer of effective powers cannot be made *all at once,* but must be pursued *progressively,* on a continuing basis, does not mean that one should or could abandon the idea of ultimately securing control of the social metabolic process in its entirety and at all levels by the associated producers. Otherwise, we would be back to the criticized illusions of the—formally democratic but substantively authoritarian—past, even if with a new version of their ultimately unworkable division of power. The initial limitations to the power of the associated producers, due to the constraints of the inherited structural determinations at the outset, are admissible only for a limited historical period of *transition,* and even then only if the *direction* of the journey, as underlined above, points unambiguously toward the full transfer of powers at the first sustainable historical opportunity. The emerging reproductive metabolism of the alternative social order could not succeed in its hegemonic aspiration on a lasting basis in any other way.

The crucial issue in, this respect, concerns the way in which the parts of the unfolding new social reproductive order—its *microcosms*—are coordinated into a qualitatively different *macrocosm.* The now established reproductive order is characterized by the incurably *adversarial* structures of its social microcosms, which, consequently, must be *subsumed* under a strictly *hierarchical* mode of overall determination in order to make possible capital's only feasible form of comprehensive coordination. This is why the established reproductive order is *authoritarian* to the core, under all circumstances. Even if some kind of "formal democratic constitutionality" can complement the unalterable material exploitative structures at the political level, in the interest of better securing the stability of the system when historical conditions permit, only to be ruthlessly discarded in periods of major crisis. The alternative social reproductive order, by contrast, is inconceivable without overcoming the authoritarian and *adversarial innermost determinations* of the microcosms inherited from capital. This becomes possible only by instituting a qualitatively new mode of reproductive interchange, based on the fully shared vital interests of the members of the restructured *non-adversarial* social microcosms. Only in that way can they be properly *coordinated* in a corresponding form of *non-adversarial macrocosm.*

This is why participation is meaningful only if the powers of decision making are actually transferred to the associated producers at all levels and in all domains. Exercising control only *locally*—embellished by the consolation prize of 'small is beautiful' and the like—is a contradiction in terms if the local decisions are subject to approval or rejection at a structurally entrenched, and thereby necessarily adversarial, *higher level.* In that case, they are not decisions at all but, at best, some kind of permissible (or not) recommendations, since decisions properly so called can be taken only by a "higher authority." The envisaged new microcosms cannot be truly democratic—and non-adversarially socialist—if contradictions can enter the stage through the "back door" of a permanently established higher authority. And vice versa. The macrocosm of such a social order cannot be non-adversarially socialist if a structurally higher level retains for itself the power of deciding and overruling.

9.2.2

What is at stake here is the vitally important relationship of *genuine non-hierarchical coordination,* as opposed to all known and feasible forms of *structurally enforced domination and subordination.*

It is one of the favorite devices of the adversaries of socialism to decree the impossibility of taking *substantive decisions*—in contrast to participating in *formalized events,* like parliamentary elections or referenda—whenever the numbers of people involved are very large and the issues themselves varied. This preconceived disqualifying device works in the same way as the earlier mentioned rejection of the possibility of *comprehensive qualitative change,* declared to be inadmissible in contrast to the only acceptable approach of "piecemeal reform." On both occasions, the *fetishism of quantity* is invoked, in order to confer plausibility on the eternization of the existing order. In the first case, the *direction* of the emancipatory journey leading to a qualitative change is smuggled out of the picture, in order to be able to turn the real issue into a mechanical caricature of contesting quantities, ascribing victory—by definition, and nothing else—to the idealized "small degrees." In the same way, in the second case, our "complexity merchants" use the fetish of quantity to declare that "beyond a certain size of a community," never really defined how small or large, substantive decision making cannot be carried out by its members, because there are too many of them. And this is supposed to completely invalidate the concept of participation in any meaningful sense of the term. This kind of reasoning is fallacious not only because right from the beginning it *assumes* the conclusion that it claims to *prove* but also, even more importantly, because it diverts attention from the real problem of what is the necessary condition for coordinating the microcosms of participatory decision making into a coherent and historically sustainable social macrocosm. This is not a question of small or large size. Even the smallest community of *two* irreconcilably quarrelling people is far too large to be really sustainable. Rather, the only feasible solution of this problem requires the supersession of the *adversarial and conflictual* inner determination of the particular social microcosms in order to combine them into a positively developing social whole.

Thus, the establishment of genuine nonhierarchical, and accordingly nonadversarial, coordination is the challenge facing us in our attempts to secure the future. For that is the only way in which effective participation at all levels of decision-making can positively prevail in the course of socialist development: through the all-embracing autonomous activity of the associated producers as the real *subject of power.*

9.3 Substantive Equality:
The Absolute Condition of Sustainability

9.3.1

Substantive equality is, to be sure, the necessary corollary to the previous point. For it would be quite absurd to leave out of consideration the question of *substantive*—and not simply *formal*—equality when assessing success or failure in our strategy of genuine participation as the necessary condition of creating an alternative social order. In a world, like ours, in which one third of the entire population must survive on just above, or indeed well below, one dollar per day, while capital's captains of industry and business obscenely reward themselves with hundred-million-dollar salaries per annum, it is nothing short of a moral outrage to talk about democracy and liberty and continue to enforce the exploitative practices of the ruling order with every means at the system's disposal, including the most violent military means of undertaking genocidal wars if need be.

It is inconceivable to remove the adversarial inner determinations of our existing social microcosms without consciously confronting the age-old problem of substantive inequality. Capital's social order is structured in a profoundly iniquitous way and it could not conceivably function in any other way. For by its very nature capital must always retain for itself all significant power of decision making, starting from the system's smallest constitutive cells all the way to the highest levels of overall societal control. This is true not only in the so-called under-developed societies—that is, in the totally integrated and structurally subordinated parts of capital's global pecking order—but also in the most privileged countries of the now dominant system of social metabolic reproduction.

What makes the historic task of radically altering the capital system's structural inequalities that much more difficult is the fact that this social order is inseparable from a very long established *culture of substantive inequality* in the constitution of which even the greatest and most progressive figures of the bourgeoisie in the ascendant were deeply implicated.[2] Naturally, there could be nothing surprising about that. For even the most far-sighted and enlightened figures of the bourgeoisie—including intellectual giants like Adam Smith, Goethe, and Hegel—viewed the world and its problems from the *standpoint of capital.* They formulated both their diagnoses of what needed to be redressed, and their solutions to the identified challenges and contradictions, well within the structurally constraining parameters and presuppositions of capital's horizon. The notion of *real equality,* fully embracing the members of all social classes, could not conceivably enter their considerations.

In the great tempest of the French Revolution of 1789, the fundamental challenge of establishing a social order of *"Liberty, Equality, Fraternity"* surfaced, and its main defining characteristics were proclaimed at the level of political ideology. However, in reality they were violated right from the beginning, as they had to be under the pressure of capital's incorrigible inner determinations. The concept of Enlightenment could not be stretched as far as to tolerate the "Liberty" of those who tried to struggle for the institution of *substantive equality.* Not surprisingly, therefore, when François Babeuf criticized in his *Tribune du Peuple* the course the revolution was taking, and tried to organize his *"Society of Equals,"* he had to be unceremoniously dragged to the scaffold and guillotined in 1797 for his unforgivable crime.

Understandably, therefore, in the course of the capital system's subsequent historical development two of the three great slogans of the French Revolution—"Equality and Fraternity"—have quietly disappeared from the horizon. And even "Liberty" had to be turned into a favorite device of vacuous political rhetoric, so as to make it in due course not only compatible with, but even the pretended *legitimator* of, the most brutal violations of its substance.

The alternative social order is not sustainable in the longer-run without the full realization of equality, in place of the existing social relations in which equality exists at best only as a *formal and legal* requirement, and nothing more than a ritualistically reiterated formal requirement. For, in reality, even the solemnly proclaimed "equality before the law" is, as a rule, twisted in favor of those who can easily afford to pay for making a *practical mockery* out of the high-sounding *formal rules.* Rousseau in his time did not hesitate to ask some pertinent questions in this regard, even if he could not offer a viable solution to the identified contradictions. This is how he voiced his critique:

> Are not all the advantages of society for the rich and powerful? Are not all lucrative posts in their hands? Are not all privileges and exemptions reserved for them alone? . . . How different is the case of the poor man! *The more humanity owes him, the more society denies him.* . . . The terms of the social compact between these two estates of man may be summed up in a few words: 'You have need of me, because I am rich and you are poor. We will therefore come to an agreement. I will permit you to have the honour of serving me, on condition that you bestow on me the little you have left, in return for the pains I shall take to command you.'[3]

As the historical ascendancy of the bourgeois order came to a close, asking embarrassing questions about social inequality became utterly incompatible with capital's standpoint. The dominant discourse on equality had to be confined to concern only with some limited aspects of the strictly formal requirement of equality, and even that only because it was relevant to the rules of capitalistically enforceable contracts. But the principal function of the discourse on equality—in its overwhelmingly formalized sense—was social apologetics and mystification.

Nothing illustrates this better than the ubiquitous cynical discourse dedicated to ruling out of order the *"equality of outcome."* For allowing to press for a meaningful change in "outcome" would involve some inconvenient interference with the established power relations, improving the ability of social individuals to effectively intervene in the substantive processes of societal decision making. This is why the very idea of advocating for "equality of outcome" must be categorically dismissed in favor of the totally vacuous formula, which promises the unrealizable condition of the *"equality of opportunity."* A totally unrealizable condition because the way in which the issue itself is defined, the proclaimed "equality of opportunity" amounts to nothing more than an *empty formal shell.* For the formula itself is explicitly premised on the callous and cynical rejection of *"equality of outcome."* And, of course, no "opportunity" can have any meaning whatsoever if the hoped for "outcome" is excluded, by definition, from the outset.

9.3.2

The full realization of substantive equality is, to be sure, an immensely difficult historic task. Indeed, perhaps it is the most difficult one, involving the transformation of the entire social order. For the creation of a truly equitable society requires radically overcoming the exploitative structural hierarchies established for thousands of years, and not only their capitalist variety.

As we all know, as regards many centuries of human history the structurally entrenched inequalities were justified, with some legitimacy, on the ground that the elementary conditions of expanded reproduction could be best secured through the command structure of class societies. For they were capable of setting aside and accumulating to a significant degree—even if in a most iniquitous way—the fruits of surplus-labor for potential productive advancement, instead of everything being consumed at once from "hand-to-mouth." Such justification has, of course, no validity at all under the immense productive powers and potentialities of our own time. Naturally, the kind of historically produced transformation achieved by humanity—incomparably for the better—in the conditions of expanded societal reproduction would indicate, in principle, the *possibility* of establishing a qualitatively different way of ordering our mode of social metabolic control, on the basis of the substantive equality of all.

But the story does not end there. The fact that a great *historical possibility* is opened up in our time does not mean at all that it will be turned into *reality* in the near, or even in the far away, future. Especially since under the conditions of capital's social metabolic control at its present stage of development, every *productive potential* is simultaneously also a threatening *destructive potential.* The latter is brought to its perilous fulfillment in our time with growing frequency and on an increasing scale, endangering not only human life but also the totality of living nature on our finite planet. This is the sobering meaning of the much-touted *capitalist globalization* in our time.

Inevitably, such a formerly unthinkable historical predicament invites a radical redefinition of many of our problems, including, high on our order of challenges, the question of real equality. For the formation of a viable socialist reproductive order demands more than simply the negation of capital's mode of ever-more-destructive social metabolic control. It cannot be sustained in the longer-run, unless it can be simultaneously articulated as a *positive alternative* to the now prevailing conditions. Substantive equality is in this regard a *necessary* feature of the positive definition of the alternative social reproductive order. For it is impossible to remove the *adversarial and conflictual* inner determination of the constituent cells of our existing social macrocosm without restructuring them on the basis of substantive equality.

A society of *structurally entrenched hierarchy*—the fundamental defining characteristic of the capital system—by its very nature must always remain adversarial and conflictual both in its constitutive microcosms and in its antagonistically combined totality. As the structural crisis of the capital system deepens, the antagonistic inner determinations can only intensify, ultimately to the point of explosion. This is why we are witnessing today a turn toward the institution of increasingly more *authoritarian* state legislative measures even in the most developed capitalist countries,[4] and their active engagement—sharply belying pretences to "democracy and liberty"—in devastating wars.

However, the now clearly observable authoritarian tendency of trying to control the accumulating explosive contradictions by more and more violent means is bound to become not only unmanageable but also counterproductive. The ultimate prospect of such developments is the destruction of humanity.

The only tenable alternative in this respect in the long run is a society in which the associated producers can unreservedly identify themselves with the aims and humanly rewarding working requirements for reproducing their conditions of existence. And that is conceivable only on the basis of substantive equality.

In other words, the solution to the explosive antagonisms, which cannot be repressed indefinitely, is feasible only in a society in which, on the one hand, work itself is *universalized*,[5] consciously involving every single individual, and, on the other hand, the potentially most generous fruits of the individuals' positive dedication to their productive objectives are *equitably shared* out among all of them. There could be no reason whatsoever why the producers should behave differently from the "reluctant labor force" (well known in the imploded Soviet-type societies) short of these two—inseparable—dimensions of substantive equality.

This is why the realization of all-embracing substantive equality, irrespective of how long it might take, is an *absolute condition* for creating a historically sustainable alternative order. And precisely because it is an absolute condition of successfully instituting and sustaining a nonantagonistic reproductive order, the aim of its realization must be an integral part of the overall strategy of social transformation right from the beginning. Without consciously adopting it as the *necessary target* of transformation—a target that simultaneously provides both the *compass* of the journey and the tangible *measure* of success on the way of reaching the chosen destination—all talk about building socialism is bound to remain an elusive political dream.

Talking about the necessary relationship between *socialism and democracy* sidesteps this vital problem. For the advocacy of "democracy" in this respect is either the *formal* reduction of the concept of democracy, as seen in a handful of "advanced capitalist" countries in the past (amounting to nothing more than the *minimal requirement* under socialist conditions), or a mystifying *evasion*, trying to confine everything in the search for solutions to the *political* sphere and thereby necessarily moving around in circles. This is how the appeal to build socialism becomes an unrealizable condition and an elusive political dream, since the postulated "democracy" has no identifiable *social content.* For politics, as constituted in and inherited from the capitalist past is, in fact, one of the greatest obstacles to the emancipation of humankind.

This is why Marx was explicit in his uncompromising advocacy of the *withering away of the state* with all of its corollaries. Only the unrelenting drive toward the realization of a society of *substantive equality* can give the required *social content* to the concept of *socialist democracy.* This is a concept that cannot be defined in political terms alone, because it must go *beyond politics itself* as inherited from the past.

Thus, *substantive equality* is also the fundamental guiding principle of the *politics of transition* towards the alternative social order. Whether it is explicitly acknowledged or not, the main business of the politics of transition is to put itself out of business by progressively transferring the powers of decision making to the associated producers, enabling them in that way to become *freely* associated producers. But politics cannot do that without finding an appropriate orienting principle beyond itself, in the unfolding alternative social order of substantive equality. This dedication to the vital historic task of realizing substantive equality is the only way in which socialist politics can fulfill its mandate for redefining and restructuring itself in the service of the great emancipatory transformation.

9.4 Planning: The Necessity to Overcome Capital's Abuse of Time

9.4.1

Socialism, the name for the necessary alternative mode of reproducing our conditions of existence on this finite planet under the present historical circumstances, is inconceivable without adopting a rational and rewarding form of social metabolic control, in place of capital's antagonistic and ever more destructive way of managing the *planetary household.*

Planning, in the fullest sense of the term, is an essential feature of the socialist mode of social metabolic control. For our mode of control must be viable not only in regards to the immediate impact of productive activity on the conditions of individual and societal reproduction, but also *indefinitely,* as far away in the future as one can and must envisage for the sake of instituting and keeping alive the appropriate safeguards.

In this respect, in capital's social metabolic order we encounter a striking contradiction. For, on the one hand, no previous mode of social reproduction has ever had an even remotely comparable impact on the vital conditions of existence—including the *natural substratum* of human life itself—not only in its *immediacy* but also even in the *long run.* At the same time the *long-term historical dimension* is completely missing from the vision of capital's mode of social metabolic control, turning it thereby into an *irrational* and utterly *irresponsible* form of husbandry. The requirement of rationality at the level of the *minutest details* is not only compatible with capital, on the time-scale of *immediacy,* but also required by it, as the elementary condition of its tenability, finding its suitable operational framework in the capitalist market. The trouble is, though, that the vitally important dimension of *overall rationality* is necessarily absent from this mode of social reproductive control. The increasing involvement of the capitalist state as a lopsided corrective is a very poor—and ultimately untenable—substitute for it.

This incorrigible structural defect of the system rules out the possibility of *historical consciousness* precisely in an age when the need for it would be the greatest: in our own historical period of *globalization.* For the unforeseen—and by the personifications of capital in principle unforeseeable—long-term impact of the system's development has by now invaded the whole of the planet. Accordingly, if once upon a time it was relatively justified to characterize the capitalist order as a system of *"productive* destruction," as depicted by some major liberal political economists like Schumpeter, it becomes a most dangerous delusion to continue to celebrate it in such terms today. That is, to misrepresent it in that way in an age when—under the impact of late-twentieth-century *historical development,* resulting in the stubbornly persisting *structural crisis* of the capital system in its entirety—it becomes absolutely unavoidable to confront the devastating impact and the fateful potentiality of *destructive* production: the diametrical opposite of the idealized *"productive* destruction."

Only a rationally planned system of social metabolic reproduction could show a way out of the contradictions and dangers of this historically produced predicament now running out of control. To remedy it would require a form of *genuine comprehensive planning* which—in order to qualify for its now absolutely necessary but never in the past practically feasible role—must be able to deal in our own time with the manifold problems and *all* dimensions of a truly *global* socioeconomic, political, and cultural development, and not only with the difficulties of coordinating and positively enhancing the productive powers of *particular countries.*

Understandably, given the deeply embedded vested interests and self-mythologizing circumstances of the dominant capitalist "market economy," the very idea of a successfully planned alternative form of economy is *a priori* ruled out of order. In their recently published powerful advocacy of socialism the Magdoffs characterized this myopic approach opposed to planning in the following terms:

> The skepticism that people feel about the efficacy or even possibility of central planning admits only the shortcomings while denying the achievements.

There is nothing in central planning that requires commandism and confining all aspects of planning to the central authorities. That occurs because of the influence of special bureaucratic interests and the overarching power of the state. Planning for the people has to involve the people. Plans of regions, cities, and towns need the active involvement of local populations, factories and stores in worker and community councils. The overall program—especially deciding the distribution of resources between consumption goods and investment—calls for people's participation. And for that, the people must have the facts, a clear way to inform their thinking, and contribute to the basic decisions.[6]

In periods of great historical emergency, as for instance the Second World War, even the capitalist decision makers are willing to incorporate into their productive strategies some elements of a planned economy, even if only of a rather limited and on the whole profit-oriented kind. Once, however, the great emergency is over, all such practices are quickly wiped out of historical memory, and the mythology of the market—proclaimed to be ideally suited to the solution of all conceivable problems—is promoted more strongly than ever before.

It would be a monumental miracle if the *normality* of capital's mode of social metabolic control, in contrast to its occasional *emergency* concessions, could be very different from that. For the idea of planning cannot be separated from the fundamental *determination of time* appropriate to the given social reproductive system. In this respect, the well-known prejudices against planning arise from *capital's necessary abuse of time*. The only modality of time directly meaningful to capital is *necessary labor-time* and its operational corollaries, as required for securing and safeguarding the conditions of *profit-oriented time-accountancy* and thereby the realization of capital on an extended scale.

As mentioned earlier, the myopic rationality of pursuing (and in a bastardized sense "planning") minute details in particular enterprises, necessarily devoid of an overall design in the economy as a whole— a practice finding its complement in the adversarial and conflictually combined market—is compatible only with *decapitated and short-circuited time*. When in a period of great historical emergency, like the Second World War, some elements of a more comprehensive rationality are introduced, in order to meet a major military challenge, this is done on the clear understanding that the conceded measures must be *strictly temporary* and will have to be removed at the earliest possible opportunity.

In complete contrast to the existing state of affairs, if we acknowledge the fact that the reproductive practices of a *globally integrated* world call for the introduction *and retention* of the effective guiding force of *overall rationality,* as we must, in order to counter the increasing dangers of uncontrollability and ensuing explosions, in that case the perverse relationship of capital to time must be radically reexamined and altered. Truly participatory *comprehensive planning* of the conditions of humanity's social metabolic reproduction—embracing *all* of its diverse constituents, including the moral and cultural ones, and not just the strictly economic dimension—is a self-evident requirement in this respect. However, to make such comprehensive planning possible at all, it is necessary to overcome the fatefully alienating and crippling condition whereby profit-oriented and myopically decapitated *"[t]ime is everything, man is nothing; he is at the most time's carcase."*[7]

9.4.2

The main reason why the normality of capital is incompatible with comprehensive planning is because the vital requirement of sustainable socioeconomic orientation arises from the *qualitative* aspects of managing a *humanly viable* reproductive order. If it were simply a question of *extending* the time involved in capital's economic operations, this would be in principle feasible from the ruling system's standpoint. What intervenes in this regard as a *prohibiting* condition for resolving the apparently intractable problem is the total absence of a proper *measure.* A measure suitable to adequately assessing the *qualitative human impact* of the adopted productive practices, even on a relatively short-term basis and not only in the long run, is absent. The highly irresponsible way in which the dominant capitalist countries, above all the United States,[8] handle even the minimal requirements of the Kyoto Protocol is a good illustration of this point.

Capital has no difficulties with impressive *quantification,* and even with self-expansive *multiplication,* provided that its projected productive expansion can be defined without any appeal to qualitative considerations either on the plane of material and human *resources* or with regard to *time.* In this sense, *growth,* as a particularly important concept both in the present and in the future, must be handled by capital within the crippling confines of *fetishistic quantification*, although in reality it cannot be sustained at all as a form of productively viable strategy without applying to it profoundly *qualitative* considerations, as we shall see in the next section. In the same way, *comprehensive planning*—in contrast to safely *selective* (as regards the particular productive targets which can be pursued) and *temporally limited* (short-term) interventions—is inadmissible because neither the *scope* nor the *time-scale* of *humanly valid* overall rationality is amenable to fetishistic quantification.

The key concept here is not rationality in and of itself but the necessary determination of the required *sustainable rationality* by the *inherent humanness* of the adopted overall measure. Readily quantifiable *partial rationality* can be fully in tune with capital's operational imperatives within its productive microcosms—but not *humanly valid overall rationality* as the orienting framework and appropriate *measure* of the system as a whole. For the only thing that can define a viable and sustainable productive system with regard to its orienting overall rationality is *human need* itself: *an inherently qualitative determination.*

Such qualitative overall determination can only arise from the reality of irrepressible, even if now capitalistically frustrated, human need. This is what is necessarily missing from the capital system's incorrigible self-definition and insurmountable overall determination. It is precisely for this reason that capital must *subordinate use-value*—which is totally meaningless without its *qualitative* relationship to clearly identifiable *human need*—to easily quantifiable *exchange-value.* The latter need not have anything at all to do with human need—only with the need of capital's extended self-reproduction. Indeed, it is thoroughly compatible with the triumph of *destructive counter-value,* as the gruesome reality of the *military-industrial complex* and its lucrative "capital-realizing" involvement in the directly *anti-human* practices of genocidal wars clearly demonstrate in our time.

9.4.3

Planning, in the deepest sense of the term, is absolutely vital for redressing these problems and contradictions. But the planning in question cannot be visualized without its corresponding dimension of *historical time.* In this respect, the concept of time required for making sense of planning in its proper—in contrast to narrowly technical—meaning is not an abstract and generic *cosmic time,* but *humanly meaningful time.* For in the course of history, and especially through the unfolding of human history, the concept of time is significantly altered in the sense that with the development of human beings—and the concomitant "humanization of nature itself" (Marx)—a radically new dimension of time enters the picture.

The fact that humanity, in contrast to the animal world, is made of historically created and, under changing conditions, historically developing *individuals,* cannot be divorced from the circumstance that human individuals, as opposed to their species, have a strictly *limited life-time.* Accordingly, thanks to a long historical development the problem of time presents itself in the human context not simply as the need to survive from day one to the last hour of the individuals' life-span, but simultaneously also as the challenge directly confronting them for the creation of a *meaningful life,* as the real *subjects of their own life-activity.* In other words, a challenge to *make sense* of their own life as real "authors" of their own acts, in close conjunction with the ever-more-enhanced collective potentialities of their society of which they themselves are an integral and actively contributing part. This is how individual and social consciousness can really come together in the interest of human advancement.

Under the rule of capital all this is impossible. The vital requirement of planning is nullified both at the comprehensive social level and in the lives of individuals. At the broadest social level comprehensive planning, in its positive orientation by human need, is disqualified in the interest of the most myopically oriented time-accountancy, carrying with it increasing dangers of destructive production. At the same time, at the level of individual consciousness, the requirement of "making sense of one's life" can enter only into the socially most ineffectual forms of religious discourse, interested in nothing but "the world of the beyond."

Capital's necessary abuse of time prevails at all cost and in all domains. In order to envisage a socialist reproductive order as the viable hegemonic alternative to the existent order, the question of planning must remain in the forefront of our attention. For there can be no lasting success without combining the broad social dimension of reproductive rationality and the individual's quest for a meaningful life.

These two fundamental dimensions of what it means to be a *real subject*, in the proper sense of the term, stand or fall together. For how could the body of freely associated producers, as a consciously self-asserting *collective force*, be the sovereign *"subject of power"* in the social world, planning and autonomously managing its productive interchanges with nature and among the members of society, if the *particular social individuals* who constitute that collective force are unable to emancipate themselves to the point of becoming "conscious subjects of their own actions," fully assuming responsibility for their meaningful life-activity? And vice versa: how could the *individuals* have meaningful lives of their own if the *overall conditions* of social metabolic reproduction are dominated by an *alien force* that frustrates their designs and, in a most authoritarian way, overrules the self-realizing aims and values which the social individuals attempt to set themselves?

The bureaucratic violations of planning in Soviet type post-capitalist societies were manifestations of the same contradiction. The paralyzing "influence of special bureaucratic interests and the overarching power of the state" in the economy—rightly deplored by the Magdoffs—had to fail. For the members of the Politburo arbitrarily assigned to themselves the exclusive role of all-powerful decision making subjects in running their decreed "planned economy," dismissing at the same time with an undisguised sense of superiority even the top planning officials of the state as "just a bunch of accountants."

A revealing interview reports a conversation Harry Magdoff had with Che Guevara:

> I said to Che, 'What's important is that when plans are made, that the planners, the ones who come up with the directions and the numbers, should be involved in thinking about the actual policy alternatives in light of practical conditions.' Whereupon he laughed and he said that when he was in Moscow, his host Khrushchev, who was then the head of the Party and the government, took him around to see places as a political tourist. Traveling through the city, Che told Khrushchev that he would like to meet with the planning commission. Whereupon Khrushchev said: *'Why do you want to do that? They are just a bunch of accountants.'*[9]

Moreover, as far as the particular individuals of society as a whole were concerned, they had even less say in the overall planning process than the arrogantly characterized "bunch of accountants." Their role, as individual subjects, was unceremoniously confined by the state authorities to carrying out the orders handed down to them from high above.

The consequences were quite devastating, and understandably so. For under the prevailing circumstances the *conscious collective subject* of the necessary comprehensive interchanges could not be constituted at all as a genuine collective subject, so as to exercise truly sustainable control over the vital processes of societal reproduction. This was impossible because the two fundamental dimensions of what it means to be a *real subject*—namely, the necessity to combine the broad social dimension of reproductive rationality with the individual objectives—were abitrarily broken and opposed to one another. In this way—under the given modality of top-down decision making—the potential constitutive members of society's valid collective subject, the *particular individuals,* were denied the autonomous control of their own meaningful life-activity, and thereby also of controlling social metabolic reproduction as a whole. The rest of the sad story has become well known through the implosion of the Soviet-type system.

Thus, radically overcoming capital's necessary abuse of time—which degrades human beings to the condition of "time's carcase," denying them the power of self-determination as real subjects—is vital for the creation of an alternative social order. Decapitated and short-circuited time cannot be remedied at the general societal level alone. The conditions of individual and social emancipation cannot be separated from—let alone opposed to—one another. They prevail or fail together, on the temporal plane of *simultaneity.* For one is as fully required for the realization of the other, as the other way round. One cannot wait for the emancipation of the individuals until even the elementary general objectives of social transformation are successfully accomplished. For who on earth could take even the first steps of a comprehensive social transformation if not the individuals who can—and do—identify themselves with their chosen society's objectives and values?

But to do that, the particular social individuals must liberate themselves from the straitjacket of decapitated time narrowly imposed upon them. They can do that only by acquiring the power of autonomous, conscious, and responsible decision making, with its proper—non-adversarially enlarged—perspective of meaningful life-activity. This is how it becomes possible to constitute an alternative social metabolic order on a historically sustainable timescale. And that is what confers true meaning on *planning* as a vital principle of the socialist enterprise.

9.5 Qualitative Growth in Utilization: The Only Viable Economy

9.5.1

Once upon a time, the capitalist mode of production represented a great advance over all of the preceding ones, however problematic and indeed destructive this historical advance turned out in the end. By *breaking* the long prevailing but constraining direct link between human use and production, and replacing it with the *commodity relation,* capital opened up the dynamically unfolding possibilities of apparently irresistible *expansion* to which—from the standpoint of the capital system and its willing personifications—there could be no conceivable limits. For the paradoxical and ultimately quite untenable inner determination of capital's productive system is that commodities *"are non-use-values for their owners and use-values for their non-owners. Consequently they must all change hands. . . .* Hence commodities must be realized as values *before they can be realized as use-values."*[10]

This self-contradictory inner determination of the system, which imposes the ruthless submission of human need to the alienating necessity of capital expansion, is what removes the possibility of overall rational control from this dynamic productive order. It brings with itself perilous and potentially catastrophic consequences in the longrun, transforming in due course a great *positive power* of previously quite unimaginable economic development into a *devastating negativity,* in the total absence of the necessary reproductive restraint.

What is systematically ignored—and must be ignored, due to the unalterable fetishistic imperatives and vested interests of the capital system—is the fact that, inescapably, we live in a *finite world,* with its literally vital *objective limits.* For a long time in human history, including several centuries of capitalistic development, those limits could be—as indeed they were—ignored with relative safety. Once, however, they assert themselves, as they emphatically must do in our irreversible historical epoch, no irrational and wasteful productive system, no matter how dynamic (in fact the more dynamic the worse) can escape the consequences. It can only disregard them for a while through reorienting itself toward the callous justification of the more or less openly destructive imperative of the system's self-preservation at all cost: by preaching the wisdom of "there is no alternative," and in that spirit brushing aside, and whenever need be, brutally suppressing even the most obvious warning signs that foreshadow the unsustainable future.

False theorization is the necessary consequence of this lopsided objective structural determination and domination of use-value by exchange-value not only under the most absurdly and blindly apologetic conditions of contemporary capitalism but also in the classical period of bourgeois political economy, at the time of the capital system's historical ascendancy. This is because under the rule of capital a *fictitiously limitless* production must be pursued at all cost, as well as theoretically justified as the only commendable one. Such pursuit is imperative even if there can be no guarantee whatsoever that: (1) the required and sustainable "changing of hands" of the supplied commodities will take place on the idealized market (thanks to the mysterious benevolence of Adam Smith's even more mysterious "invisible hand"); and that (2) the objective material conditions for producing the projected unlimited—and humanly unlimitable, since in its primary determination divorced from need and use—supply of commodities can be *forever secured,* irrespective of the destructive impact of capital's mode of social metabolic reproduction on nature, and consequently on the elementary conditions of human existence itself.

The ideal suitability of the market for rectifying the unalterable structural defect indicated in point one above is a *gratuitous afterthought,* bringing with it many arbitrary assumptions and unrealizable regulative projections in the same vein. The sobering reality underlying the market as a remedial afterthought is a set of insuperably adversarial power relations, tending to monopolistic domination and to the intensification of the system's antagonisms. Likewise, the grave structural defect of pursuing unlimited capital expansion—idealizing all-important "growth" as an end in itself—as put into relief in point two above, is complemented by an equally *fictitious afterthought* when it has to be admitted that some remedy might be in order. And the remedy thus projected—as an alternative to the system's collapse into the unredeemable negativity of the fateful "stationary state" theorized by bourgeois political economy in the nineteenth century—is simply the wishful advocacy of making *distribution* "more equitable" (and thereby less conflict-torn) while leaving the production system as it stands. This postulate, even if it could be implemented, which of course it cannot be, due to the fundamental hierarchical structural determinations of capital's social order, would not be able to solve any of the grave problems of *production* on which *also* the insurmountable contradictions of the capital system's incurable *distribution* are erected.

One of the principal representatives of liberal thought, John Stuart Mill, is as genuine in his concern about the "stationary state" of the future as he is hopelessly unreal in his proposed remedy to it. He can only offer vacuous hope in his discussion of this problem, which happens to be absolutely intractable from the standpoint of capital. He writes "I sincerely hope, for the sake of posterity, that they will be *content to be stationary*, long before necessity compels them to it."[11] In this way, Mill's discourse amounts to no more than paternalistic preaching, because he can only acknowledge, in tune with his acceptance of the Malthusian diagnosis, the difficulties arising from population growth, but none of the contradictions of capital's reproductive order. His bourgeois self-complacency is clearly visible, depriving his analysis and paternalistic reforming intent of all substance. Mill peremptorily asserts that, "it is only in the *backward countries of the world* that increased production is still an important object: in those most advanced, what is economically needed is a *better distribution,* of which one indispensable means is a *stricter restraint on population.*"[12] Even his idea of "better distribution" is hopelessly unreal. For what Mill cannot possibly recognize (or acknowledge) is that the overwhelmingly important aspect of distribution is the untouchable exclusive distribution of the means of production to the capitalist class. Understandably, given such a self-serving operational premise of the social order, a paternalist sense of superiority remains always prevalent, maintaining that no solution can be expected "until *the better minds* succeeded in educating the others,"[13] so that they accept population restraint and a "better distribution" supposedly arising from such restraint. Thus, people should forget all about changing the destructive structural determinations of the established social metabolic order that inexorably drive society toward a stagnating stationary state. In Mill's discourse the utopia of the capitalist millennium, with its *tenable stationary state,* will be brought into existence thanks to the good services of the enlightened liberal "better minds." And then, as far as the structural determinations of the established social reproductive order are concerned, everything can go on forever as before.

All this made some sense from capital's standpoint, however problematic and ultimately untenable that sense in the end had to turn out to be, due to the dramatic onset and relentless deepening of the system's structural crisis. But even that partial sense of the same wishful propositions could not be ascribed to the reformist political movement that claimed to represent the strategic interests of labor. Yet, social-democratic reformism at its inception took its inspiration from such naïve, even if at first genuinely held, afterthoughts of liberal political economy. Thus, due to the internal logic of the adopted social premises, emanating from capital's standpoint and vested interests as the unchallengeable controller of the reproductive metabolism, it could not be surprising in the least that social-democratic reformism ended its course of development the way in which it actually did: by transforming itself into "New Labour" (in Britain and its equivalents in other countries) and by abandoning completely any concern with even the most limited reform of the established social order. At the same time, in place of genuine liberalism, the most savage and inhuman varieties of *neoliberalism* appeared on the historical stage, wiping out the memory of the once advocated social remedies—including even the wishful paternalistic solutions—from the progressive past of the liberal creed. And as a bitter irony of contemporary historical development, the New Labour-type of former social-democratic reformist movements installed in government—not only in Britain but also everywhere else in the "advanced" and not-so-advanced capitalist world—did not hesitate to unreservedly identify themselves with the aggressive neoliberal phase of capital-apologetics. This transformation clearly marked the end of the reformist road, which was a blind alley from the outset.

9.5.2

In order to create an economically viable and also, on a long-term basis, historically sustainable social reproductive order it is necessary to radically alter the self-contradictory inner determinations of the established one which impose the ruthless submission of human need and use to the alienating necessity of capital expansion. This means that the absurd precondition of the ruling productive system—whereby use-values, by preordained and totally iniquitous determinations of ownership, must be divorced from, and opposed to, those who create them, so as to bring about and circularly/arbitrarily legitimate capital's enlarged self-realization—has to be permanently relegated to the past. Otherwise, the only viable meaning of *economy* as rational *economizing* with the available, necessarily finite, resources cannot be instituted and respected as a vital orienting principle. Instead, irresponsible *wastefulness* dominates in capital's socioeconomic—and corresponding political—order which invariably reasserts itself as *institutionalized irresponsibility*, notwithstanding its self-mythology of absolutely insuperable "efficiency." (To be sure, the kind of "efficiency" glorified in this way is in fact capital's ultimately self-undermining efficiency for blindly driving forward the adversarial and conflictual *parts* at the expense of the *whole*.) Understandably, therefore, the government's well-promoted fantasies of "market socialism" had to fizzle out in the form of a humiliating collapse, due to the acceptance of such presuppositions and capitalistically insuperable structural determinations.

The now dominant conception of the "economy," which happens to be quite incapable of setting limits even to the most grievous waste, in our time truly on a *planetary* scale, can only operate with self-serving *tautologies* and arbitrarily prefabricated, as well as simultaneously dismissed, *false oppositions and pseudo-alternatives*, devised for the same purpose of unjustifiable self-justification. As a blatant—and dangerously all-infecting—tautology, we are offered the arbitrary definition of *productivity as growth, and growth as productivity*, although both terms would require a historically qualified and objectively sustainable evaluation of their own. Naturally, the reason why the obvious tautological fallacy is much preferable to the required proper theoretical and practical assessment is that by arbitrarily decreeing the *identity* of these two key terms of reference of the capital system, the *self-evident validity and timeless superiority* of an extremely problematic—and ultimately even self-destructive—social reproductive order look not only plausible but absolutely unquestionable. At the same time, the arbitrarily decreed *tautological identity* of growth and productivity is shored up by the equally arbitrary and self-serving alternative between "*growth or no-growth*." Moreover, the latter is automatically prejudged in favor of capitalistically postulated and defined "*growth*."

It is projected and defined with fetishistic quantification, as befits the—in its claims absurdly timeless, though in reality strictly historical—way of *presupposing forever,* as *synonymous to growth itself,* nothing more specific and humanly meaningful than the abstract genericity of enlarged *capital-expansion* as the elementary *precondition* for satisfying human need and use.

That is where the incorrigible divorce of capitalistic growth from human need and use—indeed its potentially most devastating and destructive *counter-position* to human need—betrays itself. Once the fetishistic mystifications and arbitrary postulates at the root of the categorically decreed false identity of *growth and productivity* are peeled away, it becomes abundantly clear that the kind of growth postulated and at the same time automatically exempted from all critical scrutiny is in no way inherently connected with sustainable objectives corresponding to human need. The only connection that must be asserted and defended at all cost in capital's social metabolic universe is the *false identity* of—presupposed—*capital-expansion* and circularly corresponding (but in truth likewise presupposed) "growth," whatever might be the consequences imposed on nature and humankind by even the most destructive type of growth. For capital's real concern can only be its own *ever-enlarged expansion,* even if that brings with it the destruction of humanity.

In this vision, even the most lethal *cancerous growth* must preserve its conceptual primacy over against human need and use, if human need by any chance happens to be mentioned at all. And when the apologists of the capital system are willing to consider *The Limits to Growth,*[14] as the Club of Rome did it in its vastly propagandized capital-apologetic venture in the early 1970s, the aim inevitably remains the *eternization of the existing grave inequalities*[15] by fictitiously (and quixotically) freezing global capitalist production at a totally untenable level, blaming primarily "population growth" (as customary in bourgeois political economy ever since Malthus) for the existing problems. Compared to such callous hypocritical "remedial intent," rhetorically pretending to be concerned with nothing less than "the Predicament of Mankind," John Stuart Mill's paternalistic preaching, with its genuine advocacy of a somewhat more equitable distribution than what he was familiar with, is the paradigm of radical enlightenment.

The characteristically self-serving false alternative of "growth or no growth" is evident even if we only consider what would be the

unavoidable impact of the postulated "no growth" on the grave conditions of inequality and suffering in capital's social order. It would
mean the *permanent condemnation* of humanity's overwhelming
majority to the inhuman conditions they are now forced to endure.
For thousands of millions are now in a literal sense forced to endure
them, when there could be *created* a real alternative to it. Under conditions, that is, when it would be quite feasible to rectify at least the
worst effects of global deprivation: by putting to humanly commendable and rewarding use the attained *potential* of productivity, in a
world of now criminally wasted material and human resources.

9.5.3

To be sure, we can only speak of the positive *potential of productivity*,
and not of its existing reality, as often predicated, with green-colored
good intentions but boundless illusions, by old fashioned single-issue
reformers, wishfully asserting that we could do it "right now," with the
productive powers at our disposal today, if we really decided to do so.
Unfortunately, however, such a conception completely ignores the way
in which our productive system is presently articulated, requiring in
the future a radical re-articulation. For productivity wedded to *capitalist* growth, in the form of the now dominant reality of *destructive production,* is a most forbidding adversary. In order to turn the positive
potentiality of productive development into a much-needed reality, so
as to be able to rectify many of the crying inequalities and injustices of
our existing society, it would be necessary to adopt the *regulative principles* of a *qualitatively different* social order. In other words, humanity's now destructively negated *potential of productivity* would have to
be liberated from its capitalist integument in order to become socially
viable *productive power.*

The quixotic advocacy of freezing production at the level attained
in the early 1970s tried to camouflage, with vacuous pseudo-scientific
model-mongering pioneered at the Massachusetts Institute of
Technology, the ruthlessly enforced actual power relations of
U.S.–dominated postwar imperialism. That variety of imperialism
was, of course, very different from its earlier form known to Lenin. For
in Lenin's lifetime at least half a dozen significant imperialist powers
were competing for the rewards of their real and or hoped for conquests. And even in the 1930s, Hitler was still willing to share the fruits

of violently redefined imperialism with Japan and Mussolini's Italy. In our time, by contrast, we have to face up to the reality—and the lethal dangers—arising from *global hegemonic imperialism*,[16] with the United States as its overwhelmingly dominant power. In contrast to even Hitler, the United States as the *single hegemon* is quite unwilling to share global domination with any rival. And that is not simply on account of political and military contingencies. The problems are much deeper. They assert themselves through the ever-aggravating contradictions of the capital system's deepening *structural crisis*. U.S.–dominated global hegemonic imperialism is an—ultimately futile—attempt to devise a solution to that crisis through the most brutal and violent rule over the rest of the world, enforced with or without the help of slavishly "willing allies," now through a succession of genocidal wars. Ever since the 1970s, the United States has been sinking ever deeper into *catastrophic indebtedness*. The fantasy solution publicly proclaimed by several U.S. presidents was *"to grow out of it."* And the result: the diametrical opposite, in the form of astronomical and still growing indebtedness. Accordingly, the United States must grab to itself, by any means at its disposal, including the most violent military aggression, whenever required for this purpose, everything it can, through the transfer of the fruits of capitalist growth—thanks to the global socioeconomic, political, and military domination of the United States as the now successfully prevailing single hegemon—from everywhere in the world. Could then any sane person imagine, no matter how well armored by his or her callous contempt for "the shibboleth of equality," that U.S.–dominated global hegemonic imperialism would take seriously even for a moment the panacea of "no growth"? Only the worst kind of bad faith could suggest such ideas, no matter how pretentiously packaged in the hypocritical concern over "the Predicament of Mankind."

For a variety of reasons there can be no question about the importance of growth both in the present and in the future. But there must be a proper examination of the concept of growth not only as we know it up to the present, but also as we can envisage its sustainability in the future. Our siding with the need for growth cannot be in favor of *unqualified growth*. The tendentiously avoided real question is: *what kind of growth* is both feasible today, in contrast to the dangerously wasteful and even crippling capitalist growth visible all around us? For growth must be also *positively sustainable* in the future on a *long-term* basis.

As mentioned already, capitalist growth is fatefully dominated by the inescapable confines of *fetishistic quantification*. Ever-aggravating *wastefulness* is a necessary corollary of such fetishism, since there can be no criteria—and no viable *measure*—through the observance of which wastefulness could be corrected. More or less arbitrary *quantification* sets the context, creating at the same time also the illusion that once the required quantities are secured for the more powerful, there can be no further significant problems. Yet the truth of the matter is that self-oriented *quantification* in reality cannot be sustained at all as a form of productively viable strategy even in the short run. For it is partial and myopic (if not altogether blind), concerned only with quantities corresponding to the *immediate obstacles* hindering the accomplishment of a given productive task, but not with the necessarily associated *structural limits* of the socioeconomic enterprise itself which—whether you know it or not—ultimately decide everything. The capitalistically necessary confusion of *structural limits* with *obstacles* (which can be quantitatively overcome), in order to ignore the limits (since they correspond to the insurmountable determinations of capital's social metabolic order), vitiates the growth orientation of the entire productive system. To make growth viable would require applying to it profoundly *qualitative* considerations. But that is absolutely prevented by the unquestioning and unquestionable *self-expansionary drive* of capital, which is incompatible with the *constraining* consideration of *quality* and *limits*.

The great innovation of the capital system is that it can operate—*undialectically*—through the overwhelming domination of *quantity*. Capital subsumes *everything*, including living human labor (inseparable from the qualities of human need and use) under *abstract quantitative determinations,* in the form of value and exchange-value. Thus, everything becomes profitably commensurable and manageable for a determinate period of time. This is the secret of capital's—for a long time irresistible—sociohistorical triumph. But it is also the harbinger of its ultimate unsustainability and necessary implosion once the *absolute limits* of the system (in contrast to its *relative* limits, corresponding to productively superable *expansion-hindering obstacles*) are fully activated, as they increasingly happen to be in our own historical epoch. That is the time when the undialectical domination of quality by quantity becomes dangerous and untenable. For it is inconceivable to ignore in our time the fundamental, but under capitalism necessarily sidelined inherent connection—which must be now consciously adopted as a vital regulating orientation—of *economy as economizing* (which equals *responsible husbandry*). We are at a critical point in historical time when the ruling productive system's willing personifications are doing everything in their power to wipe out all awareness of that vital objective connection, opting for undeniable destructiveness not only in the cult of extremely wasteful productive practices but even glorifying their lethally destructive engagement in unlimited "preventive and preemptive wars."

Quality, by its very nature, is inseparable from *specificities.* Accordingly, a social metabolic system respectful of quality—above all of the needs of living human beings as its producing subjects—cannot be hierarchically regimented. A radically different kind of socioeconomic and cultural management is required for a society operated on the basis of such a qualitatively different reproductive metabolism, briefly summed up as *self-management.* Regimentation was both feasible and necessary for capital's social metabolic order. In fact, the command structure of capital could not function in any other way. Structurally secured hierarchy and authoritarian regimentation are the defining characteristics of capital's command structure. The alternative order is incompatible with regimentation and with the kind of accountancy—including the strictly quantitative operation of *necessary labor-time*—which must prevail in the capital system. Thus, the kind of growth necessary and feasible in the alternative social metabolic order can only be based on *quality* directly corresponding to *human needs:* the actual and historically developing needs of both society as a whole and of its particular individuals. At the same time, the alternative to the restrictive and fetishistic time-accountancy of *necessary labor-time* can only be the liberating and emancipating *disposable time* consciously offered and managed by the social individuals themselves. That kind of social metabolic control of the available human and material resources would—and actually could—respect both the overall limits arising from the orienting principle of economy as economizing, and at the same time would also consciously expand them as the historically developing conditions safely permitted. After all, we should not forget that "the first historical act was the creation of a new need" (Marx). Only capital's reckless way of treating the economy—not as rational economizing but the most irresponsible legitimating of boundless waste—is what *totally perverts* this historical process: by substituting to human need capital's one and only real need for enlarged self-reproduction, thereby threatening to bring to an end human history itself.

9.5.4

There can be not even *partial correctives* introduced into capital's operational framework if they are genuinely quality-oriented. For the only qualities relevant in this respect are not some abstract physical characteristics but the *humanly meaningful qualities inseparable from need.* It is true, of course, as stressed before, that such qualities are always specific, corresponding to clearly identifiable particular human needs both of the individuals themselves and of their historically given and changing social relations. Accordingly, in their many sided specificity they constitute a *coherent and well-defined set* of inviolable systemic determinations, with their own *systemic limits.* It is precisely the existence of such—very far from abstract—systemic limits which makes impossible to transfer any meaningful operating determinations and orienting principles from the envisaged alternative social metabolic order into the capital system. The two systems are radically exclusive of each other. For the specific qualities corresponding to human need, in the alternative order, carry the indelible marks of their overall systemic determinations, as integral parts of a humanly valid social reproductive system of control. In the capital system, on the contrary, the overall determinations must be inalterably *abstract,* because capital's *value relation* must reduce all qualities (corresponding to need and use) to measurable generic quantities, in order to assert its alienating historical dominance over everything, in the interest of capital expansion, irrespective of the consequences.

The incompatibilities of the two systems become amply clear when we consider their relationship to the question of *limit itself.* The only sustainable *growth* positively promoted under the alternative social metabolic control is based on the *conscious acceptance of the limits* whose violation would imperil the realization of the chosen—and humanly valid—reproductive objectives. Hence, *wastefulness* and *destructiveness* (as clearly identified limiting concepts) are *absolutely excluded* by the consciously accepted systemic determinations themselves, adopted by social individuals as their vital orienting principles. By contrast, the capital system is characterized, and fatefully driven, by the—conscious or unconscious—*rejection of all limits, including its own systemic limits.* Even the latter are arbitrarily and dangerously treated as if they were nothing more than superable *contingent obstacles.* Hence, anything goes in this social reproductive system, including the possibility—and by the time we have reached our own historical epoch also the overwhelming grave probability—of *total destruction.*

Naturally, this mutually exclusive relationship to the question of limits prevails also the other way round. Thus, there can be no "partial correctives" borrowed from the capital system when creating and strengthening the alternative social metabolic order. The partial—not to mention general—incompatibilities of the two systems arise from the *radical incompatibility of their value dimension.* As mentioned above, this is why the particular value determinations and relations of the alternative order could not be transferred into capital's social metabolic framework for the purpose of improving it, as postulated by some utterly unreal reformist design, wedded to the vacuous methodology of "little by little." For even the smallest relations of the alternative system are *deeply embedded in the general value determinations* of an overall framework of human needs whose inviolable elementary axiom is the radical exclusion of *waste and destruction,* in accord with its *innermost nature.*

At the same time, on the other side, no partial "correctives" can be transferred from the operational framework of capital into a genuinely socialist order, as the disastrous failure of Gorbachev's "market socialist" venture painfully and conclusively demonstrated. For also in that respect we would always be confronted by the radical incompatibility of value determinations, even if in that case the value involved is destructive *counter-value,* corresponding to the ultimate—necessarily ignored—limits of the capital system itself. The systemic limits of capital are thoroughly compatible with waste and destruction. For such normative considerations can only be *secondary* to capital. More fundamental determinations must take the precedence over such concerns. This is why capital's original *indifference to waste and destruction* (never a more positive posture than indifference) is turned into their most active promotion when conditions require that shift. In fact waste and destruction must be relentlessly pursued in this system in direct subordination to the *imperative of capital-expansion,* the overwhelming systemic determinant. This is all the more so the further we leave behind the historically ascending phase of the capital system's development. And no one should be fooled by the fact that frequently the preponderant assertion of *counter-value* is misrepresented and rationalized as *"value-neutrality"* by capital's celebrated ideologists.

It was therefore mind-boggling that at the time of Gorbachev's ill-fated perestroika his "Ideology Chief" (officially called by that name) could seriously assert that the capitalist market and its commodity relations were the instrumental embodiments of "universal human values" and a "major achievement of human civilization," adding to these grotesque capitulatory assertions that the capitalist market was even *"the guarantee of the renewal of socialism."*[17] Such theorists kept talking about the adoption of the "market mechanism," when the capitalist market was *anything but* an adaptable neutral *"mechanism."* It was in fact *incurably value-laden,* and must always remain so. In this kind of conception—curiously shared by Gorbachev's Ideology Chief (and others) with the von Hayeks of this world, who violently denounced any idea of socialism as *"The Road to Serfdom"*[18]— *exchange* in general was ahistorically and anti-historically equated with *capitalist exchange,* and the ever more destructive reality of the *capitalist market* with a fictionalized benevolent *"market"* in general. Whether they realized it or not, they capitulated thereby to idealizing the imperatives of a ruthless system of necessary *market domination* (ultimately inseparable from the ravages of imperialism) required by the inner determinations of capital's social metabolic order. The adoption of this capitulatory position was equally pronounced but even more damaging in Gorbachev's reform document. For he insisted that:

> There are *no alternatives to the market.* Only the market can ensure the satisfaction of *people's needs,* the *fair distribution* of wealth, *social rights,* and the strengthening of *freedom and democracy.* The market would permit the Soviet economy to be *organically* linked with the world's, and give our citizens access to all the achievements of *world civilization.*[19]

Naturally, given the total unreality of Gorbachev's "no alternative" wishful thinking, expecting the generous supply "to the people" of all those wonderful would-be achievements and benefits, in all domains, from the global capitalist market, this venture could only end, most humiliatingly, in the disastrous implosion of the Soviet type system.

9.5.5

It is not at all accidental or surprising that the proposition of *"there is no alternative"* occupies such a prominent place in the socioeconomic and political conceptions formulated from capital's standpoint. Not even the greatest thinkers of the bourgeoisie—like Adam Smith and Hegel—could be exceptions in this respect. For it is absolutely true that the bourgeois order either succeeds in asserting itself in the form of dynamic *capital expansion,* or it is condemned to ultimate failure. There can be really *no conceivable alternative* to endless capital expansion from capital's standpoint, determining thereby the vision of all those who adopt it. But the adoption of this standpoint also means that the question of *"what price must be paid"* for uncontrollable capital expansion beyond a certain point in time—once the ascendant phase of the system's development is left behind—cannot enter into consideration at all. The violation of *historical time* is therefore the necessary consequence of adopting capital's standpoint by internalizing the system's expansionary imperative as its most fundamental and absolutely unalterable determinant. Even in the conceptions of the greatest bourgeois thinkers this position must prevail. There can be no alternative future social order whose defining characteristics would be significantly different from the already established one. This is why even Hegel, who formulates by far the most profound historical conception up to his own time, must also arbitrarily bring history to an end in capital's unalterable present, idealizing the capitalist nation state[20] as the insuperable climax of all conceivable historical development, despite his sharp perception of the destructive implications of the whole system of nation states.

Thus, there can be no alternative to decreeing the pernicious dogma of *no alternative* in bourgeois thought. But it is totally absurd for socialists to adopt the position of endless (and by its nature uncontrollable) capital expansion. For the corollary idealization of—again characteristically unqualified—"consumption" ignores the elementary truth that from capital's uncritical self-expansionary vantage point there can be *no difference between destruction and consumption.* One is as good as the other for the required purpose. This is so because the commercial transaction in the capital relation—even of the most destructive kind, embodied in the ware of the military-industrial complex and the use to which it is put in its inhuman wars—successfully completes the cycle of capital's enlarged self-reproduction, so as to be able to open a new cycle. This is the only thing that really matters to capital—no matter how unsustainable might be the consequences. Consequently, when socialists internalize the imperative of capital expansion as the necessary ground of the advocated growth, they do not simply accept an isolated tenet but a whole "package deal." Knowingly or not, they accept at the same time all of the *false alternatives*—like "growth or no-growth"—that can be derived from the uncritical advocacy of necessary capital expansion.

We must reject the false alternative of *no growth* because its adoption would perpetuate the most gruesome misery and inequality now dominating the world, with struggle and destructiveness inseparable from it. The radical negation of that approach can only be a necessary point of departure. The inherently *positive* dimension of our vision involves the fundamental redefinition of *wealth itself.* Under capital's social metabolic order we are confronted by *the alienating rule of wealth over society,* directly affecting every aspect of life, from the narrowly economic to the cultural and spiritual domains. Consequently, we cannot get out of capital's vicious circle, with all of its ultimately destructive determinations and false alternatives, without fully turning around that vital relationship. Namely, without *making society—the society of freely associated individuals—rule over wealth,* redefining at the same time also their relation to *time* and to the kind of *use* to which the products of human labor are put. As Marx had written already in one of his early works:

> In a future society, in which class antagonism will have ceased, in which there will no longer be any classes, use will no longer be determined by the *minimum time of production;* but the time of production devoted to an article will be determined by the *degree of its social utility.*[21]

This means an uncompromising departure from viewing wealth as a fetishistic material entity that must ignore the *real individuals* who are the creators of wealth. Naturally, capital—in its false claim to be identical to wealth, as the "creator and embodiment of wealth"—must ignore the individuals, in the self-legitimating service of its own social metabolic control. In this way, by usurping the role of real wealth and subverting the potential use to which it could be put, capital is the *enemy of historical time.* This is what must be redressed for the sake of human survival itself. Thus, all constituents of the unfolding relationships among the historically self-determining real individuals, together with the wealth they create and positively allocate through the conscious application of the only viable modality of time—*disposable time*—must be brought together in a qualitatively different social metabolic framework. In the words of Marx:

> . . . *real wealth* is the developed productive power of all individuals. The measure of wealth is then not any longer, in any way, labor-time, but rather *disposable time*. Labor time as the measure of value posits wealth itself as founded on poverty, and disposable time as existing in and because of the antithesis to surplus labor-time; or, the positing of an individual's entire time as labor-time, and his *degradation* therefore to mere worker, *subsumption under labor.*[22]

Disposable time is the *individuals' actual historical time.* In contrast, necessary labor-time required for the functioning of capital's mode of social metabolic control is *antihistorical,* denying the individuals the only way in which they can assert and fulfill themselves as *real historical subjects* in control of their own life-activity. In the form of capital's necessary labor-time the individuals are subjected to time exercised as *tyrannical judge and degrading measure,* with no court of appeal, instead of being itself *judged* and *measured* in relation to qualitative human criteria "by the *needs* of the social individuals."[23] Capital's perversely self-absolutizing anti-historical time thus superimposes itself over human life as fetishistic *determinant* which reduces living labor to "*time's carcase,*" as we have seen above. The historical challenge is, then, to move, in the alternative social metabolic order, from the rule of capital's frozen time as *alienating determinant* to become freely *determined* by the social individuals themselves who consciously dedicate themselves to the realization of their chosen objectives their incomparably richer resources of *disposable time* than what could be squeezed out of them through the tyranny of necessary labor-time. This is an absolutely vital difference. Only the social individuals can really determine their own *disposable time,* in sharp contrast to necessary labor-time that dominates them. The adoption of disposable time is the only conceivable *and rightful* way in which time can be transformed from a *tyrannical determinant* into a autonomously and creatively *determined* constituent of the reproduction process.

9.5.6

This challenge necessarily involves the supersession of the structurally enforced hierarchical social division of labor. For so long as time dominates society in the form of the imperative to extract the surplus labor-time of its overwhelming majority, the personnel in charge of this process must lead a substantially different form of existence, in conformity to its function as the *willing enforcer of the alienating time-imperative.* At the same time, the overwhelming majority of the individuals are *"degraded to mere worker, subsumed under labor."* Under such conditions, the social reproduction process must sink ever deeper into its *structural crisis,* with the perilous ultimate implications of no possible way of return.

The nightmare of the "stationary state" remains a nightmare even if one tries to alleviate it, as John Stuart Mill proposed, through the illusory remedy of "better distribution" taken in isolation. There can be no such thing as "better distribution" without a radical restructuring of the *production process* itself. The socialist hegemonic alternative to the rule of capital requires fundamentally overcoming the *truncated dialectic* in the vital interrelationship of *production, distribution and consumption.* For without that, the socialist aim of turning work into "life's prime want" is inconceivable. To quote Marx:

> In a higher phase of communist society, after the enslaving subordination of the individual to the division of labor, and therewith also the antithesis between mental and physical labor, has vanished; after labor has become not only a means of life but *life's prime want;* after the productive forces have also increased with the *all-round development of the individual,* and all the springs of *cooperative wealth* flow more abundantly—only then can the narrow horizon of bourgeois right be crossed in its entirety and society inscribe on its banners: *From each according to his ability, to each according to his needs!*[24]

These are the *overall targets* of socialist transformation, providing the *compass* of the journey and simultaneously also the *measure* of the achievements accomplished (or failed to be accomplished) on the way. Within such a vision of the hegemonic alternative to capital's social reproductive order there can be no room at all for anything like "the stationary state," nor for any of the false alternatives associated with or derived from it. "The *all-round development* of the individuals," consciously exercising the full resources of their *disposable time,* within the framework of the new social metabolic control oriented toward the production of *"cooperative wealth,"* is meant to provide the basis of a *qualitatively* different accountancy: the necessary *socialist accountancy,* defined by human need and diametrically opposed to fetishistic quantification and to the concomitant unavoidable waste.

This is why the vital importance of *growth of a sustainable kind* can be recognized and successfully managed in the alternative social metabolic framework. In an order of social metabolic control, that is, where the antithesis between mental and physical labor—always vital for maintaining the absolute domination over labor by capital as the usurper of the role of the controlling historical subject, secured to it through its structurally pre-established expropriation of the means of production—must vanish for good. Consequently, consciously pursued productivity itself can be elevated to a *qualitatively higher level,* without any danger of uncontrollable *waste,* bringing forth genuine— and not narrowly profit-oriented material—*wealth* of which the "rich social individuals" (Marx), as autonomous historical subjects (and rich precisely in that sense) are fully in control. In the "stationary state," by contrast, the individuals could not be genuine historical subjects. For they could not be in control of a life of their own, in view of being at the mercy of the worst kind of material determinations directly under the rule of *incurable scarcity.*

Ever growing—and by its ultimate implications catastrophic— waste in the capital system is inseparable from the most irresponsible way in which the produced goods and services are *utilized,* in the service of profitable capital-expansion. Perversely, the lower their rate of utilization the higher the scope for profitable replacement, in the spirit of the absurd and in the future totally untenable equation mentioned already, whereby from capital's vantage point there can be no meaningful distinction drawn between *consumption and destruction.* For totally wasteful *destruction* just as adequately fulfils the demand required by self-expansionary capital for a new profitable cycle of production, as genuine consumption corresponding to use would be able to do. However, the moment of truth arrives when a heavy price must be paid for capital's criminally irresponsible husbandry, in the course of its historical development. That is the point where the imperative to adopt an increasingly better and incomparably more responsible *rate of utilization* of the produced goods and services—and indeed consciously produced with that aim in mind, in relation to qualitative human need and use—becomes absolutely vital. For *the only viable economy*—one *meaningfully economizing* and thereby sustainable in the near and more distant future—can only be the kind of rationally managed economy, oriented toward the *optimal utilization* of the produced goods and services. There can be no *growth of a sustainable kind* outside these parameters of rational husbandry oriented by genuine human need.

To take a crucially important example of what is incurably wrong in this respect under the rule of capital, we should think of the way in which the ever-growing numbers of automobiles are utilized in our society. The resources squandered on the production and fuelling of automobiles are immense under "advanced capitalism," representing the second highest expenditure—after the mortgage commitments—in the particular households. Absurdly, however, the rate of utilization of automobiles is less than *1 percent*, spuriously justified by the *exclusive possession rights* conferred upon their purchasers. At the same time, the thoroughly practicable real alternative is not simply neglected but actively sabotaged by the massive vested interests of quasi-monopolistic corporations. For the simple truth is that what the individuals *need* (and do not obtain, despite the heavy financial burden imposed upon them) are adequate *transport services,* and not the economically wasteful and environmentally most damaging privately owned commodity that also makes them lose countless hours of their life in unhealthy *traffic jams.* Evidently, the *real alternative* would be to develop *public transport* to the qualitatively highest level, satisfying the necessary economic, environmental, and personal health criteria well within the scope of such a rationally pursued project, confining at the same time the use of—collectively owned and appropriately allocated, but not exclusively and wastefully possessed—automobiles to specific functions. Thus, the individuals' need—in this case their genuine need for *proper transport services*—would determine the targets of the vehicles and communication facilities (like roads, railway networks, and navigation systems) to be produced and maintained, in accord with the principle of optimal utilization, instead of the individuals being completely dominated by the established system's fetishistic need for profitable but ultimately destructive capital expansion.

The unavoidable, but up to the present time tendentiously avoided, question of the *real economy,* must be faced in the very near future.

For in the so-called third world countries it is inconceivable to follow the wasteful "development" pattern of the past, which in fact condemned them to their precarious condition of today, under the rule of capital's mode of social metabolic reproduction. The clamorous failure of the much promoted "modernization theories" and their corresponding institutional embodiments clearly demonstrate the hopelessness of that approach.

9.5.7

In one respect, at least, we have seen alarm raised in this regard—characteristically pressing at the same time for the assertion and absolute preservation of the privileges of the dominant capitalist countries—in the recent past. It concerned the internationally growing need for *energy resources* and the competitive intervention of some potentially immense economic powers, above all China, in the unfolding process. Today that concern is primarily about China, but in due course also India must be added, of course, to the list of major countries unavoidably pressing for vital energy resources. And when we add to China the population of the Indian subcontinent, we are talking about more than *two-and-a-half-billion people.* Naturally, if they really followed the once grotesquely propagandized prescription of *The Stages of Economic Growth,*[25] with its simple-minded advocacy of "capitalist take-off and drive to maturity," that would have devastating consequences for all of us. For the fully automobilized society of two-and-a-half-billion people on the U.S. model of "advanced capitalist development," with more than 700 motor cars to every 1,000 people, would mean that we would be all dead before long through the global "modernizing" benefits of poisonous pollution, not to mention the total depletion of the planet's oil reserves in no time at all. But by the same token, in an opposite sense, no one can seriously envisage that the countries in question could be left indefinitely where they stand today. To imagine that the two-and-a-half-billion people of China and the Indian sub-continent could be permanently condemned to their existing predicament, still in heavy dependency to the capitalistically advanced parts of the world in one way or another, defies all credulity. The only question is: whether humanity can find a rationally viable and truly equitable solution to the legitimate demand for social and economic development of the peoples involved, or antagonistic competition and destructive struggle over resources are the way of the future, as befits the orienting framework and operating principles of capital's mode of social reproductive control.

Another respect in which the absolute imperative to adopt a qualitatively different way of organizing economic and social life appeared on the horizon in our time concerns the *ecology*. But again, the only viable way of addressing the increasingly grave problems of our global ecology—if we want to face up in a responsible way to the aggravating problems and contradictions of the planetary household, from their direct impact on such vital questions as global warming to the elementary demand for clean water resources and healthy air—is to switch from the existing order's wasteful husbandry of fetishistic quantification to a genuinely *quality oriented* one. Ecology, in this respect, is an important but subordinate aspect of the necessary *qualitative redefinition* of utilizing the produced goods and services, without which the advocacy of humanity's permanently sustainable ecology—again, an absolute must—can be nothing more than a pious hope.

The final point to stress in this context is that the urgency to face up to these problems cannot be understated, let alone minimized, as capital's vested interests, sustained by its dominant imperialist state formations in their insuperable rivalry among themselves continue to do. Ironically, although there is so much propagandistic talk about "globalization," the objective requirements for making a rationally sustainable and globally coordinated reproductive order of social interchanges work are constantly violated. Yet, given the present stage of historical development, the irrepressible truth remains that with regard to all of the major issues discussed in this section we are really concerned with ever aggravating *global challenges*, requiring *global solutions*. However, our gravest concern is that capital's mode of social metabolic reproduction—in view of its inherently antagonistic structural determinations and their destructive manifestations—is not amenable at all to viable global solutions. Capital, given its unalterable nature, is nothing unless it can prevail in the form of *structural domination*. But the inseparable other dimension of structural domination is *structural subordination*. This is the way in which capital's mode of social metabolic reproduction always functioned and always must try to function, bringing with it even the most devastating wars of which we have had much more than just a foretaste in our time. The violent assertion of the destructive imperatives of global hegemonic imperialism, through the formerly unimaginable destructive might of the United States as the global hegemon, cannot bring *global solutions* to our aggravating problems but only *global disaster*. Thus, the unavoidable necessity to address these global problems in a historically sustainable way puts the challenge of socialism in the twenty-first century—the only viable hegemonic alternative to capital's mode of social metabolic control—on the order of the day.

9.6 The National and the International: Their Dialectical Complementarity in Our Time

9.6.1

One of the greatest impediments to socialist development has been and still remains the persistent neglect of the national question. The reason for this neglect has arisen both from some contingent but far-reaching historical determinations and from the complicated theoretical legacy of the past. Moreover, given the nature of the issues involved, the two happen to be closely intertwined.

As regards the practical and historical determinations, we must remember first of all that the formation of modern nations has been accomplished under the class leadership of the bourgeoisie. This development took place in accord with the socioeconomic imperatives inherent in the self-expansionary drive of the multiplicity of capitals from their originally very limited local settings toward ever greater territorial control, in ever-intensifying conflicts with one another, culminating in two devastating world wars in the twentieth century and in the potential annihilation of humankind in our own time.

The system of inter-state relations constituted under the self-expansionary imperatives of capital could only be incurably iniquitous. It had to enforce and constantly reinforce the highly privileged position of the imperialistically poised handful of nations, and in complete contrast, it had to impose at the same time, with all available means, including the most violent ones, a structurally subordinate predicament on all the other nations. This way of articulating the international order prevailed not only against smaller nations but even when the countries concerned had incomparably larger populations than their foreign oppressors, as for instance India under the British Empire. As

regards the colonized nations, their conditions of economic and political dependency were ruthlessly enforced upon them by the dominant
imperialist powers, thanks also to the subservient complicity of their
indigenous ruling classes. Characteristically, therefore, the "post-colo-
nial" changes had no difficulty whatsoever in reproducing, in all substantive relations, the earlier modes of domination, even if in a formally somewhat modified way, thereby perpetuating the long-established
system of structural domination and dependency all the way down to
the present.

Only through the force of a monumental miracle could
capitalistic inter-state relations of structural domination and subordination have become significantly different from what they actually
turned out to be in the course of historical development. For capital,
as the controlling force of the economic and social reproduction
process, cannot be other than strictly hierarchical and authoritarian in
its innermost determinations even in the most privileged imperialist
countries. How could, therefore, a social and political system—characterized in its capitalist variety by the "authoritarianism of the workshop and the tyranny of the market" (Marx)—be equitable on the
international plane? Capital's absolute necessity to dominate internally its own labor force may well be compatible with granting some limited privileges to its indigenous working population, for the purpose
of chauvinistic mystification, from the extra margin of exploitative
advantage derived from imperialist domination. But such practices do
not introduce even the smallest degree of equality into the
capital/labor relationship of the privileged imperialist country in
which capital fully retains, and must always retain, the power of decision-making on all substantive issues. To suggest, therefore, that
despite such unalterable internal structural determinations the external—inter-state—relations of the system could be other than wholly
iniquitous would be quite absurd. For it would be tantamount to pretending that what is by its very nature deeply iniquitous produces genuine equality under the further aggravating conditions of necessarily
enforced foreign domination.

Understandably, therefore, the socialist response to such a system
had to be spelled out in terms of a most radical negation, stressing the
need for a qualitatively different relationship among the great variety
of nations, large and small, on the basis of the supersession of the prevailing antagonisms within the framework of a genuinely cooperative

international order. The matter was, however, greatly complicated in the twentieth century by the tragic circumstance that the first successful revolution, which projected the socialist transformation of society, broke out in tsarist Russia. For that country happened to be at the time an oppressive multinational empire. This is a fact that significantly contributed to its characterization by Lenin as "the weakest link of the chain of imperialism," and as such a positive asset to the potential outbreak of the revolution—an assessment in which he has been proved completely right. But the other side of the same coin was that not only the grave socioeconomic backwardness but also the terrible legacy of the oppressive multinational empire represented immense problems for the future.

Controversy raged over "socialism in a single country" for many decades after Stalin consolidated his power. However, the simple but vital consideration as a rule omitted from such discussions was that the Soviet Union was not at all a *single country,* but a multiplicity of nationalities divided by the grave iniquities and internal antagonisms bequeathed to them by the tsarist empire.

The failure to properly address the potentially explosive contradictions of national iniquity after Lenin's death carried with it devastating consequences for the future, ultimately resulting in the breakup of the Soviet Union. The contrast between Lenin and Stalin's approach to these problems could not have been greater. Lenin always advocated the right of the various national minorities to full autonomy, "to the point of secession," whereas Stalin degraded them to nothing more than "border regions," to be controlled at all cost, in strictest subordination to the interests of Russia. This is why Lenin condemned him in no uncertain terms, insisting that if the views advocated by Stalin prevailed, as later they did, "the *freedom to secede from the union*' by which we justify ourselves will be a mere scrap of paper, unable to defend the non-Russians from the onslaught of that really Russian man, the Great-Russian chauvinist."[26] He underlined the gravity of the damage caused by the policies pursued and clearly named the culprits: "The political responsibility for all this truly Great-Russian nationalist campaign must, of course, be laid on Stalin and Dzerzhinsky."[27]

After Lenin's death in January 1924, following his long-time incapacitating illness, all of his recommendations on the national question were nullified and Stalin's "Great-Russian" policies—which treated the other nationalities as subordinate "border regions"—were fully implemented, contributing greatly to the *blocked development* that subsequently characterized Soviet society. Even the approach of Gorbachev and his followers was characterized by the same sense of tendentious unreality as the other post-Lenin theorizations and practices, as I tried to stress well before the implosion of the Soviet Union.[28] They maintained the fiction of the "Soviet nation," with its allegedly *"unified self-awareness,"* naively or wantonly ignoring the explosive internal problems of the "unified Soviet nation," notwithstanding the clear signs of a gathering storm which soon enough resulted in the breakup of the far from unified Soviet Union. At the same time, they tried to justify the reduction of various national communities, including the Baltic, Byelorussian, and Ukrainian, to the status of "ethnic groups."

Under Stalin's rule, the acceptance of such wanton unreality could be imposed with the help of authoritarian repressive measures, going as far as even the deportation of entire national minorities. Once, however, that road had to be abandoned, nothing could make the terrible legacy of the oppressive tsarist multinational empire and the subsequent preservation of its antagonisms prevail. It was, therefore, only a question of what time and in what particular form the post-revolutionary Soviet state—one very far from being a "single country"—would have to disintegrate under the intolerable weight of its manifold contradictions.

9.6.2

The persistent neglect of the national question has not been, to be sure, confined to the vicissitudes of the Soviet failure to face up to its dilemmas. The tendency in the West European socialist movement to move in the direction of a blind alley, as regards the national question and the closely associated issue of internationalism, appeared well before the Russian revolution. In fact, Engels bitterly complained forty-two years earlier, at the time of the discussion of the Gotha Program in Germany, that in this document "the principle that the workers' movement is an *international movement* is, to all intents and purposes, *completely disavowed.*"[29] The necessary radical negation of capital's existing order from a socialist perspective was inconceivable without the adoption of a consistent and, in reality, fully sustainable international position. However, the opportunistic maneuver aimed at securing the unification of the political forces involved in approving the Gotha Program carried with it serious nationalistic concessions for which a very high price had to be paid in the future. The total capitulation of German Social Democracy to the forces of aggressive bourgeois chauvinism at the outbreak of the First World War was only the logical culmination of that dangerous turn in German political development, sealing thereby also the fate of the Second International.

It is important to remember here that none of the four Internationals—founded with the expectation of making the power of international solidarity prevail against capital's hierarchical structural domination of labor—have succeeded in fulfilling the hope attached to them. The First International foundered already in Marx's lifetime, as a result of the derailment of the workers' movement as an international movement towards the end of the 1870s, sharply criticized by Engels as we have just seen. The Second International carried within itself the seeds of this contradiction and turned them into inexorably growing plants, waiting only for the historical opportunity—provided by the First World War—before the members of the International sided with the rival warring parties, thereby fatefully discrediting the whole organization. This badly discredited "Workers' International," whose constituent national members throughout the war continued to identify themselves with their own bourgeoisie and thereby ceased to have anything at all to do with the vital requirements of socialist internationalism, was later reestablished as an organ of socioeconomic accommodation and the institutionalized denial of the class struggle. Rosa Luxemburg's judgment summed up with great clarity the meaning of these developments by stressing that "in refuting the existence of the class struggle, the Social Democracy has denied the very basis of its own existence."[30] It was, therefore, only a question of time before the Social Democratic parties all over the world went on adopting a position openly in defense of the established order.

Against the background of the Second International's ignominious failure, the Third International was founded in the aftermath of the October Revolution. However, as a result of the progressive imposition of Stalin's authoritarian policies, which treated international matters, including the relationship with the parties of the Third International itself, in strict subordination to Soviet state interests, also this organization failed to fulfill the role of developing genuine socialist internationalism. Its dissolution as the Communist International (the Comintern), and its metamorphosis into the Cominform—i.e., an international organization of information—did not solve anything. For even the Cominform was a one-way street. This was so because any critique of the Soviet system remained an absolute taboo during Stalin's lifetime. And even after he died, Khrushchev's severe critique of his "personality cult" and of its negative consequences failed to address the fundamental issues of Soviet-type society as a mode of social metabolic reproduction, despite its ever intensifying contradictions and crisis symptoms.

By the time the gravity of the crisis itself was acknowledged, under Gorbachev's *glasnost* and *perestroika*, the envisaged corrective efforts were conceived in a way inseparable from embarking on the road to the restoration of capitalism. As to the Fourth International, it could never attain the status of an international organization with *mass* influence, despite the intentions of its founder. Yet, if the envisaged strategic vision cannot, in Marx's words, "grip the masses," the task of developing the necessary socialist internationalism cannot be accomplished.

The national question inevitably assumed the form of polarization between the handful of oppressor states and the overwhelming majority of imperialistically oppressed nations: a most iniquitous relationship in which the working classes of the imperialist countries were deeply implicated. Nor was this relationship confined to direct military domination. The purpose of the latter—whenever it was brought into play either through some major military operations or through the exercise of "gunboat diplomacy"—was to secure the maximum feasible exploitation of labor in the conquered countries on a continuing basis, imposing thereby the characteristic mode of capital's social metabolic control ultimately in the entire world. This is why in the course of post-Second World War "decolonization" it was quite possible to abandon direct military and political control of the former empires without changing the substance of the established relationship of structural domination and subordination, as befits the capital system.

The United States was the pioneer in this respect. It exercised direct colonial-type military domination in some countries, like the Philippines, for instance, wedded to socioeconomic supremacy over the populations involved. At the same time it secured the massive domination of the whole of Latin America in the form of imposing on the countries of the continent structural dependency without necessarily intervening militarily. But, of course, the United States unhesitatingly resorted to open or covert military interventions in its proclaimed "backyard" whenever the maintenance of its exploitative domination was put into question. One of its preferred ways of imposing rule was the "indigenous" military overthrow of elected governments and the establishment of "friendly" dictatorships, with the most cynical and hypocritical justification for such acts on numerous occasions, from Brazil's military dictatorship to Pinochet's Chile.

Nevertheless, for a long time the principal strategy of the United States for asserting its exploitative interests in the post-Second World War period was through the exercise of economic domination, wedded to the deceitful ideology of "democracy and liberty." This was well in tune with a determinate phase of capital's historical development, when the political and military shackles of the old empires proved to be rather anachronistic for realizing the potentialities of capital-expansion better suited in the postwar world to neocolonial practices. The United States was in a nearly ideal position, in this regard, both as the most dynamic constituent of global capital in its drive to productive expansion, and as a country which could claim to have no need for a direct political and military domination of colonies, unlike the British and French Empires. It is therefore highly significant—and in its implications for the survival of humanity most dangerous—that in our time this "democratic" superpower has had to revert to the most wasteful and brutal form of military interventions and occupations, in response to capital's structural crisis, in a vain attempt to resolve that crisis by imposing itself on the rest of the world as the master of global hegemonic imperialism.

This newer version of imperialism was (and remains) a form of domination no less iniquitous for the great masses of the working people than its predecessor. Accordingly, it is inconceivable to realize true internationalism without the radical emancipation of the many oppressed nations, not least in Latin America, from their continued domination by the oppressor nations. This is the meaning of legitimate defensive nationalism today, as stressed from the very beginning by Lenin. The *positive* dimension of internationalism must complement this *defensive* nationalism in order for it to succeed.

9.6.3

International solidarity is a *positive potential* of capital's structural antagonist only. It is in harmony with *patriotism,* which is habitually confused in theoretical discussions even on the left with bourgeois *chauvinism.* This confusion happens to be quite often a more or less conscious excuse for denying the necessity for breaking the chains of exploitative structural dependency of which even the workers of "advanced capitalism" are undeniable beneficiaries, even if to a much more limited degree than their class antagonists. But patriotism does not mean identifying oneself exclusively with the legitimate national interests of *one's own country,* when it is threatened by a foreign power, or indeed by the capitulatory behavior of one's own ruling class for which Lenin and Luxemburg rightly advocated turning the weapons of war against the internal class exploiters. It also means *full solidarity* with the genuine patriotism of the *oppressed peoples.*

The condition of realization of such patriotism is not simply a change in the prevailing inter-state relations, countering thereby to some extent the foreign dictates of the established political, or military and political, dependency. For the condition of lasting success can only be a sustained struggle against capital's hierarchical structural domination, for as long as it takes, all over the world. Without it, also, the now and then successful casting off of the earlier political and military supremacy of the foreign power can be reestablished, in the old form or in a new one, at the next turn of events. International solidarity of the oppressed, therefore, requires the full awareness and the consistent practical observance of these vital strategic orienting principles.

Socialist internationalism is inconceivable without full respect for the aspirations of the working people of other nations. Only that respect can create the objective possibility of positive cooperative interchanges. Ever since its first formulation, Marxist theory insisted that a nation that dominates other nations deprives itself of its own freedom—a dictum Lenin never ceased to reiterate. It is not difficult to see why this should be so. For any form of inter-state domination presupposes a strictly regulated framework of social interchange in which the exercise of control is expropriated by the relatively few. A national state which is constituted in such a way that it should be able to dominate other nationalities, or the so-called peripheral and border regions, presupposes the complicity of its politically active citizenry in the exercise of domination, thus mystifying and weakening the working masses in their aspiration to emancipate themselves.

Thus, the radical negation of the long-prevailing system of most iniquitous inter-state relations is an absolutely unavoidable requirement of socialist theory. It provides the conceptual basis of *defensive* nationalism. However, the necessary positive alternative to capital's social order cannot be a defensive one. For all defensive positions suffer from being ultimately unstable, in that even the best defenses can be overrun under concentrated fire, given the suitably changed relation of forces in favor of the adversary. What is needed in this respect, in response to capital's perverse globalization, is the articulation of a viable positive alternative. That is, an international social reproductive order instituted and managed on the basis of the genuine equality of its manifold constituents, defined not in formal but in materially and culturally identifiable substantive terms. Thus, the strategy of *positive internationalism* means replacing the absolutely iniquitous—and insuperably conflictual—structuring principle of capital's reproductive "microcosms" (the particular productive and distributive enterprises which constitute the comprehensive "macrocosm" of the system) by a *fully cooperative alternative.*

The destructive drive of transnational capital cannot be even alleviated, let alone positively overcome, at the international level, only through the action of particular national governments. For the continued existence of the antagonistic "microcosms," and their subsumption under increasingly larger structures of the same conflictual type (like the giant transnational corporations, as they arise through the concentration and centralization of capital today) of necessity reproduces the temporarily placated conflicts sooner or later. Thus, positive internationalism defines itself as the strategy for going beyond capital as a mode of social metabolic control by helping to articulate and comprehensively coordinate a *non-hierarchical form of decision making*[31] at the material as well as on the cultural and political plane. In other words, by a qualitatively different form of decision-making in which the vital controlling functions of societal reproduction can be positively *devolved* to the members of the "microcosms," and, at the same time, the activities of the latter can be appropriately coordinated to embrace the most comprehensive levels, because they are not torn apart by irreconcilable antagonisms.

9.6.4

Such antagonisms proved to be insurmountable even when heroic attempts were made by Simón Bolívar to create a viable alternative. For what was necessarily required in order to succeed was the transformation of the whole fabric of society far beyond even such measures as the legal emancipation of the slaves. Thus, in his efforts to find a lasting solution for which the historical time had not yet arrived, Bolívar encountered great hostility even in the Latin American countries to which he rendered unequalled services, acknowledged by the unique title of *El Libertador* with which he had been honored at the time. As a result, he had to spend his final days in tragic isolation.

As to his adversaries in the United States, who felt threatened by the spread of his enlightened conception of *equality*[32]—both internally (as slave owners directly challenged by Bolívar's emancipation of the slaves) and by his advocacy of harmonious inter-state relations across the world—they did not hesitate to condemn and dismiss him as *"the dangerous madman of the South."*[33]

The principal impediment was the sharp contrast between the political unity of the Latin American countries advocated by Bolívar and the deeply adversarial and conflictual constituents of their social microcosms. Consequently, even the noblest and most eloquent appeals to political unity could work only while the menace presented by the Spanish colonial adversary was acute. But by itself such menace could not remedy the internal antagonisms. Nor could the situation be radically altered by Bolívar's far-sighted identification of the new danger. Namely, that "the United States of North America seem to be destined by providence to condemn America to misery in the name of Liberty." A danger even more strongly underlined, in the same spirit, by José Martí sixty years later.[34] Both were as realistic in their diagnoses of the new dangers as they were generous in advocating an ideal solution to humanity's grave problems. Bolívar, when he proposed a way of bringing all nations of humanity harmoniously together in the isthmus of Panama made the capital of the globe, in the same way "as Constantine wanted to make Byzantium the capital of the antique hemisphere,"[35] and Martí when he insisted that "patria es humanidad": *"humanity is our homeland."*

When these ideals were formulated, historical time still pointed in the opposite direction: toward the frightful intensification of the social

antagonisms and the horrendous bloodletting of two world wars arising from them. Toward the end of his life, Bolívar was forced to concede, tragically, the day of America, as he had envisaged it before, had
not yet arrived. Today the situation is very different. Bolívar's "day of
America" has arrived in the sense that the age-old conditions of Latin
America's quasi-colonial domination by the United States cannot be
maintained any longer. In this regard, the interests of the effective
national sovereignty of the Latin American countries fully coincide
with the necessary drive for overcoming national grievances everywhere, since the long prevailing national domination of many countries by a few imperialist powers has become an irreversible historical
anachronism.

The changed historical condition cannot be undone by the fact
that the former imperialist powers, and above all by far the most powerful of them the United States, are trying to turn back the wheels of
history and *recolonize* the world. Their design to such end is already
visible in the way in which they have recently undertaken some devastating military adventures under the pretext of the so-called "war
against terror." Indeed, the new panacea—namely that embarking on
what would in fact amount to a blatant re-colonizing venture—is
declared by the most aggressive powers to be the essential condition
for the success of their cynically righteous "war against international
terror" in the "new world order." But they are bound to fail in this
enterprise.

In the past, many attempts aimed at rectifying justifiable national
grievances were derailed by the pursuit of *chauvinistic* strategies. For,
given the nature of the problems at stake, the imposed national interests of the dominant countries cannot permanently prevail at the
expense of the justifiable social objectives of some other nations, vio-
lating the required *fully equitable international conditions* of inter-state
relations. Thus, the far-sighted historical validity of the Bolivarian
project, pressing for the strategic unity and equality of the Latin
American countries not simply against the United States but within
the broadest framework of the envisaged harmonious international
association of all, could not be clearer. Indeed, by realizing social and
political unity based on solidarity amongst themselves, the Latin
American countries could play a pioneering role today, in the interest
of the whole of humankind. None of them can succeed in isolation
even negatively against their powerful antagonist in North America,

but together they can show a way forward to all of us by instituting a positive confederate solution. They are all the more in a position to do that, in the spirit of *genuine internationalism,* because they are not burdened by the past of many European imperialist or quasi-imperialist traditions.

The grave problems of national contradictions are shared and suffered in different parts of the world. In this respect it is enough to think of the constantly war-torn Middle East, the violent breakup of the former Yugoslavia, the disintegration of the Soviet Union and its deeply troubled (in places like Chechnya even explosive) aftermath, the open or latent conflicts in Central Europe, the severe internal antagonisms periodically erupting on the Indian subcontinent, the still far from resolved national grievances in Canada, and the various armed confrontations in North and Central Africa. It is unthinkable to find lasting solutions to the underlying problems without fully facing up to the persistently neglected issue of equitable inter-state relations, to be instituted by respecting the dialectical complementarity of the national and the international as appropriate to our own historical time.

Given the antagonistic structural determinations of capital's mode of social metabolic control, culminating in the imperialist domination of the many by the few, only a consistent socialist approach can succeed in this respect. But the other side of the same coin must also be examined. Namely, that the vitally necessary socialist transformation of our mode of social metabolic reproduction is not feasible at all without instituting truly viable solutions to the long neglected legitimate national grievances of the dominated countries, within the framework of substantively equitable internationalism. For only the historically appropriate pursuit of the strategy—capable of bringing the national and the international dimensions of social interchange to their positive common denominator everywhere—can solve the grave structural crisis of our social order.

9.6.5

To be sure, capitalism did not invent exploitation and oppression. Brutally repressed slave revolts took place in history thousands of years ago, and major peasant uprisings—repressed with equal brutality—broke out hundreds of years before the unfolding and stabilization of capital's reproductive order. The innovation of capital was to try and make its own variety of socioeconomic and political exploitation universally acceptable and permanent. The same goes for national and ethnic discrimination and oppression. They also have much deeper historical roots than the last three or four hundred years, even if the most iniquitous—imperialist—inter-state relations of domination and subordination prevailed only under the rule of "advanced capital."

Accordingly, the problems of national and ethnic discrimination cannot be fully overcome without attending to their deeper historical roots. Just like the age-old questions of exploitation and oppression, national grievances point to a much broader picture. Considering the long history of hierarchical domination and exploitation, attacking the capitalist variety can only be part of the answer, notwithstanding the fact that it constitutes the most obvious challenge and point of departure in our time. The same is true of the most obvious national contradictions and grievances. Consequently, with regard to both sets of fundamental unresolved problems, *the socialist alternative* requires that they should be confronted in their *full historical perspective,* reaching down to their ultimate ground in search for a lasting *epochal* remedy. They must be grasped at their deepest historical roots of which the capitalist variety is only *one*—no matter how important and now globally dominant—sprout. If this is not done, a new antagonistic shoot may germinate some time in the future. Concerning the socialist alternative, it was precisely this burden of class determinations in history as a whole, and not only in its last few centuries, which made Marx sharply contrast what he called "humanity's prehistory" with *humanity's real history.* A conception of history as a qualitatively different mode of productive and distributive control consciously managed—in accord with their chosen objectives—by the social individuals as the genuine *subjects* of history.

The struggle over these vital concerns characterized human history for thousands of years, even if it was bound to assume new forms with the changing of circumstances and the corresponding change of human beings. In a magnificent poem, entitled *By the Danube* ("*A Dunánál*"), Attila József depicts this process of dramatic social and national conflicts in its full historical intensity. He does that with splendid poetic imagination by addressing and interrogating the river—"who is past, present and future," yet an inseparable part and personified witness of human history—in order to offer his own answers. By creatively representing his vision in the form of a most inspired interplay between the vantage points of the poet and the age-old mighty river, József is able to put before us with great humanity and evocative power all dimensions of historical time, together with the deeply felt burden of historical responsibility. In this way, he can bring to life the "fiercely fought" major antagonisms of the past and present among the "many nationalities," with moving advocacy of their required solutions.

This is how Attila József speaks to us in the last two stanzas of his great poem:

> I am the world, everything there was and is,
> the many nationalities bent on fateful conflict.
> The conquerors triumph with me in their death,
> and I am tortured by the agony of the conquered.
> Árpád and Zalán, Werböczy and Dózsa,[36]
> Turk, Tartar, Slovak, Rumanian swirl in this heart,
> in profound debt to the past
> with a gentle future, Oh, Hungarians of today!

> I want to work. It is hard enough
> that the past must be confessed.
> Of mighty Danube—who is past, present and future—
> the soft waves flow in calm embrace.
> The struggle fiercely fought by our ancestors
> dissolves into peace through memory.
> To attend to our shared tasks, to put them in order at last,
> that is our work; and it is not little!

At the present juncture of history we are all without exception "in pro-found debt to the past with a gentle future." Indeed, we are in such debt not only to a very, very long past, but also to the perilously threat-ening present. In debt with a permanently sustainable "gentle future," to be secured in the alternative social order of humanity's *real history,* well beyond the "fiercely fought struggles" not only of our ancestors but also of those that must still be fought against the destructive pow-ers of today. The stakes have never been higher, and they cannot be won without overcoming the persistent antagonisms and perilous conflicts arising also from national and ethnic grievances, with their multi-layered and profound roots, reproducing in our time the poisonous plant of capital's increasingly destructive inter-state relations. They exploded in two devastating world wars in the course of the twentieth century, and now they directly threaten humanity's very survival.

The solution of the age-old conflicts and antagonisms inherited from the past and intensified in the present is long overdue. But the task of overcoming national grievances cannot be achieved without extracting the multilayered roots themselves, just as the contradictions of the capital system cannot be resolved by reforms, without *eradicating,* that is, *capital itself* from the social fabric. It is not enough to "abolish wage slavery" alone, when we must target the structural determinations of *exploitation and oppression* in their long historical continuity and change. All forms and feasible varieties of exploitation and oppression must be firmly eradicated if we are to succeed, including the latent or explosive national and ethnic grievances that go very far back in history. Their memory lingers on for a long time, often contributing to the eruption of further antagonisms. Such memory cannot be remedied simply by thinking in a different way about the past. It is profoundly true that *"The struggle fiercely fought by our ancestors dissolves into peace through memory."* But only when historical memory is actually reshaped through *practical intervention,* which rectifies the national and ethnic grievances themselves on a lasting basis, will this be the case. These fundamental issues of shared concern cannot be postponed indefinitely. To say it with József: "*attend to our shared tasks, to put them in order at last, that is our work; and it is not little!*"

9.6.6

José Martí was absolutely right when he highlighted the real meaning of *patriotism* by insisting that *"patria es humanidad,"* or humanity is our homeland. For this kind of homeland—characterized by the individuals' conscious identification with the positive values of their community—is the only permanently sustainable social order which cannot be torn apart by devastating antagonisms. As such, it is not a remote ideal but the *necessary target, compass, and measure* of success of the socialist strategy of transformation, envisaging the institution of the alternative mode of social reproductive control in which there can be no room for national discrimination and concomitant grievances. It is the only viable *international* order, in the deepest sense of the term, in contrast to all attempts to impose one from outside and from above—failed in the past and destined to failure also in the future. What makes it viable and sustainable is that Martí's homeland, defined in direct relationship to humanity, arises from the *positive inner determinations* of its constitutive parts, which harmonize the many particular manifestations of genuine patriotism with their global conditions of ongoing realization. These two dimensions are inseparable in the socialist strategy, with its necessary overall target and guiding compass. There can be no sustainable global and international interchange—this, too, is an absolute must in our time—without the positive coalescence of the great varieties of the people's patriotic identification with the actual life conditions of their community, and vice versa. There can be no patriotism worthy of its name without the successful institution and strengthening of humanity's reciprocally adaptive and cooperatively harmonizing global/international homeland, which alone can confer the required positive defining characteristics on patriotism itself. In this sense, the dialectical complementarity of the national and the international remains a vital orienting principle of human interchanges in the foreseeable future.

Naturally, the organizational dimension of these problems cannot be understated. On the contrary, in the light of recent trends of socioeconomic and political developments it acquires a growing importance. For the international actions of global hegemonic imperialism, assuming by now the form of even major military adventures, represent an enormous danger for the future. Thus, they urgently call for the development of a viable socialist international framework of action. Without that the much-needed hegemonic alternative to capital's destructive mode of social reproductive and political control cannot prevail.

In terms of the necessary *strategic priorities* to be accomplished, the articulation and strengthening of such a framework of socialist international action occupies a most prominent place. It cannot be envisaged simply as the occasional and periodic *response* to international capital's most threatening developments on the economic (e.g., environmental) and political plane, but as a *coherently unfolding alternative* that must be sustained in all domains by appropriate forms of international action. In other words, what we are concerned with is the *historical actuality* (and necessity) of such organizational achievements, to be consistently pursued in their own strategic terms of reference and sustained not only when extreme challenges arise—as, for instance, on some explosive occasion when they join in the more or less spontaneously generated *mass protests* against some imperialist military operation—but on a continuing timescale.

Inevitably, one of the principal conditions required in our time for the successful articulation and strengthening of a viable international mode of action is a serious critical examination of the failures of the past in this respect. For, as mentioned earlier, all four Internationals fell very far short of accomplishing their declared objectives. If unfavorable historical conditions hindered—and worse, prevented—the successful international development of the socialist organizational alternative in the past, are conditions more favorable today?

The need for a significant advance of the radical socialist forces, as protagonists of the hegemonic alternative to capital's reproductive order, is undoubtedly very great today, in view of the escalating destructiveness of the ruling order. But such need by itself is not enough, no matter how strong or promising. For we cannot overlook the heavy burden of *internal fractures* on the *radical wing* of the socialist movement (in addition to the long-prevailing reformist derailment at the other wing), as they unfolded in the past and continue to exercise their painfully divisive and negative influence also today. The international failures of the past cannot be remedied without facing up to this problem, even if the historical conditions for developing and sustaining an organizationally viable mode of radical international action are much more favorable today than ever before.

The major difference in this regard is that we have reached the historical stage of the capital system's *structural crisis*. That means in tangible social and political terms that some avenues—which in the past enabled capital to manage its contradictions and antagonisms with relative ease under its periodic conjunctural crises—have now been blocked, producing severe complications for the future.

Among the most important blocked avenues, two stand out as directly relevant here. The first concerns the way in which capital could in the past induce reformist labor to *internalize* and actively promote the unrealizable promise of *"evolutionary socialism"*—and its twin brothers: *"parliamentary socialism"* in different parts of Europe, and the fictitious establishment of socialism by *"conquering the commanding heights of the economy"* in Harold Wilson's Britain—thereby mystifying and successfully disarming its potential adversary. However, under the heavy impact of capital's structural crisis the pretended socialist—but in truth totally capitulatory—strategies had to be finally abandoned by the reformist parties, thus turning themselves into open defenders of the ruling order, like "New Labour" in Britain. Inevitably, this development reopened the question of what course of action must be followed in the future in order to oppose the worsening conditions of life for workers even in the advanced capitalist countries, no matter how long it might take to rectify the defeatist past.

The second blocked avenue is even more important. It concerns the removal of the possibility of solving the system's aggravating problems through an *all-out war,* as it was twice attempted in the world wars of the twentieth century. I wrote at the time of the onset of capital's structural crisis, toward the end of the Vietnam war that:

> ... the system has been decapitated through the removal of its ultimate sanction: an all-out war on its real or potential adversaries ... Exporting violence is no longer possible on the *required massive scale.* Attempts at doing so on a limited scale—like the Vietnam War[37]—not only are no substitutes for the old mechanism but even accelerate the inevitable internal explosions of the system. Nor is it possible to get away indefinitely with the ideological mystification which represented the *internal* challenge of socialism: the only possible solution to the present crisis, as an *external* confrontation: a 'subversion' directed from abroad by a 'monolithic' enemy. For the first time in history capitalism is globally confronted with its own problems which cannot be 'postponed' much longer, nor can they be indeed transferred to the military plane in order to be *exported* in the form of an *all-out war.*[38]

I added in a note to the last sentence that "Of course such a war can *happen,* but its actual planning and active preparation in the open cannot function as a vital internal stabilizer."[39] This is so even if the neoconservative "vision guys" of the Pentagon—whose "theories" border on insanity[40]—are more than willing "to think the unthinkable." But even such extreme forms of irrationality cannot undo the far-reaching implications of this blocked avenue. For the underlying issue is an insoluble contradiction within the reproductive framework of the capital system. A contradiction manifest, on the one hand, through the ongoing relentless concentration and centralization of capital on a global scale, and on the other, through the structurally imposed inability of the capital system to produce the required political stabilization on a corresponding global scale. Even the most aggressive military interventions of global hegemonic imperialism—at present those of the United States—in different parts of the planet are bound to fail in this respect.

The destructiveness of limited wars, no matter how many, is very far from being enough for imposing everywhere on a lasting basis the unchallengeable rule of a single imperialist hegemon and its "global government"—the only thing that would befit the logic of capital. Only the socialist hegemonic alternative can show a way out of this destructive contradiction. That is, an organizationally viable alternative that fully respects the dialectical complementarity of the national and the international in our time.

9.7 Alternative to Parliamentarism: Unifying the Material Reproductive and the Political Sphere

9.7.1

The necessary alternative to parliamentarism is closely linked to the question of real *Participation* discussed in Section 9.2. On the face of it, the major difference is that whereas full participation is an absolutely fundamental and permanent regulative principle of socialist interrelations—no matter how advanced and how distant a form of socialist society—the need for producing a strategically sustainable alternative to parliamentarism is immediate, unavoidable, and urgently facing us. However, this is only the most obvious aspect of the important problem of how to liberate the socialist movement from the straitjacket of bourgeois parliamentarism. It has another dimension as well, concerned with the much broader and ultimately no less unavoidable challenge which is usually referred to in the socialist literature as "*the withering away of the state.*" The apparently prohibiting difficulties of that vital Marxian project apply with equal relevance and weight to both *participation*—as fully autonomous self-management of their society by the freely associated producers in every domain, well beyond the (for some time necessary) mediatory constraints of the modern political state—and to the enduring way of unifying the material reproductive and the political sphere, as the envisaged radical alternative to *parliamentarism*. Indeed, when we consider the historic task of making real "the withering away of the state," self-management through full participation, and the permanently sustainable overcoming of parliamentarism by a positive form of substantive—in opposition to politically confined formal and legal—decision-making are inseparable.

The necessity to institute a valid alternative to parliamentarism arises from the historically specific political institutions of our own time. They have been transformed—much for the worse, to the point of becoming a force of paralysis, instead of potential advancement—in the course of the twentieth century, bitterly disappointing all hope and expectations once held by the radical socialist movement. For the ironical and in many ways tragic result of long decades of political struggle within the confines of capital's self-serving political institutions—marked by the full conformity of the various organized working class representatives to the "rules of the parliamentary game,"—turned out to be that under the now prevailing conditions the working class has been *totally disenfranchised* in all of the advanced capitalist countries. In this way, social-democratic capitulation, while claiming to represent the "real interests of the working class," in fact fully completed the vicious circle of this process of complete disenfranchisement from which there can be no escape without radically overcoming—in a truly sustainable way—the historically anachronistic parliamentary system itself.

The contrast between the actually existing conditions of our time and the promises of the past could not be greater. Particularly when we remind ourselves of the political developments of the last third of the nineteenth century and labor's hope invested in them. As we all know, well before that time the working-class movement appeared on the historical stage and made its first advances as an *extra-parliamentary movement*. The last third of the nineteenth century, however, produced a significant change in that respect, with the formation and strengthening of *mass* working-class parties which began to orient themselves, in their majority, toward the gradual conquest of the political domain by electoral means, so as to introduce—through consensual legislative intervention—the required far-reaching and lasting structural reforms in society as a whole. As a matter of fact, as time went by, the mass parties of the working class were able to show some spectacular successes in strictly electoral terms, adopting and nourishing, as a result, the most problematical anticipation of a corresponding success, *"in due course,"* also in the material power relations of society. This is how social-democratic reformism became dominant in the working class parties of the most powerful capitalist countries, marginalizing at the same time the radical wing of the labor movement for several decades.

But the "due course" never arrived and never could arrive. Instituting a radically different social order within the self-serving parameters of capital's social metabolic control could be from the very beginning nothing more than a *contradiction in terms*. Whether the advocated political and social strategy was called, as by Bernstein and his followers, *"evolutionary socialism,"* or *"conquering the commanding heights of the economy,"* by Harold Wilson and others, the long-promised land repeatedly proclaimed by such strategies could only be the leisurely march toward the *never-never-land* of a fictitious future, in the end clamorously and completely *left behind* by British "New Labour"—as well as by German and many other social-democratic parties all over the world.

Moreover, what makes this problem even graver is that some of the most important and also electorally successful parties of the radical Left, constituted within the framework of the Third International, in forceful explicit condemnation of the irretrievable historical failure of the social-democratic Second International, followed—this time really *in due course*—the same disastrous path as the parties which they had strongly denounced and dismissed. It is enough to think, in this respect, of the "parliamentary road to socialism" pursued by the Italian and the French Communist Parties. Indeed, the Italian Communist Party (once the Party of no less a revolutionary figure than Antonio Gramsci)—after indulging in the other fantasy-strategy of "the Great Historic Compromise," disregarding or perhaps genuinely forgetting that it takes at least two to make a real compromise, otherwise one can only compromise oneself—rebaptised itself as the "Democrats of the Left," so as to be fully accommodated to the service of capital's "democratic" social order. And when we recall that Mikhail Gorbachev, the General Secretary of the Soviet Party—once upon a time Lenin's own Party—presumed to himself the power and the right to *dissolve the Party by decree,* and could actually get away with such an authoritarian move in the name of *glasnost* and democracy, that should be a clear indication that something fundamentally wrong must be redressed in these matters. Nostalgia for the past is not going to offer any solution to the underlying issues.

All this is not said "in hindsight." An expression customarily used in order to deflect criticism and justify the failed strategies of the past, together with the role undertaken by the people who were responsible for imposing them, as if there could be no alternative to following such a course of action until the "hindsight"—even now sidelined and disqualified with self-justifying sarcasm—appeared on the horizon. The historically documented real state of affairs could not be more different. For the most far-sighted and profoundly committed advocates of the radical socialist alternative, who were active at the time when the fateful derailment of the organized socialist movement was beginning to gather pace—Lenin and Rosa Luxemburg—clearly diagnosed the unfolding dangers, demonstrating not in hindsight but right on the spot the theoretical and political vacuity of the unrealizable "evolutionary" prescriptions. Marx, at an even earlier stage of this process of the ultimate capitulatory integration into the bourgeois parliamentary system, sounded an unmistakable warning, but his insistence, in the *Critique of the Gotha Program*, that there should be no compromise on principle remained a voice in the wilderness.

The forces of organized labor had to make their own experience, however bitter in the end such experience turned out to be. For a long historical period ahead there seemed to be no alternative to following the elusive promise of "the line of least resistance" by the great majority of the labor movement. The promises and temptations of solving the highly complex problems of society through the relatively simple processes of parliamentary legislation were too great to be ignored or bypassed until bitter experience revealed that the structurally entrenched and enforced inequality of the material power relations in capital's favor had to prevail also in the institutionalized political setting, notwithstanding the ideology of—in reality strictly *formal,* and never *substantive*—"democratic choice" and electorally safeguarded "equality." In fact, the objectively secured institutional entrapment of labor was further complicated by the corruptive impact of the electoral machinery and the "majority seeking" apologetic ideology associated with it. As Rosa Luxemburg characterized these aspects of the problem a long time ago:

> Parliamentarism is the breeding place of all the opportunist tendencies now existing in the Western Social Democracy... [it] provides the soil for such illusions of current opportunism as overvaluation of social reforms, class and party collaboration, the hope of pacific development toward socialism, etc.... With the growth of the labor movement, parliamentarism becomes a spring-

board for political careerists. That is why so many ambitious failures from the bourgeoisie flock to the banners of the socialist parties. . . . [The aim is to] *dissolve* the active, class conscious sector of the proletariat in the *amorphous mass of an 'electorate.'*[41]

Naturally, the perversely self-justifying ideology of pretended democratic respect for the mythical "electorate" could be conveniently used for the purpose of arbitrarily, and often corruptly, controlling the political parties and nullifying the possibility of instituting even minor "gradual reform," as the depressing historical record of the twentieth century clearly demonstrated, resulting in the complete disenfranchisement of the working class. It was therefore by no means accidental that attempts to introduce major social changes—in the last fifteen years in Latin America, for instance, notably in Venezuela and now in Bolivia—were coupled with a forceful critique of the parliamentary system and the establishment of constitutional assemblies as the first step toward the advocated far-reaching transformations.

9.7.2

Significantly enough, the critique of the parliamentary system is almost as old as parliament itself. The exposure of its incurable limitations from a radical perspective did not begin with Marx. We find it powerfully expressed already in Rousseau's writings. Starting from the position that sovereignty belongs to the people and therefore it cannot be rightfully alienated, Rousseau argued that for the same reasons it cannot be legitimately turned into any form of representational abdication:

> The deputies of the people, therefore, are not and cannot be its representatives; they are merely its stewards, and can carry through no definitive acts. Every law the people has not ratified in person is null and void—is, in fact, not a law. The people of England regard itself as free; but it is grossly mistaken; it is free only during the election of members of parliament. As soon as they are elected, slavery overtakes it, and it is nothing. The use it makes of the short moments of liberty it enjoys shows indeed that it deserves to lose them.[42]

At the same time, Rousseau also made the important point that although the power of legislation cannot be divorced from the people even through parliamentary representation, administrative or 'executive' functions must be considered in a very different light. As he had put it:

> In the exercise of the legislative power, the people cannot be represented; but in that of the executive power, which is only the force that is applied to give the law effect, it both can and should be represented.[43]

In this way, Rousseau had put forward a much more practicable exercise of political and administrative power than what he is usually credited with or indeed is accused of by his detractors even on the Left. In the tendentious misrepresentation of Rousseau's position both of the vitally important principles of his theory, usable in a suitably adapted form also by socialists, have been disqualified and thrown overboard. Yet, the truth of the matter is that, on the one hand, the power of fundamental decision making should never be divorced from the popular masses. At the same time, on the other hand, the fulfillment of specific administrative and executive functions in all domains of the social reproductive process can indeed be *delegated* for a determinate period of time to members of the given community, provided that it is done under rules autonomously set by and properly controlled at all stages of the substantive decision-making process by the freely associated producers.

Thus, the difficulties do not reside in the two basic principles themselves as formulated by Rousseau, but in the way in which they must be related to capital's material and political control of the social metabolic process. For the establishment of a socialist form of decision making, in accordance with the principles of both inalienable rule-determining power *(i.e., the "sovereignty" of labor not as a particular class but as the universal condition of society)* and delegating specific roles and functions under well defined, flexibly distributed, and appropriately supervised, rules would require entering and radically restructuring capital's antagonistic material domain. This is a process that would indeed have to go well beyond what could be successfully regulated by considerations derived from Rousseau's principle of inalienable popular sovereignty and its delegatory corollary. In other words, in a socialist order the "legislative" process would have to be fused with the production process itself in such a way that the necessary *horizontal division of labor*[44] should be appropriately complemented by a system of self-determined *coordination* of labor, from the local to the global levels.

This relationship is in sharp contrast to capital's pernicious *vertical division of labor*,[45] which is complemented by the "separation of powers" in an alienated, and on the laboring masses, unalterably superimposed "democratic political system." For the vertical division of labor under the rule of capital necessarily affects and incurably infects every facet also of the horizontal division of labor, from the simplest productive functions to the most complicated balancing processes of the legislative jungle. The latter is an ever-denser legislative jungle because its endlessly multiplying rules and institutional constituents must play their vital part in keeping firmly under control the actually or potentially challenging behavior of recalcitrant labor, watchful over limited labor disputes as well as safeguarding capital's overall rule in society at large. Also, they must somehow reconcile at any particular temporal slice of the unfolding historical process—to the extent to which such reconciliation is feasible at all—the separate interests of the plurality of capitals with the uncontrollable dynamics of the totality of social capital tending toward its ultimate self-assertion as a global entity.

Naturally, the fundamental changes required for securing and safeguarding the socialist transformation of society cannot be accomplished *within* the political domain as constituted and ossified during the last four hundred years of capitalist development. For the unavoidable challenge in this respect necessitates the solution of a most bewildering problem: namely that capital is the *extra-parliamentary force par excellence* of our social order, and yet at the same time it *completely dominates parliament* from the outside, while pretending to be simply a *part of it*, professedly operating in relation to the alternative political forces of the working-class movement on a *fully equitable* basis.

Although in its impact this state of affairs is profoundly misleading, our concern is not simply a question of deceptive appearance to which the political representatives of labor personally fall victim. In other words, it is not a condition from which the now-deceived people could in principle be personally extricated through the proper ideological and political enlightenment, without any need for radically changing the well-entrenched social reproductive order. Regrettably, it is much more serious than that. For the false appearance itself arises from *objective structural determinations,* and it is constantly reinforced by the dynamics of the capital system in all of its transformations.

9.7.3

In one sense, the underlying problem can be briefly characterized as the historically established *separation of politics*—pursued in parliament and in its various institutional corollaries—from society's *material reproductive dimension,* as the latter is embodied and practically renewed in the multiplicity of productive enterprises. As a matter of *contingent historical development,* capitalism as a social reproductive order had to unfold and assert itself against the then prevailing feudal-political and material-reproductive constraints. At first, this did not take the form of a unified political force frontally confronting the feudal political order—that happened relatively late, at the stage of the victorious bourgeois revolutions in some major countries, by which time the material ground favoring the capitalistic processes was well advanced in their societies—but through the emerging multiplicity of productive enterprises, free from the political constraints of feudal serfdom, as they were materially conquering an increasingly more important share of the dynamically changing overall societal reproduction process.

However, the successful advancement of the material reproductive units by themselves was very far from the end of the story, despite its one-sided theoretical conceptualizations. This was unavoidable because the political dimension was always present in some form, and in fact it had to play an ever-greater role, notwithstanding its peculiar articulation, the more fully developed the capitalist system became. For the great multiplicity of *centrifugal* material reproductive units had to be brought somehow together under the all-embracing political command structure of the capitalist state, so that the new social metabolic order should not fall apart in the absence of a cohesive dimension.

The wishful presumption of the all-powerfully regulating *"invisible hand"* appeared to be a suitable alternative explanation to the actually very important role of politics. The illusions necessarily associated with the unfolding capitalistic developments were well illustrated by the fact that at the point in time when the system was becoming ever more consolidated and also politically safeguarded in Britain by the capitalist state, after the successful defeat of the feudal adversary a century earlier in the civil war and the "glorious revolution," an outstanding figure of classical political economy, Adam Smith, wanted to ban altogether the "statesman, council or senate whatever" from significant involvement in economic affairs, dismissing the very idea of such involvement as "dangerous folly and presumption."[46]

The fact that Adam Smith adopted this position is understandable, since he held the view that the capitalist reproductive order represented *"the natural system of perfect liberty and justice."*[47] Accordingly, in a similar conception of the reproductive order there could be neither *need,* nor an admissible conceptual *space,* for the regulatory intervention of politics. For, in Smith's view, politics could only interfere with such a "natural system"—one said to be fully in tune with the requirements of liberty and justice—in an adverse and detrimental way, since it was already ideally preordained for the good of all by nature[48] and perfectly administered by the "invisible hand."

What was completely missing from Adam Smith's picture was the vital question of actually existing and *inherently conflictual power relations*—without which the dynamics of capitalist development cannot be made intelligible—whose acknowledgement, however, would make it absolutely essential to offer an appropriate form of *political* explanation as well. In Smith's theory, the place of social conflictual power relations was taken by the mythically inflated concept of the *"local situation,"* coupled with the notion of the corresponding particular enterprises locally owned by purely self-interested individuals who unconsciously—but nonetheless for the benefit of the whole of society ideally—managed their productive capital under the mysterious guidance of the "invisible hand." This local-oriented individualistic—yet harmoniously all-embracing and universally beneficial—conception of capital's insuperably conflictual power relations was very far removed from reality even in the age of Adam Smith.

The great defect of the variety of such conceptions, of which there were many, even in the twentieth century, was their failure to recognize and theoretically explain the *immanent objective connection*—which always had to prevail despite the deceptive appearance of unalterable separation—between the capital system's material reproductive and political dimension. In fact, without the immanent relationship of the two dimensions the established social metabolic order could not possibly function and survive for any length of time.

However, it is equally necessary to underline in the same context that the paradoxical interrelationship of the two vital dimensions of the capital system—deceptive in its appearance but rooted in objective structural determinations—has far-reaching implications also for successfully instituting the socialist alternative. For it is inconceivable to substantively overcome the established order through the political overthrow of the capitalist state,[49] let alone by gaining victory over the forces of exploitation within the given framework of parliamentary legislation. Attempting to do so cannot address on a lasting basis the mystifyingly compartmentalized but necessary connection between the inherited capital system's material reproductive and political dimension. This is why the historically viable radical reconstitution of the indissoluble unity of the material reproductive and the political sphere on a permanent basis is and remains the essential requirement of the socialist mode of social metabolic control.

9.7.4

Ignoring or disregarding the harsh reality of capital's conflictual power relations, from the earliest stage of the system's emergence to the "democratic" present, and above all transubstantiating the authoritarian subjection and ruthless domination of labor within those power relations into the pretended "equality" of all individuals, was an unavoidable concomitant of viewing the world from capital's vantage point even in the writings of the greatest and most progressive intellectual figures of the bourgeoisie. What was obliterated by the adoption of capital's vantage point, from the very beginning, was the blood-soaked history of the "primitive accumulation"[50] in which the emergent new ruling class continued the well-secured exploitative practices of the preceding one—the feudal landed property—even if in a new form, putting thereby into relief, again, the significant historical continuity of the varieties of age-old class oppression and exploitation.

On the common ground of that affinity, appropriately redefined in accord with the nature of capital, the *permanently necessary presupposition* of the new productive order of "free labor," the *exclusive proprietorship* of the all-important controlling means of production by a tiny minority, and the simultaneous—and ultimately by the state *politically safeguarded*—exclusion of society's overwhelming majority from them, had to be perpetuated, despite the professed creed of "freedom and equality." At the same time, the brutal reality of the materially/reproductively as well as politically/ideologically enforced exclusion of the overwhelming majority of the people from the controlling powers of the social order—which could not have been more remote from, indeed diametrically opposed to, any genuine "ethical state"—had to be kept under the seal of deep silence in the self-images of the new mode of social metabolic control. Even in the best self-images conceived from capital's self-serving vantage point. This is how the mystifying separation of politics from the material reproductive dimension could both fulfill its conservative ideological and cultural function and at the same time also be celebrated as forever unsurpassable. Thus Hegel, for instance, offered in his system the most ingenious and philosophically absolutized separation of the self-serving material reality of "civil society" and the political "ethical state" postulated as the ideal corrective to the unavoidable defects of "civil society." *Reversing the actual causal order,* Hegel mystifyingly depicted the vital determination of being *self-serving* as directly emanating from the individuals themselves, although in reality it was immanent to capital's insurmountable ontological ground, imposed on the individuals who could not opt out from operating within the framework of the given social metabolic order. Consequently, the individuals had to *internalize* the system's *objective self-expansionary imperative* (i.e., its unalterably self-serving determination to dominate every aspect of society in that way)—without which the capital system as such could not possibly survive—as if self-aggrandizement sprang out of the inner core of their nature-determined personal aims and purposes, as Pallas Athene was supposed to spring out of the head of Zeus fully armed. In this way, Hegel was able not only to produce a philosophically absolutized dualism of capital's social order but also to glorify at the same time the historical development corresponding to the claimed "realization of freedom" in it as "the true *Theodicaea:* the justification of God in history."[51]

The critique of these conceptions, in all their varieties, is highly relevant today. For, maintaining the dualistic conception of the relationship between civil society and the political state can only bring disorienting strategies, irrespective of which side of the adopted dualist vision is given precedence over the other in the envisaged course of action. The unreality of parliamentary projections is well matched in this respect by the utter fragility of the expectations attached to the idea of resolving our major problems through the naïvely postulated institutional counter-force of civil society.

The adoption of such a position can only result in being trapped by a very naive conception of the nature of "civil society" itself and by a totally uncritical attitude toward a great multiplicity of NGOs which, belying their self-characterization as "non-governmental organizations," happen to be well capable of happily coexisting with the dominant retrograde state institutions on which they depend for their financial existence. And even when we think of some organizations of far greater importance than the particular NGOs, like the trade unions, the situation is not much better in this regard. Consequently, to treat trade unions, in opposition to political parties, as somehow belonging to "civil society" alone, in virtue of which they can be used against the political state for a profound socialist transformation, is no more than romantic wishful thinking. For in reality the institutional circle of capital is made of the *reciprocal totalizations* of civil society and the political state that deeply interpenetrate and powerfully support one another. There can be no realistic strategy of socialist transformation without firmly pursuing the realization of the unity of the political and the material reproductive dimensions also in the organizational domain. In fact, the great emancipatory potential of the trade unions consists precisely in their capability to assume (at least in principle) a radical political role—well beyond the rather conservative political role which they now, on the whole, tend to fulfill—in a conscious attempt to overcome the fateful separation of labor's *"industrial arm"* (themselves) and its *"political arm"* (the parliamentary parties), split asunder under the capitalist integument of both through the acceptance of parliamentary domination by the majority of the labor movement in the course of the last one hundred and thirty years.[52]

The appearance of the working class on the historical stage was only an *inconvenient afterthought* to the parliamentary system, constituted well before the first organized forces of labor attempted to voice in public the interests of their class. From capital's standpoint the immediate response to such an inconvenient but growing "nuisance" was the rather untenable rejection and exclusion of the political groups concerned. Later, however, it was followed by the much more adaptable idea of *taming* in some way the forces of labor—at first through paternalistic parliamentary sponsorship of some working-class demands by relatively progressive bourgeois political parties, and later still by the acceptance of the legitimacy of some working class parties in parliament itself, though of course in a *strictly circumscribed* form, compelling them to conform to "the democratic rules of the parliamentary game." Inevitably, this meant to such parties nothing less than "freely consenting" to their own effective *accommodation,* even if they could maintain for a fairly long time the illusion that in the fullness of time they would be able to radically redress the situation through parliamentary action in their own favor.

This is how the original, and potentially alternative *extra-parliamentary force of labor* has been turned into a *permanently disadvantaged* parliamentary organization. Although this course of development could be explained by the obvious weakness of organized labor at the *beginning,* arguing and justifying in this way what has actually happened simply begs the question in favor of the social-democratic parliamentary blind alley. For the *radical alternative of gaining strength* by the forces of the working class organizing and asserting themselves *outside parliament*—in contrast to the strategy followed for many decades, which culminated in the *complete disenfranchisement of the working class* in the name of "gaining strength"—cannot be dismissed so facilely, as if a truly radical alternative was an *a priori* impossibility. Especially since the need for sustainable extra-parliamentary action is absolutely vital for the future of a radically rearticulated socialist movement.

9.7.5

The unreality of postulating the sustainable solution of the grave problems of our social order within the formal and legal framework and corresponding constraints of parliamentary politics arises from the fundamental misconception of the structural determinations of capital's rule, as represented in all varieties that assert the dualism of civil society and the political state. The difficulty, insurmountable within the parliamentary framework, is this that since capital is *actually* in control of all vital aspects of the social metabolism, *it can afford* to define the separately constituted sphere of political legitimation as a strictly *formal and legal* matter, thereby necessarily excluding the possibility of being legitimately challenged in its *substantive* sphere of socioeconomic reproductive operation. Directly or indirectly, capital controls *everything,* including the parliamentary legislative process, even if the latter is supposed to be fully independent from capital in many theories that fictitiously hypostatize the "democratic equality" of all political forces participating in the legislative process. To envisage a very different relationship to the powers of decision making in our societies, now completely dominated by the forces of capital in every domain, it is necessary to radically challenge capital itself as the *overall controller* of social metabolic reproduction.

What makes this problem worse for all those who are looking for significant change on the margins of the established political system is that the latter can claim for itself genuine constitutional legitimacy in its present mode of functioning, based on the historically constituted *inversion* of the actual state of the material reproductive affairs. For inasmuch as the capitalist is not only the "personification of capital" but simultaneously functions also "as the personification of the *social* character of labor, of the *total workshop* as such,"[53] the system can claim to represent the vitally necessary productive power of society *vis-à-vis* the individuals as the basis of their continued existence, incorporating the interest of all. In this way capital asserts itself not only as the *de facto* but also as the *de jure* power of society, in its capacity as the objectively given necessary condition of societal reproduction, and thereby as the constitutional foundation to its own political order. The fact that the constitutional legitimacy of capital is historically founded on the ruthless expropriation of the conditions of social metabolic reproduction—the means and material of labor—from the producers, and therefore capital's claimed "constitutionality" (like the origin of all constitutions) is unconstitutional, is an unpalatable truth which fades away in the mist of a remote past. The *"social productive powers* of labor, or *productive powers of social labor,* first develop historically with the specifically capitalist mode of production, hence appear as something *immanent* in the capital-relation and *inseparable* from it."[54]

This is how capital's mode of social metabolic reproduction becomes *eternalized and legitimated* as a lawfully unchallengeable system. Legitimate contest is admissible only in relation to some *minor aspects* of the unalterable overall structure. The real state of affairs on the plane of socioeconomic reproduction—i.e., the actually exercised productive power of labor and its absolute necessity for securing capital's own reproduction—disappears from sight. Partly because of the ignorance of the very far from legitimate historical origin of capital's "primitive accumulation" and the concomitant, frequently violent, expropriation of property as the precondition of the system's present mode of functioning; and partly because of the mystifying nature of the established productive and distributive relations. As Marx notes:

> The *objective conditions of labor* do not appear as subsumed under the work-er; rather, he appears as subsumed under them. Capital *employs* Labor. Even this relation in its simplicity is *a personification of things and a reification of persons.*[55]

None of this can be challenged and remedied within the framework of parliamentary political reform. It would be quite absurd to expect the abolition of the *"personification of things and the reification of persons"* by political decree, and just as absurd to expect the proclamation of such an intended reform within the framework of capital's political institutions. For the capital system cannot function without the per-verse overturning of the relationship between persons and things: cap-ital's alienated and reified powers dominate the masses of the people. Similarly, it would be a miracle if the workers who confront capital in the labor process as "isolated workers" could reacquire mastery over the social productive powers of their labor by some political decree, or even by a whole series of parliamentary reforms enacted under capi-tal's order of social metabolic control. For in these matters there can be no way of avoiding the irreconcilable conflict over the material stakes of *"either/or."*

Capital can neither abdicate its—usurped—social productive powers in favor of labor, nor can it *share* them with labor, thanks to some wishful but utterly fictitious "political compromise." For they constitute the overall controlling power of societal reproduction in the form of *"the rule of wealth over society."* Thus it is impossible to escape, in the domain of the fundamental social metabolism, the severe logic of *either/or.* For either wealth, in the shape of capital, continues to rule over human society, taking it to the brink of self-destruction, or the society of associated producers learns to rule over alienated and reified wealth, with productive powers arising from the *self-determined social labor* of its individual—but no longer *isolated*—members.

Capital is the *extra-parliamentary force par excellence.* It cannot possibly be politically constrained by parliament in its power of social metabolic control. This is why the only mode of political representa-tion compatible with capital's mode of functioning is one that *effec-tively denies* the possibility of contesting its *material power.* And pre-cisely because capital is the extra-parliamentary force par excellence, it has nothing to fear from the reforms that can be enacted within its parliamentary political framework.

Since the vital issue on which everything else hinges is that "the *objective conditions of labor* do not appear as subsumed under the worker" but, on the contrary, "he appears as subsumed under them," no meaningful change is feasible without addressing this issue both in a form of politics capable of *matching capital's extra-parliamentary powers* and modes of action, and in the domain of *material reproduction*. Thus, the only challenge that could affect the power of capital, in a sustainable manner, is one which would simultaneously aim at assuming the system's key productive functions, and at acquiring control over the corresponding political decision making processes in all spheres, instead of being hopelessly constrained by the circular confinement of institutionally legitimated political action to parliamentary legislation.[56]

There is a great deal of critique of formerly leftwing political figures and of their now fully accommodating parties in the political debates of the last decades. However, what is problematic about such debates is that by overemphasizing the role of personal ambition and failure, they often continue to envisage remedying the situation within the same political institutional framework that, in fact, greatly favors the criticized "personal betrayals" and the painful "party derailments." Unfortunately, though, the advocated and hoped for personnel and government changes tend to reproduce the same deplorable results.

All this should not be very surprising. The reason why the now established political institutions successfully resist significant change for the better is because they are themselves part of the *problem* and not of the *solution*. For in their immanent nature they are the embodiment of the underlying structural determinations and contradictions through which the modern capitalist state—with its ubiquitous network of bureaucratic constituents—has been articulated and stabilized in the course of the last four hundred years. Naturally, the state was formed not as a one-sided mechanical *result* but through its *necessary reciprocal interrelationship* to the material ground of capital's historical unfolding, as not only being shaped by the latter but also actively shaping it as much as historically feasible under the prevailing—and precisely through that interrelationship also changing—circumstances.

Given the insuperably centrifugal determination of capital's productive microcosms, even at the level of the giant quasi-monopolistic transnational corporations, only the modern state could assume and fulfill the required function of being the overall command structure of the capital system. Inevitably, that meant the complete alienation of the power of overall decision making from the producers. Even the "particular personifications of capital" were strictly mandated to act in accord with the structural imperatives of their system. Indeed the modern state, as constituted on the material ground of the capital system, is the *paradigm of alienation* as regards the power of comprehensive decision making. It would be therefore extremely naïve to imagine that the capitalist state could willingly hand over the alienated power of systemic decision making to any rival actor who operates within the legislative framework of parliament.

Thus, in order to envisage a meaningful and historically sustainable societal change, it is necessary to submit to a radical critique both the material reproductive and the political inter-determinations of the entire system, and not simply some of the contingent and limited political practices. The combined totality of the material reproductive determinations and the all-embracing political command structure of the state together constitute the overpowering reality of the capital system. In this sense, in view of the unavoidable question arising from the challenge of *systemic* determinations, with regard to both socioeconomic reproduction and the state, the need for a comprehensive political transformation—in close conjunction to the meaningful exercise of society's vital productive functions without which far-reaching and lasting political change is inconceivable—becomes inseparable from the problem characterized as the *withering away of the state*. Accordingly, in the historic task of accomplishing "the withering away of the state," self-management through full participation, and the permanently sustainable overcoming of parliamentarism by a positive form of substantive decision-making are inseparable.

This is a vital concern and not "romantic faithfulness to Marx's unrealizable dream," as some people try to discredit and dismiss it. In truth, the "withering away of the state" refers to nothing mysterious or remote but to a perfectly tangible process that must be initiated right in our own historical time. It means, in plain language, the progressive reacquisition of the alienated power of political decision making by the individuals in their enterprise of moving toward a genuine socialist society. Without the reacquisition of this power—to which not only the capitalist state but also the paralyzing inertia of the structurally well-entrenched material reproductive practices are fundamentally opposed—neither the new mode of political control of society as a whole by its individuals is conceivable, nor indeed the *nonadversarial* and thereby *cohesive and plannable* everyday operation of the particular productive and distributive units by the self-managing freely associated producers. Radically superseding *adversariality,* and thereby securing the material and political ground of *globally viable planning*—an absolute must for the very survival of humanity, not to mention the potentially enriched self-realization of its individual members—is synonymous with the *withering away of the state* as an ongoing historical enterprise.

9.7.6

Obviously, a transformation of this magnitude cannot be accomplished without the *conscious dedication* of a revolutionary movement to the most challenging historic task of all, capable of being sustained against all adversity, since engaging in it is bound to rouse the fierce hostility of all major forces of the capital system. For this reason the movement in question cannot be simply a political party oriented toward securing parliamentary concessions, which as a rule turn out to be nullified sooner or later by the extra-parliamentary vested interests of the established order prevailing also in parliament. The socialist movement cannot succeed in the face of the hostility of such forces unless it is rearticulated as a revolutionary *mass* movement, consciously active in *all* forms of political and social struggle: local, countrywide, and global/international, fully utilizing the parliamentary opportunities when available, limited though they might be, and above all not shirking back from asserting the necessary demands of defiant extra-parliamentary action.

The development of this movement is very important for the future of humanity at the present juncture of history. For without a strategically oriented and sustained extra-parliamentary challenge the parties alternating in government can continue to function as convenient reciprocal *alibis* for the necessary structural failure of the system toward labor, thus effectively confining the role of class opposition to its present position as an inconvenient but *marginal afterthought* in capital's parliamentary system. Thus, in relation to both the material reproductive and the political domain, the constitution of a strategically viable socialist extra-parliamentary *mass* movement—in conjunction with the traditional forms of labor's, at present hopelessly derailed, political organizations, which *badly need the radicalizing pressure and support* of such extra-parliamentary forces—is a vital precondition for countering the massive extra-parliamentary power of capital.

The role of a revolutionary extra-parliamentary movement is twofold. On the one hand, it has to formulate and organizationally defend the strategic interests of labor as a comprehensive social metabolic alternative. The success of that role is feasible only if the organized forces of labor consciously confront and forcefully negate in practical terms the structural determinations of the established *material reproductive* order as manifest in the capital-relation and in the concomitant subordination of labor in the socioeconomic process, instead of helping to *re-stabilize* capital in periods of crisis, as invariably happened at important junctures of the reformist past. At the same time, on the other hand, the open or concealed *political* power of capital which now prevails in parliament needs to be, and can be, challenged—even if only to a limited degree—through the pressure which extra-parliamentary forms of action can exercise on the legislative and the executive.

Extra-parliamentary action can be effective only if it consciously addresses the central aspects and systemic determinations of capital, cutting through the maze of fetishistic appearances through which they dominate society. For the established order materially asserts its power primarily in and through the *capital relation,* perpetuated on the basis of the mystifying *inversion* of the actual productive relationship of the hegemonic alternative classes in capitalist society. As mentioned already, this inversion enables capital to usurp the role of the *"producer,"* who in Marx's words, *"employs labor,"* thanks to the baffling *"personification of things and the reification of persons,"* and thereby legitimates itself as the unalterable precondition for realizing the "interest of all." Since the concept of the "interest of all" really matters, even if it is now fraudulently used to camouflage the total denial of its substance to the overwhelming majority of the people by the formal and legal pretences of "justice and equality," there can be no meaningful and historically sustainable alternative to the established social order without radically overcoming the all-embracing capital relation itself. This systemic demand cannot be postponed. *Partial demands* can be and should be advocated by socialists if they have a direct or indirect bearing on the absolutely fundamental demand of overcoming the capital relation, which goes to the heart of the matter.

This demand is in sharp contrast to what is now allowed to the forces of opposition by capital's faithful ideologists and political figures. Their major criterion for ruling out the possibility of even the important partial demands of labor is precisely whether they have a potential for negatively affecting the stability of the system. Thus, for instance, even local "politically motivated industrial action" is categorically excluded (even outlawed) "in a democratic society," because its pursuit might have negative implications for the normal functioning of the system. The role of reformist parties, by contrast, is welcome, because their demands either help to re-stabilize the system in difficult times—through wage-restraining industrial intervention (with the slogan of the "necessity of tightening the belt") and trade-union-curbing political and legislative agreements—and thus they contribute to the dynamics of renewed capital expansion, or are at least "neutral" in the sense that at some point in the future, even if not at the moment of their first formulation, they can be integrated into the stipulated framework of "normality."

The revolutionary negation of the capital system is conceivable only through a strategically sustained and conscious organizational intervention. While the tendentiously one-sided dismissal of "spontaneity" by sectarian presumption must be treated with the criticism it deserves, it is no less harmful to underrate the importance of revolutionary consciousness and the organizational requirements of its success. The historical failure of some major parties of the Third International, which once professed Leninist and revolutionary aims, like the Italian and the French Communist Parties, should not divert our attention from the importance of recreating on a much more secure ground the political organizations through which the vital socialist transformation of our societies can be accomplished in the future. Evidently, a forceful critical assessment of what went wrong is an important part of this process of renewal. What is amply clear right now is that the disintegrative descent of such parties on the slippery slope of parliamentary entrapment offers an important lesson for the future.

Only two comprehensive modes of social metabolic control are feasible today: capital's class exploitative reproductive order— imposed at all cost by the "personifications of capital"—which miserably failed humanity in our time, pushing it to the brink of self-destruction. And the other order, diametrically opposed to the established one: the social metabolic *hegemonic alternative* of labor not as a particular class, but as the *universal condition of existence* of every individual in society. A society managed by them on the basis of *substantive equality* which enables them to develop their productive human and intellectual potentialities to the full, in harmony with the metabolic requirements of the natural order, instead of being bent on the destruction of nature and thereby also of themselves, as capital's mode of uncontrollable social metabolic control is engaged in doing right now. This is why under the present conditions of capital's structural crisis nothing short of the *comprehensive hegemonic alternative* to capital's rule—spelled out as the dialectical complementarity of particular but *non-marginalizable immediate demands* and the *comprehensive objectives of systemic transformation*—can constitute the valid program of the conscious revolutionary organized movement all over the world.

To be sure, the conscious organized revolutionary movement cannot be contained within the restrictive political framework of parliament dominated by the extra-parliamentary power of capital. Nor can it succeed as a self-oriented sectarian organization. It can successfully define itself through two vital orienting principles. First, as just mentioned, by the elaboration of its own extra-parliamentary program oriented toward the comprehensive hegemonic alternative objectives to secure a fundamental systemic transformation. And the second, equally important in strategic organizational terms, is its active involvement in the constitution of the necessary extra-parliamentary *mass movement,* as the carrier of the revolutionary alternative capable of changing also the legislative process in a qualitative way, as a major step in the direction of the withering away of the state. Only through these organizational developments, directly involving also the great masses of the people, can one envisage the realization of the historic task of instituting labor's hegemonic alternative, in the interest of all-embracing socialist emancipation.

9.8 Education: The Ongoing
Development of Socialist Consciousness

9.8.1

The role of education could not be greater in securing a fully sustainable socialist transformation. The conception of education here referred to—envisaged not as a strictly limited period in the life of individuals but as the ongoing development of socialist consciousness in society as a whole—marks a radical departure from the dominant educational practices under advanced capitalism. It is understood to be the historically valid extension and radical transformation of the great educational ideals advocated in the more remote past. For those educational ideals were not only undermined with the passing of time but in the end completely extinguished under the impact of ever-advancing alienation and the subjection of cultural development in its entirety to the ever more constraining interests of capital-expansion and profit maximization.

Not only Paracelsus in the sixteenth century but even Goethe and Schiller[57] as late as the end of the eighteenth and the first decades of the nineteenth century still believed in an educational ideal that could guide and humanly enrich the individuals throughout their life. By contrast, the second half of the nineteenth century was already marked by the triumph of *utilitarianism,* and the twentieth century also unreservedly capitulated in the educational field to the narrowest conceptions of *"instrumental rationality."* The more "advanced" capitalist society had become, the more one-sided it became about the production of reified wealth as an end in itself and on exploiting the educational institutions at all levels, from preparatory schools to universities—in the form of "privatization," promoted with telling ideological zeal by the state—for the perpetuation of commodity society.

Unsurprisingly, this development went hand in hand with the indoctrination of the overwhelming majority of the people with the values of capital's social order as the unalterable "natural order," rationalized and justified by the system's most sophisticated ideologists in the name of "scientific objectivity" and "value-neutrality." The actual conditions of everyday life were fully dominated by the capitalist ethos, subjecting individuals—as a matter of structurally secured determination—to the imperative of adjusting their aspirations accordingly, even though they could not escape the harsh predicament of wage slavery. Thus, advanced capitalism could safely order its affairs by confining the period of institutionalized education to an economically expedient few years in the life of individuals, doing even that in a discriminatory and elitist fashion. The objective structural determinations of the "normality" of capitalist everyday life successfully accomplished the rest, "educating" people on an *ongoing basis* in the spirit of taking for granted the dominant social ethos, thereby "consensually" internalizing the proclaimed inalterability of the established "natural order." This is why even the best ideals of Kant's *"moral education"* and Schiller's *"aesthetic education"*—intended by their authors as the necessary and feasible antidotes to the advancing trend of dehumanizing alienation, counterposed to the criticized trend by the morally concerned individuals in their personal life—were condemned to remain forever in the realm of unrealizable *educational utopias*. They could be no match at all to the prosaic reality of the forces successfully imposing capital's ultimately destructive self-expansionary imperative. For the socioeconomic trend of all-engulfing alienation was powerful enough to extinguish without a trace even the noblest ideals of the age of the Enlightenment.

In this sense, we can see that although the period of institutionalized education is limited under capitalism to a relatively few years in the life of individuals, the ideological dominance of society prevails over their entire life, even if in many contexts such dominance does not have to assume open doctrinal value preferences. And that makes the problem of capital's ideological rule over society as a whole, and simultaneously over its conveniently isolated individuals, even more pernicious. Whether the particular individuals are aware of it or not, they cannot find even a tiniest spot of "value-neutral ground" in their society, although the explicit ideological indoctrination deceitfully assures them of the opposite, pretending—and inviting the individuals to "autonomously" identify themselves with such pretense—that they are fully *sovereign* in their choice of values in general, as they are said to be *"sovereign consumers"* of the capitalistically produced commodities, purchased on the basis of *"sovereign choices"* in the ever more monopolistically controlled supermarkets. All this is an integral part of capitalist education through which the particular individuals are *soaked in the values of commodity society* everywhere on a daily basis, as a matter of course.

Thus, capitalist society has its powerfully entrenched system of not only ongoing education but simultaneously also of *permanent indoctrination,* even when all-pervasive indoctrination appears to be nothing of the kind because it is treated by the "consensually internalized" ruling ideology as the legitimately shared positive belief system of the established, totally unobjectionable, "free society." What makes matters even worse is that the central core of the capital system's ongoing education is the assertion that the established order itself needs *no significant change.* It needs only "fine-tuning" at its margins, which must be accomplished through the idealized methodology of "little by little." Accordingly, the deepest meaning of the established order's *ongoing education* is the arbitrary imposition of belief in the *absolute innalterability* of its fundamental structural determinations.

Since the real meaning of education worthy of its mandate is to make individuals live up to the challenges of the historically changing social conditions—of which they are also the makers even under the most difficult circumstances—any system of education oriented toward the *uncritical preservation* of the established order at all cost can be compatible only with the most *perverted educational ideals and values.* This is why unlike the age of the Enlightenment, in the ascending phase of capitalist transformations, which could still produce noble *educational utopias,* like Kant's and Schiller's conceptions, the descending phase of capital's history, culminating in the apology of the boundless destruction brought about by monopolistic and imperialist development in the twentieth century and their extension into the twenty-first, had to bring with it an earlier inconceivable *educational crisis,* together with the most aggressive and cynical cult of *counter-value.* The latter includes in our time the pretences of *racist supremacy,* the horrendous presumption of the *"moral right to use nuclear weapons preventively and pre-emptively,"* even against countries which never had any nuclear weapons, and the most hypocritical justification of purportedly more "humane," even if inescapably destructive, *"liberal imperialism."* This new imperialism is said to be right and proper to our *"postmodern conditions."* The latter is a theory dressed up in its search for intellectual respectability in the grotesque schematism of *"premodernity-modernity-postmodernity,"* after the ignominious collapse of traditional imperialism. This is what we see advocated today, in all seriousness, by capital's self-appointed mandarins and political policy makers, projected as the necessary strategy to be imposed on the peremptorily decreed *"failed states"* and on the so-called *"axis of evil."*

These ideas are supposed to be the strategic orienting principles and values appropriate to our own historical conditions. They are meant to set the overall parameters within which the individuals must now be educated, so as to enable the dominant capitalist states to win the "ideological struggle"—a concept suddenly propagandized in positive terms with great frequency, in sharp contrast to the myths of the "end of ideology" and the happy liberal "ending of history" preached and generously promoted not so long ago—synonymous to the idea of the "war against terror." Thus, it is hard even to imagine a more complete degradation of educational ideals, compared to capital's more distant past, than what we are actively confronted with today. And all this is promoted in our time, with all means at the system's disposal, in the name of "democracy and liberty"—words that pepper the speeches of presidents and prime ministers in great abundance. Nothing could display more clearly the perverted nature of capitalist *false consciousness,* fully complemented by the ubiquitous indoctrination more or less spontaneously exercised over the individuals by commodity society in their everyday life.

9.8.2

The socialist conception of education is qualitatively different even from the noblest educational ideals of the enlightened bourgeoisie, formulated in the ascendant phase of capitalist development. For such conceptions inevitably suffered from the limits imposed on their originators by the fact that they identified themselves with the *"standpoint of capital,"* even if they assumed a critical stance toward the excesses of the emerging new order and toward the negative impact of some already visible trends on the personal development of the individuals. They did this in sharp contrast to capital's more recent ideologists who refuse to see anything wrong with their cherished society.

The major figures of bourgeois Enlightenment were in favor of the humanly fulfilling all-around development of the particular individuals. But they wanted to see it accomplished within the framework of capitalist society, freed from its threatening "prosaic" traits and their humanly impoverishing corollaries, including the "moral debauchery" against which Adam Smith raised his eloquent voice. However, viewing the world from the vantage point of capital they could not envision the *radical change* required in the social order as a whole in order to make their own ideals prevail. For the vantage point of capital adopted by them made it impossible to see the *structural incompatibility* between their own educational ideals—applied to the projected, morally and aesthetically commendable individuals of their utopian counter-images—and the triumphantly emerging social order.

It cannot be underlined strongly enough how vital is the concept of *change* in educational theory. For it is bound to set the overall horizon and the ultimate viability (or not) of every system of education. In this respect, under the prevailing historical circumstances the change envisaged by the great bourgeois enlightenment figures had to remain characteristically lopsided. For while it was radical enough in relation to the denounced *feudal order* of society dominating the *ancient régime*, with regard to the future their conception of the advocated change could only extend to the personal educational development of the particular individuals, as an illusory way of countering the negative sociohistorical trends.

Critically addressing the *structural determinations of capital's social order*—which necessarily affected, and must always affect in a most significant way, the development of the individuals—had to remain well beyond their reach. *Correctives* to the denounced trends of development could be envisaged only in individualistic terms. That is to say, in a way which in the final account left the structural framework and the growing antagonisms of the victoriously emerging capitalist order in their place. This is why the proposed "antidotes," even in the most consistently elaborated variety of the individuals' *aesthetic education,* had to remain unrealizable *utopian counter-images.* For it is quite impossible to call a halt to the *negative effects* of a powerful social trend on the formation of the *individual* without identifying—and effectively countering in appropriate *social* terms—the *causal determinations* that produce and inexorably reproduce them.

Thus the adoption of capital's vantage point as the *insuperable social premise* of their critical horizon confined even the greatest figures of the bourgeoisie in the ascendant to projecting the struggle of the particular, and rather isolated, individuals against the negative *effects and consequences* of the social forces which the representatives of the Enlightenment wanted to reform through the ideally suitable personal education of the individuals. This struggle could never be brought to a successful conclusion because a powerful *social force* cannot be subdued by the fragmented agency of *isolated individuals,* and because the *causal structural determinations* of the criticized order must be matched and countered in the *causal domain,* in their own terms of reference: i.e., by the historically sustainable force of a coherent *structural alternative.* But that would require, of course, the adoption of a radically different social standpoint by the thinkers in question. That is, a social vantage point capable of realistically assessing the inescapable limitations of capital's reforming potentiality against its own structural causal determinations. Unsurprisingly, therefore, the acceptance of capital's vantage point as the overall horizon of their own vision confined the feasible remedial measures of the great thinkers of the Enlightenment to the advocacy of hopelessly utopian counter-measures even in the still relatively flexible ascending phase of the capital system's historical unfolding. Prior to the age, that is, when the antagonistic class determinations of the fully developed commodity society have become petrified, through and through, into a reified and alienating social structure which cannot be reformed.

This is where we can clearly see the contrast between the educational ideals and practices of the past and the conceptions appropriate to the historical challenges we have to face in the course of a sustainable socialist transformation. The mandate of socialist education can never be formulated in terms of some *utopian ideals* set before the individuals to which they are supposed to conform, in a rather naïve hope of counteracting and overcoming the problems of their social life—as more or less isolated but "morally conscious" individuals—through the force of a wishfully stipulated abstract moral *"ought-to-be."* That has never worked in the past and could never do so in the future, notwithstanding the obvious need to meet the very real challenges constantly arising from altered historical conditions and from the objective constraints of the situation of the people involved, as members of their society. It would be utterly self-defeating to conceive socialist education as an individualistic antidote to the defects of social life, no matter how desirable and commendable the proposed abstract moral *ought-to-be* might appear on the face of it. The total failure of "Stakhanovite exhortations" for transforming the work ethic in Soviet society is a good illustration of the issue at stake. Such exhortations proved a failure due to the wanton ignorance of the *causal determinations* at the roots of the prevailing work ethic of the *reluctant labor force* under the given conditions, arising from the authoritarian exclusion of the workers from the decision-making process.

The success of socialist education is feasible because its evaluative standpoint—in contrast to the structural limitations inherent in adopting capital's vantage point in the past—does not have to divert it from the causally determined real problems of society (calling for appropriate social remedies) to an abstract and individualistic moral appeal which could yield only unrealizable utopian projections. Social causes must and can be faced in the socialist educational framework at their proper level: as historically arising causes and clearly identifiable as well as changeable structural determinations. And precisely because the challenge to face up to the no matter how painful demands of *significant social change* is not an inhibiting concept in this approach but, rather, a *positive* idea inseparable from an *open-ended* view of the consciously shaped future, the required educational forces can be successfully activated for the realization of the adopted aims and values of the envisaged socialist development of society by its members.

Accordingly, the ideal mandate and the practical role of education in the course of socialist transformation consists in its continuing effective intervention in the evolving social process through the activity of the *social* individuals who are conscious of the challenges they have to confront *as social individuals,* in accordance with the values required and elaborated by them for meeting their challenges. This is inconceivable without the development of their moral consciousness. But the morality in question is not an imposition on the particular individuals from outside, let alone from above, in the name of a separate and rather abstract moral discourse of "ought-to-be," like the inscription chiseled into marble in many English churches: *"Fear thy God and obey thy King!"* Nor is it the secular equivalent to such half-religious external commands superimposed on the individuals in all societies ruled by capital's imperatives. On the contrary, the morality of socialist education is concerned with rationally conceived and commended far-reaching *social change.* Its tenets are articulated on the basis of the concrete evaluation of the chosen tasks and of the share required by the individuals in their conscious determination to accomplish them. This is how socialist education can define itself as the *ongoing development of socialist consciousness* inseparable from and closely interacting with the overall historical transformation in progress at any given time. In other words, the defining characteristics of socialist education arise from, and deeply interact with, all of the relevant orienting principles of socialist development discussed in this chapter.

9.8.3

In view of its radically different attitude to *change,* applied not only to the personal development of the individuals but simultaneously also to the vital structural determinations of their society, only within a socialist perspective can the full meaning of education come to fruition. But to put this circumstance into relief is far from sufficient by itself. For the other side of the same coin is that—because of the seminal role of education in the overall change of society—it is impossible to achieve the vital aims of a sustainable historical development without the *permanent contribution* of education to the *consciously envisaged* transformative process.

The demarcation line, opposing the advocated socialist development to the constraints and contradictions of the past, is drawn by the necessary critique of *false consciousness* which runs riot in a variety of forms under capital's rule of the social metabolism. A metabolism dominated by the mystifying reversal of the actual relations of social reproductive interchange under the fetish of "productive" capital's supposedly legitimate hegemony, and capitalistically "employed" labor's total dependency, thereby successfully imposing on the consciousness of society as a whole and of its actually working and productive individuals the false consciousness of the *"personification of things and the reification of persons."*[58]

Naturally, the power of false consciousness cannot be overcome by the (no matter how well-intentioned) educational enlightenment of individuals alone. The particular individuals, as isolated individuals, are at the mercy of reifying false consciousness because the historically given actual reproductive relations into which they are inserted can only function on the basis of the "personification of things and the reification of persons." Consequently, in order to alter the mystifying and ultimately destructive reversal of the sustainable reproductive relationship of human beings, countering at the same time the dominance of reifying false consciousness over the particular individuals, an all-embracing societal change is called for. Nothing less comprehensive than that can prevail on a lasting basis.

Being contented with "gradual reform" and the corresponding partial changes is self-defeating. The issue is not whether the changes are introduced *suddenly,* or over a longer term, but the *overall strategic framework* of the consistently pursued *fundamental structural* transformation, irrespective of how long its successful realization might take. The stakes of *either/or* between the mutually exclusive—the now established and the future—forms of social metabolic control are *global* both in space and in time. This is why the socialist project can succeed only if it is articulated and consistently asserted as the *hegemonic alternative* to capital's structurally entrenched and alienating social metabolism. That is, if the socialist alternative order embraces in the course of its productive development *every society,* and does it in the spirit of securing the *historical irreversibility* of labor's hegemonic alternative to capital's established social metabolic control.

In the socialist project, due to the unavoidable and openly professed radical critique of the capital system's structurally dominant false consciousness, the adopted measures of material transformation are *inseparable* from the advocated educational objectives. This is because the orienting principles of the socialist transformation of society are unrealizable without the full involvement of education as the ongoing development of socialist consciousness. All of the orienting principles discussed earlier—from genuine participation at all levels of decision making to comprehensive planning (conceived in the sense of planning which includes autonomously "making sense of one's life"), and from the progressive realization of substantive equality in society as a whole to the globally sustainable conditions of a viable economy in a positively evolving international order—can only be translated into reality if the power of education is fully activated for this purpose.

The measures adopted at any given time are historical also in the sense that they are, and remain, always subject to change. It goes without saying that, under favorable conditions, the achievements attained can be progressively enhanced and deepened. But, of course, it equally stands to reason that reversals can never be *a priori* excluded. So much will always depend on the effective intervention of socialist education in the ongoing process of transformation. That is what decides in the final analysis whether the positive or the negative potentialities shall prevail, and to what degree.

9.8.4

There is so much talk today in advanced capitalist societies about the *"respect agenda."* It consists in the wishful projection of resolving the ever-deepening *crisis of values*—manifest in the form of growing criminality and delinquency, together with the worsening alienation of the young from their society—by a rather rhetorical direct appeal to the individuals' consciousness, postulating, in vain, the suitable "respect for the values of responsible democratic citizenship." And when all that vacuous preaching fails, as it is bound to fail, since it avoids the social causes of the denounced negative symptoms, capital's political personifications in high office, including the highest of them, begin to talk about how they can identify future delinquency already "in the mother's womb," indicating the "necessary" authoritarian state legislative measures to deal with potential future criminality at the earliest possible stage. This line of approach is not more rational or less authoritarian than the capitalist state's advocacy of "relentlessly pursuing the ideological struggle" in order to win the "war against terror." At the same time, what is absolutely excluded is the possibility of changing the structural determinations of the established social order that produce and reproduce the destructive effects and consequences. It must be categorically denied that there could be anything seriously wrong with society as it stands. Only the individuals tendentiously singled out for censure might be in need of remedial action. A corrective action that provided by a privileged group of self-appointed individuals—the willing personifications and guardians of capital's socioeconomic and political order—who claim to know *ex officio* everything better.

Thus, nothing could be more justified than the institution of the hegemonic alternative order. The educational framework of such an order is both individual and social, and *inseparably* so. The *addressee* of socialist education cannot be simply the separate individual on the model of traditional educational ideals. As indicated already, in the past, the advocated educational tenets and principles were as a rule spelled out in the form of *direct appeals* to the particular *individuals' consciousness,* usually conceived in terms of moral exhortations. By contrast, socialist education addresses the *social* individuals, and not the isolated individuals. In other words, it is concerned with the individuals whose self-definition as individuals—in contrast to the abstract generic discourse of traditional philosophy on self-referential isolated individuality—cannot be even imagined without their relationship to their actual social setting and to the specific historical situation in which their human challenges inescapably arise. For it is precisely their concrete social and historical situation which invites them to formulate values through which their active commitment to determinate forms of action can bring about the realization of their consciously adopted appropriate share—which thereby defines them as autonomous and responsible social individuals—in the ongoing major transformation. This is how the practically effective education of social individuals becomes synonymous with the deepest meaning of education as *self-education.* Marx's references to the *"rich social individual"* are meant to indicate this kind of *self-definition* as the viable framework of education.

Assuming social responsibility not as the abstract moralistic "ought-to-be" of traditional philosophical discourse, which advocates some external "ideal to which the individuals are expected to conform," but as a real force *integral* to the actual social and historical situation, is possible only on the basis of conceiving education itself as a strategically vital *social organ,* i.e., as the social practice inseparable from the *ongoing development of socialist consciousness.* And that, in its turn, is only feasible because of the *radically different attitude to change* within the framework of the hegemonic alternative order.

Nothing can be exempted from change in the new order on an *a priori* basis, in sharp contrast to capital's social metabolic framework in which the critique of the significant structural determinations of society are decreed to be illegitimate and therefore prevented with all means at the system's disposal, including the most violent ones. Altering the historically given conditions, in accord with the unfolding dynamics of social development, is not only acceptable but also vitally important in the hegemonic alternative order. Failing to do so would not only run counter to the professed socialist ethos but would also deprive society of its positive potential for development, as twentieth-century history tragically demonstrated.

The role of socialist education is very important in this respect. Its simultaneously social and individual inner determination confers upon it a unique historical role, on the basis of the *reciprocity* through which it can exercise its influence, producing a major impact on social development in its entirety. Socialist education can fulfill its mandate only if it is articulated as a conscious and effective intervention in the process of social transformation.

The *reciprocity* just mentioned is highly relevant in this regard because the social individuals, on the one hand, can actively contribute to the realization of the given tasks and challenges, and thereby to the significant transformation of their society, and at the same time, they are shaped in a meaningful way in the course of the accomplished changes. Indeed, they are legitimately shaped by their own *positive awareness* of the significance of the ongoing developments, rightly perceiving their active role in these developments. This kind of *genuine consensual internalization* of ongoing developments by social individuals marks a radical departure from the thoroughly apologetic doctrine of *"tacit consent"* which has prevailed in the political theory of the established order ever since the time of John Locke, its originator.

The active involvement of individuals in societal changes can be identified as *social interaction* in the best sense of the term. This is a meaningful social interaction, on the basis of *mutually beneficial reciprocity* between social individuals and their society. The emergence and strengthening of such mutually beneficial reciprocity would be completely out of the question if the various aspects of the hegemonic alternative order, including its most important *structural determinations,* were designated by some authority to remain beyond the reach of social individuals. Their "autonomy" in that case would amount to absolutely nothing, as in fact it means nothing in the case of the postulated "sovereign choices" made by the individuals in commodity society. Thus, the significance of socialist education, as the ongoing development of socialist consciousness—in this vital sense of *reciprocity,* which defines the particular individuals as *social individuals* (and makes clear at the same time the meaning of this defining term itself)—could not be greater. For the requirements of a historically viable development, in the spirit of the important orienting principles of socialist transformation, become real through the most active contribution of education to the process. *None* of them could fulfill their required social function without it.

9.8.5

As a representative case, we can see very clearly the seminal importance of education—evidenced in the form of the mutually beneficial reciprocity between the particular individuals and their society—in relation to the fundamental change required in order to transform the now dominant economic practices into a qualitatively different kind. The difference directly concerns the vital material reproductive domain whose health is essential for the viability of even the most mediated cultural practices. For capital's *time-imperative*, prevailing in the material reproduction process, directly affects not only the exploitative structural relationships of class society as a whole but imposes at the same time its negative, humanly impoverishing effects over every aspect of material and intellectual activity in the *life-time* of the particular individuals. Accordingly, the need for human *emancipation*, in which socialist education plays a crucial role, represents a fundamental challenge.

The reproductive practices of capitalist society are characterized by the dehumanizing time-accountancy which *compels* the working individuals—in contrast to the "personifications of capital" who are the most *willing enforcers* of the system's alienating time-imperative—to submit to the tyranny of *necessary labor-time*. In this way, as Marx complained, the working individuals—the potentially "rich social individuals" in his words—suffer the alienating consequences throughout their life because they are "degraded to mere worker, subsumed under labor."[59] Moreover, this structural dependency and corresponding degradation is by no means the end of the story. Under determinate circumstances, especially under the conditions of major socioeconomic crises, the workers must also suffer the depravity of unemployment, the cynically camouflaged and hypocritically justified hardship of "labor flexibility," and the savagery of widespread *precarization*. All of these conditions arise from the same operational determination of the capitalist labor process. They are due to the unredeemable inhumanity of capital's *time-accountancy* and the structural enforcement of the system's *unalterable time-imperative*.[60]

As we have seen, labor's hegemonic alternative is the institution of a radically different *time-accountancy*, synonymous to the humanly enriching requirements of *socialist accountancy*. Only on that basis is it possible to envisage the fully unfolding productive practices of the *"rich social individuals."* This is feasible only through a radical shift from the historically prevailing tyranny of *necessary labor-time* to the conscious adoption and creative use of *disposable time* as the orienting principle of societal reproduction.

Obviously, the idea of a shift of this magnitude carries with it far-reaching implications. For the very moment we focus attention on the need for the qualitative change involved in the adoption of disposable time as the practically effective time-accountancy capable of replacing necessary labor-time, it becomes amply clear that it is inconceivable to institute in society such a fundamental shift without fully activating the power of socialist education. This is for two principal reasons.

First, because the institution of *disposable time* as the new orienting and operational principle of the societal reproduction process requires a *conscious* adhesion to it. This is in total contrast to the tyranny of *necessary labor-time* which dominates society in the form of overall *economic compulsion,* regulated not by *conscious insight*—not even by the *strictly partial* "planning" applicable to the particular economic units introduced *in hindsight* by the personifications of capital into the labor process—but by the antagonistic contradiction between capital and labor and by the *post festum* force of the market. The workers do not have to be educated for the task of entering the operational framework of necessary labor-time. They simply cannot escape its imperatives, since such imperatives are directly *imposed* upon them, with the absoluteness of a "social destiny," corresponding to their *structurally secured subordination* in the established social order. This is why Marx aptly called such a framework "the unconscious condition of mankind." As such, *unconsciousness* ubiquitously prevailing in the capitalist labor process, on account of its blind—no matter how idealized—time-accountancy, means also *uncontrollability,* with its ultimately destructive implications.

The second, equally important reason is that the *social subject* capable of regulating the labor process on the basis of *disposable time* can only be the *consciously combined force of the multiplicity of social individuals:* the *"freely associated producers,"* as they are customarily called. Again, we can see here a striking contrast to the "subject" regulating the societal reproduction process on the basis of necessary labor-time. For necessary labor-time is not only narrowly *deterministic* but also utterly *impersonal,* in that the regulatory force of production and societal reproduction is not a proper subject at all, but the *structural imperatives of the capital system in general.* Even the most willing enforcers of the established system's *time-imperative* can only *obey them,* more or less successfully. If they are not successful in their required *conformity* to the fetishistic imperatives, they will soon enough be ejected from the framework of the system through the bankruptcy of their enterprises. Notwithstanding the fetishistic mystifications of the capital system, the real producing subject is the worker; the capitalist as the presumed controlling subject—who is in fact firmly controlled through the necessarily prevailing structural imperatives of the established order—can only be a *usurping pseudo-subject.* Con-sequently, only the actually producing subject, labor, can acquire the feasible and productively viable regulatory consciousness under the historical conditions of our time. Obviously, we are not talking about the empiricist sociological category of particular workers, who as isolated workers confront the social force of capital, but about the *labor of the consciously combined social individuals as the universal condition of life in the hegemonic alternative order.* This is the only feasible social subject capable of consciously regulating the societal reproduction process on the basis of *disposable time.* Or, to put the same dialectical correlation in another way: only through the conscious adoption of disposable time as the orienting and practically effective operating principle of our life is it possible to envisage the development of a social subject capable of appropriately controlling production and societal reproduction in the hegemonic alternative order.

The subject in question, as mentioned before, is simultaneously social and individual. This social individual is unthinkable without the educational—and self-educational—processes through which the creative requirements of the new social metabolic order can be satisfied. As society stands today, the adoption of *disposable time* everywhere as a vital operating principle of production is an *abstract potentiality* only. The future depends on our ability (or failure) to turn such *abstract potentiality* into *concrete, creative reality.*

The tyranny of necessary labor-time is an imposition on the workers, who must always remain a *reluctant labor force* within the framework of the capital system. Moreover, the imposition of necessary labor-time is also wasteful in its own terms of reference, in that its operation presupposes the establishment of a strictly hierarchical command structure, which is in some parts extremely problematical, or indeed completely parasitical, even with regard to their claimed economic functions. Compared to that, the advantages of carrying out production and societal reproduction on the basis of disposable time, dedicated to the realization of the objectives consciously chosen by the self-regulating social individuals, is undeniable. For the freely associated producers dispose over incomparably richer resources than what could ever be squeezed out of the reluctant labor force under the imposition of the structural imperatives of capital's necessary labor-time.

It must be also emphasized here that education—as the unfolding development of socialist consciousness integral to the life of social individuals in its close interaction with their historically changing social setting—is a vital force identifiable also through the major impact of education on material reproductive change. This impact directly arises from the operational shift from necessary labor-time to autonomously determined disposable time set at the disposal of their society by the working individuals. Obviously, only social individuals, as individuals, can consciously determine, by and for themselves, the nature (i.e., the qualitative dimension) and the amount of *their own disposable time* from which the creative achievements of their society can successfully emerge. All of that concerns both the number of hours and the intensity of work dedicated by them to the relevant productive task. No separate authority can decide or impose such requirements on them, in contrast to the formerly inescapable dominance of necessary labor-time.

The only force capable of positively contributing to the new transformative process is *education* itself, fulfilling thereby its role as the earlier mentioned *social organ* through which the *mutually beneficial reciprocity* between the individuals and their society becomes real. Nothing can be imposed here either *in advance* (as a pre-established norm) or with restrictive *finality.* We see in the positively open-ended reproductive process of the hegemonic alternative order the manifestation of a genuine *interaction.* Through the intermediary of socialist education the productive power of the individuals is extended and enhanced, simultaneously also enlarging and rendering more emancipatory the overall reproductive power of their society as a whole. This is the only historically sustainable meaning of *increasing social wealth,* in contrast to the fetishistic cult of ultimately destructive *capital-expansion* in our finite world, which is inseparable from the fateful wastefulness of the capital system.

The domination of use-value by exchange-value, and thereby the systematic callous denial of human need in our global order can be redressed only on the basis of the radical shift to the socialist orienting principle of disposable time consciously adopted and exercised by social individuals. Their education as *value-oriented self-education,* inseparable from the ongoing development of their socialist consciousness in its dialectical reciprocity to the historic tasks and challenges which they have to face, makes them grow in their productive powers as well as in their humanity. This is what provides for them the necessary ground for creative self-fulfillment as autonomous subjects who can make sense of (and at the same time give sense to) their own life as particular social individuals, fully aware of their stake in—and responsibility for—securing the historically sustainable positive development of their society. And, of course, this is what confers true meaning on the expression *"rich social individual."*

9.8.6

The same considerations apply to all of the vital orienting principles of the hegemonic alternative social order in the integral link of their reproductive requirements to socialist education. For only through the most active and constant involvement of education in the process of social transformation—accomplished through its ability to activate the increasingly more conscious dialectical reciprocity between the individuals and their society—is it possible to turn into an effective, historically unfolding and *concrete operative force* what can be at first only *general orienting principles and values.*

Social individuals will consciously determine the improving nature and amount of their disposable time freely dedicated to the realization of their chosen social objectives, which only they themselves can autonomously determine on a continuing basis. In the same way, they alone can define the meaning of *real participation* at all levels of decision making. For creatively liberating and productive participation is conceivable only by properly understanding the nature of the tasks involved, including their historic *raison d'être,* and at the same time seeing the necessity of the conscious acceptance of the great *responsibility* inseparable from a fully participatory way of regulating their social order on a sustainable basis.

Similarly, the meaning of *substantive equality* can be turned from a valid general *orienting principle* into a creatively sustainable and humanly enriching *social reality*—and into the corresponding unreserved positive identification of the members of society with the underlying *value-determinations* and their genuine justification—only through self-transforming education as the ongoing development of socialist consciousness. This is a form of education which must be capable of not only consciously confronting and redressing the structurally entrenched and fatefully damaging social reproductive relations of *material and social and political inequality* inherited from the past, but simultaneously also of overcoming the deeply embedded mystifying force of the age-old *culture of substantive inequality* which still permeates our social consciousness.

The deplorable failure of economic *planning* in Soviet-type social systems was due to the bureaucratic attempt to impose it on society in a most authoritarian way, *from above*, ignoring the need to secure the willing cooperation of the social individuals with the plan announced by the state. Conscious positive cooperation was an essential requirement impossible to achieve without the positive intervention of practically effective education as self-education—in the form and spirit of the earlier mentioned reciprocity between the working individuals and their broader societal commitments—for the purpose of obtaining the conscious identification of the particular individuals with the fulfillment of their chosen productive objectives. Without it the individuals could not creatively interact with the overall plan itself in order to autonomously contribute to the process of transformation in a critically important domain.

And to take one more example, when we think of the dialectical complemetarity of the national and the international dimensions of society in our time, it immediately transpires that the role of education as consciously pursued consensual education is overwhelmingly important. To quote Fidel Castro:

> To the measure in which we succeed in profoundly educating our people in the spirit of *internationalism and solidarity*, rendering it conscious of the problems of our world today, to the same extent we shall be able to rely on our people to fulfill its international obligations. It is impossible to speak of solidarity among the *members of a people* if solidarity is not created simultaneously also *among the peoples*. Failing to do so we risk falling into *national egotism*.[61]

The highly negative and divisive legacy of the past still weighs all too heavily on the consciousness of the peoples, actively contributing to the constant eruption of conflicts and destructive confrontations in different parts of the world today. It is inconceivable to extricate ourselves from these contradictions and antagonisms without the creative power of education autonomously exercised by social individuals as the ongoing development of socialist consciousness. For only such education can enable them to have clear insight into the nature and significance of the issues at stake, and inspire them at the same time to assume full responsibility for their own positive part in bringing under control the destructive trends in our globally intertwined—and in our historical time inescapably national and international—social order.

In all these matters, we are concerned with the vital need for a radical and all-embracing structural change of our social reproductive order. This cannot be accomplished through the blind material determinations that had to prevail in past historical development. Moreover, the great problems and difficulties of our own historical conditions are further intensified and aggravated by an undeniable *urgency of time,* never experienced in earlier historical epochs.

It is sufficient to point in this respect to two literally vital differences that put sharply into relief the urgency of time in our own age. First, the formerly unimaginable *power of destruction* at humanity's disposal today, whereby the complete extermination of humankind is now easily achievable through a variety of military means. This is gravely underlined by the fact that in the last century we witnessed both the ever-increasing scale and the ever-growing intensity of actual military conflagrations, including two extremely destructive World Wars. Moreover, in the last few years of the chaotic "new world order" the most absurd and cynical pretenses were—and are being—used for embarking on genocidal wars, threatening us at the same time even with the "morally justified" use of nuclear weapons in projected future "preventive and preemptive" wars. And the second gravely threatening condition is that the destructive nature of capital's social metabolic control in our time—manifest through the ever-greater predominance of *destructive production* in contrast to the traditionally self-justifying capitalist mythology of *productive destruction*—is in the process of devastating the natural environment, thereby directly endangering the elementary conditions of human existence on this planet.

If nothing else, these conditions forcefully underline both the dramatic urgency of time in our own historical epoch and the impossibility of finding viable solutions to the grave problems involved without *consciously* confronting the dangers and committing ourselves to the only *rationally* feasible—and in the deepest sense of the term *cooperative*—search for remedies. Thus, because of the unprecedented magnitude of the tasks at stake, and the historically unique urgency of our time pressing for their enduring solution, the role assigned to the ongoing development of socialist consciousness is absolutely fundamental.

The necessity of a radical and comprehensive structural change in the established social metabolic order carries with it the need for the *qualitative redefinition* of society's *systemic determinations* as the overall perspective of transformation. No partial adjustments and marginal improvements to the existing social reproductive order are sufficient to meet the challenge. For they could only reproduce on an enlarged scale—and indeed with the passing of our heavily constrained historical time necessarily aggravate as well—the clearly identifiable dangers both in the domain of economic and military destruction and on the ecological plane. This is why only the institution and consolidation of the *hegemonic alternative* to capital's social metabolic control can offer a way out from the contradictions and antagonisms of our time.

As we have seen above, what distinguishes the contending hegemonic alternatives in the most striking way is their radically different attitude to change. Capital's social metabolic control is absolutely incompatible with any idea of structurally significant change, despite all evidence for its urgency. By contrast, the hegemonic alternative order of social labor cannot function at all without *positively*—and *consciously*—embracing the dynamic forces of change at all levels of individual and social life, including the structurally vital determinations of society's material and cultural reproduction. This is realizable, on a continuing and comprehensive societal basis, only through the necessary pursuit of *planning worthy of its name,* consciously designed and autonomously brought to fruition by social individuals.

In this sense change is feasible in the hegemonic alternative order not as a particular step or steps adopted with a claim to finality and closure (there is always some new challenge generated and indeed welcome in the course of socialist transformation) but only through the ongoing—*never definitively completed*—development of socialist consciousness. Thus, the hegemonic alternative mode of social metabolic control defines itself not less in terms of the enduring impact of its freely adopted and operationally important orienting principles—which turn into reality the power of individual and social consciousness—than through the effective capability of material production and all-embracing societal reproduction. In fact, the latter could not proceed at all without its constant interaction with the projects and designs consciously formulated by human beings in their changing socio-historical situation, in close conjunction with their value-determinations and conscious commitment to meeting the encountered challenges and to improving their conditions of existence. And the improvements here referred to arise not simply in material terms but in accord with the full meaning of "self-developing rich social individuals."

The consciousness of the social individuals at work in these relations of contending claims between the established social metabolic order and its hegemonic alternative is in the first place their consciousness of the need for successfully instituting a historically sustainable alternative to the growing destructiveness of capital's mode of social reproductive control. At the same time, with regard to the self-awareness and historically appropriate self-definition of the people involved, the required consciousness of the social individuals engaged in the process of transformation is their positive awareness that they are actively engaged in the institution of the only feasible hegemonic alternative order under the prevailing circumstances. Nothing short of this kind of self-definition—asserted with uncompromising determination and consistency—can succeed. We are concerned here with a unique mandate for an all-embracing qualitative transformation arising at a critical juncture of human history. At a formerly inconceivable juncture, when nothing less than the very survival of the human species is directly at stake.

The only social organ capable of fulfilling the vital historical mandate in question is education firmly oriented toward the ongoing development of socialist consciousness.

9.8.7

Since the idea of structural change is *a priori* excluded when viewing the world from the standpoint of capital, in view of the necessarily constraining conceptual parameters of the system, the dimension of the *future* suffers the consequence that it must be curtailed in the vision of absolutely everyone whose historical horizon is set by capital's vantage point. Accordingly, even a philosophical genius, like

Hegel, could offer only a *truncated dialectic of time* when he reached the present in his monumental conception of world history. Tellingly, he barred the road before the possibility of any structurally significant future change by insisting in an apologetic way—which in the end had to turn out to be in its spirit also anti-historical—that "The History of the World travels from East to West, for *Europe is absolutely the end of History.*"[62] And he added, for good measure, that this process of development to its climax and ideal completion is "the true *Theodicaea,* the justification of God in History."[63]

From the ultimately self-defeating vantage point of capital, the prospects of development must be adjusted in such a way that concern with *immediacy* dominates the time horizon. All envisaged change is admissible and legitimate only if the potentially altered conditions can readily fit into the established structural framework of the capital system and of its corresponding value-determinations.

The educational orientation of individuals—including their material aspirations and social values—is guided in the same way, directly dominated by the problems of capitalist immediacy. Their time-consciousness, as far as the "future" is concerned, is restricted to the constantly renewed *present tense* of their struggle with the fetishistic and constraining power of immediacy in their everyday life: a struggle which they cannot possibly win under the rule of capital's necessary labor-time. *Localism* and *immediacy* must therefore prevail everywhere. The concept of materially and socially feasible *overall structural change,* not to mention its *desirability and legitimacy,* must remain in terms of the dominant educational system absolute *taboos.*

The capitalistically convenient cult of the *local* and the *immediate* prevail and go inseparably together. Thus, in the conceptions which conform to the vantage point of capital's self-mythologizing allegedly permanent "natural order," the missing dynamics of *comprehensive* and transformative objectives and ideals, which would have to envisage at some future juncture the necessity—or at least the possibility—of fundamental sociohistorical change, cannot be made intelligible without bearing in mind the unavoidably *truncated time-horizon* of individuals in their everyday life. There is a perverse reciprocity here, producing a vicious circle in the relationship of the two. The truncated time-horizon of individuals excludes the possibility of setting themselves comprehensive and transformative objectives, and vice versa, the absence of comprehensive transformative determinations from their vision condemns their time-consciousness to remain locked into the narrowest time-horizon of immediacy.

Socialist education, by contrast, cannot fulfill its historic mandate without giving due weight to the vitally important comprehensive and transformative objectives linked to their appropriate time-horizon. To be sure, this does not mean that the most fundamental objectives of structural change must be or can be left to a distant future, on account of their unavoidably long-term perspective for full realization. On the contrary, it is a prominent characteristic of the issues that must be confronted in the course of socialist transformation that the immediate tasks cannot be separated and conveniently isolated from, let alone in a self-justifying way opposed—as done in the past—to the long-term and more comprehensive challenges. The issues themselves are so closely intertwined, because of the unique historical character of the required all-embracing structural change, that action concerning even the most distant *fully* realizable transformative objectives—like, for instance, the institution of *substantive equality* everywhere, in the full meaning of the term—cannot be left to some remote future date. The road leading to the all-inclusive realization of substantive equality must be embarked upon today if we are serious at all about the successful completion of the uncompromising activity required for the institution and consolidation of such a radical material and cultural change.

It is a historically unique feature of the socialist advocacy of qualitative structural change that the consciousness—and self-consciousness—of individuals must focus on the *comprehensive* and *all-embracing* nature of the required social transformation and of their own part in it as *integral to the overall objectives* in question, rather than being compartmentalized in the private domain of some more or less fictitious isolated individuality. In this way also the time-horizon of the particular social individuals is inseparable from the comprehensive—no matter how long-term—historical time of their dynamically developing society in its entirety. Thus, for the first time ever in the course of human history, individuals are expected to become really *conscious* of their part in human development both as regards its positively feasible *comprehensive and transformative objectives* and of the *time scale* of their own actual involvement and specific contribution to the unfolding change of their societies.

In this sense, the consciousness and self-consciousness of the particular individuals of their role as responsible social individuals—their clear awareness of their *immediate,* but autonomously chosen, *specific contribution* to the ongoing *all-embracing* transformation—is an *integral and essential* part of all feasible success. For they cannot properly accomplish even their relatively limited objectives without self-consciously viewing and evaluating the relevance of their particular activity in the broader transformative framework—which in this way they themselves autonomously constitute and shape—as integral to the all-encompassing historical time created on an ongoing basis by a succession of generations, including themselves. Only within this perspective can they become fully aware of the vital significance of their own *disposable time,* as "freely associated producers." This is the only way in which they can autonomously dedicate their disposable time—which is simultaneously their *real historical time* as particular social individuals who can make sense of, and give sense to, their own life—to the creation of a qualitatively different as well as historically sustainable social metabolic order.

In this radical transformation, nothing less than the literally vital need for the creation of a viable new society is at stake. This is a transformation whose success is inconceivable without consciously securing the—historically inescapable—*rational design of the new order's overall parameters* on a continuing basis, and without the *self-consciousness* of the social individuals as creators and re-creators of that overall design across generations. And it stands to reason that the creation and the appropriate renewal of the required overall design is inconceivable without the self-conscious and autonomous value-determinations of social individuals who are able and willing to identify themselves with their society's historically unfolding transformation.

The role of education, properly defined as the ongoing development of socialist consciousness, is obviously a crucial constituent of this great process of transformation.

9.8.8

Given the unprecedented urgency of our historical time, socialism in the twenty-first century cannot avoid facing up to the dramatic challenges arising from these imperatives.

In a general sense, they appeared already in Marx's lifetime, even if in those days the total destruction of humanity—in the absence of the military means and modalities for easily accomplishing such destruction, in close conjunction to the capital system's inescapable structural crisis, as it is experienced everywhere in our time—was not yet a globally threatening reality.

Marx himself was passionately trying to explore ways for realizing the all-embracing transformative changes necessary in order to counter, on a historically sustainable basis, the capital system's advancing trend of destruction. He was fully aware of the fact that without the conscious dedication of the people to the realization of the monumental historic task of instituting a radically different and viable social metabolic order of reproduction there could be no success. The intellectual and persuasive power of theoretical insight, no matter how well founded, was by itself not enough. The way he had formulated this problem, with a great sense of reality, was to acknowledge that: "*It is not enough for thought to strive for realization, reality must itself strive toward thought.*"[64]

He knew well that the increasingly destructive material force of capital, in the descending phase of the system's development, had to be matched and positively overcome by the material force of the historically viable hegemonic alternative. Thus, underlining the way in which theoretical work could aspire at being meaningful, he added to the sentence just quoted that "theory also becomes a material force as soon as it has gripped the masses."[65] Naturally, not just any theory can do that. Since it is a question of constituting an appropriate relationship between theory committed to the idea of a fundamental societal change and the material force which could make the difference, some vitally important conditions have to be satisfied without which the advocated idea of "theory gripping the masses" amounts to nothing more than rather vacuous moralistic sloganising, as has frequently been the case in sectarian and elitist political discourse. Thus, Marx concluded his reflections on the subject by firmly stressing that "Theory can be realized in a people *only insofar as it is the realization of the needs of that people.*"[66]

Theory cannot reach the people in question by books alone, nor by simply addressing, even with the best of intentions, an occasional crowd of individuals. Radical thought cannot succeed in its mandate of changing social consciousness without an adequate *organizational articulation.* A coherent organization—to provide the historically developing framework of interchange between the needs of the people and the strategic ideas of their realization—is essential for the success of the enterprise of transformation. It is, therefore, by no means surprising that Marx and his close companion Engels, as young revolutionary intellectuals, joined the most radical social movement of their time and were responsible for writing the *Communist Manifesto* which advocated the required uncompromising organized intervention in the unfolding global historical process.

It is also essential to have a clear idea of the strategic orientation of developing consciousness, i.e., its necessary focus without which it could be diverted from the realization of its historic task. This is why Marx stressed *"communist consciousness"* would be able to fulfill its historic mandate only if it was "the consciousness of the *necessity of a fundamental revolution."*[67]

Moreover, an equally important consideration is the question of *how wide* this communist consciousness must be diffused in society, in order to stand a chance of subduing its adversary, alongside the corollary question of the still-missing *conditions of its diffusion* under the prevailing circumstances, given the long historical conditioning of the people involved which mitigates against the wide-scale adoption of communist consciousness. For the ultimately self-defeating temptations of *vanguardism* did not originate in recent times. They were already prominent well before the time of Marx. This applied not only to the ignorance of the question of *"how are the educators themselves educated?"*—presuming some kind of a "birthright" or *ex officio* superiority to the self-appointed "educators"—but in more general terms: to the vital issue of *decision making* which excludes the great masses of the people. Besides, such elitist conceptions are always condemned to futility and failure because without mobilizing the great masses of the people there can be no hope of success against the odds overwhelmingly in capital's favor under the prevailing historical conditions.

In opposition to all conceivable elitist misrepresentations of the challenge, of which we have seen several damaging embodiments in the past, Marx emphasized:

> Both for the production on a *mass scale* of this communist consciousness, and for the success of the cause itself, the alteration of men on a *mass scale* is necessary, an alteration which can only take place in a *practical movement, a revolution;* the revolution is necessary, therefore, not only because the ruling class cannot be overthrown in any other way, but also because the class over-

throwing it can only in a revolution succeed in *ridding itself* of all the muck
of ages and become *fitted to found society anew.*[68]

These considerations remain valid also for the present and the future.
Sectarian vanguardism can never match up to the magnitude of the
historic task, which involves both the constitution of a revolutionary
mass movement capable of successfully overcoming its adversary and
at the same time "ridding itself" of the paralyzing muck of ages, so as
to become *fitted to found society anew.* This is why Marx contrasts the
need for *communist mass consciousness* with the *"abstract ideal* to
which the people were supposed to conform." Whether the advocates
of such approaches are aware of it or not, *sectarian vanguardism* was
always—and could never be anything else than—precisely the attempt
to impose on the great masses of the people the abstract ideal deplored
by Marx, while arrogantly or at least naïvely dismissing the valid alternative of *communist mass consciousness* as "populism" or something of
the kind. And the externally imposed "abstract ideal" of sectarian vanguardism can not be considered less damaging just because some of its
dedicated advocates themselves would be personally willing to conform to it.

Paradoxically, in some periods of the twentieth century *"reality
itself was striving toward thought,"* to use Marx's expression, but
"thought"—as it should be embodied in the social and political strategies of the required radical transformation, together with their corresponding organizational articulations—was not up to the challenge.
In order to counter the possibility of failing to take advantage of the
favorable conditions arising in the midst of capital's deepening structural crisis, two seminally important questions must be remembered.
With regard to both, the role of education—as the much needed
development of socialist consciousness without which even the grave
structural crisis of capital's social metabolic order is very far from
being sufficient to activate the process of "founding society anew"—is
paramount.

The first concerns the necessary *transition* from the ruling order
to the historically sustainable society of the future. As we have seen
before, capital's now deeply entrenched social metabolic order is characterized by the dominance of *counter-value*—i.e., by the positive con-
notation perniciously given to waste and destruction—carrying with
it the degradation of "education" to the conformist conditioning of the

people who must "internalize" the capital system's destructive and suicidal requirements, in the spirit suited to the maintenance and extension of counter-value. In this sense, moving toward the new social metabolic order, in the *transitional* society, is inseparable from the necessity to overcome the *inherited social ethos* of capital's reproductive order. Only through education conceived as the radical *self-education* of social individuals, in the course of their *"alteration* which can only take place in a *practical movement, a revolution,"* can the social individuals become simultaneously both educators and educated. This is the only conceivable way to overcome the conservative dichotomy of all elitist conceptions that divide society into the select few mysteriously superior "educators," and the rest of society consigned to their permanently subordinate position of "the educated," as highlighted by Marx. In this respect, we must constantly bear in mind that the advocated "alteration of the people to become *fitted to found society anew"* is feasible only through the development of *"communist mass consciousness,"* embracing the overwhelming majority of society.

This development takes place in a *transitional society,* with its given characteristics which cannot be wished out of existence in order to suit some idealized future postulate. The actually available mediatory leverages—the identifiable practical *mediations* [69] between the present and the sustainable future—are the only ways and means through which the *general orienting principles* of socialist transformation can be turned into *operative forces,* increasingly enhancing the perceived positive potentialities and reducing the power of the inherited negative constituents. For the success of this process it is necessary to rely on the practical dialectic of both change *and continuity,* by consolidating the positive potentialities and achievements as the necessary ground on which one can successively build. Naturally, the proper way of taking hold of the available mediatory leverages in a transitional society includes consciously adapting to our own design the progressive aspirations of the more remote past—as we have earlier seen them with reference to the unrealized educational ideals of the great enlightenment thinkers—and thereby recreating a lost *historical continuity* to which capital is absolutely inimical at the present stage of its systemic crisis. Successful *transition* is a vital historical process, unfolding within the sustainable dialectic of continuity and change. By abandoning either of the two valid dialectical constituents of such a process, not to mention suppressing both of them, one can only *destroy history,* as capital is bent on doing today. The autonomous role of self-educating education in grasping and suitably adapting the transitional society's mediatory leverages is the necessary builder of positive continuity. It is *living history*, as it unfolds in the direction of the chosen future, and at the same time the social individuals' conscious way of living their own history in the difficult period of transition.

The second question concerns the *international challenge* facing us. For no one can seriously deny that the cult of localism—from the naïve romanticism of *"small is beautiful"* to the self-defeating and one-sided, even if rhetorically tempting slogan, "think globally, *act locally*"—is totally powerless against capital's global resources of domination and destruction. At the same time, it is also very difficult to deny that past attempts to organizationally counter capital's global power by the force of socialist internationalism did not live up to their declared objectives. One of the principal reasons for the failure of Internationals was their most unrealistic—even if historically conditioned—presupposition of *doctrinal unity* as their starting point and necessary mode of operation, and its attempted *enforcement* in a variety of self-defeating ways, leading to *derailments* and ultimate implosion. To consciously rectify this problem, in accord with the requirements and potentialities of our historical time, represents a major challenge for the future.

On the other side, capital's ideological domination in the international domain was forcefully supported by the *culture of substantive inequality*. It promoted the self-serving myth of the *"world-historical nations"*—a handful of capitalistically powerful countries coming to dominance under determinate historical circumstances—at the expense of the smaller nations allegedly destined to be forever subordinated to the "world-historical" countries. This view elevated, in abstract philosophy, an obvious *historical contingency* to the lofty status of some kind of *a priori ontological necessity*, culminating in the apologetic dictum according to which the "world-historical nations" of Europe represented "absolutely the end of history." In this way, the totally unjustifiable system of domination and structural subordination was justified through the speculative travesty of the contingently established but historically changeable brute relation of forces into the postulated permanence of substantive inequality.

The role of education is also crucial in this respect. For, on the one hand, it is necessary to expose—through the demystifying power of socialist education—the apologetic character of the long established culture of *substantive inequality,* in all of its forms, in order to bring nearer the realization of a permanently sustainable human relationship of *substantive equality* in the historically changing global order. And on the other hand, the positive intervention of education in the elaboration of ways for successfully countering capital's global domination, through the establishment of *organizationally viable forms of socialist solidarity,* is vital for meeting the great *international challenge* of our historical time.

10. Why Socialism? Historical Time and the Actuality of Radical Change

In his contribution to the first issue of *Monthly Review,* in 1949, Albert Einstein asked the question: *"Why Socialism?"* Einstein forcefully underlined in his answer that "human society is passing through a *crisis,* its stability has been *gravely shattered."* He insisted that the stakes to be secured were very high in our globally interlocking social order because "it is only a slight exaggeration to say that mankind constitutes even now a *planetary community* of production and consumption." Nor did he wish to underrate the problems that had to be faced in the future. On the contrary, he stressed with a sober sense of responsibility that "The achievement of socialism requires the solution of some extremely difficult socio-political problems." And he concluded his reasoning with these words: "Clarity about the aims and problems of socialism is of the greatest significance in *our age of transition."*[1]

It has been almost sixty years, and since these words were written the crisis Einstein referred to has become much greater: it is a veritable *structural crisis* of our entire social reproductive system. Also, no one could wish to deny today that we must concern ourselves with the complex predicament of a *planetary* order, even if the fashionable term for the ongoing trends of development of that order—used often with self-serving evasion—is *globalization.* Moreover, with the implosion of the Soviet-type system in the mid 1980s, with painful repercussions for countless millions, Einstein's judgment that "the achievement of socialism requires the solution of some extremely difficult sociopolitical problems" has been dramatically highlighted.

Thus, more than ever before, *our age of transition* is in need of finding a historically viable solution to its contradictions and devastating confrontations, in order to remedy its gravely shattered stability, brought about by the antagonisms at the roots of two devastating world wars in the twentieth century, and foreshadowing the total destruction of humanity in the event of a third. Only the most uncritical defenders of the established order could maintain that everything can go on indefinitely as we have seen it before. Thus, in view of the deepening structural crisis of capital's social metabolic order, the question of "why socialism" can be—and must be—legitimately raised anew.

Why socialism then? The primary reason is because capital by its very nature is incapable of addressing the perilous problems of its structural crisis. The capital system is eminently—and even uniquely—*historical* in character. However, its personifications refuse to admit this, in the interest of *eternalizing* the rule of their mode of social reproductive control, despite its by now all too obvious dangers even with regard to the destruction of nature and the undeniable implications of such destruction for human survival itself.

The insuperable difficulty is that the capital system, as a mode of societal reproductive control, must follow at whatever cost its own logic, corresponding to its objective structural determinations. Capital's self-expansionary drive cannot restrain itself by conceding any human consideration just because that might appear morally more palatable, as the self-mythology of "caring capitalism" and "peoples' capitalism" would wish to make us believe. On the contrary, capital's logic is characterized by self-serving destructiveness, since everything that stands in the way of the system's ruthless expansionary drive must be brushed aside, and even crushed if need be, as a matter of course. Otherwise capital would quickly drive to a halt in its self-expansionary advancement, and before long it would also totally implode as a mode of social metabolic control.

This is by no means a novelty, asserting itself only under the present historical circumstances of the system's structural crisis, rather it is the other way round. We are confronted by the perilous conditions of capital's structural crisis because this form of social metabolic control is no longer in a position of readily *displacing* its inherent contradictions and antagonisms without activating at the same time the unsurpassable limits of the system. This predicament is in sharp contrast to capital's past ability to encroach over everything and overcome with relative ease the encountered obstacles in the ascending phase of its systemic development.

Given the objective limitations of our planetary household and the antagonistically competing forces over its resources, capital's customary way of ruthlessly subduing everything had to be an increasingly more problematical way of displacing the contradictions constantly generated on an ever-growing scale. In the twentieth century, the ultimately untenable displacement of contradictions included the extreme destructiveness of two world wars with the fatefully prohibitive implications of a potential Third World War. Obviously, however, once the possibility of such destructive displacement on an appropriate global scale is ruled out, the systemic contradictions and antagonisms can only intensify, bringing with them the insurmountable structural crisis of the whole system.

To be sure, the absence of human considerations from capital's relentless self-expansionary drive was in evidence ever since the time of early capitalistic developments, as the blood-soaked history of the so-called primitive accumulation abundantly demonstrated. In England, for instance, under the reign of Henry VIII alone, 72,000 human beings were exterminated as "vagrants" and "vagabonds"—as "surplus to requirements"—after being deprived of their former livelihood on the common land expropriated for the purpose of profitable sheep farming. That was the reason why Sir Thomas More exposed with biting irony the inhuman conditions under which "sheep are eating men"[2] in the lucrative service of wool production.

No one should have any illusions that under the aggravating conditions of the established order's structural crisis capital could acquire a different attitude to the human impact of its ruthless self-assertion. The painful fact is that, notwithstanding all self-justifying promises, capital has failed to satisfy, up to the present even, the elementary requirements of the overwhelming majority of humankind. Accordingly, the great challenge for the future is how to overcome in a positive way capital's systemic determinations, which have *always* imposed their adversarial self-expansionary drive on society without any consideration for the human consequences. This is why socialism is on the historical agenda as the radical alternative to capital's rule over society.

10.1 Conflicting Determinations of Time

10.1.1

When we address the question of time at the present juncture of history, the principal consideration regarding the requirements of a historically sustainable social order can only be the radical supersession of capital's destructive adversariality. The latter was described by Kant as "the antagonism of men in society," allegedly arising from the incorrigible "asocial sociability" of their human nature. Our necessary rejection of the circular escape clause of human nature—because it would not explain anything at all by itself but condemn us, instead, to doing nothing about the criticized condition—can only be the starting point. Also, fighting against capital's destructive adversariality constitutes, on its own, only the negative side of the historic task.

The truth of the matter is that the unavoidable negation of capital's adversariality cannot possibly succeed without being complemented by the positive side of the same undertaking. And that involves the creative harmonization of the time of social individuals with the *open ended* historical time of humanity. Unless it is genuinely open-ended, "historical time" is not historical at all.

This view is in sharp contrast to the arbitrarily closed temporality of the *"eternal present"* which is supposed to characterize the established order's *"rational actuality,"* as postulated by Hegel. Nothing could justify the speculative rationalization of capital's eternalized present. Any attempt to do so can amount to no more than the uncritical support for the perpetuation of the *irrational actuality* of an untenable—structurally most iniquitous and incorrigibly antagonistic—social order, even if the Hegelian *closure of historical time* is presented by the great German philosopher with a tone of consenting resignation.

The necessary harmonization of historical time here referred to means, in the first place, the adoption of humanity's objectively feasible *positive potentialities* by social individuals as the orienting principles and values of their own life-activity, in opposition to capital's deterministically imposed *counter-values.* Naturally, this is conceivable only on the basis of strategies and consciously chosen aims arising from the historically determinate challenges of the social groups to which the particular individuals belong. But their awareness of *endan-*

gered humanity is a necessary requirement of their self-definition in our time. Without that the overall horizon of their perceived historical predicament—directly relevant precisely to their actions as conscious social individuals—would be missing a most vital dimension. As Attila József put it in his great poem:

> Real matter created us,
> coal, iron and petrol,
> thrown us into the mould
> of this horrible society,
> ardently and untrammeled,
> to make our stand for humanity,
> on the eternal soil.[3]

Moreover, as József put it into relief in this poem, the social individuals who are called upon now to make their stand for humanity must do that in full awareness of the need to observe the objectively necessary laws which are capable of securing the continued historical development of the human species. For only as *"faithful listeners to the laws"*—*"fieles oidores de las leyes,"* in the Spanish translation[4]—can they prevail over the dangerously advancing trends of capital's self-assertion today which foreshadow the degradation and destruction of nature. This is why—in a poem written with great foresight in 1933—the last two lines of the stanza quoted above directly link *"our stand for humanity"* with the vital respect for the irreplaceable natural ground of human existence, indicated by the words: *"on the eternal soil,"* where our stand for humanity must be made.

That demand is inseparable also from the need to have profound respect for what constitutes the positive values in the historical progression of humanity. They must be observed in the spirit of the dialectical relationship between *continuity and change.* In other words, the demand in question means the understanding of, and the support for, the socially viable and meaningful *continuity in change,* and the historically appropriate and sustainable *change in continuity.* To quote the lines that immediately follow "on the eternal soil" in the poem:

> After priests, soldiers and burghers,
> thus we became at last
> the faithful listeners to the laws:

this is why the sense of all
human work throngs in us
like the deep viola.[5]

This is how the time of the consciously acting social individuals and the time of humanity can be brought together under our endangered historical predicament. But, of course, such harmonization of the individual's lifetime with the historical time of humanity—in contrast to the ontologically insuperable dichotomies projected by classical German philosophy through its conveniently presumed "asocial sociability" which is supposed to directly arise from fixed "human nature"—cannot be taken for granted. It is feasible only if the very real, and not speculatively postulated, conflicting determinations of time which deeply affect the fate of humanity—and with it inevitably also the life of the totality of individuals—are resolved in favor of a historically sustainable social order by successfully overcoming capital's, in our age, all too obvious destructive trends of development.

10.1.2

To be sure, the objectively conflicting determinations of time are inseparable from the nature of the social forces competing on the historical stage, opposing each other on the basis of their socially constituted interests and antagonisms. József had no illusions that a direct appeal to individual consciousness could provide the required solution to these conflicts. He clearly realized that the individuals' perception of historical time arises from the position which they occupy—not simply by birth but through their more or less consciously renewed self-definition—in relation to the fundamental hegemonic alternatives of the given social order. A truly feasible solution is therefore inconceivable without confrontations involving the major social forces as carriers of the actually available—whether already fully articulated and entrenched or yet in the process of emerging and potentially prevailing—historical alternatives of the epoch. And that determination carries with it a significant difference in terms of the individuals' attitude to historical time, together with their contrasting self-definition in terms of the actions oriented toward an emancipatory transformation of society or, on the contrary, toward the preservation of the established order. As József put it in one of his earlier poems:[6]

Time is lifting the fog,
so that we can better see our summit.
Time is lifting the fog,
we have brought time with us,
we brought it with our struggle,
with our reserves of misery.

The defenders of the established order, armed also with powerful *fog-generators*, do everything in their power to mystify their historical adversary by denying the conflicting determinations of time. However, "time is lifting the fog," due to the irrepressible struggle over structurally enforced inequality and misery, no matter how cynically the ideologists of the ruling order lie about the pretended successful elimination of the fundamental social interests and antagonisms in their characteristically undefined "modern world." They have been unashamedly preaching for well over a century that "the classes are *merging* into one another" and that "we are all becoming *middle class*." But—in the midst of the ever-more obvious growth of inequality and exploitation directly affecting the overwhelming majority of humankind—they studiously avoided and continue to avoid the question: *the middle of what?* For them history has already been brought to a happy completion, and therefore there can be no meaningful dispute, let alone socially grounded objective confrontation, over historical time.

The basic line of demarcation in relation to time is drawn between those who want to *eternalize* the established mode of social metabolic reproduction, despite its growing destructiveness, and those who will have to institute and render humanly gratifying the necessary *radical alternative* to it on a historically sustainable scale. Thus, the stakes are truly epochal, excluding the possibility of resolving the capital system's structural antagonisms by patching up here and there the existing order. That has been tried and totally failed over the duration of much more than a century of "reformist" promises.

The attitude of the apologists of capital's rule over society is to deny the relevance of historical time—that is, as a set of clearly identifiable and objectively contestable temporal determinations—to our problems. They try to do this in a number of different ways, and not only by projecting the exchange relations of commodity-society way back into the past, so as to be able to envisage all the more easily its timeless persistence in an unalterable future.

Perhaps their most revealing approach is the attempt to turn *historical time-determinations*—and corresponding social developments—into fictitious *natural determinations*. They seem to be convinced that by arguing in that way, the historically created—and historically changeable—*structural hierarchies* of society can be safely proclaimed to be the preordained and the absolutely unalterable work of nature. Thanks to this kind of reasoning, the most reactionary social interests can be perversely defended and even glorified by exempting them from any *historical* scrutiny in the name of being sanctioned forever by *nature*.

To give a telling example, the fact of *diversity (or difference)* in nature—including the obvious but by no means *ipso facto* socially discriminatory diversity among human beings—is used as the falsely decreed eternal justification for the historically instituted and *structurally entrenched inequality* of the prevailing social order. Thus, the apologists of the ruling reproductive system do not hesitate to fallaciously equate, with cynical *conservative* intent, the neutral concept of *diversity* with the socially created and totally unjustifiable conditions of *structural domination and subordination*. At the same time, and by the same token, they dismissively condemn any attempt aimed at challenging and changing the established conditions of gruesome inequality and discrimination as nothing more than a mere *"shibboleth of equality,"*[7] as if such attempts represented an unforgivable affront to nature. This is how they justify the unjustifiable with their conservatively inspired violation of logic.

Naturally, the conservative forces here mentioned are not simply those formal organizations that—for the sake of an available political label—conveniently take that name. Self-characterizations of that kind can readily change according to how the political wind blows in the course of adjusting the respective positions of the established parties in their efforts to take advantage of the shifting parliamentary opportunities, for instance. What we can witness in this way among the traditional conservative parties is true also on the claimed "progressive" side of parliamentary political transformations. Through these changes, we reach a situation in which some of the earlier reform-oriented political parties of the Left become indistinguishable from the long-established conservative parties of the Right, or become even more entrenched in hopelessly conservative positions, more or less openly abandoning even their postwar pretences to reforming the social system. The metamorphosis of the British Labour Party into Tony Blair's "New Labour" is a good illustration of this kind of development.

However, these political conjunctural changes reveal very little, if anything, about the conflicting determinations of historical time, because they are not concerned at all with the fundamental hegemonic alternatives of our actual historical predicament. In fact, the political programs announced for changing the social order through reformist adjustments—from Edward Bernstein's advocacy of "evolutionary socialism" to its ever more dubious imitations elsewhere—were *never* theoretically articulated, let alone practically attempted, as the necessary hegemonic alternative to the established mode of social metabolic reproduction. On the contrary, they all adopted as their fundamental animating principle the—at first naïve but increasingly more vacuous—belief that the only kind of change feasible had to be *strictly gradual* ("piecemeal," "little by little," etc.), and it had to be instituted well within the confines of capital's established structural framework. Anything more radical than this had to be condemned and categorically rejected as Marxian "dialectical scaffolding," in Bernstein's notorious words. No wonder, therefore, that social-democratic Labourism ended up with completely abandoning even its mild reformist program, finding itself on the same side—and in some prominent cases even considerably to the right—of its erstwhile conservative political adversary.

In reality, the meaning of *conservative* as it is relevant to its historical time is closely linked to the question of actually existing hegemonic alternatives, irrespective of the conjunctural political changes. That meaning is objectively defined by the historical fact that once the capital system is firmly established (in the sense of becoming the all-embracing and dominant mode of societal reproduction), capital cannot help being *conservative* in the fundamental sense of the term, categorically opposing and fighting all attempts directed at instituting major changes in society. From that point onwards only *marginal* adjustments are admissible, and even those only in order to strengthen the capital system.

The generally promoted and enforced ethos of *"there is no alternative"* is understandable on that basis. Likewise it is understandable, but of course very far from justifiable, that according to the conservative "conviction politicians" of our time, including Prime Minister

Margaret Thatcher, the advocates of *structural change* must be fought with the full power of the capitalist state as *"the enemy within."* It was, therefore, a most telling demonstration of the unholy consensus of the political forces which were supposed to be on the opposite side of the parliamentary barricade that the British coal miners, engaged in a year-long strike action, were in the end defeated thanks to the active contribution of the Labour Party in favor of Margaret Thatcher's repressive action against them. Whenever we witness even a remote possibility of hegemonic confrontation, the traditional political parties—be they Conservative or Labour—find themselves, as a rule, lined up on the same side of the social divide against the forces oriented toward the institution of the historically required radical alternative.

But despite all of these negative circumstances and *conjunctural* political accommodations, the actually conflicting determinations of historical time cannot be eliminated by force, nor indeed turned into the *permanent* wishfully uncontestable solution of the deep-seated—structurally irreconcilable—social antagonisms. For so long as the destructive contradictions of our established social order continue to intensify—and now to the point of directly threatening the very survival of the human species—the necessity to institute a sustainable hegemonic alternative to capital's mode of social metabolic reproduction is bound to remain on the historical agenda.

10.1.3

The attempt to confine historical time to the domain of the gradual and the piecemeal, so as to conform to the capital-apologetic prescription of little by little, and to expect from such procedure the lasting results of social progress, was always a theoretical absurdity and a practical non-starter. For the "gradual" and "piecemeal" institution of "little by little," devoid of an appropriate *comprehensive* frame of reference, makes no sense at all. This is so because it is totally blind without an envisaged and in the light of ongoing developments suitably modifiable *strategic framework,* one firmly oriented from its inception toward a radical socialist transformation.

We all know, from the bitter experience of the labor movement, that gradually appending little by little to the result of some former partial moves brings with it just as easily *disaster* and *self-defeat* as the slightest degree of even tactical—and most certainly never strategic—improvement. The ubiquitously promoted propaganda of "reform by slow degrees" advanced by twentieth-century reformism could in fact amount to nothing more than the *preservation* and even the strengthening of the established order.

The real intent behind such "evolutionary" strategies—from the Bernsteinian beginnings to their more recent permutations—was always the *crusading hostility* against "holism," that is, against any attempt aimed at radically instituting and consolidating some badly needed comprehensive changes in society. Characteristically, the actual record of the whole approach, which once promised the gradual realization of socialism, was the clamorous defeat and the effective disenfranchisement of the working class movement through the unreserved capitulation of its parliamentary political representation to its class adversary.

Given the fact that the metabolic control of the social order cannot be fragmented and divided among forces pulling in *diametrically opposite directions,* it is unthinkable that capital—structurally linked to and confronted by labor, as the subject of emancipatory transformation and therewith the only historically feasible alternative mode of all-embracing societal control—could hand over its hegemonic power of self-expansionary reproduction to its structural antagonist 'little by little.' Especially since the vital historical stakes—in view of the capital system's deeply entrenched and increasingly more destructive vested interests—have never been greater than they are in our time. This is why the conflicting determinations of historical time are set in such a way that the antagonism between the mutually exclusive *hegemonic alternatives* of capital and labor must be resolved in the form of '*either/or.*' And we have by now a fairly clear view of the fateful implications of their possible "resolution" in favor of capital's unsustainable social metabolic order. No amount of reformist fantasy or deliberate deception could alter or nullify these weighty structural and historical determinations.

Thus, the only viable historical alternative to the incurably *conservative* interests directly emanating from capital's mode of social metabolic control is the *revolutionary* restructuring of the entire social order. The changing political self-definitions of "conservative" and "liberal" are quite irrelevant in this respect. Once upon a time, "liberalism" and "utilitarianism" were promising social change through the 'enlightenment' of the mind of the people to whom they addressed their discourse. In its distant origin, Liberalism itself was part of the movement of the Enlightenment. However, the social reforming intent of the Enlightenment could not be carried forward after the antagonisms latent in the heterogeneous formation of the 'Third Estate' broke out into the open after the French Revolution. As, indeed, they had to break out into the open because of the failure to fulfill pre-revolutionary expectations precisely of the more radical social constituents of the Third Estate.

Inevitably, therefore, the liberal discourse directly addressed to the mind of the enlightened people had to become ever more problematic. For it was—and had to be on account of the class position of the addressees—premised on the *preservation* of the established hierarchical structural relations of capital's social order. Indeed, as the antagonisms continued to sharpen, expecting their solution through individual enlightenment became totally unreal. So much so in fact that we could witness in the second half of the twentieth century the transformation of liberalism into aggressive *neoliberalism* and worse. Today it would be most difficult, if not impossible, to distinguish between the self-professed *"neoliberals"* and the *"neocons,"* especially in the United States. Both of these crass ideological orientations are perfectly happy to go along with the U.S. government's reckless and adventurist strategy of openly threatening the *preemptive use of nuclear weapons* even against non-nuclear powers. And in some ways also in Europe, we have been recently presented, in all seriousness, with the influential idea of imposing on the world a *liberal imperialism,* grotesquely justifying such project on the basis that only that kind of global inter-state relationship could properly match the requirements of the "postmodern" conditions.

We should not forget that the time horizon of *imperialism*—now the open advocacy of verbally palatable "liberal imperialism"—was always regressive, retrograde, and violently reactionary. It was characterized by the ultimately unsustainable attempt to *interfere in a permanent way with historical time.* Only the dominant subjects of great power imperialism alternated among themselves, according to the periodically changing relation of forces—due to the internal dynamics of the comparative development of the principal actors and to the outcome of the immense military confrontations they were periodically engaged in—but not their orientation. Through their military confrontations they were not only attempting to gain relative advantage for themselves but also simultaneously trying to *reverse* the objective trends of historical development pointing toward an ever greater intensification of the internal and international antagonisms and toward the unfolding of the capital system's insuperable structural crisis. Throughout the nearly a century-and-a-half-long history of modern imperialism the principal actors were always characterized by the ruthless adoption of *destructive counter-value*. They ignored or deliberately defied even the most dangerous consequences, without any regard for the necessarily antagonism-generating implications of the two horrendous world wars experienced in the twentieth century.

All this was well in line with capital's deepest class interest to render impossible the self-assertion of the hegemonic alternative to the given social metabolic order. And capital's undoubted successes in this regard were achieved by no means without the revealing complicity of the reformist forces of labor which adopted "the line of least resistance," instead of dedicating themselves to the much more difficult historic task of radically restructuring the established social system. In this sense it was not at all accidental that the organized forces of German social-democratic reformism humiliatingly capitulated to their class adversary right at the outbreak of the First World War, shortly after promising the realization of "evolutionary socialism."

And now the historical stakes are incomparably higher than even in the two world wars. The structural crisis of the capital system is getting deeper, calling for a historically viable solution. But the strategy that expects a solution and the establishment of a stable "new world order" by seriously advocating, and indeed also claiming moral justification for, the use of nuclear weapons against non-nuclear powers, as the spokesmen of global hegemonic imperialism do today, represents the height of insanity, even compared to Hitler.

This is how we have reached a critical stage in human development when the issue is no longer the paradoxical and speculative philosophical closure of history, as we have seen it with reference to Hegel. We are now confronted by the acute danger of the termination of human history altogether; by military means or by global ecological destruction, or indeed by a combination of the two. This is the only way in which capital can actually bring to an end historical time, recklessly in tune with its negation of history ever since the end of the ascending phase of its systemic development.

10.1.4

Labor, as the only feasible social subject of emancipatory transformation, cannot fulfill its mandate without remaining always deeply committed to an *open-ended* conception of history. There can be no compromises and excuses in that respect, in sharp contrast to what we have experienced—coupled with a variety of equally untenable justifications—in the past, from early social-democratic reformism to dogmatic Stalinist voluntarism, and from the Italian Communist Party's utterly defeatist "great historic compromise" to Gorbachev's capitulation to capitalist historical closure.

Being committed to the *radical openness of history* does not mean, of course, that the socialist project of *conscious intervention* in the ongoing historical process can be put on the back burner until more favorable conditions arise and solve our problems. Given the capital system's ever-escalating destructiveness in our time, such wishfully postulated conditions favoring the socialist alternative can never simply "arise." They must be combatively *conquered* and defended against the retrograde forces by labor, as capital's hegemonic antagonist, under the existing undoubtedly difficult conditions, no matter how unfavorable they might appear for the time being.

What is absolutely certain is that capital, as the unyielding controller of the societal reproduction process in its entirety, cannot be willingly amenable even to tactical compromises which, according to historical evidence, it must always break at the first opportune moment if conjuncturally forced into them. Naturally, capital would be even less amenable to the fulfillment of its own share of any postulated *historical* compromise: a most unreal notion. Representatives of the Left who think and act otherwise compromise only themselves. For we are concerned here with a vitally important *mutually exclusive principle*, and not with some marginal *mutual convenience* on the basis of which some compromises are made feasible and legitimate. As Marx forcefully underlined it, already at the time of his *Critique of the Gotha Program*: "there can be *no bargaining about principles*."

The sober acknowledgement of objective constraints does not have to amount to unprincipled capitulation, in contrast to the way in which Gorbachev and his supporters yielded to it under the self-justifying excuse of *perestroika*, without any strategic plan at all for the institution and consolidation of the much needed alternative social order. The radical restructuring of our entire mode of societal reproduction is an absolute must. But such restructuring can succeed only if it is pursued on the basis of firmly maintained principles. Otherwise, the Gorbachev type entrapment in the blind alley of capitalist restoration, legitimated by arbitrarily decreeing "the equality of all types of property"—i.e., in plain English, *the juridical restoration of the rights of capitalist private property*—is the deplorable outcome.

In one of the epigraphs to Part Two of *Beyond Capital*—entitled "Historical Break and Transition in the Marxian Heritage"—I quoted a passage from Goethe's autobiographical work, *Dichtung und Wahrheit*, in order to illustrate an absolutely inescapable historical constraint of our time:

> In Frankfurt, as in most old towns, it had been the practice to gain space in wooden buildings by making not only the first but also the higher stories project over the street, which incidentally made narrow streets, in particular, somber and depressing. Finally a law was passed permitting only the first story of a new house to project over the ground floor, while the upper stories had to keep within the ground floor limits. In order to avoid losing the projecting space in the second story, my father *circumvented this law,* as others had done before him, by shoring up the upper parts of the house, taking away one story after another from the bottom upwards and as it were *slipping in the new structure,* so that although *finally none of the old house was left,* the whole new building could be considered as mere renovation.[8]

The point of this epigraph was to underline that the process of socialist transformation—because it must embrace all aspects of the materially grounded complex interrelationship between *capital, labor,* and the *state*—is conceivable only as a form of transitional *restructuring based on the inherited and progressively alterable leverage of material mediations.* As in the case of Goethe's father, even if for fundamentally different reasons, it is not possible to pull down the building in which we all live and erect a wholly new edifice in its place on totally new foundations. Life must go on in the shored-up house during the entire course of rebuilding, "taking away one story after another from the bottom upwards, slipping in the new structure, so that in the end *none of the old house should be left.*" Indeed, the task is even more difficult than that. For the decaying timber frame of the building must be also replaced in the course of extricating humankind from the perilous structural framework of the capital system.

Thus, there can be "no bargaining" over the envisaged goal of *radical restructuring* without which even the elementary conditions of humanity's survival cannot be secured. The conflicting determinations of time themselves have drawn the line of demarcation in this uncompromising way under the present historical circumstances. They have made imperative the pursuit of the kind of radical restructuring which is capable of constituting both the *destination* of the journey and the necessary *compass* leading to the chosen destination, providing at the same time also the *measure of success* in approaching—or being diverted from—the fundamental socialist objectives decided upon.

The vital condition of success with regard to the socialist open-ended conception of history is the conscious adoption of a fully *comprehensive* strategic orientation. Following the allegedly prudent advice of "little by little," devoid of any idea of how the partial efforts would add up in time, or indeed whether they would add up to anything sustainable at all, would be blind and self-defeating. For it arises from the nature of the objective historical challenge—concerned with the great difficulties of an *all-embracing historical transformation*—that at any particular point in time it is necessary to properly size up what has been already achieved and what obstacles remain to be overcome toward the overall aim of instituting the necessary and also in the long-run sustainable hegemonic alternative to the established mode of social metabolic reproduction.

This is why *planning* in the full sense of the term—that is, not simply directed at some partial aspects of *economic* life but toward the comprehensive demands of societal transformation, embracing the aspirations of the totality of social individuals and enabling them to set meaningful aims to themselves, as *real subjects of their own life-activity*—is so vital at all phases of socialist development. Consciously pursued *comprehensive design* and the *planning* of the realizable social objectives as they arise from the *determinations of the particular social individuals,* rather than imposed on them by some alien authority, are inseparable from one another. The necessary travesty and failure of planning in all forms of the capital system is due to the absence of these two vital conditions.

Once the important condition of sustainable planning is objectively ruled out in the course of actual social development, the possibility of resolving the difficulties inherent in the relationship between the *immediate* and the *long-term* determinations of time are also deeply affected. Capital's short-termism is a well-known characteristic of this mode of societal reproduction. Unfortunately, the pressures of the short-term continue to exercise a disproportionate influence in the period of transition toward the alternative social reproductive order.

To be sure, the immediate, too, has its relative validity and relatively justifiable claim to committed action. Obviously, we ignore this circumstance at our own peril. But one cannot forget—or ignore, let alone deliberately disregard, in the interest of self-justification, as too often happens to be the case—the unavoidably *long-term* timescale of transformations, even when acting under the pressure of *short-term* determinations. For the relative validity of the immediate concerns in question can only be properly assessed within the broader framework of transformation. Even if the temptation to yield to immediate determinations is considerable, it would produce derailment if the immediate concerns prevailed *at the expense* of the strategically more vital long-term aspirations. That would be detrimental to the chosen objective of radical restructuring and thereby to the chances of success of the whole undertaking. Thus, also in this respect, only a consistently pursued comprehensive strategy can show a way out of this very real dilemma.

Another important question of time directly concerns the seminal *orienting principles of socialism.* These orienting principles inevitably involve *different time-scales,* with regards to their conditions of realization, for, understandably, some of the advocated changes are feasible considerably earlier than some others. However, it cannot be emphasized strongly enough, that it is absolutely vital to be conscious of *all of them,* right from the beginning, as necessary to the success of the socialist undertaking in its entirety, and to remain conscious of their ultimate inseparability throughout the process of radical restructuring.

The building we all live in cannot be pulled down. Naturally we know very well that the "personifications of capital"—whether *neocons* or *neoliberals*—are busily engaged in trying to destroy it. It depends on the success or failure of radical restructuring which side of the unavoidably conflicting determinations of historical time will prevail. Any attempt to yield to the perilously retrograde side of capital's personifications in the form of another fictitious "historic compromise" would be as insane as their own active engagement in trying to pull down the building. For only on a firmly socialist basis is a historically viable solution conceivable, fully addressing both the existing antagonisms and the *longest-term* interests of humanity's survival on the basis of the individuals' commitment to creatively sustainable values.

In contrast to irresponsibly short-sighted compromises, only the proper understanding of the broad historical perspective, under the grave conditions of the capital system's deepening *structural crisis,* can provide the framework of *principled cooperation* with the social forces—including the progressive religious forces—which are genuinely interested in finding a way out of the greatest crisis ever experienced by humankind. Even when there are setbacks, as there are very likely to be, our commitment to the positive values of human development is bound to prevail in due course against capital's destructive counter-values. What renders impossible the sustainable solution of the closely intertwined problems of our time within the horizon of the required hegemonic alternative order is not our faithfulness to the socialist principles but any opportunistic deviation from them. To quote a Liberation theologian and a very great poet, Ernesto Cardenal: "I belong to that type of Sandinismo which maintains its *commitment to the principles and the ideals of the revolution.*"[9] That is the only way for a sustainable future. It is, and remains, the necessary condition of success not only of the most fundamental objectives but also of the more limited but lasting achievements.

10.2 Why Capitalist Globalization Cannot Work

As a rule, the question of globalization is discussed in the dominant media of the established order with typical self-complacency. It is simply proclaimed that the glorified "world market" can provide the enduring answers to our fundamental global problems both on the economic and on the political plane. Thus, the Governor of the Bank of England, Mervyn King, writes with understandable class-conscious solidarity in praise of a book written by the associate editor of London's *The Financial Times:*[10] "Wolf provides not just a devastating intellectual critique of the opponents of globalization, but a civilized, wise and optimistic view of our economic and political future. It is vital that his message be widely read and understood." And the laudatory judgment on the same book by Lawrence H. Summers, President of Harvard University, is written in the same spirit, asserting: "Wolf's book will be the definitive statement of the case for market-based globalization."

The real issue of *capitalist* globalization is thus wantonly misrepresented as plain "globalization," or just as misleadingly as plain "market-based globalization." Much like in Gorbachev's years of tenure, when the real problem of Soviet capitulation to capitalist restoration was camouflaged as simply the introduction of the "market mechanism" and the happy adoption of "market efficiency," in the same way we are now supposed to lull ourselves into believing that "the market," once it becomes fully "globalized," will forever do away with the deep-seated antagonisms and ultimately explosive inequalities of capital's established order. Even if it was by no means capable of doing anything of the kind—rather the opposite—in its former permutations. It is, therefore, necessary to consider first the real nature and prospects of the capital system before having a closer look at the kind of "civilized, wise, and optimistic" transfiguration of actual developments which we find in Wolf's highly promoted "vital message" and "definitive statement."

In truth the question is not "globalization or no globalization," just as our problem is not the same kind of false dichotomy of "growth or no growth" which we are regularly presented with in the bourgeois financial press. Rather, our real concern is *what kind* of the posited alternatives regarding global integrative development and growth are pursued in a historically sustainable way. As a matter of fact, more than a century before the propagandists of capitalist globalization were even born, Marx was already anticipating the *inexorable trend* of capital's development toward the system's *global integration.* But he was doing that not only well before anybody else but also *critically,* as indeed it should be done in relation to a matter of such magnitude and potentially catastrophic impact. Marx approached the subject in sharp contrast to the contemporary apologists of *capitalist* "globalization" who fashionably postulate the happy global outcome without even sizing up, let alone indicating a way out of the worsening maze of antagonisms and contradictions of our existing order. *Capitalist* globalization as we experience it is decidedly *not working* and *cannot work* for the overwhelming majority of humanity, even if it greatly favors the dominant economic and political forces and thereby intensifies the underlying contradictions. This is the real issue that must be addressed sooner or later in a tangible way.

10.2.1

The ruling ideology maintains its grip over popular consciousness by successfully preaching the timeless validity of the established order. In this view only small marginal changes are required by this system, to be accommodated well within its ahistorical and forever adequate structural framework of societal reproduction.

Everything is totally reversed in this discourse. It not only distorts the truth but also offers for general consumption its exact opposite. For notwithstanding all self-justifying mystification that attempts to represent capital as a *natural* and *eternal* system, we are in actuality talking about a *historically limited and uniquely time-bound* mode of social metabolic reproduction. This happens to be the case for three principal reasons:

1. The imperative of *growth* as the *self-expansion of capital*, whatever the consequences. In other words, the unrestricted pursuit of capital-accumulation, no matter how damaging, and even utterly destructive, might be the necessary consequences.

2. Capital's tendency toward *global integration* on the *economic plane* is sharply contradicted by the necessary implications of that trend on the *political plane*, due to the system's permanent *modus operandi* in the form of *domination and subordination* in all respects, including the necessary subjugation of the weaker *nation states* by the stronger ones under the rule of modern imperialism. The ultimate—and utterly mad—logic of this development is that one "superpower" submits to itself *all* of the others, in the vain hope of asserting its own unchallengeable domination as *the state of the capital system in general.*

3. The vicious circle of *competition and monopoly*, prevailing in the ultimately untenable sense of competition generating monopoly, and at the same time monopoly (generated in this uncontrollable way) bringing with it ever fiercer and ever more destructive competition, in an unstoppable process of reciprocal determinations.

In all three respects, we are concerned with the capital system's unsurpassable *self-contradictory inner determinations* that have become *fully activated and intensified* in our own time. This is what confers *extreme urgency* on these matters, calling for the *imperative of radical interventions* in order to overcome the destructive trends.

It is important to stress here that the historical viability of capital is seriously affected, in the negative sense, not only by the system's *absolute limits* but also by its total inability to admit the existence of *any limit.* The absolute limits are in evidence with regard to the following considerations:

1. The *time-horizon* of the system is necessarily *short-term.* It cannot be other than that in view of the derailing pressures of competition and monopoly and the ensuing ways of imposing domination and subordination, in the interest of *immediate* gain.

2. This time-horizon is also *post festum* in character, capable of adopting corrective measures only after the damage has been done; and even such corrective measures can only be introduced in a most limited form.

As a result of the two considerations just mentioned, the system is incompatible with *planning* in any other than the most myopic sense of the term. This is so even when we consider the giant, quasi-monopolistic transnational enterprises. Even the biggest corporations can only institute some *limited post festum* planning in their *particular* enterprises (if that), and they are unable to control on their own the *global market* of their operation, except in an extremely limited conflictual, and adversarial way. The importance of this systemic limitation cannot be overstated, especially under the historical circumstances of the now-observable tendency toward global economic integration, wedded to its fateful contradictions, when the need for a workable form of *comprehensive planning* would be absolutely vital.

The relationship between *cause and effect* is structurally vitiated in the capital system. This is because capital's innermost causal determinations can never be put under serious critical scrutiny. In other words, this system relentlessly drives itself forward, unquestioningly and absolutely unquestionably, as *causa sui.* Consequently, capital is structurally incapable of addressing historically arising *causes as causes.* It must operate, even in its most serious attempts to introduce some corrective *post festum* measures, in the form of responding to (good or bad) *effects* by piling up *effects upon other effects,* as a rule in the form of repeatedly problem-generating *counter-effects,* in tune with the constraints of the established order's extremely short-term time-horizon. Accordingly, what is frequently and wrongly described as redressable *"manipulation"* is in actuality not a more or less easily corrigible *contingent* feature of the capital system. It is one of its *fundamental* determinations that could only be remedied by adopting a radically different way of relating to *causes as structurally significant causes*, instead of dealing with them as more or less *arbitrarily treatable effects*. For this alternative solution, however, it would be necessary to overcome the structural constraints of capital by transcending them toward a higher social metabolic order of production and reproduction. After all, the meaning of *structural imperatives* is precisely that it is impossible to significantly alter them without envisaging a *qualitatively different structural framework*. In our case, one free from the necessary destructive constraints of the established order. By contrast, conceptualizing the world from capital's vantage point remains an insurmountable drawback even for the greatest thinkers who identify themselves with capital's standpoint.

The final point to mention is the wanton eternalizing of a historically specific, indeed unique, order of social metabolic control, as not only not subject to well identifiable *temporal determinations* but also as itself standing *above history* and capable of playing the role of the final arbiter *over history*. In the course of capitalistic developments, even the partial acknowledgement of the historical dimension by the great thinkers who conceptualized the world from the standpoint of capital had to be left behind in favor of the unreserved liquidation of historical time consciousness, as we have seen it earlier.

The uniqueness of the capital system is manifest in the structural imperative to *"grow inexorably or perish."* No other system of social metabolic reproduction in the whole of human history had even remotely resembled this inner determination of capital. This structural determination also reveals the complete self-serving fallacy of misrepresenting capital's reproductive order as the insurmountable *universal rule*, arbitrarily projected backwards into long-past history and forwards into an eternalized capitalist future. An arbitrarily decreed universal rule to which, in the well-known slogan of the system's apologists, *"there can be no alternative."*

What makes this whole development extremely problematic is the fact that the primary determinations of the capital system are oriented, in a perversely upside-down way, toward the *self-expansion of capital*, and only coincidentally toward the growth of use-values corresponding to genuine human need. This is why a dynamic characteristic that at an earlier phase of capital's historical unfolding represents a *positive* advancement, in as much as it goes at that time hand in hand with the satisfaction of legitimate human need, in our own times turns into a potentially most destructive determination. For the contradictory interest of capital's self-expansionary drive must prevail at all cost and under all circumstances, even when the profitable use-values produced by that drive are the infernal war material of the military-industrial complex (whose only "use-value" is destruction), capable of exterminating the whole of humanity with the *real* weapons of mass destruction of global hegemonic imperialism.

The same overturning of an erstwhile positive characteristic is in evidence in the course of capitalistic developments also as regards *competition*, marked by the ever-more-dominant role assumed by *monopoly*, as a result of the increasingly more negative inter-determinations of a historically unique system. Since the vicious circle of competition tending to monopoly, and monopoly resulting in ever fiercer competition, cannot be broken, the necessary outcome is the increasing concentration and centralization of capital and the constitution of more and more powerful enterprises—the giant transnational corporations—which dominate the stage, without the slightest decrease in their appetite for gobbling up their competitors. Thus, growth, as the self-expansion of capital, becomes the overpowering *end in itself,* excluding all consideration of the inherent worth of the adopted targets in relation to genuine human objectives. The total absence of a proper human measure for assessing the long-term viability of the production and reproduction process, and its replacement by capital-accumulation as the all-dominating end in itself, opens the door dangerously wide to the inexorable advancement of cancerous *growth*, pursued in the interest of profitable expansion and the promise of further advantage in the contest for quasi-monopolistic domination.

The destructive consequences of this perverse logic are twofold. First, on the economic plane the imperative of growth, which must be pursued even when it takes the form of *cancerous growth*, leads to a complete disregard for safeguarding the elementary conditions of human existence. This is manifest in the widespread productive practices directly endangering even the *natural substratum* of human life in the long run: a grave concern usually expressed with reference to *environmental destruction*.[11] This is an *absolute condition* of sustainable social reproduction, although its callous disregard, fully in tune with the *incurably short-term time horizon* of the capital system, denies it with the most grotesque arguments of evasion and rationalization wedded to the corresponding dangerous practical measures.[12]

The second vital aspect of cancerous growth subordinated to the ultimately destructive imperative of uncontrollable capital-expansion, and the concomitant vicious circle of monopoly and competition, is in evidence on the political and military plane. For the drive toward monopolistic domination can never fully succeed in its global aspirations. Even the most powerful transnational corporations cannot achieve more than a *quasi*-monopolistic, and not an all-embracing monopolistic, position in the global order.

This is, of course, no cause for confidence and rejoicing. The dangerous destructive dimension of the trend itself is not diminished by such a limitation. The limitation in question only means that the struggle for global domination must intensify, in line with the relative success of the giant transnsational enterprises in their own countries and on the international stage. Consequently the *states* of the imperialistically dominant countries must *directly* enter the picture, sustaining by all means at their disposal their giant *national*/transnational enterprises in their confrontations with their rivals. Thus, the question of the "military-industrial complex" is not confined to the immensely wasteful determinations of militaristic *production*. It also assumes a *direct military and political* form, as the vicissitudes of imperialism in the twentieth century—and in accord with the now prevailing trend even more dangerously in the twenty-first century—demonstrate. The new phase of *global hegemonic imperialism*, with the United States as its overwhelmingly dominant force,[13] indicates a frightening intensification of the dangers. Not simply as a matter of contingent and alterable "big power politics" but, much more importantly, as the manifestation of a fundamental *systemic* determination at the present phase of capital's historical development, requiring urgent attention on the proper plane.

Naturally, all these tendencies are closely intertwined in the innermost determinations of a historically unique system. The convenient denial of their historical character finds its explanation in the desire to perpetuate the overpowering exploitative interests of the ruling order which can be readily rationalized through the postulates of the "one and only viable" reproductive system's *eternalization*. However, the uncomfortable truth is that capital is quite incapable of acknowledging its own limits even when the question that must be addressed is how to remedy in a humanly sustainable way the fateful contradictions and dangers of its uncontrollable growth.

Such a consideration is quite inadmissible because the relationship to growth constitutes the system's ultimate vicious circle. For capital *drives forward* growth, in an absolutized and uncontrollable way, and at the same time is *driven by* growth at all cost, as the condition of its own—ultimately totally untenable—survival.

Today the system's apologists either wantonly deny that there can be any serious problem due to the prevailing modality of growth which would call for rational constraints, or engage in the conservative fantasies about "The Limits to Growth." In the latter case, they take capital's pernicious determinations for granted and quixotically offer as a "remedy" the imposition of an even more iniquitous social order than the present one.

It is impossible to find viable solutions to any of the problems we encounter on capital's terrain without full awareness of the system's historical determinations and corresponding structural constraints, in contrast to all theories aimed at eternalizing even its most problematical and indeed destructive features. It is also important to bear in mind that the historical determinateness of this mode of social metabolic reproduction is simultaneously both *epochal*—in the sense of embracing its centuries long timespan in its entirety—and characteristic of a *particular phase* of its development. The two can be quite different not in an absolute sense but precisely in their significance for the kind of action that must be undertaken in attempting to confront with any chance of success the identified problems themselves.

To take one crucial example, the pursuit of ultimately uncontrollable *growth* was *always* a fundamental characteristic of capital, as a matter of innermost systemic determination. Without it this unique mode of social metabolic control could not have conquered the historical stage the way in which it actually did. Moreover, the intensely *problematic* character of growth oriented toward capital-accumulation was not a more-or-less accidental addition later on. It was from the system's inception inseparable from the nature of capital as the most dynamic way of controlling the social metabolic order of reproduction known to human beings in history up to the maturation of this system, culminating at the point in time when it reached the end of its ascending phase of development.

And that is where the second, more specific dimension of capital's historical temporality becomes acutely relevant. For the *same systemic characteristic* of inexorable growth, deeply embedded in the very nature of capital from the moment of its constitution, through the alienation and expropriation of labor as an increasingly all-embracing control system, turns at a certain *phase* of capital's historical development into a potentially most devastating determination.

It is the historical specificity of this threatening present historical phase that imposes upon us the task of a radical reassessment of the question of growth. Not in the sense of the self-serving pseudo-alternative of "growth or no growth," which would leave the monstrous iniquities of our social world intact, or make them even worse than ever before. Growth must be reassessed by successfully mobilizing the material and human resources of a radical mass movement for practically reorienting our production practices for the realization of much needed socially legitimate objectives. This is inconceivable without bringing under rational control the destructive forces inseparable from the now-prevailing modalities of capital's uncontrollable growth.

10.2.2

The successful conquest of the planet by capital was *primarily* due to its *internal dynamics*, even if the militaristic advantage of some dominant countries—especially England and France—played a significant additional role during the first, *early modern colonial empire building stage*, of imperialism. What secured capital's global penetration and far-reaching impact on the conquered territories on a lasting basis was precisely the incomparable transformative dynamic of the system. For it was transferable in a characteristically altered but still dynamic form—as *structurally subordinated* but *internally expandable* economic corollaries of the "mother" or "metropolitan" countries—to the colonially conquered areas. This kind of dynamic, the primary source of capital's lasting success, was in sharp contrast to earlier military conquests which sooner or later had to run out of steam, in the absence of such power. It also meant that the wasteful cost of militarily controlling the colonial territories could be incomparably smaller in relative terms under the rule of capital than in former colonial empires, since some of the fundamental control functions were most effectively fulfilled for a very long time by the capital system's appropriately transplanted "invisible hand."

The principal source of capital's global advancement was the major difference between capital's *material command structure* and its *political command structure*, with the forcefully prevailing *primacy of the first* throughout the *ascending* phase of the system's development. This is why Adam Smith could eloquently insist on the need to keep politicians (and the state) out of the affairs of economic development. However, after the conclusion of the ascending phase, matters have become much more complicated, necessitating the ever-more-direct involvement of the capitalist state in promoting the imperialist aspirations of the dominant countries, during the second, *redistributive stage*, of imperialism,[14] antagonistically contested by a number of major powers on behalf of their quasi-monopolistic corporations even in the form of massively destructive world wars. Naturally, the third stage of imperialism, characteristic of our own time—namely *global hegemonic imperialism*, with the United States as its overwhelmingly dominant force—is not only most problematical but totally untenable, in view of the *suicidal* dangers with which it is heavily overburdened.[15]

The separate but closely interconnected dual command structure of capital represented a great advantage for a long time in the global unfolding and consolidation of the capital system. The internalized adoption of capital's material command structure in colonial territories carried with it a condition beneficial to further expansion on a global scale. Namely that some of the most important social metabolic control functions did not have to be imposed by the force of arms of a *hostile foreign political and military power* but could emerge (with some prodding and political and military intervention, of course) from the native material ground. Naturally, this kind of development was possible because the indigenous ruling classes played a most active self-interested role in the internal social metabolic process of transformation.

However, the end of capital's historical ascendancy made it necessary for the all-embracing political command structure of the system to assume an ever-greater role. At the same time, the capitalist state could not really fulfill such a role without an increasingly more wasteful use of violence. In the colonially dominated countries, too, this regressive determination resulted in the articulation of anti-colonial political movements, most significantly among them in the most pop-

ulous country of India. And even though the indigenous ruling classes—including those of India—were very far from attempting to institute a *systemic change* in the postwar period of "neo-imperialism," nevertheless they introduced some ultimately insoluble complications
into the global functioning of the capital system. The fact that the most
reactionary capitalist forces in our time are more or less openly pressing for the *recolonization of the world*—hypocritically thundering
against "ethnic pandemonium," the "axis of evil," "failed states,"[16] or
whatever else, when they are singing the praises of their allegedly
"enlightened" future variety of *liberal imperialism*—can only underline this point.

Inevitably, with the end of capital's historical ascendancy, the
contradictions and antagonisms of the whole system—both in the
dominant "metropolitan" countries and in the colonial territories—
are sharpened, calling for the *reversal* of the original pattern of expansionary development. For in the ascending phase—from the time of
Henry VIII to the beginning of the nineteenth century—the role of
direct political intervention shows a *diminishing trend,* whereas after
the end of the ascending phase an *ever increasing trend.* This type of
development reaches the point of the most aggressive management of
global imperialist wars on the *international* plane, and the increasingly
more extreme *state bureaucratic control* of matters on the *internal*
plane. Thus, the "invisible hand" is unceremoniously pensioned off
and only its cynically used myth is perpetuated by the ruling ideology
for the purposes of mystification, in contrast to Adam Smith who really believed in the insuperable power of the "invisible hand."

Under the new circumstances, the separate material command
structure of capital could no longer offer sufficient scope to the ruling
classes of the colonially dominated countries for their further economic development and its relatively autonomous control. This was so
because the savage new international competition for exclusive military conquest and direct control of the colonial territories firmly ruled
that out already during the second, redistributive stage of imperialism.
In this way, the *inter-state antagonisms* always latent in the capital system were fully activated and intensified, becoming clearly insoluble
despite the dominant states' most irresponsible engagement in
extreme military adventures, like the two world wars of the twentieth
century. Naturally, this contradiction became even more acute under
the conditions of global hegemonic imperialism when the *naked recol-*

onization of the world reappeared on the agenda, with the added complication that such designs could not simply be imposed by the available military means on the rest of the world in view of the absolutely suicidal nature of a potential third global war.

This is where capital's inability to *create the state of the capital system as such* asserts its insuperable limit. One hundred and fifty years of modern imperialism could achieve nothing whatsoever even to diminish the capital system's inter-state antagonisms, not to mention their wishfully and apologetically propagandized complete elimination. On the contrary, they could only intensify them, to the point that ever greater military confrontations were actually needed in order to come to terms with them on a strictly temporary basis.

A typical propagandistic misrepresentation of this problem is offered in Martin Wolf's book—praised to the sky by those who have the same vested interests as the author of *Why Globalization Works?* They praise it not only as "a civilized, wise and optimistic view of our economic and political future" but even as "a definitive analysis."[17] For Wolf offers this kind of obligingly "optimistic" explanation of ongoing developments: "all the great powers have abandoned the *atavistic notion* that prosperity derives from territorial gains and plunder rather than internal economic development and peaceful exchange. One of the striking features of today's war against terrorism is that all the world's *great powers* are on the same side."[18]

Thus, we are expected to believe that imperialism existed because some great powers were once captive of an *"atavistic notion"* which has been now happily consigned forever to the past because they have been converted to the idea of "internal economic development and peaceful exchange." And the proof of this "civilized, wise and optimistic definitive analysis" is the ridiculous *non sequitur* that the world's great powers find themselves on the same side in the 'war against terrorism.' This is a conclusion worthy of the 'atavistic notion' hypothesis. Thanks to such 'definitive analysis,' from now on we can live happily ever after, undisturbed even by the shadow of a thought concerning imperialist rivalry and the exploitative domination of the weaker countries. But what about the weaker countries—Wolf's imperialistically subservient saga only speaks of "the world's great powers!"

The uncomfortable truth of the matter is that capitalist globalization could not possibly work unless it succeeded in *creating the state of the capital system as such*. But in order to do that it would be necessary to radically overcome the contradictions and antagonisms at the roots of the destructive history of imperialist development. Yet, the inner *systemic* contradictions—and the concomitant unavoidable inter-state antagonisms—assert themselves forcefully even as things stand now. Moreover, they are gravely complicated by the circumstance that the insurmountable material limitation regarding the *finiteness* of our *planetary resources*—which was only *latent* in the more remote past— is now becoming not only blatantly obvious, even when irresponsibly denied and ignored by the most powerful states, above all by the United States, but ever more *acute*. Accordingly, we must now soberly reckon with a formerly even unimaginable potential *intensification* of the imperialist antagonisms, instead of wishfully consigning them to the past. For this time the issue is not only the rivalry concerning the colonial domination of some weaker countries but simultaneously also the *capitalistically insoluble* and potentially catastrophic competition over our finite planetary resources.

In order to persuade us to shut our eyes to the disturbing trends of contemporary development, the apologists of imperialism offer misdiagnoses and totally unreal solutions. Not surprisingly, therefore, Wolf argues in this way:

> Let us consider the biggest obstacle to a more even spread of global prosperity and the provision of essential global public goods. That obstacle is neither global economic integration nor transnational companies, as the critics allege, but the *multiplicity of independent sovereigns.*[19]

Wolf adds for good measure that "far and away the most important source of inequality and persistent poverty is: the fact that humanity is *locked into almost 200 distinct countries.*"[20] Obsessively, Wolf insists that the "principal explanation" of our problems "is the *world's political fragmentation.*"[21] True to form, therefore, he pronounces against the only positive potentiality of the WTO, demonstrated in Cancun, by saying that it "brings into the negotiations a *large number of small countries* with negligible impact on world trade and gives them *disproportionate power.*"[22]

Naturally, Wolf is in favor of the concentration of real decision-making power in the hands of "the world's great powers," as we have seen earlier. To justify such view he does not hesitate to deny even the obvious—namely that the big transnational corporations, predominantly under the control of the United States, are *national* companies—"proving" his obfuscating propagandist declaration with the help of another priceless *non sequitur.* "In most modern industries— including services—the largest companies are *not national.* Is a Toyota factory in the United States any less-or-more American than a General Motors factory in China?[23] The real answer is, of course, that the question makes no sense at all because Toyota factories are everywhere *national/*transnational *Japanese,* just like General Motors factories are *national/*transnational *American,* wherever they might be located, including China.

The climax of Wolf's propagandistic reasoning in favor of the "never again atavistic great world powers" is equally revealing. This is how it goes:

> If we ask further what would be the most powerful mechanism for ensuring that the forces of economic convergence overwhelm those of divergence, the answer has to be *jurisdictional integration.* . . . if the commitment to protecting prosperity and allowing capital to move freely were credible everywhere, the movement of capital to poor countries would greatly increase. Again, if people could move freely from poor and failing countries to richer ones, global inequality and extreme poverty would certainly fall substantially.[24]

Thus, "jurisdictional integration"—i.e., the firm imperialist state control of the entire world by a handful of great powers—is the decreed solution to our ever-aggravating problems and antagonisms. And the miraculous remedies do not even end there. For this is how the passage just quoted continues:

> We can go even further. *Imagine jurisdictional integration* not just in the sense of the contemporary EU, but in the sense of a contemporary federal state, say, the United States. Imagine that the United States was not one of the world's countries, but had become a *global federation offering equal voting rights for all.* Far greater resources would then flow to the poorer regions of this imaginary world—including United States, to finance infrastructure, education, health and the machinery of law and order. That should not be surprising. We know very well that money is spent by a country on those *with a political voice.*

But why should we not imagine on top of all of these imaginary achievements also the generous fall of *manna from heaven?* For that would perhaps solve even the one still remaining problem. Namely, that notwithstanding Wolf's totally unfounded assertion, the actually existing "equal voting rights" are very far from being able to secure a proper *"political voice"* to the voters in our liberal democracies, even if they are supposed to deliver the listed free-flowing benefits according to the author. Many millions of British pensioners, for instance, who have the same political voting rights as the other British citizens, have been trying for decades to obtain parity for their annual pension increases in line with what is conceded to average wages. But they have encountered the firmest rejection of their demand by the capitalist governments of the country, Conservative or Labour (and not only New Labour).

In Wolf's world, every difficulty is to be overcome by the virtues of a fictitiously equitable—in reality imperialistically dominated— *world market,* in sharp dismissal of its critique. Thus, we are told: "The critique allows protectionists to claim that they benefit the poor of the world as they deprive them of the opportunity to earn their living in *world markets.*"[25] The fact that the overwhelming majority of humankind failed to earn a decent living for centuries in the really existing world market is of no interest to Wolf. All that matters is that we should agree with Wolf's jurisdictionally improved "civilized, wise, and optimist view" according to which the ongoing process of capitalist globalization works to the benefit of all. In case some people continue to maintain doubts to the contrary, they are sledgehammered by Wolf with the ultimate, apparently irrefutable, argument in the last paragraph of the book, thundering against "the return of all the old anti-capitalist clichés *as if the collapse of Soviet communism had never happened.*"[26] Obviously, Martin Wolf never paid the slightest attention to the long-standing and deeply committed *socialist critique* of Soviet-type development.

In reality Wolf's 'vital message' and 'definitive analysis' is a transparent propaganda exercise fully in tune with the most retrograde vested interests. Kenneth Rogoff's wholesome endorsement of his book on its back cover illustrates also the contrast with Joseph Stiglitz, former chairman of President Clinton's Council of Economic Advisers and former Chief Economist at the World Bank. But how far can we go along with Stiglitz's undoubtedly less starry-eyed view of globalization, indicated by his book's title?

To be sure, in *Globalization and its Discontents* there are several partial criticisms of the negatively interfering economic and political control mechanisms of present-day globalization that we can share with the author, especially Joseph Stiglitz's account of the International Monetary Fund's role. Similarly in his subsequent book, *The Roaring Nineties,* his critique of the fraudulent behavior of some giant transnational corporations is firm and clear. However, as befits Bill Clinton's principal economic advisor, his approach remains always tied to the presuppositions and conclusions of capitalist globalization, even if he would like to have the process implemented "with a more human face." Thus, in the end his critique culminates in rhetoric—perhaps well-meaning rhetoric—instead of tangible proposals for materially and structurally secured significant change. We can see both the well-meaning rhetoric and the obvious limitations of Stiglitz's approach in a typical passage of his book advocating "democratic globalization":

> But *democratic globalization* means that these decisions must be made with the full participation of *all the peoples of the world.* Our system of global governance without global government can only work *if* there is an acceptance of *multilateralism.* Unfortunately, the past year has seen an increase in *unilateralism* by the government of the world's richest and most powerful country. *If* globalization is to work, this too *must change.*[27]

As we can see, Stiglitz's advocacy is built on "ifs" and "musts," but no indication whatsoever of "how" the desired objectives could be reached. It is no use to talk about *"democratic globalization"* unless the manner in which an alternative to the ongoing—ruthlessly authoritarian and imperialistically dominated—process of globalization could be actually achieved is substantively analyzed. Unfortunately, but by no means surprisingly, in Stiglitz's account the *word* "democratic" is supposed to be able to solve the problem, removing the need for explaining the difficult question of "how" the desired objectives are to be reached.

We find the same well-meaning rhetoric and at the same time avoidance of the difficult substantive issues in Stiglitz's *The Roaring Nineties,* whose subtitle is "Why We're Paying the Price for the Greediest Decade in History." Again there is no shortage of good intentions. But this is what they all amount to:

> *Perhaps* the next American administration will avoid the pitfalls into which America has fallen. *Perhaps* the next administration will have more success in addressing the long-term needs of America and the world. At the very least,

> *perhaps* citizens in the rest of the world will be more wary about succumbing to the myths that have guided so much thinking about economic policy over recent years. *Perhaps* together, America and Europe, and the developed and the developing world, can forge a *new form of global democracy,* and a new set of economic policies—policies which will ensure a *new-found prosperity* which will be shared by *all the citizens of the world.*[28]

Thus, we are offered the unfounded hope of "perhaps" not once but four times, but with absolutely nothing to back it up. This is why the projection of a "new form of global democracy" (did we have an old form of global democracy, ever?) which is supposed to "ensure a new-found prosperity" for "all the citizens of the world" remains nothing more than a pious desideratum, in the total absence of any analysis of what could turn it into reality. Stiglitz is *never* willing to consider, let alone combatively confront, the massive *structural impediments* that militate against the realization of the necessary and historically viable alternatives. Fundamentally important structural determinations of the ruling order are *systematically avoided.* Stiglitz never criticizes the *capitalist nature and framework* of the ongoing globalization. He is only concerned with its "management," expecting the remedy from rectifying the criticized "mismanagement" by a more enlightened and less "greedy" form of capitalist management, of his own kind, without any need whatsoever for some *structural change* in the established social order.

Understandably, therefore, Stiglitz's policy recommendations are rather anemic, to put it mildly. He writes in his general assessment of *The Roaring Nineties*:

> If there is a single, simple message to this book it is this: there needs to be a *balance* between the role of *government and the market.* A country can suffer from underregulation just as it can from overregulation, from too little public investment just as it can from too much public expenditure; the government can help stabilize the economy—but badly designed policies can make fluctuations worse. . . . This broader understanding means that *countries should feel greater freedom in their choice of economic policies.*[29]

We often hear that a proper *balance* should be made between the role of the government and the market, but this is advocated in vain. For the underlying *causal determinations* and weighty *structural impediments* tending to act against it are as a rule ignored.

However, even if the items enumerated on Stiglitz's list are "balanced," as he says that we should balance them, how would that solve any of the grave structural problems of our world in the slightest, not to mention the creation of "a *new-found prosperity* shared by *all the citizens of the world*"? And what should we make of Stiglitz's ultimate policy recommendation that "*countries should feel greater freedom in their choice of economic policies*"? What if they do, but *systematically fail* to turn that feeling into reality, due to the massive *structural impediments* of the capital system that simply do not exist in Stiglitz's books? He is often praised as the 'supreme insider,' which he certainly is. The trouble is, though, that despite Stiglitz's good intentions his insider position makes him captive of the—ultimately most dubious—vantage point of the structurally entrenched but historically untenable "inside."

Our problem is not the need for globalization, which is undeniable, but the systematic failure of capitalist globalization due to the destructive antagonisms generated and intensified under the existing order. For even at the most favorable point of capital's historical ascendancy this mode of social metabolic reproduction—as a result of its innermost adversarial structural determinations that no "caring capitalist management" could alter—necessarily failed to introduce in global terms a minimally tolerable level of equality. Now even the apologist Wolf must concede that if the current trends are maintained, "not only the absolute difference in standards of living but even relative gaps in living standards will continue to grow between the richest and the poorest countries in the world. Today, that ratio is some *seventy-five to one*. A century ago, it was about *ten to one*. In half a century, it could all too easily be *one hundred and fifty to one*."[30]

Thus, the real problem is human *emancipation* and the necessary conditions of its realization, and not "market-based globalization." To expect the solution of our burning issues of structurally entrenched exploitation and class domination from the supposedly all-round beneficial *world market* was always absurd, if not a bare-faced cynical lie. No reality ever corresponded to it because—far from being even-handed—the world market was *imperialistically dominated* from the time of its inception and has remained so ever since. It was constituted from the very beginning as a set of most iniquitous *power relations,* working always to the advantage of the stronger to maintain the ruthless control—if need be even the most brutal military repression—of the weaker parties.

In the past, many problems could be postponed through relatively undisturbed productive *capital accumulation,* even if characteristically inflated by the ruling ideology through promising an "ever growing cake for all" in the future. In our time, however, under the conditions of the capital system's *structural crisis,* we must face also the profound crisis of capital accumulation. It deeply affects even the most powerful capitalist country, the United States, with far-reaching implications for the rest of the world. This crisis of capital accumulation carries with it everywhere the dominance of the most parasitic form of *finance capital,* busily engaged in building dream castles in quicksand with its pretences to sound globalization. Nor should we forget the fundamental need for rationally managed *genuine economy* arising from the limitations of our finite planet, as set against the irresponsible wastefulness of capital's long-established husbandry. Moreover, the destructive inner determinations of global hegemonic imperialism greatly aggravate these problems, offering to the overwhelmingly dominant single hegemon the self-deluding "ultimate solution" not only in terms of endless capital accumulation but also of grabbing the lion's share of planetary resources through the use of extreme military violence, even if doing so foreshadows the total destruction of humankind. Bearing in mind all these problems gives a good idea of the magnitude of the historic task.

Capitalist globalization never worked and never could work in a sustainable way. The only *viable hegemonic alternative* to it would have to be a radically different socioeconomic and political order; one that would have to be based on a very different relationship to nature itself, with qualitatively different demands for energy and prime material resources as well as to agricultural needs; one fully respectful of the objective requirements of the historically sustainable reproduction process in our planetary household. This order could prevail only if instituted and maintained on the basis of *substantively equitable* relationships both *internally*—by putting an end to adversarial class relations and thereby releasing immense, now completely wasted, human resources—and *internationally,* with regard to the adoption of genuinely *cooperative inter-state relations.* But the institution of any one of the defining characteristics of such an order is inconceivable within the incurably exploitative framework of capitalist globalization, even if imaginarily freed from its "managerial discontents."

10.3 The Structural Crisis of Politics[31]

10.3.1 Symptoms of a Fundamental Crisis

It is necessary to underline here the very disquieting—indeed world-wide threatening—developments in the field of politics and the law. I wish to mention that it was no less than twenty-three years ago that I became personally acquainted in Paraiba, Brazil with the painful circumstances of explosive food riots. Twenty years later, at the time of President Lula's electoral campaign, I read that he had announced that the most important part of his future strategy was his determination to put an end in the country to the grave social evil of famine. The two intervening decades, from the time of those dramatic food riots in Paraiba, were obviously not sufficient to solve this chronic problem. And even today, I am told, the improvements are still very modest in Brazil. Moreover, the somber statistics of the United Nations constantly put into relief that the same problem persists, with devastating consequences, in many parts of the world. This is so despite the fact that the productive powers at the disposal of humankind today could relegate forever to the past the now totally unforgivable social failure of famine and malnutrition.

It might be tempting to attribute these difficulties, as frequently happens in traditional political discourse, to more or less easily corrigible political contingencies, postulating thereby the remedy through changes in personnel at the next suitable and strictly orderly electoral opportunity. But that would be a customary evasion and not a plausible explanation, for the stubborn persistence of the problems at stake, with all of their painful human consequences, point to much more deeply rooted connections. They indicate some apparently uncontrollable force of inertia which seems to be able to turn, with depressing frequency, even the good intentions of promising political manifestoes into the paving stones of the road to hell, in Dante's immortal words. Thus, the challenge is to face up to the underlying causes and structural determinations which tend to derail by the force of inertia many political programs devised for corrective intervention, even when it is originally admitted by the authors of such programs that the existing state of affairs is unsustainable.

Let us consider a few striking examples which clearly demonstrate that there is something dangerously affecting the way in which we regulate our societal interchanges and that the observable trend is the intensification of the dangers toward the point of no return.

At a public lecture delivered in Athens in October 1999, I remarked: "In all probability the ultimate form of threatening the adversary in the future—the new 'gunboat diplomacy,' exercised from the 'patented air'—will be nuclear blackmail. But its objective would be analogous to those of the past, while its envisaged modality could only underline the absurd untenability of trying to impose capital's ultimate rationality on the recalcitrant parts of the world in that way."[32] In the six years since this lecture, such potentially lethal policy-making practices of global hegemonic imperialism have become not only a general possibility but also an integral part of the openly admitted neoconservative "strategic conception" of the U.S. government. And the situation is even worse today. In the last few weeks, in relation to Iran,[33] we have entered the actual planning stage of a course of action which could threaten not only Iran itself but the whole of humanity with a nuclear disaster. The customary cynical device employed in making public such threats is "neither to confirm, nor to deny them." But no one should be fooled by that kind of ploy. In fact, this recently materialized very real danger of nuclear disaster is what induced a group of distinguished American physicists, among them five Nobel Laureates, to write an open letter of protest to President Bush in which they stated: "It is gravely irresponsible for the United States as the greatest superpower to consider courses of action that could eventually lead to the widespread destruction of life on the planet. We urge the administration to announce publicly that it is taking the nuclear option off the table in the case of all non-nuclear adversaries, present or future, and we urge the American people to make their voices heard on this matter."[34]

Are the legitimate political institutions of our societies in a position to redress even the most perilous situations by democratic intervention in the process of actual decision making, as traditional political discourse keeps reassuring us, despite all evidence to the contrary? Only the most optimistic—and rather naïve—could assert and sincerely believe that such a happy state of affairs happens to be the case. For the principal Western powers have, quite unimpeded, embarked in the last few years on devastating wars by using authoritarian devices—like the "executive prerogative" and the "Royal Prerogative"[35]—without consulting their peoples on such grave matters, and ruthlessly brushing aside the framework of international law and the appropriate decision making organs of the United Nations. The United States arrogates to itself as its moral right to act as it pleases, whenever it pleases, even to the point of using nuclear weapons—not only preventively but even preemptively—against whichever country it pleases, whenever its claimed "strategic interests" so decree. And all this is done by the United States as the pretended champion and guardian of "democracy and liberty," slavishly followed and supported in its unlawful actions by our "great democracies."

Once upon a time, the acronym MAD (Mutually Assured Destruction) was used to describe the existing state of nuclear confrontation. Now that the neoconservatives can no longer pretend that the United States (and the West in general) are threatened by nuclear annihilation, the acronym has been turned into literal MADness, as the legitimate policy orientation of institutionalized military and political insanity. This is in part the consequence of neoconservative disappointments about the Iraq War. For "American neocons had hoped the invasion of Iraq would set in train a domino effect across the region, with the people of Iran and other oil-rich states rising up to demand Western-style freedoms and democracy. Unfortunately the reverse has been true, in Iran at least."[36] But it is much worse than even that, because a whole system of institutionally entrenched and secured "strategic thinking," centered on the Pentagon itself, lurks behind it. This is what makes the new MADNESS so dangerous for the entire world, including the United States whose worst enemies are precisely such "strategic thinkers."

We can see this very clearly in a book published in 2004 by Thomas Barnett,[37] reviewed in *Monthly Review* by Richard Peet. To quote Peet:

> September 11, 2001, was an amazing gift, Barnett says, twisted and cruel as that may sound. It was an invitation from history for the United States to wake from the dream-like 1990s and *force new rules on the world*. The enemy is neither religion (Islam), nor place, but the condition of *disconnectedness*. To be disconnected in this world is to be isolated, deprived, repressed, and uneducated. For Barnett these symptoms of disconnectedness define danger. Simply put, if a country was losing out to *globalization*, or rejecting much of its cultural content flows, chances are that the United States would end up sending troops there. . . . Strategic vision in the United States needs to focus

on 'growing the number of states that recognize a stable set of rules regard-ing war and peace'—that is, the conditions under which it is reasonable to wage war against identifiable enemies of *'our collective order.'* Growing this community is a simple matter of identifying the difference between good and bad regimes and encouraging the bad ones to change their ways. The United States, he thinks, has a responsibility to use *its tremendous power* to make *globalization truly global.* Otherwise portions of humanity will be con-demned to an outsider status that will eventually *define them as enemies.* And once the *United States has named these enemies,* it will invariably *wage war on them,* unleashing *death and destruction.* This is *not forced assimilation,* Barnett claims, nor the extension of empire; instead it is the *expansion of free-dom.*[38] (emphasis added)

Evidently, this "vision" borders on insanity. Its brutal implications are spelled out in an interview given by Barnett to *Esquire* magazine: "What does this new approach mean for this nation and the world over the long run? Let me be very clear about this: The boys are never coming home. America is not leaving the Middle East until the Middle East joins the world. It is that simple. No exit means, no exit strategy."

Indeed, it hardly could be put more clearly than Barnett does here and in his book. In this way, we can see the gratuitous idealization of the absurd presumptions of U.S. "tremendous power" and the corre-sponding projection of globalization as naked American domination, openly acknowledging its vehicles as "death and destruction." And if anybody might think that Barnett was an inconsequential pen-pusher, they will be rather alarmed by the facts. For Barnett is Senior Strategic Researcher at the U.S. Naval War College in Newport, Rhodes Island, and a "vision guy" in the Office of Force Transformation attached to the Secretary of Defense.

Sadly, the highest echelons of "strategic thinking" in the United States are populated by such "vision guys," who are determined to add their massive paving blocks of not good but most aggressive bad inten-tions to Dante's road to hell. For the great Italian poet never suggested that the road to hell he was talking about is paved exclusively with good intentions. According to another one of these dangerous "vision guys," Max Boot—who is a Senior Fellow at the prestigious U.S. Council on Foreign Relations—"Any nation bent on imperial policing will suffer a few setbacks. The British army, in the course of Queen Victoria's little wars, suffered major defeats with thousands of casual-ties in the First Afghan War (1842) and the Zulu War (1879). This did not appreciably dampen British determination to defend and expand the empire; it made them hunger for vengeance. If Americans cannot adopt a similarly bloody-minded attitude, then they have no business undertaking imperial policing."[39]

In this kind of aggressive "strategic vision" we are offered the open idealization of British Empire–building, including its most brutal aspects. Cynically, in the name of spreading "democracy and liberty," the unreserved adoption of past colonial violence is recommended as the model for the United States for its empire-building today.

What makes all this particularly disturbing is that concerning all matters of major importance—some of which may result in the destruction of humanity—we find at the highest levels of political decision making in the United States an utterly unholy consensus, despite the periodic electoral rituals for the presidency as well as for the Congress and the Senate, which are supposed to offer real alternatives. However, claimed differences in such vital matters are, as a rule, only pretended differences. As I commented in December 2002, well before the invasion of Iraq, "Democratic President Clinton adopted the same policies as his Republican successor, even if in a more camouflaged form. As regards the Democratic Presidential Candidate, Al Gore, he declared recently that he supported without reservation the planned war against Iraq because such a war would not mean a 'regime change' but only 'disarming a regime which possessed weapons of mass destruction.'"[40] Also, we should not forget that the first U.S. President who bombed Afghanistan was none other than the often ludicrously idealized Bill Clinton. It is, therefore, very far from surprising that Al Gore's successor as Democratic Presidential Candidate, Senator John Kerry hastened to declare in the last presidential race, echoing the words of his Republican opponent George W. Bush, that "Americans differ about whether and how we should have gone to war. But it would be unthinkable now for us to retreat in disarray and leave behind a society deep in strife and dominated by radicals." It is understandable, therefore, that the distinguished American writer and critic, Gore Vidal, described U.S. politics, with bitter irony, as a *one-party system with two right wings*.

Unfortunately, the United States is by no means the only country capable of being characterized in such terms. There are many others, as well, in which the political decision-making functions are monopolized by very similar self-legitimating consensual institutional arrangements, with negligibly little (if any) difference between them, notwithstanding the occasional change in personnel at the top level. I will confine myself to the discussion of one prominent case, the United Kingdom. This particular country—traditionally promoting itself as the "Mother Country of Democracy" on account of the historical document of the "Magna Carta"—under the Premiership of Tony Blair eminently qualifies as a "one-party system with two right wings." The Iraq War was rubber stamped in the British parliament by both the Conservative Party and New Labour, with the help of more or less obvious legal manipulations and violations. Thus, we can now read that "transcripts of evidence given in private by the attorney general, Lord Goldsmith, to an official inquiry suggest that the crucial advice on the legality of war, presented to parliament in his name, was written for him by two of Tony Blair's closest allies. . . . The former foreign secretary Robin Cook said last night that having resigned the day before the war started, he had never heard Lord Goldsmith make the legal case in cabinet. 'I now think he never formally wrote a second opinion,' he told *The Guardian*."[41] Naturally, the subsequent public exposure and condemnation of such practices by prominent legal experts, concerning "Bush and Blair's illegal war,"[42] makes no difference whatsoever. For the vested interests of global hegemonic imperialism—unhesitatingly and humiliatingly served by the political consensual system of a former major imperialist power—must prevail at all costs.

The consequences of this way of regulating social and political interchanges are far-reaching. Indeed, they can have devastating implications for the claimed democratic credentials of the whole system of the law. Three important cases should suffice here to illustrate the point.

The first concerns the alarm raised by a famous writer, John Mortimer, who was in the past a passionate supporter of the British Labour Party, and by no means a radical figure. However, in the light of recent legal and political developments, and in particular because of the abolition of the crucially important legal safeguard of the *habeas corpus*, he felt the need to protest with equal passion, writing in a newspaper article that "now the ugly fact has emerged that New Labour's idea of 'modernization' is to force us back to before the Magna Carta and the Bill of Rights, dark days when we hadn't achieved the presumption of innocence. . . . Tony Blair appears to be in favor of summary convictions handed out by the police without the necessity of any trial at all in a large number of cases. So centuries of the constitution in which we take so much pride are dismissed."[43]

The second case shows how the British government responds to severe criticism even by the highest organs of the judiciary: by authoritarian rejection. As it was made clear recently: "A high court judge branded the government's system of control orders against terrorism suspects 'an affront to justice' yesterday and ruled that they breached human rights laws. . . . The Home Office rejected the court's ruling."[44]

As regards the third case, it indicates a matter of the greatest legislative importance: the authority of parliament itself, under threat by the New Labour government's "Reform Bill." To quote John Pilger: "The Legislative and Regulatory Reform Bill has already passed its second parliamentary reading without interest to most Labour MPs and court journalists; yet it is utterly totalitarian in scope. . . . It will mean that the government can secretly change the Parliamentary Act, and the constitution and laws can be struck down by decree from Downing Street. The new bill marks the end of true parliamentary democracy; in its effect, it is as significant as the U.S. Congress last year abandoning the Bill of Rights."[45]

Thus, the manipulation and violation of internal and international law, in the service of justifying the unjustifiable, carries with it considerable dangers even for elementary constitutional requirements. The negative changes—removing some vital legal scrutiny and safeguards from the legal and political framework of their "allies"—cannot be confined to the international (U.S.-imposed) context. They tend to undermine constitutionality in general, with uncontrollable consequences for the operation of the internal legal systems of the "willing allies," subverting their legal and political traditions. Arbitrariness and authoritarianism can run riot as a result of such highly irresponsible changes that do not hesitate to wreak havoc even on the established constitution. Current debate in Japan offers a striking case in point:

> A grave situation has arisen in which the political forces for adverse constitutional revision are actually competing with each other to draft a new constitution. The LDP [the long ruling Liberal Democratic Party] 'draft of a new Constitution' . . . deleted the second paragraph of Article 9 of the Constitution and added a provision allowing Japan to 'maintain a self-defense military' tasked to perform 'internationally coordinated activities to secure the peace

and security of the international community', thus paving the way to allow Japan to use force abroad. It also contains a clause to restrict fundamental human rights in the name of 'public interest and public order' which amounts to denying constitutionalism. In addition, it is also serious that the LDP draft of a Constitution makes it easier to make further adverse amendments to the Constitution by easing the requirement for the initiation of amendments by the Diet from the present two-thirds majority to just a majority of all members of each house.[46]

The immediate purpose of such changes is, obviously, to make the Japanese people become "willing" cannon fodder in the ongoing and future wars of U.S. imperialism. But can anybody offer reassurances and guarantees—particularly given the painful evidence of Japanese imperialist adventures in the past, together with their internally most repressive history—that there will be no other consequences in the long-run?[47]

In the meantime, so many grave problems are crying out for genuine solutions, solutions that could be well within our reach. Some of them have been with us for several decades, imposing terrible suffering and sacrifices on millions of people. Colombia is an outstanding example. For forty years the forces of oppression—internal and U.S.-dominated—have tried to suffocate the struggle of the Colombian people, without success. Attempts to reach a negotiated settlement—"with the participation of all social groups, without exception, in order to reconcile the Colombian family,"[48] in the words of the leader of FARC—have been systematically frustrated. As Manuel Marulanda Vélez wrote in an open letter addressed recently to a presidential candidate: "No government, liberal or conservative, produced an effective political solution to the social and armed conflict. The negotiations were used for the purpose of changing nothing, so that everything should remain the same. All of the political schemes of the governments were using the Constitution and the laws as a barrier, to make sure that everything continues the way as we had it before."[49]

Thus, when the dominant social interests dictate it, "constitutionality" and the rules of "democratic consensus" are used in Colombia (and elsewhere) as cynical devices for evading and forever postponing the solution of even the most burning issues, no matter how immense might be the scale of suffering imposed, as a result, on the people. And by the same token, in a different social context but under the same kind of deeply embedded structural determinations, even the most blatant and openly admitted violations of established constitutionality are disregarded, despite the periodic ritual lip-service paid to the necessity to respect the constitutional requirements. In this sense, when the U.S. Congressional Committee investigating the "Iran-Contra Affair" had concluded that the Reagan Administration was responsible for "subverting the law and undermining the Constitution," absolutely nothing happened to condemn, let alone to remove, the guilty President. And in yet another case—as we have seen in the ruling LDP government's determination to subvert the Japanese Constitution—when the original constitutional clauses appear to be obstacles to embarking on perilous new military adventures, the dominant social and political interests of the country impose a new legal framework whose principal function is to liquidate the once proclaimed democratic safeguards and turn what was formerly decreed unlawful into arbitrarily institutionalized "constitutional lawfulness." Nor should we forget what has been happening in a most adverse and dangerously authoritarian sense to British and U.S. constitutionality during the last few years.

We cannot attribute the chronic problems of our social interchanges to more or less easily corrigible political contingencies. So much is at stake, and we have historically rather limited time at our disposal in order to redress, in a socially sustainable way, the all too obvious grievances of the structurally subordinated social classes. The question of *why*—concerning substantive matters, and not simply the contingent personal failures, even when they happen to be serious, as the frequently highlighted instances of widespread political corruption are—cannot be avoided indefinitely. It is necessary to investigate the social causes and deep-seated structural determinations at the roots of the disturbing negative trends in politics and the law, in order to be able to explain their stubborn persistence and worsening at the present time. This question of "why" is what I wish to pursue now.

10.3.2 The Nature of Capital's Structural Crisis

In this respect it is necessary to clarify the relevant differences between *types* or *modalities* of crisis. It is not a matter of indifference whether a crisis in the social sphere can be considered a *periodic and conjunctural crisis*, or something much more fundamental than that. Obviously, the way of dealing with a fundamental crisis cannot be conceptualized in terms of the categories of periodic or conjunctural crises.

To anticipate my main point here, as far as politics is concerned the crucial difference between the two sharply contrasting types of crises in question is that the periodic or conjunctural crises unfold and are more or less successfully resolved within a given framework of politics, whereas the fundamental crisis affects that framework itself in its entirety. In other words, in relation to a given socioeconomic and political system we are talking about the vital difference between the more or less frequent crises *in* politics, as against the crisis *of* the established modality of politics itself, with qualitatively different requirements for its possible solution. It is the latter that we are concerned with today.

In general terms, this distinction is not simply a question of the apparent severity of the contrasting types of crises. For a periodic or conjunctural crisis can be dramatically severe—as the great world economic crisis of 1929–1933 happened to be—yet capable of a solution within the parameters of the given system. Misinterpreting the severity of a given conjunctural crisis as if it was a fundamental systemic crisis, as Stalin and his advisors did in the midst of the world crisis of 1929–1933, is bound to lead to mistaken and indeed voluntaristic strategies, like declaring social-democracy to be the "main enemy" in the early 1930s, which could only strengthen, as in fact it tragically did strengthen, Hitler's forces. And in the same way, but in the opposite sense, the "nonexplosive" character of a prolonged structural crisis, in contrast to the "thunderstorms" (Marx) through which periodic conjunctural crises can discharge and resolve themselves, may also lead to fundamentally misconceived strategies, as a result of the misinterpretation of the absence of "thunderstorms," as if their absence was the overwhelming evidence for the indefinite stability of "organized capitalism" and of the "integration of the working class." This kind of misinterpretation, to be sure heavily promoted by the ruling ideological interests under the pretences of "scientific objectivity," tends to reinforce the position of those who represent the self-justifying acceptance of the reformist approach in institutionalized—once upon a time, genuinely oppositional—working-class parties and trade unions (now, however, "Her Majesty's Official Opposition," as the saying goes). But even among the deeply committed critics of the capital system, the same misconception regarding the indefinitely crisis-free perspective of the established order can result in the adoption of a self-paralyzing defensive posture, as we have witnessed in the socialist movement in the last few decades.

It cannot be stressed enough, the crisis of politics in our time is not intelligible without being placed in the context of the broad overall social framework of which politics is an integral part. This means that in order to clarify the nature of the persistent and deepening crisis of politics all over the world today we must focus attention on the crisis of the capital system itself. For the crisis of capital we are experiencing—at least since the beginning of the 1970s[50]—is an all-embracing structural crisis.

Let us sum up, as briefly as possible, the defining characteristics of the structural crisis we are concerned with today.

The *historical* novelty of today's crisis is manifest under four main aspects:

1. Its *character* is *universal*, rather than restricted to one particular sphere (e.g, financial, or commercial, or affecting this or that particular branch of production, or applying to this rather than that type of labor, with its specific range of skills and degrees of productivity, etc.);
2. Its *scope* is truly *global* (in the most threateningly literal sense of the term), rather than confined to a particular set of countries (as all major crises have been in the past);
3. Its *time scale* is extended, continuous—if you like: *permanent*—rather than limited and *cyclic*, as all former crises of capital happened to be;
4. Its *mode* of unfolding might be called *creeping*—in contrast to the more spectacular and dramatic eruptions and collapses of the past—while adding the proviso that even the most vehement or violent convulsions cannot be excluded as far as the future is concerned: i.e, when the complex machinery now actively engaged in 'crisis-management' and in the more or less temporary 'displacement' of the growing contradictions runs out of steam.

... [Here] it is necessary to make some general points about the criteria of a structural crisis, as well as about the forms in which its solution may be envisaged.

To put it in the simplest and most general terms, a structural crisis affects the *totality* of a social complex, in all its relations with its constituent parts or sub-complexes, as well as with other complexes to which it is linked. By contrast, a non-structural crisis affects only some parts of the complex in question, and thus no matter how severe it might be with regard to the affected parts, it cannot endanger the continued survival of the overall structure.

Accordingly, the displacement of contradictions is feasible only while the crisis is partial, relative, and internally manageable by the system, requiring no more than shifts—even if major ones—*within* the relatively autonomous system itself. By the same token, a structural crisis calls into question the very existence of the overall complex concerned, postulating its transcendence and replacement by some alternative complex.

The same contrast may be expressed in terms of the limits any particular social complex happens to have in its immediacy, at any given time, as compared to those beyond which it cannot conceivably go. Thus, a structural crisis is not concerned with the *immediate* limits but with the *ultimate* limits of a global structure. . . . [51]

Thus, in a fairly obvious sense nothing could be more serious than the structural crisis of capital's mode of social metabolic reproduction that defines the ultimate limits of the established order. But even though profoundly serious in its all-important general parameters, on the face of it the structural crisis may not appear to be of such a deciding importance when compared to the dramatic vicissitudes of a major conjunctural crisis. For the "thunderstorms" through which the conjunctural crises discharge themselves are rather paradoxical in the sense that in their mode of unfolding they not only discharge (and impose) but also resolve themselves, to the degree to which that is feasible under the circumstances. This they can do precisely because their partial character does not call into question the ultimate limits of the established global structure. At the same time, however, and for the same reason, they can only "resolve" the underlying deep-seated structural problems—which necessarily assert themselves again and again in the form of the specific conjunctural crises—in a strictly partial and temporally also most limited way. Until, that is, the next conjunctural crisis appears on society's horizon.

By contrast, in view of the inescapably complex and prolonged nature of the structural crisis, unfolding in historical time in an *epochal* and not episodic and instantaneous sense, it is the cumulative interrelationship of the whole that decides the issue, even under the false appearance of "normality." This is because in the structural crisis everything is at stake, involving the all-embracing ultimate limits of the given order of which there cannot possibly be a "symbolic and paradigmatic" particular instance. Without understanding the overall systemic connections and implications of the particular events and developments, we lose sight of the really significant changes and of the corresponding levers of potential strategic intervention to positively affect them, in the interest of the necessary systemic transformation. Our social responsibility, therefore, calls for an uncompromising critical awareness of the emerging cumulative interrelationship, instead of looking for comforting reassurances in the world of illusory normality until the house collapses over our head.

Given the structural crisis of capital in our time, it would be an absolute miracle if that crisis did not manifest itself—and indeed in a profound and far-reaching sense—in the domain of politics. For politics, together with its corresponding framework of the law, occupies a vitally important position in the capital system. This is due to the fact that the modern state is the totalizing political command structure of capital, required (for as long as the now established reproductive order survives) in order to introduce some kind of cohesion (or effectively functioning unity)—even if a most problematical and periodically broken one—into the multiplicity of the centrifugal constituents (the productive and distributive "microcosms") of the capital system.

This kind of cohesion can only be unstable because it depends on the always prevailing, but by its very nature changing, relation of forces. Once that cohesion is broken, due to a significantly changed relation of forces, it must be somehow reconstituted, so as to match the new relation of forces. Until, that is, it gets broken again. And so it goes on and on, as a matter of course taken for granted. This kind of problematically self-renewing dynamic applies both internally, among the dominant forces of the particular countries, and internationally, requiring periodic readjustments according to the changing power relations of the multiplicity of states in capital's global order. This is how U.S. capital could acquire its global dominance in the twentieth century, in part through the internal dynamics of its own development, and in part through progressively asserting its imperialist superiority over the greatly weakened former imperialist powers—above all Britain and France—during and after the Second World War.

The big question in this regard is: for how long can this kind of breaking and reconstituting of the given system's effectively functioning cohesion be carried on without activating capital's structural crisis? The forced readjustment of the inter-state relation of forces does not seem to constitute an ultimate limit in this respect. After all, we must remember that humanity had to, and did, endure the horrors of two world wars without calling into question the suitability of capital to remain the systemic controller of our social metabolic reproduction. This could be considered not only understandable but, worse than that, also acceptable, because it always belonged to the normality of capital to stipulate "there must be war if the adversary cannot be subdued in any other way." The trouble is, though, that such "reasoning"—which was never more "reasoned" than the categorical assertion that "might is right, whatever the consequences"—is now totally absurd. For a Third World War could not stop at the point of subduing the denounced adversary only. It would destroy the whole of humanity. When Albert Einstein was asked, what kind of weapons the Third World War would be fought with, his answer was that he could not tell that, but he would absolutely guarantee that all subsequent wars would be fought with stone axes.

The role of politics in reconstituting the required cohesion has always been great in the capital system. Quite simply, such a system could not be maintained without it. For it would tend to fall to pieces under the centrifugal force of its constituent parts. What appears in general under the normality of capital as a major political crisis, is in a deeper sense due to the need to produce a new cohesion at the overall societal level, in accord with the materially changed—or changing—relation of forces. Thus, for instance, monopolistic trends of development cannot be left simply to themselves without causing massive problems all around. They must be somehow brought into a relatively cohesive framework by politics—the totalizing command structure of capital. This must be done even if the demonstratively adopted regulatory steps often amount to no more than a blatant ideological rationalization and justification of the new relation of forces, to be further relaxed in favor of monopolistic (or quasi-monopolistic) corporations as the underlying trend dictates it. Naturally, international monopolistic developments take place on the basis of the same kind of determinations. But all of these processes are in principle compatible with capital's normality, without necessarily resulting in the system's structural crisis—nor, indeed, in the structural crisis of politics. For, as far as the question of crisis is concerned, we are still talking about crises *in* politics—that is, particular crises unfolding and resolving themselves within the manageable parameters of the established political system—and not about the crisis *of* politics.

Established political institutions have the important function of managing, in a sense even of making routine, the most convenient and durable way of reconstituting the required societal cohesion, in tune with the ongoing material developments and correspondingly changing relation of forces, activating at the same time also the available cultural and ideological arsenal in the service of that end. In capitalist democratic societies, this process in the political domain is usually managed in the form of more or less genuinely contested periodic parliamentary elections. Even when the need for the necessary reconstituting readjustments cannot be contained within such orderly parameters, due to some major changes in the underlying relation of forces, bringing with them dictatorial types of political and military intervention, we may still talk about crises in politics containable by capital, provided that sooner or later we see a return to the "democratic constitutionality" characteristic of capital's normality. Moreover, such developments are frequently controlled to a major extent from abroad, as the numerous instances of U.S.–inspired and –managed authoritarian rule in Latin America testify.

It is, of course, a very different matter when deeply authoritarian processes and trends of development begin to prevail not in subordinate regions but in the inner core—the structurally dominant parts— of the global capital system. In that case, the former pattern of "double bookkeeping," which consists in ruthlessly (even militarily imperialistically) dominating other countries while conforming at home to the "democratic rules of the game," including the full observance of constitutionality, becomes unmanageable. The displacement of contradictions is a systemic aspiration of capital, for as long as it is practicable. Given the structural hierarchies that prevail and must prevail at any given time also in inter-state relations, it is part of the system's normality that the dominant countries attempt to export—in the form of violent interventions, including wars—their internal contradictions into other, less powerful, parts of the system. This they do in the hope of internally securing, and in the midst of major collisions intensifying even across class boundaries, the required social cohesion.[52]

However, this becomes increasingly difficult—notwithstanding all the self-serving mythology about "universally beneficial globalization"—the more globally intertwined the capital system becomes. As a result, significant changes must unfold, with serious consequences everywhere. For the primary concern of the overwhelmingly dominant country, at the present time the United States, as the supreme power of global hegemonic imperialism, is to secure and retain control over the global capital system. But in view of the prohibitive material and human costs involved, which must be paid for, one way or another, this design for global domination inevitably carries with it immense dangers as well as implied resistance, not only internationally but also internally. For that reason, in order to maintain authoritarian control over the capital system as a whole, under the conditions of a deepening structural crisis inseparable from capitalist globalization in our time, unmistakable authoritarian trends must intensify not only on the international plane but also inside the dominant imperialist countries, in order to subdue all likely resistance. The grave violations of constitutionality we have already seen in the United States and in the legal and political framework of its close allies, and what we are even more likely to see in the future, as presaged in the measures and legal clauses codified to date, or still under rather one-sided "consideration" in the cynically manipulated legislative pipeline, are clear indications of this dangerous trend, under the impact of capital's structural crisis.

A revealing example of the tendentious legislative manipulation is the way in which important laws are drafted by the executive branch of government. Not surprisingly, therefore, a High Court judge in Britain had to complain about a vital issue of human rights by saying that "the laws passed had been drafted in a way that prevented the courts overturning control orders. . . . The judge said, Charles Clarke [the British Home Secretary at the time] had made his decision to issue the order on one-sided information, but he was unable to envisage the circumstances allowing the court to quash the Home Secretary's decision. As a result, the judge said, he would have to leave the order in place, even though he ruled that it contravened human rights law."[53]

In the period following the Second World War, "the end of imperialism" was celebrated, somewhat hastily and naively. For, in reality, we saw only a long-overdue readjustment in the international relation of forces, in line with the way in which the socioeconomic and political power relations had been objectively reshaped before and during the Second World War, as projected already in a key passage of President Roosevelt's First Inaugural Speech advocating the "open door policy" everywhere, including the then colonial territories. The postwar readjustment carried with it, of course, the relegation of the former colonial powers to the second and third division, as subordinate forces of American imperialism. However, for a considerable number of years—in the postwar period of reconstruction and relatively undisturbed economic expansion which helped the successful establishment and financing of the welfare state—the major change heralded by the forcefully instituted "open door policy" (open to the United States, that is) was coupled with the illusion that imperialism itself had been forever relegated to the past. Moreover, it was also coupled with the broadly diffused ideology, heavily infecting not only intellectuals but also some important organized movements of the traditional left, according to which the crises of the established socioeconomic and political order (admitted to only shortly before the war), belonged irretrievably to the past. This ideology was promoted—together with its ideological twin brother preaching "the end of ideology"—on the gratuitous assumption that we now lived in the world of "organized capitalism" which succeeded in mastering its contradictions on a permanent basis.

There had to be a rude awakening, also in politics and ideology, as the all-embracing and deepening structural crisis of the capital system asserted itself. In 1987, when there was a big crisis on the international stock exchanges, European merchant bankers were arguing in a televised public discussion that the reason for that crisis was the U.S. refusal to do something about its astronomical debt. An American banker aggressively retorted in the discussion that they should just wait until the United States begins to do something about its debt, and then they will see how enormous a crisis will explode in their face. And in a sense he was right. For it was extremely naïve to imagine that Europe could conveniently isolate itself from the brutal all-round impact of the chronically unresolved global structural crisis of which the U.S. debt is only one aspect, fully involving the self-interested complicity of the creditor countries.

In the last two decades we have seen the return of palpably blatant imperialism with a vengeance, after being successfully camouflaged as the postcolonial world of "democracy and liberty" for a very long time. And under the now-prevailing circumstances it has assumed a particularly destructive form. It dominates the historical stage wedded to the open assertion of the necessity to engage in "unlimited wars." Moreover, it does not shy away even from decreeing the "moral legitimacy" of using nuclear weapons—in a "preventive" and "preemptive" way"—against countries which do not possess such weapons.

Since the onset of capital's structural crisis at the very beginning of the 1970s, the grave problems of the system have been accumulating and worsening in every field, not least in the domain of politics. Although, contrary to all evidence, the wishful thinking of "universally beneficial globalization" continues to be propagandized everywhere, we do not possess viable international political organs that might be able to redress the clearly visible negative consequences of the ongoing trends of development. Even the limited potential of the United Nations is nullified by American determination to impose Washington's aggressive policies on the world, as happened at the time of embarking on the Iraq War under false pretences.

Acting in that way, the U.S. government arbitrarily presumed the unchallengeable role of being the global government of the capital system as a whole, untroubled by the thought of the necessary ultimate failure of such a design. For it is not enough to unleash "overwhelming force," as the dominant military doctrine prescribes, destroying the other side's army and inflicting in the course of the undertaken military adventures immense "collateral damage," as it is obscenely called, on the entire population. The sustainable permanent occupation and domination—including the untroubled and profitable economic exploitation—of the countries attacked in that way is a totally different matter. To imagine that even the greatest military superpower could do that, as a matter of "forced normality" imposed upon the whole world, and stipulated in that sense as the unalterable predicament of the "new world order," is a totally absurd proposition.

Unfortunately, events and developments have been pointing in that direction for a very long time. It was not President George W. Bush but President Bill Clinton who arrogantly declared: "there is only one necessary nation, the United States of America." The "neocons" only wanted to live up to, and to enforce, that belief. But even the so-called liberals could preach nothing more positive than the same pernicious creed, on the whole in the same spirit. They were complaining that we have in the world today "too many states," and they were advocating a "jurisdictional integration"[54] as the viable solution of such problem. That is to say, a grotesquely named "jurisdictional integration" which would actually mean the pseudo-legitimation of an authoritarian direct control of the deplored "too many states" by less than a mere handful of imperialist powers, above all the United States. This conception, despite its obfuscating terminology, is not very different from Thomas Barnett's theorization of how to deal with the deplored "condition of disconnectedness" quoted above.

If there are "too many states" today, they cannot be wished out of existence. Nor can they be destroyed through military devastation, so as to establish on that basis the global happiness of the "new normality." Legitimate national interests cannot be repressed indefinitely. Of all places in the world, the people of Latin America can eloquently testify to this simple truth.

The structural crisis of politics is an integral part of the capital system's long festering structural crisis. It is ubiquitous, and consequently, it cannot be resolved by tampering in a self-perpetuating and apologetic way with any one of its isolated political aspects. Least of all could it be resolved by tampering with constitutionality itself, of which we can see many alarming instances. Not even by subverting and abolishing constitutionality altogether. If British High Court judges and Italian magistrates can protest against such attempts, no matter how aggressively the Berlusconis of this world denounce them even three days before a general election,[55] so can we all do the same, with critical awareness of what is at stake. Our established mode of social metabolic control is in profound crisis, and it can be remedied only by instituting a radically different one, based on substantive equality that becomes actually feasible in our time, for the first time ever in history.

Many people rightly criticize the painfully obvious failures of parliamentary politics. But also in that respect, the necessary rethinking of the past and present of parliamentarism cannot lead to sustainable results without being inserted in its broad setting, as an integral part of the envisaged new social metabolic order, inseparable from the requirements of substantive equality.

It is not too difficult to recognize today that—because of its escalating destructiveness on the environmental plane, as well as in the sphere of production and wasteful capital accumulation, not to mention the growing direct manifestations of the most irresponsible military destruction—our social metabolic order is not viable in the long run. However, what must be brought into the forefront of our critical awareness of the ongoing trends of developments and of their cumulative impact is the fact that the long run is becoming ever shorter in our time. Our responsibility is to do something about it before we run out of time.

10.4 New Challenges on Our Horizon and the Urgency of Time

10.4.1

Six years of the war in Afghanistan have passed, and four years of the Iraq War, causing immense destruction and human suffering. But there is no end in sight, despite the frequently heard hypocritical—or utterly brutal[56]—talk about an "exit strategy." And even if in the future the advocated face-saving solutions for a "proper exit" can be temporarily devised for some of the ongoing military conflicts, on account of a conjuncturally pressing and well calculated political convenience (like a future American presidential election, for instance), that can be no cause for rejoicing. For the underlying grave causal determinations of global hegemonic imperialism will produce other genocidal military interventions by our "great democracies" (above all the United States) not only in the Middle East but also in other parts of the world. And such aggressions will be coupled, to be sure, with the cynical invention of all kinds of *false pretenses* to justify the unjustifiable, as happened in the past on more than one occasion, from the "Tonkin incident" during the Vietnam War under Lyndon Johnson's presidency to Iraq's non-existent *"weapons of mass destruction"* which were supposed to be ready to be launched "in 45 minutes" according to Prime Minister Blair's totally misleading speech in the British Parliament legitimating the war.

Given the total conformity of the media to the ruling ideology, its highly ranked representatives can distort everything the way they please in order to make the interest of the ruling order prevail, misrepresenting even the most blatant forms of military *aggression* as self-justifying *defense*. Thus, hard as it may seem to believe, one of Blair's inspirers describes the war in Afghanistan as *"defensive imperialism,"* without any fear that hell might open up under his feet and swallow him, as it swallowed Don Giovanni at the end of one of Mozart's operas. In Robert Cooper's view, if states like Afghanistan "become too dangerous for established states to tolerate, it is possible to imagine a *defensive imperialism*. It is not going too far to view *the West's response to Afghanistan* in this light."[57]

Again we are not talking about an inconsequential pen-pusher. This is how *The Observer* introduces Robert Cooper's just quoted highly influential, openly pro-imperialist, article:

Senior British diplomat Robert Cooper helped to shape British Prime
Minister Tony Blair's calls for a new internationalism and a new doctrine of
humanitarian intervention which would place *limits on state sovereignty.* . . .
Cooper's call for a new *liberal imperialism* and admission of the need for *double
standards in foreign policy* have outraged the left but the essay offers a rare
and candid unofficial insight into the thinking behind British strategy on
Afghanistan, Iraq and beyond.

Naturally, one should not exaggerate Cooper's personal importance.
He is relevant only as an outspoken representative of the characteristic "party line" of global hegemonic imperialism. We have seen the
same type of approach he voices over Afghanistan in Barnett's denunciation of the alleged "disconnectedness" of the imperialistically dominated areas and in Wolf's call for sovereignty-limiting "jurisdictional
integration" of the "too many countries" of our "fragmented world."
Cooper's intellectually rather grotesque "pre-modern and post-mod-
ern" schematism is in this respect beside the point. It neither adds nor
takes anything away from the aggressive substance of his celebrated
article. It is simply used as a 'scholarly' justification of the naked imperialist orientation of his approach. Cooper's peculiar references to
postmodernity serve exactly the same purpose as Barnett's scheme of
"disconnectedness and connectedness," envisaging in both "theories"
as the ultimate solution of the identified problems the use of force by
the imperially dominant powers, even if the British diplomat's reasoning is much more convoluted than that of his American cohort.

Cooper's article offers a characteristic rationalization not only of
the "thinking behind British strategy on Afghanistan and Iraq" but also
of the thinking behind global hegemonic imperialism which recklessly plays with fire—potentially even with nuclear fire. It is worth quot-
ing an extensive passage:

> While the members of the postmodern world may not represent a danger to
> one another, both the modern and pre-modern zones pose threats. . . . The
> challenge to the postmodern world is to get used to the idea of *double stan-
> dards.* Among ourselves, we operate on the basis of laws and open coopera-
> tive security. But when dealing with more old-fashioned kinds of states out-
> side the postmodern continent of Europe, we need to revert to the rougher
> methods of an earlier era—*force, pre-emptive attack, deception,* whatever is
> necessary to deal with those who still live in the nineteenth century world of
> every state for itself. Among ourselves, we keep the law but when we operate

in the jungle, we must also *use the laws of the jungle*. . . . The challenge posed by the pre-modern world is a new one. The pre-modern world is *a world of failed states*. . . . It is precisely because of the *death of imperialism* that we are seeing the emergence of the pre-modern world. Empire and imperialism are words that have become a form of abuse in the postmodern world. Today, there are no colonial powers willing to take on the job, though the opportunities, perhaps even *the need for colonization*, is as great as it ever was in the nineteenth century. . . . All the conditions for imperialism are there, but both the supply and demand for imperialism have dried up. And yet *the weak still need the strong* and the strong still need an *orderly* world. A world in which the *efficient* and well governed *export stability and liberty*, and which is open for investment and growth—all of this seems eminently desirable. What is needed then is a *new kind of imperialism*, one acceptable to a world of *human rights and cosmopolitan values*. We can already discern its outline: an imperialism which, like all imperialism, aims to bring *order and organization* but which rests today on the *voluntary principle*.

In case some naïve people might take seriously the notion of the "voluntary principle," they must be quickly brought back to their senses by Cooper's enthusiastic support for the "voluntary imperialism of the global economy," under the iron rule of the IMF and the World Bank, and the domination exercised in the name of international aid. In this respect he makes it clear that "If states wish to benefit, they must open themselves up to the *interference of international organizations and foreign states*." (Naturally, to the interference by the big and "efficient" states which can "export stability and liberty.") He is also greatly in favor of what he calls *"the imperialism of neighbors,"* giving as an example the U.S. and EU military intervention in the Balkans, justifying it on the basis that failure to do so would have "pose[ed] a threat to Europe."

Astonishingly, however, he also decrees that the need for the new imperialism had arisen "because of the *death of imperialism*." Evidently Cooper never heard about American imperialism and about the way in which it successfully relegated British and French imperialism—not to mention the Dutch and Portuguese varieties—to the second and third division during and immediately after the Second World War. Consequently, the senior British diplomat's scheme of things is completely fanciful. Not satisfied with the rewards British military subservience is able to obtain by hanging on to the coattails of the U.S. military, Cooper is trying to squeeze out a somewhat more elbow room for the British state on the terrain of the future "Liberal imperialism" with the help of his vision— *"the vision,"* modestly called by that name by the author at the end of his article. As if the actual relation of forces of *global hegemonic imperialism,* with the United States as its overwhelmingly dominant power, did not exist and did not exercise today the potentially deadliest imperial strategy all over the world in the whole of human history.

No doubt Cooper's fanciful pleading for "a new kind of imperialism," with a prominent place to be assigned to the well experienced old British imperial power "volunteering" for that role, explains his reported influence in British government circles, including with Prime Minister Tony Blair, said to be eager for a "historical legacy." Tellingly in this respect, in the whole article there are only sporadic references to the United States,[58] despite the absolutely overbearing, often quasi-dictatorial role that country unhesitatingly exercises in international affairs. Accordingly, the United States can secure to its military adventures the submission not only of the *"willing allies"* but also of many "unwilling" states, as demonstrated by the Iraq War and by the participation of even the constitutionally constrained and reluctant NATO countries—like Germany—in the war in Afghanistan.

The truth of the matter is that imperialism never died. It only assumed a more aggressive and ever more perilous form as the global hegemonic imperialism of our time, with the United States exercising the role of the single *hegemon* for as long as it can (but certainly not forever). The unfolding of the Iraq War and the humiliating role played by Britain at the United Nations in the hypocritical preparatory process, with its pretenses to securing international legality for the American military adventure which came to absolutely nothing, forcefully underlined the total vacuity of "postmodern voluntary imperialism." The brute force of traditional imperialism had to be the operative principle unceremoniously imposed by the United States, as the "neocons" made it amply clear from the very beginning, finding no use whatsoever for the British legalistic fig leaf because they were always prepared to treat the United Nations with total contempt. The attempt to apply Cooper's pretentious "postmodern" schematism to actually existing—global hegemonic—imperialism is quite absurd. No matter how hard he tries to fit the United States into the fanciful postmodern attire, Cooper is able to come up only with this feeble result:

The U.S.A. is the more doubtful case since it is not clear that the U.S. government or Congress accepts either the necessity or desirability of interdependence, or its corollaries of openness, mutual surveillance and mutual interference, to the same extent as most European governments now do.

The qualifications "not clear" and "not to the same extent as most European governments" totally distort—and forcibly embellish—the picture. For the opposite is, in fact, *amply clear.* Namely that the U.S. government and Congress *categorically refuse* to accept the postulated constraints to *any extent,* whether we talk about the *International Criminal Court*[59] or the scandalously treated Kyoto and other international protocols. But if so, what is the explanatory value of "the vision" from which by far the most powerful country of today's world must be left out because it cannot fit the fanciful picture of the "new kind of imperialism," with its postulated *"openness* and *mutual* interference," or its *"human rights and cosmopolitan values"*? Obviously, it has no value at all. This is why the kind of "not clear" and "not to the same extent" misleading qualifications must be made which are also meant to accommodate the United States in the author's vision, even if the reality of global hegemonic U.S. imperialism contradicts every one of the defining criteria of the projected postmodern variety of imperialism.

There can be no preferential role assigned to British "postmodern imperialism" in the American scheme of global domination. The strictly subordinate position of the British army in the Afghan and Iraq Wars, and the suffering and sacrifices imposed also on its military personnel, just like on the other "willing allies," eloquently testify to this simple truth. The actual conditions of political and military development are in fact extremely serious today, given the deepening structural crisis of the capital system. Add to the Middle East wars imposed by the United States on the world, and to the other recently highlighted deplorable treatments of international law by the American government, also the shameful capitulation of all Western democracies—belying their proudly voiced claims against torture regimes—to the degrading practice of the so-called "rendition" of people by the CIA on behalf of the U.S. administration.[60] Only the most uncritical defenders of the established order can deny who dictates the conditions of actually existing imperialism and who must obey them with hardly any murmur of dissent.

10.4.2

To be sure, from the vantage point of imperialism it seems to be obvious that the best way to govern the smaller countries—whether you call them "failed states" or "jurisdictionally fragmented too many states," or indeed "the weak who still need the strong"—is the totally authoritarian imposition of all significant decisions on them, with no court of appeal. The fact that in the past this way of regulating and ruling the international order by a mere handful of imperialist states generated not only resentment but also active resistance does not seem to give food for thought to the most aggressive "neocons." They arrogantly assume that in the age of global hegemonic imperialism, the United States, as the single hegemon, can through the most brutal—openly declared to be unlimited—use of military force readily overcome the problems which proved to be insurmountable to the major powers which competed among themselves for pre-eminence at an earlier stage of imperialism.

However, the openly decreed and jealously guarded doctrine of U.S. preeminence raises the military stakes ever higher, to the point of foreshadowing the specter of humanity's total annihilation. And the fact that the Cold War is declared to be over makes no difference in this respect. General Pervez Musharraf reported, in a television interview given in Washington in 2006, that Richard Armitage, the American Deputy Secretary of State, threatened that Pakistan *"will be bombed back to the Stone Age"* if his government does not obey U.S. orders. Can anyone imagine a big country like Pakistan being bombed back into the Stone Age without the extensive use of nuclear weapons?

In the same way, the well-known U.S. neocon Richard Perle pontificated, in support of former Secretary of Defense Donald Rumsfeld, that his military strategy in Iraq was perfectly adequate. Only the necessary "political will" and the right kind of political decision to "deal with Iran and Syria" were missing, and that caused the "difficulties in Iraq." Perhaps it would be feasible "to deal with Syria" by the use of massive but non-nuclear military weaponry, even if that would create serious additional problems in the Iraq War. But to subdue Iran militarily by the use of traditional weaponry alone—which had been tried without success for eight years by Saddam Hussein's Iraq, with American and other Western support—is beyond all credulity. In fact, the idea of using "tactical nuclear weapons" against Iran is frequently voiced in the United States and in pro-U.S. circles. But who can offer any guarantee about the "suitably limited outcome" of such a reckless nuclear military intervention, with potentially catastrophic consequences not only on the military plane but also in the economic domain?

The aggressive strategic plans in the service of global domination are fully matched by the production of military hardware, including the well- publicized "bunker-busting tactical nuclear weapons" all too frequently advocated for use against Iran. But well beyond that, unhindered, easily reachable targeting of potential U.S. war objectives is in active preparation—both for the purpose of blackmail, including nuclear blackmail, and for actually unleashing some devastating military action—even for the most remote corners of the world. Yesterday's "Star Wars" could still be pretended to be a "defensive shield," even if in reality it was nothing of the kind. However, its heavily updated successor, codenamed "FALCON" (Force Application and Launch from the Continental United States), by no stretch of the imagination could be considered anything other than a blatantly offensive system of weaponry, to be deployed against the entire world. The first operational phase of this system was completed in 2006, and the initial tests took place in 2004. The fully developed unmanned delivery vehicles are reported to be able to "strike targets 9,000 nautical miles distant in less than two hours." Moreover, they will "carry a payload of up to 12,000 pounds and could ultimately fly at speeds of up to 10 times the speed of sound." The purpose of this infernal war machine is to enable the United States to *go it alone* against whichever country it pleases to subdue or destroy, in its design to achieve world domination as the unchallenged and unchallengeable ruler of global hegemonic imperialism. As John Pike, head of Washington think-tank GlobalSecurity.org, commented on the new weapons system: *"It is about blowing people up on the other side of the planet even if no country on earth will allow us to use their territory."* [62]

Thus, we face the *urgency of time* not least on account of the already planned as well as the ongoing aggressive war-practices arising from the perilous conditions and contradictions of our time. What makes these issues particularly grave is that the dangerous actions undertaken by global hegemonic imperialism are *neither* capable of being brought to a lasting conclusion, *nor* is it feasible that they will be abandoned in favor of a more sustainable and even minimally rational course of development. For notwithstanding the unlimited arrogance of militarily backed state power, the uncomfortable fact remains that it is very far from being sufficient for securing a historically sustainable outcome to destroy the central military position of the arbitrarily decreed enemy "by overwhelming force," in the words of the favorite strategic doctrine, as the Americans are now forced to recognize, even if not to admit, in Iraq. Occupying a country on a permanent basis, and generating the required resources for a profitable occupation as a matter of course, is a prohibitively complicated matter, not to mention the total absurdity of extending direct imperial domination—with the weapons of mass destruction abundantly possessed by the United States—to major areas of our planet. No doubt, the aggressive adventures of global hegemonic imperialism are fully capable of and may indeed actually succeed in destroying human civilization. But they are absolutely incapable of offering a sustainable solution to the grave problems of our time.

One cannot underline strongly enough how serious it is that even the growing aggressiveness cannot produce the wishfully anticipated results on a lasting basis, no matter how immense might be the resources invested in it by the dominant imperialist state. And the problem is further complicated by the fact that the prodigally invested resources are derived to a large extent out of escalating U.S. indebtedness, at the expense of the rest of the world, ironically now including in a prominent place China. But no matter how much is wasted, and how aggressive and humanly destructive the military strategy pursued, even if it assumes genocidal forms, the actual results will fall far short of the projected imperialist expectations. The structural crisis of the capital system as a whole deepens also in that respect.

Nevertheless, for the time being global hegemonic U.S. imperialism can dominate with relative ease its potential rivals. But can this state of affairs be assumed to endure forever? The inter-state relation of forces was never permanent in the past and could never become permanent in the capitalist future. Inevitably, there are always significant costs involved in securing one state's dominance over another, which must therefore remain strictly transitory, not to mention the implications of a single state's postulated domination of the rest of the world in accord with the arrogant neoconservative vision of the "American Millennium." The relative material productive power of the potential rivals is a most important factor in this respect, and only a fool could take for granted the permanence of an existing propor-tionality among the major countries, at the unalterable advantage of a much smaller country, like the United States, vis-à-vis China, for instance. It is no secret that in the most aggressive circles in Washington a great deal of effort is constantly invested in advocating a "proper way to deal with the Chinese threat" to U.S. supremacy in the future, including the anticipated use of large-scale military destruction.

Whatever may be the success of such design in the near future by the old and not so old "China lobby," the problem itself is certainly not going to disappear. For China's economic power is bound to become far greater than that of the United States within a relatively short space of time. Already today, if China decided to withdraw its almost astro-nomical magnitude of financial assets from the United States, that would cause a massive economic earthquake not only in the United States but also throughout the entire world. This problem, with all of its political and potentially even military corollaries, must be faced soon in a *rational* and sustainable way, if we want to avoid the destruc-tive impact of the strategies favored by the China lobby and by its unrelenting broader Washington allies.

Moreover, as regards a somewhat more distant future, also the growing—and potentially also very great—developmental promise of India must be reconsidered in accord with its true significance. It is not enough to notice China and India for the transparently self-serving purpose of the Western capitalist countries which already blame them on account of the worsening ecological conditions of our planet. The existing relation of forces in our global order is totally untenable in the long-run. Nor is it possible to attribute the slightest degree of ration-ality to the U.S. military plans to deploy a new anti-missile system in Poland, with the transparent pretence that the placement of such weaponry next door to Russia is a "defensive shield" for the United States "against al-Qaida." Russian protests voiced against that plan made it amply clear that they do not take the offered justification seri-ously for a moment. Could anybody consider this kind of U.S. military measure, set in place with the full complicity of Poland,[63] as anything other than recklessly playing with fire?

The now discernible and aggressively pursued strategies of global hegemonic imperialism can only make matters worse, because impe-rialism, as the anachronistic sworn enemy of historical time, cannot function without imposing on its ruthlessly controlled dependencies the most iniquitous forms of domination. By contrast, only the genuine advocacy of responsibly facing up to the grave problems of capital's deepening structural crisis in the spirit of *substantive equality* (feasible only in a socialist order)—which could make the paradoxically "small country" of the United States the uncontested *equal* of the big countries of India and China—is an absolute requirement for the future. For only the generally adopted spirit of substantive equality can offer a historically sustainable solution to the now prevailing and potentially most destructive inter-state relation of forces.

10.4.3

The potentially catastrophic military dangers by no means exhaust the major challenges on our horizon. Capital's uncontrollable encroachment on nature represents an equally great danger for the future of humanity, despite the recent attempts to capitalistically exploit every possible aspect of the identifiable deterioration of ecological conditions by pretending to offer—of course commercially profitable— "*green solutions.*" At the same time, we see, on the one hand, the continuing refusal of by far the worst offender—the United States—to face up to its responsibility in this matter. On the other hand, to make their dubious contribution to these apparently intractable problems, also the countries which publicly declare their acceptance of the necessary constraints and international protocols in reality fail to live up to the announced targets. They fail even in relation to the single issue of global warming, arbitrarily exempting some of the most harmful actual figures—like the massive and still increasing damage caused by fuel-guzzling aviation—from their convenient calculations. None of them are willing to consider—let alone to acknowledge and to begin to behave accordingly—that a fundamental change would be required in the existing order of production and distribution if we really wanted to secure the necessary safeguards in this respect for humanity's future.

To be sure, the threats to the vital relationship of humankind with nature are incomparably greater and more complex than what is one-sidedly highlighted under the fashionable headlines dedicated to "global warming." Even in terms of global warming the fundamental issue is not the "carbon imprint" of individuals—propagandistically

favored by capitalist governments for generating for them good political headlines while obfuscating the fact that they as governments do
virtually nothing about the major negative share of big business in
producing the damage on a growing scale—but the necessity to adopt
a *responsible and long-term sustainable energy policy,* with the maximal
possible development of *renewable energy resources* now most actively
hindered by capitalist vested interests. Naturally, this problem is further complicated by the insurmountable short-term time horizon of
capital. It is rendered quite tangible by the fact that no one can seriously deny any longer the long term unsustainable negative symptoms
which today clearly indicate the potentially irreversible damage and
the need for far-reaching corrective action while there is still time. Yet,
the personifications of capital are incapable of producing any answers,
other than the hot air contained in government-sponsored reports
talking in total vacuity about how the required targets will be reached
in 2050.

But well beyond even the genuine concern embracing all dimensions of the required long-term energy needs, together with the necessary steps to be taken against the irreversibly rapacious capitalist
exhaustion of our planet's vital strategic material resources, the most
difficult issue is how to make sure that the best use is made of the actual and feasible scientific inroads inevitably made into the objective
determinations of nature. That is, how to make sure that such inroads
are made for enhancing the positive potentialities of humanity, instead
of promoting the destructive counter-values now successfully exploited, on a monumental scale, with irresponsible wastefulness and
destructiveness, by the military industrial-complex and by the other
varieties of strictly profit-oriented but historically most retrograde
"productive" embodiments of the capital system's alienating second-
order mediations. Only a profound commitment to a positively
inspired way of handling the results of scientific and potential technological developments can measure up to the task.

The capitalist state is the essential facilitator of monopolistic developments even when it pretends to legislate against them, but never
really does so in other than a strictly marginal way. In the same sense,
the state is the facilitator of not only the relatively harmless but also the
most problematical and damaging forms of capital expansion—
including, of course, the military industrial-complex—even when the
dominance of counter-value in the facilitated or actively state-spon-

sored ventures is obviously undeniable. It would be astonishing if it could be otherwise. For the modern state is the all-embracing political command structure of the capital system and thus cannot exercise its substantive (rather than marginal) political functions against the vital material determinations of capital for securing its self-realizing expansion, no matter how extremely narrow-minded (indeed even blindly damaging) might be the prospective short-term profitable accumulation. This is why historically sustainable ecological considerations must be firmly ruled out—with the help of all kinds of false pretences—from the policies adopted by the rhetorically pro-ecological capitalist governments. This incestuous relationship between capital's material vested interests and its self-legitimating political command structure strongly underlines the inescapable need for a genuine *systemic change* if we are determined to counter the now even officially acknowledged ecological dangers.

Naturally, the same is true of the all-too-obvious military dangers of our time. Without a fundamental systemic change there can be no hope of leaving historically behind us the potentially deadliest phase of global hegemonic imperialism. We should never forget that the diverse phases of imperialism were closely connected with the corresponding phases of capitalist development. All varieties of imperialism are of course arbitrary and authoritarian in the way in which they treat their dependencies, but their overall mode of operation is unintelligible without fully taking into account the social roots and determinations of the imperial "mother countries." Without radically overcoming such internal social determinations all talk about the "death of imperialism" belongs to the realm of pure—or, rather, utterly self-interested—fantasy. Nor is it conceivable to overcome such deep-seated social determinations in the present phase of capital's historical development without a profound *systemic change.* By replacing, that is, the now dominant and incurably antagonistic mode of social metabolic reproduction by the socialist hegemonic alternative. The unavoidable imperialist inter-state system of domination is incomprehensible without the material ground from which it arises—namely, the capital system's only conceivable mode of productive (and reproductive) operation in the form of domination and subordination.

In the age of global hegemonic imperialism the notion of "Liberal Imperialism"—in which Britain would play the role of an equal—is not purely fictitious. It is fictitious in the sense that the overwhelmingly dominant U.S. partner is only willing to assign the role of Trojan horse to its British subordinate, needed for legitimating it as "the most willing ally" of U.S. international military measures and adventures. But the Liberal Imperialism proposal is also symptomatic in two senses. First, it represents an *aspiration* in the interest of reviving in some form the old imperial role for Britain. And second, it represents as an openly acknowledged *full complicity* in the imperialist way of regulating inter-state relations by making the naked relation of forces ruthlessly prevail over the less powerful countries. In this respect, it would be very naïve to imagine that the same kind of aspiration as well as disposition to the imperialist way of regulating inter-state relations and asserting presumed national interests must be alien ideas in former French colonial circles. At the same time, it would be equally naive to disregard the potential implications of such still lingering imperialist aspirations of the former major colonial powers for future conflicts with U.S. imperial domination.

Understandably, in the age of global hegemonic imperialism, massively dominated by the United States in military terms, the traditional forms of inter-imperialist rivalry had to become on the whole *latent*, but by no means extinguished. It is only a question of time and circumstance before the latent antagonisms, rooted in rival vested interests—real and potential—are likely to come to the fore in a more openly adversarial way. For the underlying social determinations in capital's social metabolic order dictate the *structurally secured* reality of domination and subordination in all domains, including of course the *political* sphere. This means that in terms of inter-state relations the stronger states must always try to impose their interests by dominating the weaker countries. It is unthinkable that the big countries could operate in any other way within the framework of the capital system.

This is true also of such twentieth-century inter-state formations as the European Union. The people who imagine that the small countries of the European Union are fully equal in their power of decision-making to the three big countries—Germany, Britain, and France—as the mystifying ideology of the "Union" declares, can only deceive themselves. Substantive equality in inter-state relations is inconceivable as long as capital's mode of social metabolic control prevails. And since the internal structure of the European Union, just like that of its potentially rival state formations, is articulated in the form of hierarchical domination and subordination, it is impossible to draw a line of demarcation beyond which *structurally secured and safeguarded adversariality* would conveniently turn into *harmonious inter-state arrangements* for the sake of regulating the *global inter-state relations* of the major powers and blocs of countries. A historically sustainable system of inter-state relationships, therefore, requires the supersession of the structurally secured adversariality of the capital system. That is the only conceivable way of overcoming the destructive logic of domination and ensuing imperialist rivalry in the future. Without it there can be no hope for consigning to the past on a permanent basis the potentially deadliest phase of global hegemonic imperialism.

Under the present circumstances, the former major imperialist powers are perfectly willing to tacitly or explicitly support the gross violations of international law by the United States not only in Guantanamo Bay but also wherever the infamous "rendition" process is practiced by the CIA, with hundreds of illegal prisoner transporting flights reported by the United Nations over the territories of major Western democracies slavishly tolerated and cynically denied by the respective governments. Our "liberal democracies" can—and do—clearly demonstrate a disposition to take for granted the authoritarian way of regulating inter-state relations, submitting to the supremacy of the practices enforced by the most reactionary neocon approach to international affairs. We have seen already, in the discussion of the structural crisis of politics above, that even grave violations of constitutionality are more than acceptable in that respect. The instances of such violations of formerly idealized "democratic principles and safeguards" continue to multiply, despite all protest by people (including senior lawyers and judges) who try to defend the once-established forms of civil liberty. Indeed, the state management of these matters does not hesitate to engage in the violation of the principles of democracy and civil liberty while cynically claiming that all such action is pursued "for the sake of democracy and liberty." No one should underestimate the seriousness of these developments as manifestations of the capital system's deepening structural crisis.

10.4.4

The challenge and burden of historical time could not be greater than under the present circumstances. For the stakes themselves could not be greater in that the established mode of social metabolic reproduction—which is prevented by its own fundamental structural determinations from functioning in any other way—now directly threatens the very survival of humankind.

Two decades ago, in the aftermath of Gorbachev's internationally celebrated *perestroika* venture, we heard a singing of the praises of the *"new world order"* and of its promises for a stable and much more productive future, including the benefits to be derived from the *"peace dividend"* which was supposed to flow with great abundance from *"the end of the Cold War."* The reality turned out to be very different. No peace dividend whatsoever (rather the opposite), and nothing even remotely resembling an acceptable order in the so-called new world order. Instead, we witnessed the most aggressive denunciation of a large number of states—as "failed states" and constituents of the "axis of evil"—because they were found objectionable by the global hegemonic imperialist power, followed by the eruption of conflict after conflict. True to the logic of such developments, the underlying senseless strategy of dealing with these matters by militarily deploying "overwhelming force" soon enough assumed the form of genocidal adventures in Afghanistan and in the Middle East. And it could not even stop there. It was followed by the openly announced prospect of using *nuclear weapons* by the United States, outrageously claiming at the same time even *moral justification* for their threatened use. And since the most aggressive militaristic strategy advocating unlimited destructive actions is in store for us in the future, irrespective of the consequences, it is more than legitimate to ask the questions: *Where is it all going to end? Where are the non-transgressable limits? Are there any? Is there any guarantee that humanity can survive the irresponsible destructiveness of global hegemonic imperialism that can decree—without fear of meaningful censure—that it stands above international law and above all responsibility?*

The expectations attached to the loudly proclaimed 'new world order' were totally gratuitous from the beginning. For they were supposed to emerge within the framework of the same social metabolic order of reproduction—without changing in the slightest its structural foundations and determinations—which *necessarily generated* (and continues to generate) the contradictions and antagonisms declared to be disappearing with the end of the Cold War. The capital system is absolutely incapable of admitting *causal changes* to its structural framework. All adjustments must be confined to the domain of manipulable and reversible *effects*. This is why the frequently voiced proverbial belief of capital's personifications is that "there can be no alternative." Naturally, the deepening structural crisis of the capital system could only aggravate the situation and make any corrective intervention—even at the level of marginal effects, as the disastrous collapse of the social-democratic reformist movements all over the world clearly demonstrated—less feasible. Thus, there could be nothing surprising about the actual intensification of systemic antagonisms and about the dominant imperialist state's engagement in genocidal wars, with the subservient support of its "willing allies," in place of the promised blessings of the "new world order" and of its "peace dividend."

The challenge and burden of historical time are inseparable from our necessary awareness of *endangered humanity*. For it is not too difficult to see the grave implications of a failure to counter the ongoing destructive trends of development which impose their power not only in the military domain but also in economic production and in humanity's relationship to nature. Thus, the burden we are talking about indicates both the great *difficulties* arising from the clearly identifiable historical challenge, underlined by the undeniable *urgency of time* for undertaking the necessary corrective action, and the *responsibility* of every individual to contribute to a successful outcome.

In view of capital's incorrigible systemic constraints and contradictions, only the socialist alternative can offer a historically sustainable way out of our dangerous predicament. To make it feasible requires a critical examination of the past as well as the reassessment of some strategies even today still followed by the labor movement.

As we know, "evolutionary socialism" promised the reform of society by way of its partial demands, without questioning the overall structural framework of the capital system. We also know the complete failure of such design and its disorienting consequences. Yet several constituents of the traditional framework of trade unions and political parties remain organizationally the same as before, and indeed weakened by losing many members on account of their inability to gain success even for their limited demands.

This circumstance underlines the painful truth that there can be no significant success without the radical reorientation of the socialist movement in terms of asserting its fundamental strategic aim as the structurally secured *hegemonic alternative* to capital's social metabolic order. The fulfillment of the traditional trade union demands is now completely frustrated and nullified by the acceptance of the economic and political *presuppositions* of the reproductive system which prescribe the general rule of making only "realistic demands," and by the economy "affordable gains" (if any), leaving thereby capital fully in control of the socioeconomic and political order as before.

Thus, the labor movement's only viable alternative strategy has turned out to be the exact *opposite* of the once proposed (but later humiliatingly abandoned) reformist approach. For in the light of constant defeats and reversals suffered by the organized labor movement it has become clear that a fully conscious articulation of the socialist hegemonic alternative to capital's mode of control is the necessary *precondition* of even *partial* achievements. Inevitably, the necessary re-articulation of the labor movement involves a radical reexamination of the failed promise of *"parliamentary socialism"* and the elaboration of viable strategies of organization—both in the field of direct political action and in the redefined mode of formerly trade-unionistically constrained forms of potential transformatory socioeconomic activity—in order to institute the historically required and sustainable change.

Given the urgency of our historical time only the most consistently radical redefinition of transformative objectives can offer any hope of success. The hegemonic alternative to capital's rule implies the need for an irreversible revolutionary transformation. Naturally, the "realists" always pontificate that such strategy is "premature" and should be postponed to the arrival of "more favorable conditions." But what could be less premature than an uncompromising radical intervention in the historical process, given the conditions of the greatest possible danger that we must now face? Or, to put it in another way, when could such intervention be considered not premature, if not under the urgency of our own historical time? The spurious objections raised against premature forms of action are as a rule pushed to the point of condemning them as "adventurism." Some "Marxists" and "communists" castigated even Che Guevara in that way. Fidel Castro answered them in unmistakable terms by stressing on the occasion of the first publication of Che Guevara's Bolivian diaries that:

> Among those who may be interested in keeping the diary unpublished are the pseudo-revolutionaries, opportunists, and charlatans of every stripe.

These people call themselves Marxists, communists, and other such titles. They have not, however, hesitated to call Che a mistaken adventurer or, when they speak more benignly, an idealist whose death marked the swan song of revolutionary armed struggle in Latin America. . . . After Che's death Zamora[64] became one of his most venomous 'Marxist-Leninist' critics.[65]

Naturally, the truth is that all revolutionary intervention in the historical process is and remains in a sense necessarily premature until there is a radical change in the overall relation of forces in favor of labor's hegemonic alternative against capital. That kind of change means not simply a temporary shift in the prevailing relation of forces—which can be undermined and reversed by forces and tendencies of restoration—but a far-reaching, reinforced, and consolidated transformation, sustainable (at least in principle) on an enduring basis. To achieve it involves a coherent strategy to go beyond capital, in contrast to the insufficiency of "negating capitalism" or "overthrowing the capitalist state." In the absence of such sustained strategy aimed at eradicating capital from the social metabolic process on an irreversible basis, capitalist restoration, with its disastrous consequences—as the Gorbachev era made amply clear—can be only a question of time.

The conclusion cannot be avoided: only a consistently pursued international perspective of revolutionary transformation can be historically sustained. Fidel Castro forcefully underlined the far-reaching implications of this approach not only for Latin America but simultaneously also for the prospects of global development:

> Only the revolutionary transformation of Latin America will enable the people of the United States to settle their own accounts with imperialism. At the same time, and in the same way, the growing struggle of the people of the United States against imperialist policy can become a decisive ally of the revolutionary movement in Latin America.[66]

Thus, the challenge and burden of our historical time is to make the *dialectical reciprocity* of socialist internationalism prevail. The house in which we all live cannot be pulled down but needs a truly radical restructuring. The requirements of revolutionary transformation are deeply interconnected throughout the world. Only on that basis can globalization work for the benefit of humankind.

Without the adoption of a viable socialist international perspective the labor movement cannot acquire its required strength. The critical reassessment of the history of the past Internationals is no less important than the radical critique of the "parliamentary road to socialism." In fact, the unfulfilled promises of these two strategic approaches are closely connected. The failure to realize the necessary conditions of success in one deeply affected the prospects of the other, and vice versa. On the one hand, without a strong self-assertive international socialist movement there was no chance of making the socialist perspective prevail in the national parliaments. On the other hand, the overwhelming dominance of capital in the national setting, and the ensuing accommodation of internationally most inadequately organized labor to the given parliamentary constraints and to the nationalistic temptations (clamorously highlighted by the capitulation of the social-democratic parties to their national bourgeoisies at the outbreak of the First World War), there could be no question of turning the radical Internationals into a cohesive and strategically effective organized force.

Thus, the unfortunate history of the radical Internationals was by no means accidental. It was to a large extent due to their unrealistic assumption of the necessity of a *doctrinal unity*—and its attempted *enforcement*—while operating within a political framework that imposed on the overwhelming majority of the labor movement the need for parliamentary accommodation. Indeed, the pursuit of these two strategic lines of approach alongside one another was *self-contradictory*. Accordingly, necessary change in the future is not feasible without critically addressing the problems of both.

As Marx wrote in one of his early works,[67] "the first historical act was the creation of a new need." In that sense, some important historical acts are now called for because it is impossible to successfully respond to the challenge and burden of our historical time without the creation and consolidation of the needs capable of securing not only humanity's survival but also its positive development in the future.

In conclusion, let it suffice to point to the new historical acts absolutely necessary under the urgency of our time for the creation of two vital needs from which others naturally follow.

The first is the need for the adoption of *responsible husbandry* in our productive system. Only the socialist hegemonic alternative to capital's mode of social metabolic control can provide this.

And the second is the consciously pursued determination to overcome—on a historically sustainable basis—the *antagonistic adversari-*

al nature of the capital system, producing ultimately uncontrollable destruction on a potentially catastrophic scale.

Obviously, the role of socialist education is immense in this respect. But the issue itself cannot be avoided. For only through the adoption of these vital needs by social individuals as really their own can individual and social consciousness come together in the interest of positive human advancement.

Notes

Foreword

1. Karl Marx and Frederick Engels, *Collected Works*, vol. 3 (New York: International Publishers, 1975), 182.

2. István Mészáros, *The Necessity of Social Control* (London: Merlin, 1971), later included as an appendix to *Beyond Capital* (New York: Monthly Review Press, 1995). See also Mészáros, *Marx's Theory of Alienation* (London: Merlin, 1975), 10.

3. For Mészáros it is essential to recognize that Marx directed his critique against *capital* as an all-encompassing social relation or system of social metabolic control, rather than simply against *capitalism* as a specific institutional order (mode of production). In this regard it is unfortunate, in his view, that the first English translation of *Capital* under Engels's supervision translated the subtitle of volume 1 as "A Critical Analysis of Capitalist Production" rather than correctly as "The Process of Production of Capital." See István Mészáros, *Beyond Capital*, 912.

4. Daniel Singer, "After Alienation," *The Nation*, June 10, 1996.

5. Mészáros, *Beyond Capital*, 423, 493. See also the present volume.

6. Chávez quoted in Mészáros, *Beyond Capital*, 711. See also István Mészáros, "Bolivar and Chávez: The Spirit of Radical Determination," *Monthly Review*, vol. 59, no. 3 (July-August 2007), 55–84.

7. Michael Lebowitz, *Build It Now: Socialism for the Twenty-First Century* (New York: Monthly Review Press, 2006), 107–08; Mészáros, *Beyond Capital*, 758–60.

8. Albert Einstein, "Why Socialism?," *Monthly Review*, vol. 1, no. 1 (May 1949), 14.

9. Marx and Engels, *Collected Works*, vol. 6, 127.

10. Rodríguez quoted in Richard Gott, *In the Shadow of the Liberator* (London: Verso, 2000), 116.

11. Barbarism, according to early socialist thought, was seen as carried forward and refined rather than fully transcended under capitalist "civilization" and was associated particularly with the most extreme forms of exploitation and deprivation of human rights through slavery, forced labor, the brutal subjuga-

tion of women, arbitrary arrest, imperial wars, "extirpation of indigenous populations," and environmental destruction. It is barbarism in this sense that the capital system, Mészáros suggests, is bringing back to the fore on an even larger scale. See John Bellamy Foster and Brett Clark, "Empire of Barbarism," *Monthly Review*, vol. 56, no. 7 (December 2004), 1–15.

12. Mészáros's remarkable insights in this respect stand out even more when compared to the empty claims regarding the end of imperialism that underpin Michael Hardt and Antonio Negri's much-acclaimed *Empire*. See John Bellamy Foster, "Imperialism and 'Empire,'" *Monthly Review*, vol. 53, no. 7 (December 2001), 1–9.

13. Simón Bolívar, "Message to the Congress of Bolivia, May 25, 1826," *Selected Works*, vol. 2 (New York: The Colonial Press, 1951), 603.

14. Here Mészáros draws on Harry Magdoff and Fred Magdoff, "Approaching Socialism," *Monthly Review*, vol. 57, no. 3 (July-August 2005), 19–61.

15. "On the Edge of the City," in Attila József, *The Iron-Blue Vault* (Newcastle upon Tyne: Bloodaxe Books, 1999), 100. Actual English translation used follows Mészáros in the present work, section 10.1.1.

Introduction

1. This text was chosen as the Epigraph by the MST (the Brazilian Landless Movement) on their 20th anniversary for their "Agenda 2004" (São Paulo: Instituto de Filosofia e Ciências Humanas, 2004).

2. "*Per vent'anni, dobbiamo impedire a questo cervello di funzionare*" from the Fascist Procurator's Memorandum, June 2, 1928. Quoted in Giuseppe Fiori, *Antonio Gramsci: Life of a Revolutionary* (London: NLB, 1970), 230.

3. Attila József, "*Ős patkány terjeszt kórt miköztünk*" ("Primeval rat spreads the plague among us"), 1937.

4. A major Hungarian writer, Dezsö Kosztolányi (1885–1936) had died of cancer a short time earlier.

5. "*Saludo a Thomas Mann*," 1937. Translated by Fayad Jamís. "*Thomas Mann üdvözlése*" in Attila József, *Poesías* (Budapest: Eötvös József Könyvkiadó, 1999), 55.

6. "Il tempo è la cosa più importante: esso è *un semplice pseudonimo della vita.*" Quoted in Giuseppe Fiori, *Vita di Antonio Gramsci* (Bari: Editori Laterza, 1966), 324.

7. "*Il pessimismo dell'intelligenza e l'ottimismo della volontà*," quoted in ibid., 323.

8. Attila József, "*Szocialisták*" ("Socialists"), 1931.

9. "*Helada*," 1932. Translated by Fayad Jamís. Attila József, "*Fagy*," op. cit., 27.

10. "*Al border de la ciudad*," 1933. Translated by Fayad Jamís. Attila József, "*A város peremén*," op. cit., 35.

11. See Marx, "The Eighteenth Brumaire of Louis Bonaparte," in Marx and Engels, *Collected Works*, vol. 11 (London: Lawrence and Wishart, 1979), 106.

12. Fidel Castro, "Interview with Tomás Borge" (1992), in David Deutschmann, ed., *Che: A Memoir by Fidel Castro* (New York: Ocean Press, 2006), 215–216.

13. Fidel Castro, "20th Anniversary of Che's Death" (October 8, 1987), ibid., 194.

The Tyranny of Capital's Time Imperative

1. This means in socialist theory that one can depict the negated aspects of social development as historical in the meaningful sense that envisages their *practical supersession.*

2. Kant, "Idea for a Universal History with Cosmopolitan Intent," in Carl J. Friedrich, ed., *Immanuel Kant's Moral and Political Writings* (New York: Random House, 1949), 119.

3. Ibid., 118.

4. Ibid., 123.

5. Ibid., 120.

6. In Kant's own words: "The *general equality* of men as subjects in a state coexists quite readily with the *greatest inequality* in degrees of the *possessions* men have, whether the possessions consist of corporeal or spiritual superiority or in material possession besides. Hence the general equality of men also coexists with *great inequality of specific rights* of which there may be many. Thus it follows that the welfare of one man may depend to a very great extent on the will of another man, just as the *poor are dependent on the rich* and the one who is *dependent must obey* the other as a *child* obeys his parents or the *wife* her husband or again, just as one man has command over another, as one man serves and another pays, etc. Nevertheless, all subjects are equal to each other before the law which, as a pronouncement of the general will, can only be one. This law concerns the *form* and not the *matter* of the object regarding which I may possess a right." Kant, "Theory and Practice," in ibid., 415–416.

7. Values as such are supposed to concern the individuals as mere individuals only. This is how Weber puts it: "One thing is the Devil and the other God as far as the individual is concerned, and the individual must decide which, *for him,* is God and which the Devil. And this is so throughout the orders of life. . . . let us go to our work and satisfy the 'demand of the day'—on the human as much as the professional level. That demand, however, is plain and simple if each of us finds and *obeys the demon* holding the threads of *his* life." Quoted in Lukács, *The Destruction of Reason* (London: Merlin Press, 1980), 616–618.

8. It is impossible to go into detail at this point. The interested reader can find this discussed in Chapter 4 of my *Beyond Capital: Towards a Theory of Transition* (New York: Monthly Review Press, 1995).

9. Hegel, *Philosophy of Right,* (Oxford: Clarendon Press, 1942), 130.

10. Marx and Engels, *Collected Works,* vol. 6 (London: Lawrence and Wishart, 1976), 126–7.

11. Hegel, op. cit., 10.

12. Sir Lewis Namier, *Vanished Supremacies: Essays on European History, 1812–1918* (Harmondsworth: Penguin Books, 1962), 203.

13. Ibid., 7.

14. Hegel, *The Philosophy of History,* (New York: Dover Publications Inc.), 103.

15. Ibid., 53.

16. See note 6.

17. Marx, *Grundrisse* (Harmondsworth: Penguin Books), 832.

18. Ibid., 528.
19. Ibid., 540.

The Uncontrollability and Destructiveness of Globalizing Capital

1. This chapter was first published as the Introduction to the Farsi edition of my *Beyond Capital* in autumn 1997.
2. Marx, *Grundrisse* (Harmondsworth: Penguin Books), 278.
3. Above all, by overcoming the prohibition on the sale and purchase of both land and labor, securing thereby the triumph of alienation in every domain.
4. Vast numbers are just surviving (if they do) "hand-to-mouth" in the "traditional economy," and the number of those who remain completely marginalized, even if still hoping—mostly in vain—for a job of some kind in the capitalist system, almost defies comprehension. Thus, "While the total number of unemployed persons registered with employment exchanges stood at 336 million in 1993, the number of employed persons in the same year according to the Planning Commission stood at only 307.6 million, which means that the number of registered unemployed persons is higher than the number of persons employed. And the rate of percentage increase of employment is almost negligible." Sukomal Sen, *Working Class of India: History of Emergence and Movement 1830–1990* (Calcutta: K. P. Bagchi & Co., 1997), 554.
5. Paul Sweezy and Harry Magdoff have highlighted the chronic crisis of accumulation as a grave structural problem on several occasions.
6. Hegel, *The Philosophy of History* (New York: Dover Publications Inc.), 39.
7. Ibid., 223.
8. Ibid., 214.
9. Schumpeter used to praise capitalism—rather self-complacently—as a reproductive order of "*productive destruction;*" today it would be much more correct to characterize it as ever-increasingly a system of "*destructive production.*"

Marxism, the Capital System, and Social Revolution

1. This chapter is based on an interview given to the Persian Quarterly *Naghd* (*Critique*) on June 2, 1998; published in issue no. 25, spring 1999.
2. See "The Intensification of the Rate of Exploitation" in Section 7 of "The Necessity of Social Control" in my *Beyond Capital: Towards a Theory of Transition* (New York: Monthly Review Press, 1995), 890–892.

Socialism or Barbarism: From the "American Century" to the Crossroads

1. Sections 1 and 2 of this chapter were presented in Athens on October 19, 1999 at a conference organized by the Greek bimonthly magazine ΟΥΤΟΠΙΑ and printed in Greek in this magazine, edited by E. I. Bitsakis, in March 2000. The full text was first published in book form in Italian, by the Milan publishing house Punto Rosso, in September 2000, and the first complete English edition appeared in June 2001, published by Monthly Review Press, New York. This study is dedicated to Harry Magdoff and Paul M. Sweezy, whose contribution

in the last fifty years—in their books and as editors of *Monthly Review*—to our awareness of imperialism and monopolistic developments has been second to none.

2. Mészáros, *The Power of Ideology* (London: Harvester/Wheatsheaf, 1989), 462–470.

3. "Marxism Today," an interview published in *Radical Philosophy*, no. 62, autumn 1992; reprinted in Part IV of *Beyond Capital*.

4. Marx, *Grundrisse* (Harmondsworth: Penguin Books), 488.

5. Ibid., 408 and 410.

6. Ibid., 540.

7. Walt Rostow, *The Stages of Economic Growth* (Cambridge: Cambridge University Press, 1960), 155.

8. See a prominent editorial article in London's *The Economist*, entitled "Time to Bury Keynes?," July 3, 1993; a question answered by the editors of *The Economist* with an emphatic "yes."

9. *The Economist*, December 31, 1991.

10. A striking example of the differential rate of exploitation is given in an essay by a major Filipino historian and political thinker, Renato Constantino: "Ford Philippines, Inc., established only in 1967, is now [four years later] 37th in the roster of [the] 1,000 biggest corporations in the Philippines. In 1971 it reported a return on equity of 121.32 percent, whereas its overall return on equity in 133 countries in the same year was only 11.8 percent. Aside from all the incentives extracted from the government, Ford's high profits were mainly due to cheap labor. While the U.S. hourly rate for skilled labor in 1971 was almost $7.50, the rate for similar work in the Philippines was only $0.30." Renato Constantino, *Neo-Colonial Identity and Counter-Consciousness: Essays in Cultural Decolonization* (London: Merlin Press, 1978), 234. The relative privileges enjoyed in the past by the working classes in the capitalistically advanced countries have started to erode in the last three decades, as a result of capital's narrowing margins of productive accumulation and of its ongoing transnational globalization. This downward equalization of the differential rate of exploitation is a most significant trend of development in our time, and it is bound to assert itself with increasing severity in the coming decades.

11. Luxemburg prophetically emphasized the growing import of militarist production, noting in 1913: "Capital itself ultimately controls this automatic and rhythmic movement of militarist production through the legislature and a press whose function is to mould so-called 'public opinion.' That is why this particular province of capitalist accumulation at first seems capable of infinite expansion." Rosa Luxemburg, *The Accumulation of Capital* (London: Routledge, 1963), 466.

The role of Nazi Fascism in further extending militarist production is obvious enough, as indeed is the prodigious (and quite prodigal) "extraneous help" provided to capital in "Western democracies" and elsewhere by the military-industrial complex after the Second World War. An equally important, even if a somewhat different kind of, extraneous help was supplied to capital by all varieties of Keynesianism in the postwar decades. What is less obvious in this respect is the conscious dedication of F. D. Roosevelt to the same objective already before his election to the presidency. He even anticipated a condemnation of what later became known as "neoliberalism," insisting—in a speech made on July 2, 1932—that "we should repeal immediately those provisions of law that compel the federal government to go into the market to purchase, to sell, to speculate in farm products in a futile attempt to reduce farm surpluses. And they are the people who are talking of *keeping Government out of business*" ("The New Deal Speech before the Democratic Convention"). This and all subsequent quotations from Roosevelt's speeches are taken from in B.D. Zevin, ed., *Nothing to Fear: The Selected Addresses of Franklin Delano Roosevelt*, 1932-1945 (London: Hodder & Stoughton, 1947).

12. Paul Baran, *The Political Economy of Growth* (New York: Monthly Review Press, 1957), vii.

13. *The Economist*, November 17, 1957.

14. *The Observer*'s comment on Roosevelt's "First Inaugural Address," delivered in Washington D.C., March 4, 1933; quoted in Zevin, op. cit., 13.

15. "First Inaugural Address," March 4, 1933, ibid.

16. "Annual Message to Congress," Washington D.C., January 11, 1944.

17. P.C. No. 992, February 23 1995. Quoted in Thomas H. Greer, *What Roosevelt Thought: The Social and Political Ideas of Franklin D. Roosevelt* (London: Angus & Robertson, 1958), 169.

18. Ibid.

19. "Address on the Fiftieth Anniversary of the Statue of Liberty," New York City, October 28, 1936.

20. Harry Magdoff, *The Age of Imperialism: The Economics of U.S. Foreign Policy* (New York: Monthly Review Press, 1966), 15.

21. Roosevelt did not try to hide that he wanted to justify his actions in the name of a war-like emergency. As he had put it: "I shall ask the Congress for broad Executive power to wage a war against the emergency, as great as the power that would be given to me if we were in fact invaded by a foreign foe" ("First Inaugural Address").

22. "Second Inaugural Address," Washington D.C., January 20, 1937. Roosevelt also argued, in the same spirit, that little of the generated profit was "devoted to the reduction of prices. The *consumer was forgotten*. Very little of it went into increased wages; *the worker was forgotten*, and by no means an adequate proportion was even paid out in dividends—*the stockholder was forgotten*" (Roosevelt's New Deal Speech). The question *why* they were forgotten was not asked. The only thing that mattered was that now they are *remembered*, and therefore everything can and will be put right. What is missing from such discourse is the acknowledgement of overwhelming objective *incompatibilities*. This is what makes such discourse on numerous occasions unrealistically rhetorical.

23. Daniel B. Schirmer, *Republic or Empire: American Resistance to the Philippine War*, (Rochester, Vermont: Schenkman Books Inc.), 1–3. The author also

makes it clear, faithful to its original historical context, why the anti-imperialist movement at the turn of the century had to fail: "In 1902 George S. Boutwell, the chairman of the anti-imperialist league and erstwhile associate of Lincoln, concluded that the leadership of a successful struggle against imperialism was to lie in the hands of labor. He told a Boston audience of trade unionists: 'The final effort for the salvation of the republic is to be made by the laboring and producing classes.' If this was to be the case, it was obvious that American labor, at the moment, was not ready to shoulder its responsibility, dominated as it was by men like [Samuel] Gompers, who were unfolding a policy of conciliation with the trusts and support for their foreign policy. Whatever the future would hold for Boutwell's belief, at the time he spoke, the anti-imperialists were declining in influence; they represented an ideology without a stable and growing social base" (ibid., 258).

24. The issue was not confined to French Indo-China. Roosevelt's attitude was equally dismissive of would-be French aspirations for retaining possession of their North African colonies, notably Morocco. See his letter to Cordell Hull on January 24, 1944, quoted in Greer, op. cit., 168.

25. See U.S. Democratic Senator Daniel Patrick Moynihan's notorious book, *Pandaemonium: Ethnicity in International Relations*, (New York: Oxford University Press, 1993).

26. Noam Chomsky, "The Current Bombings," *Spectre*, no. 7, summer 1999.

27. Jeffrey Sachs, "Helping the world's poorest," *The Economist*, August 14, 1999.

28. Characteristically, *The Economist*, in an editorial article on poverty in the "underdeveloped world," lays the stress on municipal matters ("reliable water supplies"—to be obtained through "water sellers," rather than "by struggling to install expensive piped supplies to the home"—"safe drains" and "regular rubbish collections"), concluding that "the *main answers* lie in making *local government* more efficient and more accountable" ("Helping the Poorest," August 14, 1999). The truth is, of course, that the local governments of the countries in question are hopelessly handicapped by the resources made available to them by their national governments, which in their turn are most iniquitously locked into the self-perpetuating structural hierarchies of the global capital system.

29. Michael Heseltine's ministerial resignation statement, January 9, 1986, quoted in Mészáros, "The Present Crisis" (1987), reprinted in Part IV of *Beyond Capital*, 952–964.

30. Ibid., 952.

31. Ibid., 954–958.

32. The good intentions of Jeffrey Sachs are clear when he writes that "the global regime on intellectual property rights requires a new look. The United States prevailed upon the world to toughen patent codes and cut down on intellectual piracy. But now transnational corporations and rich-country institutions are patenting everything from the human genome to rainforest biodiversity. The poor will be ripped off unless some *sense and equity* are introduced into this runaway process" (J. Sachs, op. cit., 22). However, he becomes hopelessly

unrealistic where he describes the determinations behind the criticized policies as "*amazingly misguided*" (ibid., 16). There is nothing "misguided" about
such policies, let alone "amazingly misguided," which suggests that they can be
remedied by a good dose of rational illumination (like Roosevelt's "remem-
bering" of what has been "forgotten"). On the contrary, they are embodiments
of callously deliberate, well calculated, and ruthlessly imposed decisions, emanating from capital's structurally safeguarded hierarchies and objective imperatives. Again, the real issue is not the absence of the—now happily supplied—
rational insight but the reality of overpowering *incompatibilities:* in Sachs's
case that between "sense and equity." For what "sense" would recommend, the
radical exclusion of all possible considerations of "equity" must absolutely
deny. This is why Jeffrey Sachs's article—given the author's reverent attitude to
"market society" (which cannot be even called by its proper name of capitalist market)—ends up with a totally fictitious "market solution."

33. Renato Constantino, *Identity and Consciousness: The Philippine Experience*
    (Quezon City: Malaya Books, 1974), 6. The Americans relinquished direct
    control of the Filipino educational system in 1935, by which time they were
    exercising a very effective control over it indirectly.

34. On the disastrous U.S. involvement in Vietnam, see Gabriel Kolko's seminal
    book, *Vietnam: Anatomy of a War, 1940–1975* (London: Allen & Unwin,
    1986).

35. Andreas Papandreou told me in 1973 how he was released from the colonels'
    jail. A former member of President Kennedy's brain trust, John Kenneth
    Galbraith, to his honor, went to see President Lyndon Johnson and pleaded
    with him on behalf of his old Harvard University friend. Johnson called in his
    secretary and asked her to connect him with the U.S. Ambassador in Athens.
    It was done on the spot and Johnson said to the Ambassador: "Tell those sons
    of a bitch to release this good man, Papandreou, immediately"—which they
    did. For they knew very well who was really in charge in Greece. A few weeks
    before the overthrow of Mobutu's regime, *The Economist* quoted a U.S. state
    department official: "We know that he is a son of a bitch, but he is *our* son of
    a bitch."

36. Mészáros, "Radical Politics and Transition to Socialism: Reflections on Marx's
    Centenary," first published in the Brazilian periodical *Escrita Ensaio,* Anno V,
    no. 11–12, summer 1983. A shorter version of this article was delivered as a
    lecture in Athens in April 1983. The article is reprinted in full in Part IV of
    Beyond Capital, 937–951. The quotation is from 943–944 of the latter.

37. Shoji Niihara, "Struggle Against U.S. Military Bases," *Dateline Tokyo,* no. 73,
    July 1999.

38. József Ambrus, "A polgári védelem feladatai" (The Tasks of Civil Defense), in
    a special issue of *Ezredforduló,* dedicated to the problems of Hungary's entry
    into NATO, *Strategic Enquiries of the Hungarian Academy of Sciences,* (1999).

39. For a notable exception, see John Manning's letter to *Spectre,* no. 6, spring
    1999. On a related issue, see *U.S. Military Bases in Japan: A Japan U.S.
    Dialogue,* report from the Boston Symposium, April 25, 1998, Cambridge, MA.

40. Tetsuzo Fuwa, "Address to Japan Peace Committee in its 50th Year," *Japan Press Weekly*, July 3, 1999. Comparing Japanese Prime Minister Obuchi to leading opposition figure Fuwa, *The Economist* grudgingly wrote: "Events so far tended to show Mr Obuchi as a bumbling amateur, especially when grilled by consummate professionals such as Tetsuzo Fuwa" ("A Pity about Uncle Obuchi," November 1999).

41. This is already happening as Japan is compelled to pay for the massive cost of U.S. military occupation through their numerous bases in the country. "Costs that the Japanese government bore in 1997 for maintaining U.S. bases in Japan reached 4.9 billion U.S. dollars, ranking first among other countries of the world (according to the 'Allied Contribution to the Common Defense, 1999 Report'). For each U.S. soldier stationed in Japan, this is 122,500 U.S. dollars" (S. Niihara, op. cit., 3).

42. *Akahata*, November 1, 1999; quoted in *Japan Press Weekly*, November 6, 1999.

43. S. Niihara, op. cit., 3.

44. Quoted in "Washington tells China to back off or risk Cold War," *The Daily Telegraph*, May 16, 1999. The same article also notes: "The spate of espionage stories seems to have been leaked by figures within the Republican Party or the Pentagon who see it in the long-term interests of the United States to have one big enemy." Obviously, Saddam Hussein is not big enough as regards the ideological requirements and the increasing military expenditure corresponding to the long-term design of the aggressive U.S. imperialist posture.

45. Jonathan Story, "Time is running out for the solution of the Chinese puzzle," *Sunday Times*, July 1, 1999.

46. Ibid. [Story's article is an extract from his book *The Frontiers of Fortune* (London: Financial Times/Prentice Hall, 1999).]

47. The importance of Turkey as a U.S. "local assistant" was dramatically exposed this spring with the ignominious consignment of Ocalan, the leader of the Kurdish PKK, to Ankara, under great U.S. pressure, humiliating the various European "local assistants" involved in this affair. See Luigi Vinci, *La socialdemocrazia e la sinistra antagonista in Europa* (Milan: Edizioni Punto Rosso, 1999), 13. See also Fausto Bertinotti interviewed by Giorgio Riolo, *Per una società alternativa: Intervista sulla politica, sul partito e sulle culture critiche*, (Milan: Edizioni Punto Rosso, 1999), 30–31.

48. The quotations are all from "The New Geopolitics," *The Economist*, July 31, 1999.

49. David Watts, "Howard's "Sheriff" Role Angers Asians," *The Times*, September 27, 1999.

50. Ibid.

51. Ibid.

52. Story, op. cit., 33.

53. See David Cay Johnston, "Gap Between Rich and Poor Found Substantially Wider," *The New York Times*, September 5, 1999.

54. "Worried in Beijing," *The Economist*, August 7, 1999.

55. Ibid. [The necessary overthrow of China is several times eagerly prognosticated in this editorial article.]

56. See a thought-provoking discussion of these problems in Luigi Vinci's volume quoted in note 47 above, in particular pages 60–66.

57. "Superpower Europe," *The Economist,* July 17, 1999.

58. Rupert Cornwell, "Europe warned not to weaken NATO," *The Independent,* October 8, 1999.

59. Ibid.

60. For an illuminating and up-to-date history of the American labor movement see Paul Buhle, *Taking Care of Business: Samuel Gompers, George Meany, Lane Kirkland, and the Tragedy of American Labor* (New York: Monthly Review Press, 1999), in particular pages 17–90 and 204–263. An insightful account of the strategic role of unionized labor today is given by Michael D. Yates, *Why Unions Matter* (New York: Monthly Review Press, 1998).

61. To be sure, acknowledging the existence of unfavorable objective circumstances cannot provide a blanket justification for the often self-imposed contradictions of the "subjective side." Michael Yates rightly stresses the historical impact and responsibility of the individuals who were in a position of making decisions as protagonists of the American labor movement. He writes in a recent article that "Gompers did not have to betray IWW and the militant socialist cadre to the police, but then again leading socialists did not have to ally themselves with Gompers and eventually become as rabidly conservative as he. Gompers and his progeny did not have to commit themselves to U.S. imperialism and undermine progressive workers' movements throughout the world, taking money from the CIA even as this agency of death was encouraging the murder and imprisonment of union leaders around the globe. CIO leaders did not have to join in the witch hunts, making the CIO virtually indistinguishable from the AFL by the time of their merger in 1955. But neither did the communists have to urge the government to lock up the Trotskyists and slavishly follow the directives of Stalin. All of this is not to say that the actions of some radicals and those of Gompers, et al., are on the same plane, but to say that radicals made their own history, too." Michael D. Yates, "The Road Not Taken," *Monthly Review,* 51:6, November 1999.

62. Denis Noble, "Academic Integrity," in Alan Montefiore and David Vines, eds., *Integrity in the Public and Private Domains* (London & New York: Routledge, 1999), 184.

63. Quoted in Otto Nathan and Heinz Norden, eds., *Einstein on Peace* (New York: Schocken Books, 1960), 343. Einstein's message could only be published posthumously.

64. Ibid., 107.

65. Ibid., 116.

66. Ibid., 344.

67. Quoted in Ronald W. Clark, *Einstein: The Life and Times* (London: Hodder and Stoughton, 1973), 552. The Congressman who violently denounced Einstein in the House of Representatives was John Rankin (D-Mississippi)

68. "The Poverty of Philosophy" in Marx and Engels, *Collected Works,* vol. 6 (New York: International Publishers, 1976), 210.

69. Ibid., 212.

70. See Chapter 18 of *Beyond Capital*, 673–738.

71. We should not forget that anti-labor legislation in Britain started under Harold Wilson's Labour government, with the legislative venture called "In place of strife," at the initial phase of capital's structural crisis. It continued under Edward Heath's short-lived government, and then again under Wilson's and Callaghan's Labour governments, ten years before receiving an openly neoliberal stamp under Margaret Thatcher.

72. Vinci, op. cit., 69.

73. Luxemburg, op. cit., 466

74. Written between December 10, 2002 and January 6, 2003.

Unemployment and "Flexible Casualization"

1. "Underground Economy," *The Nation*, January 12–19, 1998.

2. *Japan Press Weekly*, May 16, 1998.

3. "The Necessity of Social Control," Isaac Deutscher Memorial Lecture, delivered at the London School of Economics and Political Science on January 26, 1971. Reprinted in my *Beyond Capital: Towards a Theory of Transition* (New York: Monthly Review Press, 1995).

4. We should recall in this context that "while the total number of unemployed persons registered with employment exchanges stood at *336 million* in 1993, the number of employed persons in the same year according to the Planning Commission stood at only *307.6 million*, which means that the number of registered unemployed persons is higher than the number of persons employed. And the rate of percentage increase of employment is almost negligible." Sukomal Sen, *Working Class of India: History of the Emergence and Movement 1830-1990* (Calcutta: K.P. Bagchi & Co., 1997), 554.

5. "Waterloo in Asia?," January 12–19, 1998. U.S. interests are cynically pursued and imposed wherever the opportunity permits. Thus, "American officials, who effectively vetoed the creation of an Asian Regional Fund independent of the IMF, and therefore of Washington, have also made it known—most recently in the case of Korea—that no U.S. direct aid will be forthcoming until the ailing countries acquiesce in IMF demands. So far, Thai authorities have agreed to remove all limits on foreign ownership of financial firms and are pushing ahead with legislation to allow foreigners to own land, long a taboo. Even before it sought help from the IMF, Jakarta abolished its restrictions on foreign ownership of publicly traded stock, a move replicated by Seoul when it granted foreign investors access to the $64 billion long-term, guaranteed corporate bond market, access they had been seeking for years." Walden Bello, "The End of the Asian Miracle," *The Nation*, January 12–19, 1998.

6. IMF congratulations, to be sure, mean very little, if anything, even in their own terms of reference. Characteristically, "when the Thai economy was headed for trouble, the IMF was still praising the government's 'consistent record of sound macroeconomic management policies'" (Bello, op. cit.). Similarly, in the few months since the IMF "rescued" the South Korean economy, unem-

ployment has actually *doubled* in the country. See also an insightful article by János Jemnitz, "A review of Hungarian politics 1994–1997," *Contemporary Politics*, vol. 3, no. 4, 1997.

7. See Gabriel Kolko's fine book, *Vietnam: Anatomy of a Peace* (London and New York: Routledge, 1997). See also Nhu T. Le's passionate rejoinder in his review of Kolko's book in *The Nation*, "Screaming Souls," November 3, 1997.

8. Anthony Kuhn, "268 million Chinese will be out of jobs in a decade," *The Sunday Times*, August 21, 1994.

9. See Lord Beveridge's book of the same title. Beveridge played an important role in the establishment of the British "welfare state."

10. Marx and Engels, *Manifesto of the Communist Party* (Moscow: Progress Publishers, 1971), 44. See Marshall Berman's deeply appreciative article on the 150th Anniversary of the Manifesto, "Unchained Melody," *The Nation*, May 11, 1998.

11. "Jobless told: join Army or lose benefits," Stephen Castle, *Independent on Sunday*, May 10, 1998. Another headline on the same page reports reactions to the miserable level at which the minimum wage has been introduced by the British New Labour government under the title: "Union fury as Labour sets minimum wage at £3.60."

12. Susan Bell, "Paris passes law on 35-hour week," *The Times*, May 20, 1998.

13. "Neither resigned nor softened on the question of 35 hours, the industrialists' President is more determined than ever to promote a repealing referendum" ("*Né rassegnato, né ammorbidito sul tema delle 35 ore, il presidente degli industriali è più deciso che mai a promuovere un referendum abrogativo*"). Vittorio Sivo, "Referendum sulle 35 ore," *La Repubblica*, April 22, 1998.

14. Ibid.

15. "The working week: Fewer hours, more jobs?," *The Economist*, April 4, 1998.

16. Ibid.

17. Michiyo Nakamoto, "Revolution coming, ready or not," *Financial Times*, October 24 1997. See in the same issue of the *Financial Times* an article by John Plender, "When capital collides with labour," written in the same spirit.

18. David Coe and Dennis Snower, "Policy Complementation: The Case for Fundamental Labour Market Reform," IMF Staff Paper, volume 44, no. 1, 1997. Reviewed in *The Economist*, November 15, 1997. Tellingly, the title of the review article is *"All or nothing: Piecemeal labour-market reforms will not cure Europe's unemployment problem. Governments need to go the whole way."*

19. *Japan Press Weekly*, February 14, 1998. In the April 18, 1998 issue of *Japan Press Weekly* we find: "The main objectives of the bill are to increase the application of discretionary work schedules, to ease restrictions on the existing system of varied (flexible) working hours and to make short-term employment contracts legal."

20. *Japan Press Weekly*, February 14, 1998.

21. *Japan Press Weekly*, March 28, 1998.

22. *Japan Press Weekly*, April 4, 1998.

23. Akira Inukai, "Attack against workers' rights," *Dateline Tokyo*, no. 58, April 1998.

24. Ibid.
25. Ibid.
26. *The Necessity of Social Control,* 56–59. Republished in *Beyond Capital,* 890–892.
27. "Trentacinque ore della nostra vita," an appeal of intellectuals signed by Mario Agostinelli, Pierpaolo Baretta, Heinz Birnbaum, Carla Casalini, Marcello Cini, Giorgio Cremaschi, Pietro Ingrao, Oskar Negt, Paolo Nerozzi, Valentino Parlato, Marco Revelli, Rossana Rossanda, Claudio Sabattini and Arno Teutsch. *Il Manifesto,* February 13, 1998.
28. The interventionist role of the state is in evidence both on the economic and on the political plane. In the economic domain the funds generously dished out to major capitalist enterprises are measured in hundreds of millions of pounds. Thus British Aerospace, for instance, received nearly £600 million for one of its ongoing ventures, in addition to countless millions semi-fraudulently obtained from the state in the not too distant past, also on an occasion when the company was pretending to put on sound economic footing the now again bankrupt Rover enterprise. As to the latter, the massive funds needed to save Rover today are expected again to be provided by the state—and no one seems to hail right now the miraculous virtues of *private enterprise*—while leaving the profits, of course, to the capitalist part of the so-called "Private Public Partnerships" so much favored by New Labour. Equally, if not more important, is the role of state intervention on behalf of capital on the political plane. For the capital system badly needs the authoritarian anti-labor legislation—obligingly introduced by conservative and social-democratic governments alike (indeed, most tellingly about the gravity of the system's structural crisis, even by some governments presided over by former Communist parties, as in Italy)—in order to maintain its neoliberal rule over society at the present stage of historical development.
29. As Marshall Berman observes in his article quoted in note 10 above, "crass cruelty calls itself liberalism (we are kicking you and your kids off welfare for your own good)," and you are "laid off or fired—or *deskilled, outsourced, downsized.* (It is fascinating how many of these crushing words are quite new.)"
30. See a powerful chapter on the challenges facing the labor movement: "Beyond Labor and Leisure," in Daniel Singer, *Whose Millennium?,* (New York: Monthly Review Press, 1999).
31. "The Worker Backlash," *Sunday New York Times,* quoted in a letter sent to the readers and supporters of *Monthly Review* by its editors in October 1997.
32. Ibid.
33. Jeff Faux, "Hedging the neoliberal bet," *Dissent,* fall 1997. A review of Dani Rodrick's *Has Globalizaion Gone Too Far?* (Washington, DC: Institute for International Economics, 1997).
34. Ibid.
35. Quoted in Marx, *Grundrisse* (Harmondsworth: Penguin Books, 1973), 397.
36. The appeal referenced in Note 27 above rightly speaks of the need to "promote

a *mass mobilization* in favor of the 35-hour week, to affect both the world of work as that of politics, and culture as much as the world of associations." (*"promuovere una mobilitazione di massa a favore delle 35 ore che tocchi il mondo del lavoro cosi come quello della politica, quello della cultura come quello delle associazioni."*)

Economic Theory and Politics—Beyond Capital

1. This chapter is based on a paper presented at the Conference on "Types of Economic Thought and Their Relevance for the World of Today," organized by the editor of *Revista BCV*, Asdrúbal Baptista, held in Caracas, September 10–12, 2001.

2. "American productivity: Measuring the new economy," *The Economist*, August 11–17, 2001.

3. Ibid.

4. István Mészáros, *Szatira és valóság (Satire and reality)*, (Budapest: Szépirodalmi Könyvkiadó, 1955), 53.

5. Ibid., 55.

6. Quoted in Moshe Lewin, *Stalinism and the Seeds of Soviet Reform: the Debates of the 1960s* (London: Pluto Press, 1991), 148.

7. Vadim Medvedev, the chairman of the Soviet Party's Ideological Commission and a member of Gorbachev's Politburo, was officially called "the Ideology Chief." In this capacity he proclaimed that "*Joint-stock companies* are in no way contrary to Socialist economic principles. We regard a far-reaching reorganization of *property relations* and the diversity and equality of all of its forms as a *guarantee of the renewal of socialism*." Vadim A. Medvedev, "The Ideology of Perestroika," in Abel G. Aganbegyan, ed., *Perestroika Annual*, vol. 2 (London: Macdonald & Co. Ltd., 1990), 32. He also proclaimed that the new course taken by the economy, with its capitalistically reorganized property relations and joint-stock companies, would "*ensure the country's social democratic progress*" (ibid., 27). Naturally, none of the wishful projections made by Gorbachev's ideologists ever came to fruition.

8. In fact the shaky theories about "market socialism" and about "the social market economy" very quickly gave way to the advocacy of even the most conservative version of neoliberal capitalism. As *The Economist* approvingly commented: "'A market economy without any adjectives.' That is what Mr. Vaclav Klaus insists is needed in Czechoslovakia, where he has been finance minister since early December. Not for him the 'social market economy,' a phrase being bandied about elsewhere in Eastern Europe. This soft-spoken but smilingly confident 48-year-old economist believes that half measures will be worse than useless. To bring the market in quickly, Mr. Klaus and his ministry are preparing a slew of new laws to permit western-style financial markets ... Mr. Klaus and his fellow Czechoslovak delegates in Davos were anxious to distance themselves from the 1968 reforms. [i.e., from 'The Prague Spring,' I. M.] But they were happy to cosy up to Western business. Equity capital and not aid is what they are after, and they appear unfussed about whether it arrives through

joint ventures, greenfield investments or direct purchases of Czech firms. As a good Friedmanite, Mr. Klaus shows no interest in dictating the outcome of market forces: his role is to keep prices stable while business does its work" ("Financial Reform in Czechoslovakia: A Conversation with Vaclav Klaus," February 10, 1990). It could not come as a surprise that the Friedmanite Vaclav Klaus was quickly promoted to the Prime Ministership of Czechoslovakia (later the Czech Republic). He occupied that key position, to the delight of the big business circles of the Western "market societies," for a very long time.

9. Harry Magdoff, "Are there lessons to be learned?," *Monthly Review,* February 1991, 13–17.

10. "World Economy: Nowhere to hide. Economies almost everywhere are looking sick." *The Economist,* August 18–24, 2001.

11. Ibid. [The most up-to-date figures of industrial recession are: in Malaysia *10%*, in Taiwan *12%*, and in—what used to be for a long time considered exemplary—Singapore no less than *17%*.]

12. Ibid.

13. This is not said in hindsight, following the collapse of the Soviet system, I tried to discuss in considerable detail the reasons why the much more difficult approach—to go beyond capital—needs to be adopted, together with the conditions under which it can be realized, in a book entitled *Beyond Capital: Towards a Theory of Transition* (New York: Monthly Review Press, 1995); in Spanish, *Más allá del Capital: Hacia una teoria de la transición* (Caracas: Vadell Hermanos, Editores, 2001). The book took twenty-five years to write, and it anticipated the restoration of capitalism in the Soviet-type system way back in the mid 1970s.

14. See in this respect Chapters 17 ("Changing Forms of the Rule of Capital") and 20 ("The Line of Least Resistance and the Socialist Alternative") of *Beyond Capital.*

15. As Adam Smith put it: "The statesman, who should attempt to direct private people in what manner they ought to employ their capitals, would not only load himself with a most unnecessary attention, but assume an authority which could safely be trusted, not only to no single person, but to no council or senate whatever, and which would nowhere be so dangerous as in the hands of a man who had folly and presumption enough to fancy himself fit to exercise it." A. Smith, *An Inquiry into The Nature and Causes of The Wealth of Nations* (Edinburgh: Adam and Charles Black, 1863), 200.

16. "As every individual endeavors as much as he can both to employ his capital in the support of domestic industry, and so to direct that industry that its produce may be of the greatest value, every individual necessarily labors to render the annual revenue of the society as great as he can. He generally, indeed, neither intends to promote the public interest, nor knows how much he is promoting it. By preferring the support of domestic to that of foreign industry, he intends only his own security; and by directing that industry in such a manner as its produce may be of the greatest value, he intends only his own gain,

and he is in this, as in many other cases, *led by an invisible hand to promote an end which was no part of his intention. . . .* By pursuing his own interest he frequently *promotes that of the society more effectually than when he really intends to promote it*" (ibid., 199–200).

17. See John Maynard Keynes, *The General Theory of Employment, Interest, and Money* (London: Macmillan & Co., 1957), 320.

18. Ibid., 380–381.

19. Hayek, "The Moral Imperative of the Market," in Martin J. Anderson, ed., *The Unfinished Agenda: Essays on the Political Economy of Government Policy in Honour of Arthur Seldon* (London: The Institute of Economic Affairs, London, 1986) 147–149.

20. In the same article Hayek complains about "The failure of a large number of people to accept the moral principles which form the basis of the capitalist system . . . The vast majority of people (I do not exaggerate) no longer believes in the market."

21. Ibid., 148.

22. Ibid., 146.

23. Ibid., 148.

24. "The essential basis of the development of modern civilization is to allow people to pursue their own ends on the basis of their own knowledge and not be bound by the aims of other people" (Hayek, ibid., 146). Anybody who talks in terms like these, in all seriousness, does not live in the "modern civilization" of "modern society," not even on the same planet as the rest of us.

25. See John Kenneth Galbraith, *The New Industrial State* (Princeton: Princeton University Press, 2007).

26. Significant change in this respect would be feasible only in circumstances when—due to some major economic and political crisis—the pressure of the popular masses, in conjunction with the readiness of the more progressive forces of state legislation, could counter forcefully enough and long enough the obvious hostility of the dominant business circles toward comprehensive regulatory intervention. But, of course, such a situation would be analogous to the state of emergency experienced during the Second World War, even if on a smaller scale.

27. See Ludwig von Mises's book *Socialism: An Economic and Sociological Analysis* (New Haven: Yale University Press, 1951).

28. Idealized by many, including Schumpeter, as "productive destruction," when in reality *destructive production* is becoming more and more dominant.

29. The interested reader can find these issues discussed, in passim, in Chapters 14–20 of my book, *Beyond Capital.* (In the Spanish edition, *Más allá del Capital,* 605–1003.)

30. The title of an influential book by Lord William Beveridge.

31. See Marx, *Critique of the Gotha Programme* (New York: International Publishers, 1977).

32. The subtitle of my own book, *Beyond Capital,* is not without good reason

called "*Toward a Theory of Transition.*"

33. Harry Magdoff, "China: new theories for old," *Monthly Review*, May 1979.

34. The Chinese economist Han Deqiang, in a lecture delivered at the workshop of the European Parliament's Green Group on "China's Accession to the WTO," held in July 2001, paints a depressing picture of Western capital's negative impact on Chinese economic developments. See "The Advantages and Disadvantages of China's Accession to the WTO," available on the Internet.

35. "China's economy: Persuading the reluctant spenders," *The Economist*, August 25–31, 2001.

The Challenge of Sustainable Development

1. This chapter is based on a lecture delivered at the Cultural Forum of the Latin American Parliaments' "Summit on the Social Debt and Latin American Integration," held in Caracas, Venezuela, July 10–13, 2001. It is dedicated to the memory of Daniel Singer with whom we often conversed about the untenability of our order of structural inequality.

2. It is enough to think of two recent examples: (1) the practical disenfranchising of countless millions, due to apathy or manipulation, and the electoral farce witnessed after the last U.S. presidential election and (2) the lowest-ever participation of voters in the June 2001 General Election in Britain, producing a grotesquely inflated parliamentary majority of 169 for the Government party with the votes of less than 25 percent of the electorate. The spokesmen of the winning party, refusing to listen to the British electorate's clearly warning message, boasted that New Labour had achieved a "land-slide victory." Shirley Williams aptly commented that what we were witnessing was not a *landslide* but a *mudslide*.

3. See David Cay Johnston, "Gap Between Rich and Poor Found Substantially Wider," *New York Times*, September 5, 1999.

4. Henry Home (Lord Kames), *Loose Hints Upon Education, Chiefly Concerning the Culture of the Heart* (Edinburgh & London, 1781), 284.

5. Diderot's entry on *Journalier* in the *Encyclopédie*.

6. Rousseau, *A Discourse on Political Economy* (London: Everyman), 264. Rousseau also categorically stated that "*liberty cannot exist without equality,*" in *The Social Contract* (London: Everyman), 42.

7. Vico, *The New Science* (New York: Doubleday & Co., 1961), 3.

8. Thomas Münzer, *Hochverursachte Schutzrede und Antwort wider das geistlose, sanftlebende Fleisch zu Wittenberg, welches mit verkehrter Weise durch den Diebstahl der heiligen Schrift die erbärmliche Christenheit also ganz jämmerlich besudelt hat* (1524), quoted by Marx in his essay on *The Jewish Question*.

9. In other words, we end up with a double circularity, produced by the most iniquitous actual historical development: "liberty" is defined as (abstractly postulated but in real substance utterly fictitious) "contractual equality," and "equality" is exhausted in the vague desideratum of a "liberty" to aspire at being granted nothing more than the formally proclaimed but socially nullified "equality of opportunity."

10. From Part Two, Act 5, of Goethe's *Faust* (Harmondsworth, Middlesex: Penguin Classics, 1959). English quotations are taken from pages 267–270 of this volume.

11. The direct inspiration for Balzac's novella was a tale by an Irish Anglican clergy, the descendant of a French Huguenot priest who fled France after the revocation of the Edict of Nantes. This work, by Charles Robert Maturin, the curate of St. Peter's, Dublin, entitled *Melmoth the Wanderer*, was first published in Dublin in 1820, and immediately translated into French. There is a recent edition published by the Folio Society, London, 1993, with an Introduction by Virendra P. Varma. The big difference is that, while Maturin's wandering Melmoth in the end cannot escape hell, Balzac's very different way of approaching the Faust legend, with devastating irony and sarcasm, transfers the story onto a radically different plane, putting into relief a vital determination of our social order.

Education—Beyond Capital

1. This chapter is based on my Opening Lecture at the *Fórum Mundial de Educação*, Porto Alegre, Brazil, July 28, 2004.

2. Paracelsus, *Selected Writings* (London: Routledge & Kegan Paul, 1951), 181.

3. José Martí, "Libros," in *Obras Completas*, vol. 18 (La Habana: Editorial de Ciencias Sociales, 1991), 290–91.

4. Marx, *Theses on Feuerbach*, in Marx and Engels, *Collected Works*, vol. 5 (London: Lawrence and Wishart, 1975), 7.

5. For a detailed discussion of Bernstein's reformist strategy see the chapter entitled "Bernstein's representative blind alley" in my book: *The Power of Ideology* (London: Harvester/Whetsheaf, 1989); in Portuguese: *O Poder da Ideologia*, enlarged edition (Sâo Paulo: Boitempo Editorial, 2004).

6. Adam Smith, *Lectures on Justice, Police, Revenue, and Arms* (1763) in Herbert W. Schneider, ed., *A. Smith's Moral and Political Philosophy*, (New York: Haffner Publishing Co. 1948), 318–21.

7. Ibid., 319–20.

8. Robert Owen, *A New View of Society and Other Writings* (Everyman edition), 124.

9. Ibid., 88–89.

10. Ibid., 124.

11. See note 3.

12. Fidel Castro, *José Martí: El autor intelectual* (Havana: Editora Política, 1983), 162. See also page 150 of the same volume.

13. Marx, *Capital*, vol. 1(Moscow: Foreign Languages Publishing House, 1959), 713–14 and 734–36.

14. Locke, "Memorandum on the Reform of the Poor Law," in H.R. Fox Bourne, *The Life of John Locke*, vol. 2 (London: King, 1876), 378.

15. Ibid., 383.

16. Neal Wood, *The Politics of Locke's Philosophy* (Berkeley: University of California Press, 1983), 26.

17. Locke in Bourne, op. cit., 380.
18. Ibid.
19. Ibid., 383.
20. Ibid., 384–85.
21. "Public," in this context, means *private* in Britain, referring to exorbitant *fee-paying* schools.
22. Antonio Gramsci, "The formation of intellectuals," in *The Modern Prince and Other Writings* (London: Lawrence and Wishart, 1957), 121.
23. "The difficulty is that the 'moment' of radical politics is strictly limited by the nature of the crises in question and the temporal determinations of their unfolding. The breach opened up at times of crisis cannot be left open forever and the measures adopted to fill it, from the earliest steps onwards, have their own logic and cumulative impact on subsequent interventions. Furthermore, both the existing socioeconomic structures and their corresponding framework of political institutions tend to act against radical initiatives by their very inertia as soon as the worst moment of the crisis is over and thus it becomes possible to contemplate again 'the line of least resistance' . . . . Paradoxical as it may sound, only a radical self-determination of politics can prolong the moment of radical politics. If that moment is not to be dissipated under the weight of immediate economic pressures, a way must be found to extend its influence well beyond the peak of the crisis itself (the peak, that is, when radical politics tends to assert its effectiveness as a rule). And since the temporal duration of the crisis as such cannot be prolonged at will—nor should it be, since voluntaristic politics, with its artificially manipulated 'states of emergency', may only attempt to do so at its own peril, thereby alienating the masses of the people instead of securing their support—the solution can only arise from successfully turning 'fleeting time' into *enduring space* by means of restructuring the powers and institutions of decision making." Mészáros, *Beyond Capital*, 950–51.
24. "*Al borde de la ciudad,*" translated by Fayad Jamís. "*A város peremén*" in Attila József, *Poesías* (Budapest: Eötvös József Könyvkiadó, 1999), 55.
25. Renato Constantino, *Neo-Colonial Identity and Counter Consciousness: Essays on Cultural Decolonization,* (London: Merlin Press, 1978).
26. Ibid., 20–21.
27. Ibid., 23.
28. Quoted in Jorge Lezcano Pérez, *José Martí: 150 Aniversario,* (Brazil: Casa Editora de la Embajada de Cuba en Brasil, 2003), 8.
29. Intended by Martí as an ongoing project, lack of financial support allowed only four issues to be published. All four issues are now reproduced in volume 18 of José Martí's *Obras Completas,* 299–503. (La Habana: Editorial de Ciencias Sociales, 1991).
30. Marx, *The Poverty of Philosophy* (London: Martin Lawrence Ltd.), 123.
31. "We are condemned to the vale of tears" in one version, and "we are condemned to the anguish of freedom" in another.
32. Bernstein's polemic against Marx presents an utter caricature of the latter's

perspective. Instead of engaging in a proper theoretical discussion, he prefers to follow the path of throwing gratuitous insult, condemning, without any argument at all, Marx's and Hegel's "dialectical scaffolding," as if the transformation of the weighty problems of dialectical reasoning into a disqualifying swearword could by itself settle the important social and political issues in dispute. The interested reader can find a fairly detailed discussion of this controversy in Chapter 8 of my *The Power of Ideology* (London: Harvester/ Whetsheaf, 1989). The term *"grandes narratives,"* in postmodern thought, is used analogously to Bernstein's "dialectical scaffolding."

33. Fidel Castro in *José Martí: El autor intelectual* (La Habana: Editora Política, 1983), 224.

34. Even the hostile U.S. government had to acknowledge this achievement in a lopsided way: by granting to an American drug company in California the right to conclude a significant—multi-million dollar—commercial deal with Cuba, in July 2004, for the distribution of a life-saving anti-cancer drug, suspending thereby in this respect one of its savage blockading regulations. Of course, even then the U.S. government maintained its hostility by denying the right to transfer in "hard currency" the funds involved, compelling its own company to negotiate some kind of "barter" arrangement instead, supplying American agricultural or industrial products in exchange for the path-breaking Cuban medicine.

35. Paracelsus, *Selected Writings* (London: Routledge & Kegan Paul, 1951), 176–77, 189, and 183.

36. See Paracelsus, *Leben und Lebensweisheit in Selbstzeugnissen* (Leipzig: Reclam Verlag, 1956), 134.

37. See the article on "Education" in the thirteenth edition (1926) of the *Encyclopaedia Britannica.*

38. See Harry Braverman, *Labor and Monopoly Capital: The Degradation of Work in the Twentieth Century* (New York: Monthly Review Press, 1974). A television documentary on Detroit assembly-line autoworkers interviewed a group of them, asking how long it took to learn their skills. They looked at each other and they started to laugh, responding with undisguised contempt: *"eight minutes; that's all!"*

39. F. W. Taylor, *Scientific Management* (New York: Harper and Row, 1947), 29. See Chapters 2 and 3 of *The Power of Ideology*, op. cit, especially Sections 2.1: "Postwar Expansion and 'Post-Ideology,'" and 3.1: "Managerial Ideology and the State."

40. Minqi Li, "After Neoliberalism: Empire, Social Democracy, or Socialism?," *Monthly Review*, January 2004.

41. Martin Wolf, *Why Globalization Works,* (New Haven: Yale University Press, 2004).

Socialism in the Twenty-First Century

1. Marx, "The Eighteenth Brumaire of Louis Bonaparte," in Marx and Engels, *Collected Works*, vol. 11 (London: Lawrence and Wishart, 1979), 107.

2. See Chapter 7 of this book: "The Challenge of Sustainable Development and

the Culture of Substantive Equality," a lecture delivered at the Cultural Forum of the Latin American Parliaments' "Summit on the Social Debt and Latin American Integration," held in Caracas, Venezuela, July 10–13, 2001.

3. Rousseau, *A Discourse on Political Economy* (Everyman edition), 262–264.

4. See, for instance, Jean-Claude Paye, "The End of *Habeas Corpus* in Great Britain," *Monthly Review*, November 2005. As the author characterizes the recent pernicious legal developments in the British Parliament: "The law attacks the formal separation of powers by giving to the secretary of state for home affairs judicial prerogatives. Further, it reduces the rights of the defense practically to nothing. It also establishes the primacy of suspicion over fact, since measures restricting liberties, potentially leading to house arrest, could be imposed on individuals not for what they have done, but according to what the home secretary thinks they could have done or could do. Thus this law deliberately turns its back on the rule of law and establishes a new form of political regime." See also Chapter 10 of the present study, especially the discussion of "The Structural Crisis of Politics."

5. This requirement for the socially equitable universalization of work appeared several centuries ago in the writings of some great visionary thinkers, but to no avail, given the overpowering dynamics of ongoing socioeconomic development in their time. See my discussion of Paracelsus in Chapter 8 above.

6. Harry Magdoff and Fred Magdoff, "Approaching Socialism," *Monthly Review*, July/August 2005.

7. Marx, *The Poverty of Philosophy* (London: Martin Lawrence Ltd.), 47.

8. The unhappy Kyoto Saga is only the latest phase of these developments. I argued more than a decade ago that "Any attempt to deal with the reluctantly acknowledged problems must be conducted under the prohibitive weight of the fundamental laws and structural antagonisms of the system. Thus the 'corrective measures' envisaged within the framework of big international jamborees—like the 1992 gathering in Rio de Janeiro—amount to absolutely nothing, since they must be subordinated to the perpetuation of the established global power relations and vested interests. Causality and time must be treated as a plaything of the dominant capitalist interests, no matter how acute the dangers. Thus the future tense is callously and irresponsibly confined to the narrowest horizon of immediate profit expectations." Mészáros, *Beyond Capital*, 148. "Characteristically, even the feeble resolutions of the 1992 Rio de Janeiro Conference—watered down almost to the point of meaninglessness under the pressure of the dominant capitalist powers, primarily the United States whose delegation was headed by President George H. W. Bush— are used only as an *alibi* for carrying on as before, doing nothing to meet the challenge while pretending to 'fulfill the obligations undertaken'" (ibid., 270).

9. Harry Magdoff, interviewed by Huck Gutman, "Creating a Just Society: Lessons from Planning in the U.S.S.R. & the U.S.," *Monthly Review*, October 2002.

10. Marx, *Capital*, vol. 1 (Moscow: Foreign Languages Publishing House, 1959), 85.

11. John Stuart Mill, *Principles of Political Economy,* (London: Longmans, Green, and Co., 1923), 751.

12. Ibid., 749.

13. Ibid.

14. To quote this book with its full, utterly pretentious, title, *The Limits to Growth: A Report for the Club of Rome Project on the Predicament of Mankind,* A Potomac Associates Book (London: Earth Island Limited, 1972).

15. Tellingly, the principal theoretical figure behind this "growth limiting" venture, Professor Jay Forrester, of the Massachusetts Institute of Technology, contemptuously dismissed all concern with equality as a mere "shibboleth of equality." See his interview in *Le Monde,* August 1, 1972.

16. See Chapter 4 of the present book, especially Section 2: "The Potentially Deadliest Phase of Imperialism."

17. Vadim Medvedev, "The Ideology of Perestroika" in Abel Aganbegyan, ed., *Perestroika Annual,* vol. 2 (London: Futura/Macdonald, 1989), 31–32.

18. The title of Hayek's most famous crusading book.

19. Gorbachev quoted in John Rettie, "Only market can save Soviet economy," *The Guardian,* October 17, 1990.

20. To quote one of Hegel's idealizing postulates: "The *nation state* is mind in its substantive rationality and immediate actuality and is therefore the *absolute power* on earth." Hegel, *The Philosophy of Right* (Oxford: Clarendon Press, 1942), 212.

21. Marx, *The Poverty of Philosophy* in Marx and Engels, *Collected Works,* vol. 6 (London: Lawrence and Wishart, 1976), 134. Quoted in Chapter 19 of *Beyond Capital* ("The Communitarian System and the Law of Value in Marx and Lukács"). See also Chapter 15 ("The Decreasing Rate of Utilization Under Capitalism") and Chapter 16 ("The Decreasing Rate of Utilization and the Capitalist State") of *Beyond Capital,* which deal with some important related issues.

22. Marx, *Grundrisse* (Harmondsworth: Penguin Books), 708.

23. Ibid.

24. Marx, *Critique of the Gotha Programme,* in Marx and Engels, *Selected Works,* vol. 2 (Moscow: Foreign Languages Publishing House, 1958).

25. See Walt Rostow, *The Stages of Economic Growth: A Non-Communist Manifesto* (London: Cambridge University Press, 1960). Rostow was a prominent member of President Kennedy's "brain trust."

26. Lenin, *Collected Works,* vol. 36 (London: Lawrence and Wishart, 1960), 606.

27. Ibid., 610.

28. See my discussion of these problems in "The dramatic reappearance of the national question," part of an article entitled "Socialismo hoy dia," written between December 1989—January 1990 for the Venezuelan quarterly periodical *El ojo del huracán* and published in its February/March/April 1990 issue. Republished in English in Part IV of *Beyond Capital.*

29. Engels, *Letter to August Bebel,* March 18–28, 1875.

30. Rosa Luxemburg, *Junius Pamphlet* (Colombo: Young Socialist, 1967), 54.

31. See Section 2 of the present chapter, on Participation.
32. Bolívar called equality *"the law of laws,"* adding that "without equality all freedoms, all rights perish. For it, we must make sacrifices." (*"La ley de las leyes: la Igualdad. Sin ella perecen todas las libertades. A ella debemos hacer los sacrificios."*)
33. *"El peligroso loco del Sur."*
34. See José Martí, *"Discurso,"* pronounced in Hardman Hall, New York, October 10, 1890 and *"La Verdad Sobre los Estados Unidos,"* *Patria*, April 17, 1884.
35. *"Acaso sólo allí podrá fijarse algún día la capital de la tierra, como pretendió Constantino que fuese Bizancio la del antiguo hemisferio."*
36. Each pair of names stands for conquerors and conquered. Árpád was the Chief of the Hungarian tribes who in the ninth century triumphed over Zalán in the Karpathian Basin, and Werbőczy was the early sixteenth century Hungarian statesman who brutally avenged the 1514 peasant uprising of György Dózsa.
37. Here we may add the Middle East wars.
38. Mészáros, *Marx's Theory of Alienation* (London: Merlin Press, 1970), 310.
39. Ibid., 342.
40. See my article: "The Structural Crisis of Politics," *Monthly Review,* September 2006.
41. Rosa Luxemburg, "Organizational Questions of the Russian Social Democracy," in *The Russian Revolution and Leninism or Marxism"* (Ann Arbor: The University of Michigan Press, 1970), 98.
42. Rousseau, *The Social Contract* (Everyman edition), 78.
43. Rousseau, Ibid., 79.
44. Discussed in some detail in Chapter 14 of *Beyond Capital.*
45. Ibid.
46. Adam Smith, *The Wealth of Nations,* (Edinburgh: Adam and Charles Black, 1863), 200.
47. Ibid., 273.
48. It is worth recalling here the great moral indignation with which Thomas Münzer, the Anabaptist leader of the German peasant revolution, denounced, two and a half centuries earlier, the unfolding system of "natural" and universal commodification and alienation. Münzer noted how intolerable it was "that every creature should be *transformed into property*—the fishes in the water, the birds of the air, the plants of the earth." Quoted in Chapter 7.1 of this text.
49. Lenin made it amply clear that *"political* revolutions can under no circumstances whatsoever either obscure or weaken the slogan of a *socialist* revolution . . . which should not be regarded as a *single act,* but as a *period* of turbulent political and economic upheavals, the most intense class struggle, civil war, revolutions, and counter-revolutions." Lenin, "On the Slogan for a United States of Europe," in *Collected Works,* vol. 21 (London: Lawrence and Wishart, 1960), 340. Whereas Lenin always retained his awareness of the fundamental difference between the political and the ongoing social revolution, even when

he was irrevocably forced into defending the bare survival of the political revolution as such after the dying down of the revolutionary wave in Europe, Stalin obliterated this vital distinction, pretending that the unavoidable *first step* in the direction of the socialist transformation represented socialism itself, to be simply followed by stepping onto the "highest stage of Communism" in an encircled state.

50. As Marx put it, in the course of so-called primitive accumulation capital emerges "dripping from head to foot, from every pore, with blood and dirt." See Part VIII of Marx's *Capital*, vol. 1: "The So-Called Primitive Accumulation."

51. Hegel, *The Philosophy of History* (New York: Dover Publications, Inc., 1956), 457.

52. On this issue see Section 3 ("Historical Challenges Facing the Socialist Movement") of Chapter 4 above, as well as Chapter 18 of *Beyond Capital*).

53. *Economic Manuscripts of 1861–63* in Marx and Engels, *Collected Works*, vol. 34 (London: Lawrence and Wishart, 1994), 457. Another important qualification that must be added here is that "productive labor—as value producing—always confronts capital as the labor of *isolated* workers, whatever social combinations those workers may enter into in the production process. Thus, whereas capital represents the social productive power of labor towards the workers, productive labor always represents towards capital only the labor of the *isolated* worker" (ibid., 460).

54. Ibid., 456.

55. Ibid., 457.

56. From "The Need to Counter Capital's Extra-Parliamentary Force," Section 18.4 of *Beyond Capital*, 734–5.

57. See Chapter 8 of the present study and Chapter 10 ("Alienation and the Crisis of Education") of my book *on Marx's Theory of Alienation* (London: The Merlin Press, 1970).

58. *Economic Manuscripts of 1861–63*, op. cit., 457.

59. Marx, *Grundrisse*, 708.

60. See the discussion of some important related issues in Chapter 5 above.

61. Fidel Castro Ruz, Speech in Katowice, Poland, June 7, 1972, Quoted in Carlos Tablada Pérez, *Economia, etica e politica nel pensiero di Che Guevara* (Milan: Il Papiro, 1996), 165.

62. *The Philosophy of History*, op. cit., 103.

63. Ibid., 457.

64. Marx and Engels, *Collected Works*, vol. 3, 184.

65. Ibid.

66. Ibid.

67. Marx and Engels, *Collected Works*, vol. 5, 52.

68. Ibid., 52–53.

69. In philosophical terms, the category of *mediation* acquires a particularly great importance in the historical period of transition toward the new social order.

Why Socialism? Historical Time and the Actuality of Radical Change

1. Albert Einstein, "Why Socialism?," *Monthly Review,* May 1949.
2. See Sir Thomas More, *Utopia,* published in 1516.
3. Attila József, "*A város peremén*" ("On the outskirts of the city"), 1933.
4. Translation by Fayad Jamís.
5. The Spanish translation renders these lines of József's poem: "*Tras los sacer-dotes, los soldatos y los burgueses, / al fin nos hemos vuelto fieles / oidores de las leyes: / por eso el sentido de toda obra humana / zumba en nosotros / como el vio-lón profundo.*"
6. Attila József, "Szocialisták" ("Socialists"), 1931.
7. See the remark to this effect by Professor Jay Forrester—the main figure behind the Club of Rome's propaganda efforts heavily promoted by the vest-ed interests—quoted in Chapter 9.5.2 above.
8. Quoted in Mészáros, *Beyond Capital,* 423.
9. Ernesto Cardenal, interview with *Carta Maior,* January 25, 2007. See also a book by another Liberation Theologian, François Houtart, *Délégitimer le cap-italisme: Reconstruire l'espérance* (Brussels: Colophon Éditions, 2005). See especially Chapter 4: "*La place du croyant dans les luttes sociales.*"
10. Martin Wolf, *Why Globalization Works? The Case for the Global Market Economy* (New Haven: Yale University Press, 2004). Quotations by King and Summers are taken from the promotional blurbs on the back cover of Martin Wolf's book.
11. I have discussed these problems since 1971. See the Section on "Capitalism and Environmental Destruction" in my Isaac Deutscher Memorial Lecture, *The Necessity of Social Control,* held at the London School of Economics in January 1971, first published as a volume by Merlin Press in London in 1971, and later reprinted in Part IV of my *Beyond Capital.*
12. See John Bellamy Foster's penetrating study, *Marx's Ecology* (New York: Monthly Review Press, 2000). See also Joel Kovel's powerful book, *The Enemy of Nature: The End of Capitalism or the End of the World?* (London: Zed Books Ltd., 2002).
13. To be sure, this domination—no matter how ruthlessly enforced today—can-not be maintained indefinitely. It is necessary to underline not only the dan-gerous character of U.S. domination but also its historical instability and ulti-mate failure. In due course, the complex problems at the roots of such deter-minations must be resolved in order to remove that instability, or else the trend toward an ever more aggressive assertion of U.S. dictates can lead to the destruction of humankind.
14. Named by Lenin "the highest stage of capitalism."
15. See the discussion of these problems in Chapter 4, especially in Section 4.2, "The Potentially Deadliest Phase of Imperialism."
16. Martin Wolf is no exception in reactionary substance even if more diplomat-ic in language. Adopting with pious subservience the supposedly self-justifi-catory notion of "the global community"—in the name of which the most brutal violation of elementary human rights is constantly committed by U.S.

imperialism and its "willing allies"—Wolf, predictably, insists that "the *global community* also needs the *capacity and will to intervene where states have failed altogether*" (Wolf, op. cit., 320).

17. This phrase is used in a promotional blurb provided by Kenneth Rogoff, the chief economist of the IMF and a Harvard University professor, on the back cover of Wolf's book. Rogoff proved his impeccable establishment credentials as a bitter adversary of even John Stiglitz. See Stiglitz's account of their sharp confrontation in the Afterword to the Penguin edition of his book *Globalization and Its Discontents* (Harmondsworth: Penguin Books, 2004).

18. Wolf, op. cit., 309.

19. Ibid., 313.

20. Ibid., 316.

21. Ibid., 317.

22. Ibid., 319.

23. Ibid., 311.

24. Ibid., 315.

25. Ibid., 319.

26. Ibid., 320.

27. Stiglitz, op. cit., 274.

28. Joseph Stiglitz, *The Roaring Nineties* (Penguin Books, 2004), 346.

29. Stiglitz, ibid., XIV.

30. Wolf, op. cit., 314.

31. Sections 10.3.1 and 10.3.2 were delivered in Maceió, Brazil, on May 4, 2006, as the opening lecture at the 13th Congresso Nacional dos Magistrados da Justiça do Trabalho and the 30th Anniversary of their Association. This lecture was first published in English in *Monthly Review*, September 2006.

32. See also my *The Alternative to Capital's Social Order: Socialism or Barbarism* (Kolkata: Bagchi & Co., 2001), 39; in the Monthly Review Press edition, 40.

33. "Seymour Hersh reports that one option involves the use of a bunker-buster tactical nuclear weapon, such as the B61-11, to ensure the destruction of Iran's main centrifuge plant at Natanz." Sarah Baxter, "Gunning for Iran," *The Sunday Times*, April 9, 2006.

34. This letter, dated April 17, 2006, together with the email addresses of the prominent signatories, can be read online at http://www.globalresearch.ca/. The April 17, 2006 initiative was preceded in the autumn of 2005 by a petition signed by more than 1,800 physicists that repudiated new U.S. nuclear weapons policies that include preemptive use of nuclear weapons against non-nuclear adversaries.

35. John Pilger rightly castigated Prime Minister Tony Blair on this score. He wrote: "Blair has demonstrated his taste for absolute power with his abuse of the Royal Prerogative, which he has used to bypass parliament in going to war" (*New Statesman*, April 17, 2006). We could also add that such devices as the "Royal Prerogative," as well as their equally problematic equivalents in other constitutions, have been invented on the whole precisely for the purpose of being abused, as self-legitimating authoritarian escape clauses which can

arbitrarily overrule democratic demands under difficult circumstances, instead of extending the power of democratic decision making, as should be the case in situations of major crisis.

36. From Sarah Baxter's *Sunday Times* article quoted above.

37. Thomas P.M. Barnett, author of *The Pentagon's New Map: War and Peace in the Twenty-First Century* (New York: G.P. Puttnam's Sons, 2004).

38. Richard Peet, "Perpetual War for a Lasting Peace," *Monthly Review,* January 2005.

39. Max Boot, *Savage Wars of Peace* (a title drawn from Rudjard Kipling's *The White Man's Burden*), quoted in "The Failure of Empire," review of the month by the editors of *Monthly Review,* January 2005.

40. Boitempo (São Paulo) edition of *O século XXI, socialismo ou barbárie,* 10.

41. "Transcripts show No 10's hand in war legal advice," *The Guardian,* February 24, 2005. It should be mentioned here by way of clarification that Lord Goldmith's first opinion was highly skeptical of the legality of the envisaged war.

42. See Philippe Sands, *Lawless World: America and the Making and Breaking of Global Rule* (London: Penguin Books, 2005).

43. John Mortimer, "I cannot believe that a Labour Government would be so ready to destroy our law, our freedom of speech and our civil liberties," *The Mail on Sunday,* October 2, 2005.

44. "Terror Law an affront to justice," *The Guardian,* April 13, 2006.

45. "John Pilger sees freedom die quietly," *New Statesman,* April 17 2006.

46. *Japan Press Weekly,* Special Issue, March 2006.

47. As Kazuo Shii warned recently: "How did Japan head down the wrong path of territorial expansionism? For victim nations, it was the history of losing their home countries in humiliation and suffering ravages. It is not masochistic to recognize this fact. If Japan is courageous enough to squarely face the past history and acknowledge its wrongdoing, it can gain the trust of other Asian nations and Japanese people can face the future with confidence. On the contrary, turning a blind eye to past wrongdoings leads to committing the same errors again." *Japan Press Weekly,* September 2, 2006.

48. Manuel Marulanda Vélez, *Carta enviada pelo líder histórico das FARC da Colômbia a Álvaro Leyva, candidato às Eleições Presidênciais marcadas para 24 de Maio de 2006, resistir. info,* April 2006.

49. Ibid.

50. I wrote in November 1971, in the Preface to the Third Edition of my book *Marx's Theory of Alienation,* that the unfolding events and developments "dramatically underlined the intensification of the global structural crisis of capital."

51. This quotation is taken from Section 18.2.1 of *Beyond Capital,* 680–682.

52. Kant suggested an ideal solution to the problem of inter-state antagonisms by postulating the realization of "perpetual peace" in the future through the good services of "moral politics." Hegel, by contrast, considered inter-state conflict a positive asset. He summarily dismissed Kant's wishful alternative with a sense of realism, bordering on cynicism, by saying that "corruption in nations

would be the product of prolonged, let alone 'perpetual' peace." Hegel, *Philosophy of Right* (Oxford: Clarendon Press, 1942), 324.

53. "Terror Law an affront to justice," *The Guardian*, April 13, 2006. Another article in the same issue of *The Guardian*, by Tania Branigan, the paper's political correspondent, reported: "Critics claimed that the Legislative and Regulatory Reform Bill would allow the government to change almost any law it wished—even introducing new criminal offences or altering the constitution—without scrutiny. . . . Tories and Lib Dems had dubbed it the 'parliamentary scrutiny abolition bill.'"

54. See Wolf, op. cit.

55. See the April 7, 2006 issue of *La Republica,* in particular an article by Giorgio Ruffolo: "Un paese danneggiato."

56. As exemplified by Barnett's discourse quoted above.

57. Robert Cooper, "The New Liberal Imperialism," *Observer Worldview Extra,* Sunday April 7, 2002. All of Cooper's quotations are taken from the same article.

58. While forgetting the actual history of the "end game" of the Balkan war under the decisions taken and the military orders imposed by President Bill Clinton, and at the same time illusorily asserting the "postmodern" primacy of the European Union in the region, Cooper nevertheless has to concede in one of his rare references to the United States that "the U.S. presence is an indispensable stabilizing factor."

59. The *International Criminal Court* is one of Cooper's idealized examples of postmodern institutions. Yet his schematism is not disturbed by the fact that the U.S. refuses to accept for itself the Court's authority.

60. In Italy, today, twenty-three CIA operatives are indicted for the kidnapping and for the "rendition" of someone politically disliked by the U.S. administration. Yet the U.S. government, convinced of its entitlement to stand above international law, has already declared that it will refuse to extradite any one of them.

61. See in Section 4.2.9 above the discussion of this problem, with reference to former U.S. Deputy Secretary of State Strobe Talbot's sharp warning about the necessity to respect the "global pre-eminence of the United States" at an important meeting of the Royal Institute of International Affairs in London. Strobe Talbot was a member of President Clinton's administration. Thus, the concern about imposing U.S. global pre-eminence is by no means confined to the extreme neo-conservative right-wing of the Republican Party. Democratic President Clinton's hair-raising remark that "there is only one necessary nation, the United States" puts into relief the same belief in the uncontestable legitimacy of American global domination.

62. Julian Borger, "U.S.-based missiles to have global reach," *The Guardian,* July 1, 2003.

63. According to well-sourced reports, Poland and Romania are also facilitating the CIA "rendition" of people to torture regimes and operating in their country illegal detention camps on behalf of the U.S. At the time of the United Nations debate on the Iraq War, Donald Rumsfeld was praising these coun-

tries as representatives of the "New Europe" while arrogantly condemning "Old Europe" which at the time rejected the claimed legality of the war.

64. One of the leaders of the Bolivian Communist Party.

65. Fidel Castro Ruz, "A Necessary Introduction" (1968) in David Deutschmann, ed., *Che: A Memoir by Fidel Castro,* (New York: Ocean Press, 2006), 105–110.

66. Ibid., 116.

67. In *The German Ideology.*

Index